The Corporate Objective

CORPORATIONS, GLOBALISATION AND THE LAW

Series Editor: Janet Dine, *Director, Centre for Commercial Law Studies, Queen Mary College, University of London, UK*

This new and uniquely positioned monograph series aims to draw together high quality research work from established and younger scholars on what is an intriguing and under-researched area of the law. The books will offer insights into a variety of legal issues that concern corporations operating on the global stage, including interaction with WTO, international financial institutions and nation states, in both developing and developed countries. Whilst the underlying foundation of the series will be that of company law, broadly-defined, authors are encouraged to take an approach that draws on the work of other social sciences, such as politics, economics and development studies and to offer an international or comparative perspective where appropriate. Specific topics to be considered will include corporate governance, corporate responsibility, taxation and criminal liability, amongst others. The series will undoubtedly offer an important contribution to legal thinking and to the wider globalisation debate.

Titles in the series include:

Corporate Governance and China's H-Share Market
Alice de Jonge

Corporate Rescue Law – An Anglo-American Perspective
Gerard McCormack

Multinational Enterprises and Tort Liabilities
An Interdisciplinary and Comparative Examination
Muzaffer Eroglu

Perspectives on Corporate Social Responsibility
Edited by Nina Boeger, Rachel Murray and Charlotte Villiers

Corporate Governance in the 21st Century
Japan's Gradual Transformation
Edited by Luke Nottage, Leon Wolff and Kent Anderson

National Corporate Law in a Globalised Market
The UK Experience in Perspective
David Milman

Transnational Corporations and International Law
Accountability in the Global Business Environment
Alice de Jonge

The Corporate Objective
Andrew Keay

The Corporate Objective

Andrew Keay

Professor of Corporate and Commercial Law, Centre for Business Law and Practice, University of Leeds, UK

CORPORATIONS, GLOBALISATION AND THE LAW

Edward Elgar

Cheltenham, UK • Northampton, MA, USA

Published by
Edward Elgar Publishing Limited
The Lypiatts
15 Lansdown Road
Cheltenham
Glos GL50 2JA
UK

Edward Elgar Publishing, Inc.
William Pratt House
9 Dewey Court
Northampton
Massachusetts 01060
USA

A catalogue record for this book
is available from the British Library

Library of Congress Control Number: 2010939255

ISBN 978 1 84844 771 4

Typeset by Servis Filmsetting Ltd, Stockport, Cheshire
Printed and bound by MPG Books Group, UK

Contents

Preface

Large public companies dominate the world in which we live, and have become increasingly important over the past century. Despite this fact there has never been unanimity amongst scholars, practitioners and directors as to what the objective of such companies is and should be. For many years there has been robust and, at times, caustic debate over the matter. While there has been much written on the topic I believe that there is still room for scholars to contribute to the debate, especially if they are not merely re-hashing the main points that have been made thus far.

This book seeks to consider the issue of the corporate objective normatively and to investigate what in fact should be the corporate objective. The book proposes an approach that is titled, the Entity Maximisation and Sustainability model. It is an ungainly title, perhaps, but it is descriptive of that which is proposed. Before articulating the model and seeking to apply and justify it, I discuss the two theories that have dominated the field, the shareholder primacy and stakeholder theories. It is necessary to do this for two reasons. First, I seek to synthesise, and provide in one place, the arguments for and against each theory. Hitherto, for a comprehensive appreciation of the two theories, from the viewpoint of various academic disciplines, one had to read a large volume of articles. Second, before propounding a fresh approach one must, as a matter of respect to other scholars and as a requirement for good scholarship, consider and assess the views that have been put forward for many years.

The fact that the debate is long-standing should not pre-empt further study, especially where there is not a simple re-hashing of the arguments already propounded. This work seeks to make a break from the existing situation, namely polarisation of arguments around one or other of the two predominant theories. The literature has focused on aspects of these theories, whereas this book seeks to move away from that and proposes a fresh approach, through the development of a new model, and to investigate its effects in a corporate setting.

It is acknowledged that this work will not end the debate, and it does not purport to do so. It is hoped that it will lead to further study. The value of the work is not necessarily in that it will change practical management in the short term. It is submitted that it might, however, form the foundation for further work by, and consideration of, academics, law-makers and directors. It is hoped that work will provide an underpinning for the further development of corporate governance guidelines, mechanisms or regulation.

It is further hoped that this work will lead to a fresh consideration of the role and position of investors (often known as 'stakeholders') and new approaches to issues such as how companies should distribute the profits which they accumulate. Furthermore, previous theories have focused almost solely on how the managers should act in relation to either the shareholders or all stakeholders while the model that is being proposed in the book introduces a different way of approaching how companies should be run, and what issues should be considered by the directors. It will demonstrate that the corporate objective does not have to be assessed from the standpoint of the groups with interests in the company, but by asking how the company entity should act for its own enhancement.

Some of the material in the book draws on five articles which I have written and published, and where permission of the publishers has needed to be sought I have kindly been given the permission of the publishers (named below) to use them. The articles are:

- 'The Ultimate Objective of the Public Company and the Enforcement of the Entity Maximisation and Sustainability Model' (2010) 10 *Journal of Corporate Law Studies* 35–71 (Hart Publishing).
- 'Ascertaining the Corporate Objective: An Entity Maximisation and Sustainability Model' (2008) 71 *Modern Law Review* 663–698 (Blackwell Publishing).
- 'Shareholder Primacy in Corporate Law: Can It Survive? Should It Survive?' [2010] *European Company and Financial Law Review* 369–413 (De Gruyter).
- 'Stakeholder Theory in Corporate Law: Has It Got What It Takes?' (2010) 9 *Richmond Journal of Global Law & Business* 240–300 (University of Richmond).
- 'Getting to Grips With the Shareholder Value Theory in Corporate Law' accepted for publication in the *Common Law World Review* (Vathek Publishing).

The initial research that I undertook in relation to this project was supported by a grant from the British Academy, for which I am very thankful. I am thankful to the School of Law at the University of Leeds for granting me study leave to develop the book. I wish to thank several friends and colleagues who have provided me with feedback on aspects of the material that is found within this book. In particular, I thank Harry Rajak, Chris Riley, Gerry McCormack and Joan Loughrey. I am responsible for all errors and the aforementioned parties should not be regarded as in any way responsible for what I have written.

I have appreciated the support of Ben Booth from the publisher over the time I have been writing the book.

Andrew Keay
Leeds
1 January 2011

Table of cases

1. Public companies: context, theory and objectives

The aim of this Chapter is simply to set the scene for the balance of the book. It seeks to consider general issues such as the power and nature of large public companies, their position in society, the objective of the book and why the focus of the book is important.

1. THE CONTEXT

The business company is a ubiquitous part of today's society. Such entities have great effects on our daily lives and have an influence over just about all that we do. The business company has been with us now in its present form, or close to it, for over 150 years. As the Honourable Justice Michael Kirby (a judge of the High Court of Australia at the time of speaking) said extra-judicially, and in relation to public companies:

> [T]he idea of an independent corporation, governed by directors and accountable to shareholders, was a brilliant one. It permitted people to raise capital from the public, to invest it without, in most cases, a danger of personal risk and to engage in entrepreneurial activity which, otherwise, would probably not occur.[1]

Michael Jensen has emitted similar sentiments and said that the public company lowered the risk of capital and permitted the spread of financial risk over the portfolios of large numbers of investors.[2] Nevertheless, the nature and operation of such companies has caused no end of discussion, argument and litigation, and the most fundamental issues relating to the company still elude us.[3] This is undoubtedly partly due to their

---

[1] 'The Company Director, Past, Present and Future,' address to the Australian Institute of Directors, Hobart, 31 March 1998.

[2] 'Eclipse of the Public Corporation' (1989) *Harvard Business Review* 61 at 64.

[3] C. Brunner, 'The Enduring Ambivalence of Corporate Law' (2008) 59 *Alabama Law Review* 1385 at 1385.

fundamental role as the most important institutions for social wealth creation in capitalist economies.[4]

It is trite to say that companies play critical roles in the carrying on of commerce across the world. Undoubtedly, a large element of economic activity is undertaken by companies in most, if not nearly all, of the world's nations,[5] and they have been and are the dominant economic institutions in the world. In the United States companies account for nearly 100 per cent of all national output,[6] although this includes private companies (close corporations). It is fair to say that the role of companies in society has changed remarkably over time, from small business ventures to the gigantic multinational enterprises which we see today. Leslie Hannah has stated, in relation to Great Britain, that with the developments in the twentieth century alone, British industry went from: 'a disaggregated structure of predominantly small, competing firms to a concentrated structure dominated by large, and often monopolistic, corporations.'[7] But for well over a century the public company has been 'one of the primary institutions of capitalism'[8] and has established a well-used vehicle for the ownership and control of property, the accumulation of capital and the organisation of production.[9] Clearly companies in general are the most used structure invoked by businesses around the world for running their activities.[10]

The public companies of today often are part of a complex corpo-

---

[4] M. Blair, 'For Whom Should Corporations Be Run?: An Economic Rationale for Stakeholder Management' (1998) 31 *Long Range Planning* 195 at 195.

[5] M. Blair, *Ownership and Control* (Washington DC, Brookings Institute, 1995) at 17.

[6] R. Estes, *Tyranny of the Bottom Line: Why Corporations Make Good People Do Bad Things*, 1996 at 86 and referred to in C. Bagley and K. Page, 'The Devil Made Me Do It: Replacing Corporate Directors' Veil of Secrecy with the Mantle of Stewardship' (1999) 16 *San Diego Law Review* 897 at 899.

[7] L. Hannah, *The Rise of the Corporate Economy*, 2nd ed (London, Methuen, 1983) at 1.

[8] J. McCahery, S. Picciotto and C. Scott, 'Introduction: Corporate Control: Changing Concepts and Practices of the Firm' in J. McCahery, S. Picciotto and C. Scott (eds), *Corporate Control and Accountability* (Oxford, Clarendon Press, 1993) at 2.

[9] J. McCahery, S. Picciotto and C. Scott, 'Introduction: Corporate Control: Changing Concepts and Practices of the Firm' in J. McCahery, S. Picciotto and C. Scott (eds), *Corporate Control and Accountability* (Oxford, Clarendon Press, 1993) at 2.

[10] O. Couwenberg, 'Corporate Architecture and Limited Liability' (2008) 4 *Review of Law and Economics* 621 at 622.

rate grouping where the group operates in several sectors of industry and commerce, and with such groups there are often many layers of subsidiary companies. They have a professional management and a sophisticated organisational structure. Many companies continue to have a growing influence globally. In 2000, the Institute for Policy Studies released a study that showed that of the world's 100 largest economic entities, 51 were corporations and 49 were countries,[11] and 22 American corporations had market capitalisations at the end of the 1990s that were greater than the gross domestic product of 22 countries and this included reasonably significant economies such as Spain and Poland.[12] Hitachi, listed 16th on the Fortune 500 (which is Fortune Magazine's listing of the largest companies in the United States) in the late 1990s, had a larger annual revenue than the Philippines, which at the time was listed as the 40th largest country in terms of gross national product.[13] And things do not seem to be changing, for data in 2002 suggested that the number of companies in the world's 100 largest economic entities had in fact increased to 52.[14]

All companies, whether they are large or small, multinational or local, play a fundamental, multidimensional and evolving role in promoting economic growth.[15] Public companies, one major type of company and the type of company with which this study is concerned, undoubtedly have a significant amount of power in society and what they do is clearly important to us all. They conduct many businesses, some of them operating globally and netting millions of pounds, dollars, euro, yen etc per annum. In fact it has been asserted that without the company much of

---

[11] S. Anderson and J. Cavanagh, 'Top 200: The rise of corporate global power,' Institute for Policy Studies, 2000, < http://www.ips-dc.org/downloads/Top_200.pdf > and referred to by the Australian Parliamentary Joint Committee on Corporations and Financial Services, *Corporate Responsibility: Managing Risk and Creating Value*, June 2006 at para 2.39.

[12] G. Morgenson, 'A Company Worth More Than Spain' *New York Times*, 26 December 1999, at 1 and referred to in L. Mitchell, *Corporate Irresponsibility* (New Haven, Yale Press, 2001) at 2.

[13] D. Logan, 'Corporate Citizenship in a Global Age' (1998) 146 *Royal Society of Arts Journal* 64 at 66 and referred to in S. Wheeler, *Corporations and the Third Way* (Oxford, Hart Publishing, 2002) at 9.

[14] S. Anderson et al, *Field Guide to the Global Economy*, 2nd ed (2005) at 69 and referred to by K. Greenfield, 'Defending Stakeholder Governance' (2008) 58 *Case Western Reserve Law Review* 1043 at n4.

[15] Department of the Treasury (Australia), *Submission 134*, p1, and referred to in para 2.34 of the Australian Parliamentary Joint Committee on Corporations and Financial Services, *Corporate Responsibility: Managing Risk and Creating Value*, June 2006.

people's enterprise would have remained locally owned and managed.[16] But companies are not merely giants in relation to economic affairs; their influence and reach is such that they feature in all aspects of social and political life as well as the economic.[17] For example, companies can be regarded as private forums in which social planning can be conducted, in such a way as to serve their own decisional criteria.[18] They own large tracts of land and significant assets, make huge numbers of contracts, and employ many millions of people. Companies have, in their function of employer, a critical role in interpreting and applying government policy in many sectors, and they can exert leverage when dealing with the communities in which they operate, often leading to concessions and other benefits. It has even been said that the United States is 'governed by international corporations which [do] not take politicians seriously.'[19] Moreover, their investment decisions can determine the rate of growth of particular sectors of business.[20] Undoubtedly many companies wield substantial power and enjoy strong bargaining positions. An example of this is the fact that the large supermarkets in western countries are able to demand that farmers who wish to be retained as suppliers provide food items at low prices.

Clearly large companies generally can dictate what is produced, how it is produced, when it is produced, and in what quantities it is produced,[21] and this has given companies something of a chequered reputation. The Confederation of British Industry stated as far back as 1973 that: 'Our style of life is determined by the activities and style of business; and the style of business is largely determined by the activities and style of our

---

[16] N. Long, 'The Corporation, Its Satellites, and the Local Community' in E. Mason (ed), *The Corporation in Modern Society* (Cambridge, Massachusetts, Harvard University Press, 1970 reprint) at 202.

[17] S. Bottomley, *The Constitutional Corporation* (Aldershot, Ashgate, 2007) at 3; C. Kaysen, 'The Corporation: How Much Power? What Scope' in E. Mason (ed), *The Corporation in Modern Society* (Cambridge, Massachusetts, Harvard University Press, 1970 reprint) at 99; D. Votaw, 'The Mythology of Corporations' (1962) (Spring) *California Management Review* 58 at 68.

[18] J. Parkinson, *Corporate Power and Responsibility* (Oxford, Oxford University Press, 1993) at 1.

[19] 'Vidal votes for chaos on his way to heaven' *Sydney Morning Herald*, 24 January 1997 and quoted in J. Hill, 'Visions and Revisions of the Shareholder' (2000) 48 *American Journal of Comparative Law* 39 at 53.

[20] C. Kaysen, 'The Corporation: How Much Power? What Scope?' in E. Mason (ed), *The Corporation in Modern Society* (Cambridge, Massachusetts, Harvard University Press, 1970 reprint) at 92.

[21] See J. Parkinson, *Corporate Power and Responsibility* (Oxford, Oxford University Press, 1993) at 15.

companies.'[22] This statement is even truer today than it was 40 years ago. All of this means that it endows great power on those who manage such businesses, for typically, today, the company's articles of association or by-laws will vest the board of directors with general management powers[23] concerning the affairs of the company, and this will determine the power distribution in a company. Where directors have been given wide-ranging powers, then they alone can exercise them, and in some jurisdictions the only thing that the members can do is to pass a special resolution to amend the articles or by-laws.[24] Elsewhere, such as in the United States, not even a unanimous vote of shareholders can control the directors and what they do within their considerable powers.[25]

The reach of many large companies can be seen in their involvement in, and influence over, the mechanisms of government that determine what laws will be applied to society.[26] It has been said that 'the corporation provides the legal framework for the development of resources and the generation of wealth in the private sector.'[27] Also, some companies carry out critical 'public services' such as providing telecommunications, water, electricity and gas. Thomas Donaldson[28] has noted that 'large corporations are capable of influencing mainstream societal events and this power is not only economic, but social and political'.[29] A good example is when a large company decides either to reduce its workforce, something being seen during the recent global recession, or to relocate a factory. The ability, on the part of large companies, to exercise what the

---

[22] Confederation of British Industry, *The Responsibilities of the British Public Company*, 1973 at 8 and quoted in J. Parkinson, *Corporate Power and Responsibility* (Oxford, Oxford University Press, 1993) at 3.

[23] For example, see in the UK, The Companies (Tables A–F) Regulations 1985, Art 70 of Table A and The Companies (Model Articles) Regulations 2008, SI 2008/3229, reg 2, Sch 1, art 5 (private companies); reg 4, Sch 3, art 5 (public companies). In the United States, see Delaware General Corporation Law, s.141(a) (2009) and Model Business Corporation Act, s.8.01 (2008).

[24] *John Shaw & Sons (Salford) Ltd v Shaw* [1935] 2 KB 113.

[25] S. Bainbridge, *The New Corporate Governance* (New York, Oxford University Press, 2008) at 34.

[26] L. Mitchell, *Corporate Irresponsibility* (New Haven, Yale Press, 2001) at 7.

[27] *Teck Corporation v Millar* (1972) 33 DLR (3d) 288 at 314 per Berger J.

[28] *Corporations and Morality* (Englewood Cliffs, NJ, Prentice Hall, 1982) at 7.

[29] For further discussion concerning the political nature of a large company, see S. Bottomley, 'From Contractualism to Constitutionalism: A Framework for Corporate Governance' (1997) 19 *Sydney Law Review* 277, and his subsequent monograph, *The Constitutional Corporation* (Aldershot, Ashgate, 2007).

late John Parkinson described as 'social decision-making power,'[30] raises concerns for the reason that 'companies are able to make choices which have important social consequences: they make private decisions which have public results.'[31] Nevertheless, Sally Wheeler makes the point that it is not accurate to say that companies are all-powerful for there are instances of governments and courts limiting the power of large companies.[32] And companies do depend upon many elements that exist in the world in which they operate, including the political, social and economic environment. Having said all of that, there are clearly examples of companies operating at a level that is 'beyond that of national law,'[33] and acting so as to influence government policy and law-making.[34] All of this might lead to companies being able to extract inducements that constitute market and political benefits.[35] This has led some to assert that companies are not really private institutions, but rather they should be seen as public institutions with public obligations, and as being responsible in some of the ways in which we ordinarily associate with governments.[36] In Europe, in particular, there has been a focus on companies having a responsibility in relation to the public interest, and it has been stated that the public interest of a company increases the larger it becomes.[37] In the distant past, companies clearly stated in their charters of incorporation what the company's purpose was to be, and

---

[30]   J. Parkinson, *Corporate Power and Responsibility* (Oxford, Oxford University Press, 1993) at 22.

[31]   Ibid at 10. Also, see L. Mitchell, *Corporate Irresponsibility* (New Haven, Yale Press, 2001) at 6; S. Sunder, 'Value of the Firm: Who Gets the Goodies?' Yale ICF Working Paper No. 02-15, August 2001 at 4, available at < http://papers.ssrn.com/abstract_id=309747 > (last visited, 16 June 2009).

[32]   S. Wheeler, *Corporations and the Third Way* (Oxford, Hart Publishing, 2002) at 10.

[33]   Ibid, and referring to F. Johns, 'The Invisibility of the Transnational Corporation: An Analysis of International Law and Legal Theory' (1994) 19 *Melbourne University Law Review* 893.

[34]   J. Parkinson, *Corporate Power and Responsibility* (Oxford, Oxford University Press, 1993) at 19.

[35]   C. E. Lindblom, *Politics and Markets*, 1977 at 173 and referred to in J. Parkinson, *Corporate Power and Responsibility* (Oxford, Oxford University Press, 1993) at 20.

[36]   For example, see D. Branson, 'The Death of Contractarianism and the Vindication of Structure and Authority in Corporate Governance and Corporate Law' in L. Mitchell (ed), *Progressive Corporate Law* (Boulder, Westview Press, 1995) at 93.

[37]   M. Kaye, 'The Theoretical Basis of Modern Company Law' [1976] *Journal Business Law* 235 at 239.

the charter of the British East India Company, which, of course, had great influence in the eighteenth and nineteenth centuries, was: 'serving public interests.'[38]

The fact of the matter is that companies not only play a critical role in markets and the commercial world, but they influence the lives of 'ordinary people' because they are employed by them, buy goods from them as consumers and are citizens in communities from where the companies operate. Mary Stokes sums it up neatly when she states:

> [T]he company has become an organization whose significance almost rivals that of the state. It is the primary institution for organizing and employing much of our capital and labour resources and the primary supplier of goods and services in our community.[39]

The significance of large companies can be seen in many ways, not least in the fact that their collapse can create havoc. This has occurred on many occasions in many different countries. An example is the HIH Insurance Group, which operated in Australia. It collapsed in 2001.[40] Such was the impact on Australian society, the Australian government established a Royal Commission to look into the company's management and demise. The Royal Commissioner, Justice Owen, described some elements of the impact when he said:

> HIH was one of Australia's biggest home-building market insurers. Its collapse left the building industry in turmoil. Home owners were left without compulsory home warranty insurance; the owners of residential dwellings have found that cover for defective building work has vanished; builders are unable to operate because they cannot obtain builders' warranty insurance. The cost to the building and construction industry alone has forced state governments to spend millions of dollars of public money to prevent further damage to the industry. There are thousands of other cases of personal and community hardship, each one no less devastating for those affected by it.[41]

---

[38]   J. Cohan, "'I didn't know' and "I was only doing my job": has corporate governance careered out of control?' (2002) 40 *Journal of Business Ethics* 275 at 292.

[39]   'Company Law and Company Theory' in S. Wheeler (ed), *The Law of the Business Enterprise* (Oxford, Oxford University Press, 1994) at 107.

[40]   It involved the largest corporate collapse in Australian history.

[41]   *The Failure of HIH Insurance: A Corporate Collapse and its Lessons*, Royal Commission, conducted by Justice Owen, April 2003, vol 1, (Commonwealth of Australia, Canberra) at pxiii, and accessible at <http://www.hihroyalcom.gov.au/finalreport/Front%20Matter,%20critical%20assessment%20and%20summary.HTML#_Toc37086537> (last visited, 5 April 2010).

And compared to the demise of a giant like Lehman Bros, the huge global financial services corporation, HIH's demise was relatively small, but to the many Australians, and some foreigners, who were affected by the collapse, the impact was massive.

It is established,[42] since the seminal work of Adolf Berle and Gardiner Means in the early 1930s, that in the United Kingdom and the United States, and in other countries adopting similar laws and commercial practices, public companies are marked by the principle of separation of ownership and control. That is, the people who own the company, or at least the shares in it, do not control it. Control is vested in specialist managers, often known as executives or managers. This is due to the fact that in the UK and the US the shareholding is dispersed amongst a large range of shareholders, and so not all shareholders can be involved in the management process.[43] Yet in other countries, notably Germany and Japan, shareholding is concentrated amongst a relative few, primarily banks, insurance companies and other institutions. Such shareholders are known as blockholders.[44]

2.   THE NEED FOR OBJECTIVE

All purposeful activity requires some objective, and the work of a company is no different. It has been said that a company is an entity whose 'defining

---

[42]   There have been recent challenges to the thesis of the work. See, for example, L. Hannah, 'The Divorce of Ownership From Control From 1900: Recalibrating Imagined Global Historical Trends' (2007) 49 *Business History* 404 at 423; C. Holderness, 'The Myth of Diffuse Ownership in the United States' (2009) 22 *Review of Financial Studies* 1322. But note the response in B. Cheffins and S. Bank, 'Is Berle and Means Really a Myth?' ECGI Law Working Paper No 121/2009 and accessible at <http://ssrn.com/abstract =1352605> (last visited on 16 November 2009).

[43]   Recent statistics suggest that the range of shareholders is not as broad in the UK and the US as it once was. There are indications that institutional investors have been taking a greater portion of shares in public companies. This is certainly the case in the US, for in 2008 it was reported that the portion of institutional investor ownership in the US had increased to 66 per cent (C. Brancato and S. Rabimov, *The Conference Board*, 2008, Institutional Investment Report 6, 9, 20). But the statistics in the UK are somewhat confusing and the increase of the proportion of shares held by institutional investors may not be as high as once was thought. See, A. Keay, 'Moving Towards Stakeholderism? Constituency Statutes, Enlightened Shareholder Value and All That: Much Ado About Little?' (2011) 22 *European Business Law Review* 1.

[44]   For a discussion of blockholders, see C.Holderness, 'A Survey of Blockholders and Corporate Control' (2005) *FRBNY Economic Policy Review* (April) 51.

characteristic is the attainment of a specific goal or purpose.'[45] As Michael Jensen has said: 'Every organisation attempting to accomplish something has to ask and answer the following question: what are we trying to accomplish?'[46] Specifically, it has been pointed out that in order to construct a system of corporate governance one needs to commence with purpose.[47] Notwithstanding the importance of public companies, there has been uncertainty for many years as to what is the actual objective of companies, because arguably the company law in most jurisdictions fails to articulate the purpose of the company. It is acknowledged that every company, through its board, will set its own basic goals, as a necessity of successfully operating a business,[48] and these will undoubtedly differ. Also, companies regularly include in their constitutions or charters the general goals for which the company was incorporated, such as 'to carry out the business of a building contractor' or 'to operate the business of a clothes retailer.'[49] Having said that, the practice has been, for many years, to use standard boilerplate clauses providing for a very wide range of purposes. The priorities of companies will, obviously, change as a company's size, focus and strategy changes. Directors might consider, as part of their management strategy, concentrating on variables, such as accounting profitability, stock returns, customer value, market share, company growth, employee satisfaction, supplier surplus or attaining social performance.[50] Whatever the various aims directors have for a company, it is the argument of this book that all companies need to have an ultimate objective, and whatever is formulated by the directors in terms of goals, it must be congruent with the interests of society as a whole.[51] The book seeks to formulate an objective later.

---

[45]   T. Parsons, *Structure and Process in Modern Scientific Societies* (Glencoe, Free Press, 1960) at 63

[46]   'Value Maximisation, Stakeholder Theory, and the Corporate Objective Function' (2001) 7 *European Financial Management* 297 at 298.

[47]   J. Carver, 'A Case for Global Governance Theory' (2010) 18 *Corporate Governance: An International Review* 149 at 149, 150.

[48]   P. Drucker, 'Business Objectives and Survival Needs: Notes on a Discipline of Business Enterprise' (1958) 31 *Journal of Business* 81 at 87.

[49]   Of course those involved might have their own goals for the company, and these will rarely be expressed: M. Metzger and D. Dalton, 'Seeing the Elephant: An Organizational Perspective on Corporate Moral Agency' (1996) 33 *American Business Law Journal* 489 at 516.

[50]   S. Thomsen, 'Corporate Values and Corporate Governance' (2004) 4 *Corporate Governance* 29 at 34.

[51]   M. Blair, *Ownership and Control* (Washington DC, Brookings Institute, 1995) at 14.

Robert Clark, the renowned American law professor, said, in his major and influential work on corporate law, that the corporate purpose is an '"extremely varied, inclusive and open-ended" concept.'[52] This is because the law does not lay down the objective of the company, save for providing that what it engages in must be for lawful purposes. It has been said by an associate editor of the journal, *Organization Science,* that ascertaining the corporate objective is the 'most important theoretical and practical issue confronting us today,'[53] and is the subject, directly or indirectly of a substantial amount of literature in many disciplines, including law, finance, economics, organisational behaviour, ethics and sociology. The ascertainment of the objective is critical for a number of reasons. For example, it underpins the kind of corporate governance that needs to be implemented and determines what responsibilities are imposed on directors. The problem in dealing with this issue is, according to John Farrar, that 'we lack a clear idea of the legitimate ends of corporation [sic].'[54]

The issue of the objective of the company is far from being a new one. Debate as to what should be the goal or purpose of a company has gone on for years[55] and has generally revolved around argument as to whether one of two dominant theories, namely shareholder primacy theory or stakeholder theory, should be followed. Although it has been said that the issue of the corporate objective has been debated 'ad nauseam,'[56] it is persistent[57] and debate concerning it is far from at an end.[58] One reason

---

[52] R. Clark, *Corporate Law*, 1986 at 17 and quoted to in M. Blair and L. Stout, 'Specific Investment: Explaining Anomalies in Corporate Law' (2006) 31 *Journal of Corporation Law* 719 at 731.

[53] J. Walsh, 'Introduction to the "Corporate Objective Revisited" Exchange' (2004) 15 *Organization Science* 349 at 349.

[54] J. Farrar, 'Frankenstein Incorporated or Fools Parliament? Revisiting the Concept of the Corporation in Corporate Governance' (1998) 10 *Bond Law Review* 142 at 158.

[55] J. Cohan, '"I didn't know" and "I was only doing my job"': has corporate governance careered out of control?' (2002) 40 *Journal of Business Ethics* 275 at 291.

[56] See H. N. Butler and F. S. McChesney, 'Why They Give at the Office: Shareholder Welfare and Corporate Philanthropy in the Contractual Theory of the Corporation' (1999) 84 *Cornell Law Review* 1195 at 1195.

[57] W. Allen, J. Jacobs and L. Strine, 'The Great Takeover Debate: A Meditation on Bridging the Conceptual Divide' (2002) 69 *University of Chicago Law Review* 1067 at 1067.

[58] A. Sundram and A. Inkpen, 'The Corporate Objective Revisited' (2004) 15 *Organization Science* 350; H. Hu, 'Buffet, Corporate Objectives, and the Nature of Sheep' (1997) 19 *Cardozo Law Review* 379 at 380.

for the longevity of the debate about it is that it is a very complex issue and its study is continually pointing up new questions and aspects that require consideration.[59]

It is often said that the aim of business companies is to make profits, with some emphasising the need to maximise profits.[60] To say that that is the aim of companies is fine as a very basic statement,[61] as profits are essential for a business, but it tends to be too glib, providing no definite and identifiable content. While this might be all well and good for private (closely-held) companies, it is not appropriate and adequate for public companies that are large and complex and which have profound effects on the interests of a wide range of people, and even nations. Elaine Sternberg has criticised[62] fixation on profits on the basis that they are, as with all accounting measures, a slippery notion, and can be 'massaged' to suit the purposes of management.[63] Also, she asserts that profits usually, as a measure, means that the focus of a company's board is on short-term gains.[64] Charles Handy has called it a myth that profit is the purpose of a company.[65] And as far back as 1959 Robert Anthony criticised economics texts for assuming that the company's objective is profit maximisation.[66] But, the renowned economist Milton Friedman famously argued in 1970 that the objective of a company is to produce profit.[67] Others have said

---

[59] See, H. Hu, 'Buffet, Corporate Objectives, and the Nature of Sheep' (1997) 19 *Cardozo Law Review* 379 at 380.

[60] For instance, see H. Manne, *The Modern Corporation and Social Responsibility* (Washington DC, American Enterprise Institute, 1972) at 8. Some, such as Henry Simon, have argued for companies merely making satisfactory profits (*Models of Man* (New York, John Wiley, 1957) at 204ff). This is known as 'profit-satisficing'.

[61] Although J. Galbraith in 'Galbraith and the theory of the corporation' (1984) 7 *Journal of Post Keynesian Economics* 43 at 56 regards it only as an assumption at best and some have seen it as an untenable assumption: R. Nelson, S. Winter and H. Schuette, 'Technical Change in an Evolutionary Model' (1976) 90 *Quarterly Journal of Economics* 90.

[62] E. Sternberg, *Just Business*, 2nd ed (Oxford, Oxford University Press, 2000) at 45.

[63] In this regard, see Chapter 8 below.

[64] E. Sternberg, *Just Business*, 2nd ed (Oxford, Oxford University Press, 2000) at 45–46.

[65] 'What is a Company For?' (1993) 1 *Corporate Governance* 14 at 14. Peter Drucker essentially agrees ('Business Objectives and Survival Needs: Notes on a Discipline of Business Enterprise' (1958) 31 *Journal of Business* 81 at 84).

[66] 'The Trouble with Profit Maximization' (1960) *Harvard Business Review* 126 at 126.

[67] 'The Social Responsibility of Business is to Increase its Profits' *New York Times*, 13 September 1970, Section 6 (Magazine), 32 at 33.

that the purpose of the corporate form is to foster social wealth.[68] The problem with this latter proposition is that it is vague and far from clear what is meant by social wealth. It also begs the question: how is this to be attained? Another commentator[69] has even argued for the happiness of the shareholders as being the objective of the company, divorcing this from the usual approach of simply focusing on the financial position of shareholders. The central question which this book addresses is: what model should be used in defining the objective of a public company? If a model can be arrived at, a second question is posed, one that scholars have found difficult to resolve, namely: how would the model operate?

The debate about the issue of the corporate objective is often said to have commenced with two American law professors, Adolph Berle and E. Merrick Dodd, in the early 1930s. Since that time the debate has become more intense, and particularly, as mentioned above, in the past 25–30 years. Advocates of the two predominant theories often trace their positions back to either Berle or Dodd. Putting it very glibly, Berle took the view that the managers of the company held the property of the company for the benefit of the shareholders and they acted in order to maximise shareholder wealth,[70] whilst Dodd argued that managers acted as trustees for the corporate enterprise and that they had to be concerned with broader interests.[71] But the fact is overlooked that Berle indicated[72] that he, like Dodd, favoured an approach closer to what we know as stakeholder theory today, but he confessed that he could not see it being workable. His inevitable conclusion from his thinking was that you cannot abandon an emphasis on: 'the view that business corporations exist for the sole purpose of making profits for their shareholders until such time as [you] are prepared to offer a clear and reasonably enforceable scheme of responsibilities to someone else.'[73] Berle saw shareholder primacy as a second-best solution as a way of mitigating the amount of

---

68   For example, T. Glynn, 'Communities and Their Corporations: Towards a Stakeholder Conception of the Production of Corporate Law' (2008) 58 *Case Western Reserve Law Review* 4 at 4; K. Greenfield, 'Saving the World With Corporate Law' (2008) 57 *Emory Law Journal* 947 at 963.

69   J. McConvill, 'The Separation of Ownership and Control under a Happiness-based Theory of the Corporation' (2005) 26 *The Company Lawyer* 35 at 36.

70   A.A. Berle Jr, 'For Whom Corporate Managers are Trustees: A Note' (1932) 45 *Harvard Law Review* 1365 at 1367.

71   E.M. Dodd, 'For Whom Are Corporate Managers Trustees' (1932) 45 *Harvard Law Review* 1145 at 1147–1148.

72   A.A. Berle Jr, 'For Whom Corporate Managers are Trustees: A Note' (1932) 45 *Harvard Law Review* 1365.

73   Ibid at 1367.

opportunism[74] in which managers might engage, but it was more practicable than stakeholder theory.

Relating to the work of Berle and Dodd, a critical issue that this book tackles, and one that has been regularly asked, is: how are directors to act in managing the affairs of a public company? This is because it is inextricably linked to the corporate objective question. It is the directors who will seek to meet the corporate objective and what the objective is will determine how directors should act. Another major issue has been what happens to the profit that is generated by companies? It has been said that there is 'no greater policy issue in corporate law than to whose benefit corporate production is intended to redound.'[75] The issue is discussed in detail in Chapter 8.

3.   THE COMPANY

What is striking about companies is that they are rather peculiar structures. Whilst obviously not human, they are legal persons, legal personality being conferred as a result of the process of incorporation (registration), and are able to do many things which can be done by humans, such as owning property, making contracts, instituting legal proceedings and, most importantly, and unlike humans, enjoying perpetual succession. This last feature of companies means that they may, conceivably, never cease to exist. Indeed we have operating in the world of commerce many companies that have existed not only for decades, but centuries.

The company is a mechanism that people who want to carry on business collectively can use effectively and productively. When producing large quantities of goods or services it is normal to need a wide variety of inputs, including financial resources, risk-bearing services and decision-making.[76] The public company is well suited to meeting this need as it avoids the costs associated with market transactions involving individuals; the company can handle all of the transactions and this reduces transaction costs and is more economically efficient. According to Ronald Coase,

---

[74]   In this work this term, consistent with the way that it is used by Oliver Williamson (*The Economic Institution of Capitalism* (1985) at 47–49)) is employed to describe self-interested behaviour that includes features of guile, misrepresentation, deception or bad faith.

[75]   C. Brunner, 'The Enduring Ambivalence of Corporate Law' (2008) 59 *Alabama Law Review* 1385 at 1426.

[76]   L. Putterman, 'Ownership and the Nature of the Firm' (1993) 17 *Journal of Comparative Economics* 243 at 245.

the renowned economics theorist, the company permits the collection of various resources, such as capital and labour, without the need to negotiate the terms for each and every use of the resources.[77] This can, of course, be repeated for later transactions, and when it does so the cost of incorporation and the running of the company are paid for by the saving of transaction costs.

The book does not address in any real way the issue of whether the company is wholly a private institution with no public concerns as advocated by most contractarians, or whether it is a public institution with public obligations, as argued for by the communitarians, although these issues are mentioned and considered briefly from time to time. The book also does not indulge in any significant consideration of the responsibility of the company save where it is pertinent in examining the shareholder primacy and stakeholder theories and again when mapping out the objective of the company that is argued for in the book. This is not meant to suggest that the issue of corporate responsibility is not an important matter. On the contrary, it is a critical issue. For the most part the book notes that companies do have responsibilities, but it is not intended to adumbrate them and to examine them.[78] It is submitted that 'responsibilities' and 'objectives' are not synonymous.

It is clear that in the past companies existed for the public benefit,[79] and in the early days of the American corporation there was a tendency to see corporations as social organisations.[80] UK legislation has never indicated how the company should be perceived. The law left it to the courts to interpret the 'mystical utterances'[81] in the legislation. The House of Lords did this to a certain extent in the famous case of *Salomon v Salomon and Co Ltd*.[82] This case and its effects are discussed in Chapter 5.

Likewise the book does not examine in any detail the power that is vested in and exercised by companies. It suffices to say, as indicated earlier, that companies wield a significant amount of social, political and

---

[77] See R. Coase 'The Nature of the Firm' (1937) 4 *Economica* 386.

[78] This is done by, for instance, J. Brummer, *Corporate Responsibility and Legitimacy* (New York, Greenwood Press, 1991); J. Parkinson, *Corporate Power and Responsibility* (Oxford, Oxford University Press, 1993); L. Mitchell, *Corporate Irresponsibility* (New Haven, Yale University Press, 2001).

[79] J. Hurst, *The Legitimacy of the Business Corporation* (Charlottesville, 1970), The University Press of Virginia, Chapters 1 & 2.

[80] E. M. Dodd, 'For Whom are Corporate Managers Trustees?' (1932) 45 *Harvard Law Review* 1145 at 1148–1149.

[81] (1897) 13 LQR 6.

[82] [1897] AC 22.

economic power in individual and national communities, and some exercise power in global terms.[83]

Finally, we can say that public companies involve the pooling of resources thereby enabling the process of amassing capital to exploit economies of scale.

4. THE SPECIFIC ISSUES IN THE BOOK

The central question which the book seeks to address is: what should be the ultimate objective of large public companies? This is largely a normative study which aims to analyse the existing dominant theories that address the above question and to explain and justify a new model for defining the corporate objective, which arguably has not been unequivocally laid down by the law. It then seeks to articulate how the managers of a company are to act in employing the model and how the model can address some of the more difficult questions that have been posed in relation to the manner in which companies are to engage in business.

The book focuses on public companies. There is clearly a different context, flavour and dynamic to closely-held (private) companies which do in fact constitute the vast majority of companies in most jurisdictions, but they do not possess the same power as public companies and particularly the same range of power.

5. THE BACKGROUND TO THE STUDY

The issue of the corporate objective has been dominated, for a long time, by two theories, the shareholder primacy (or value) theory and the stakeholder theory, and, as mentioned earlier, most of the relevant literature has polarised around these two approaches. The approaches have diametrically opposed ways of tackling the issue of the corporate objective, as well as the corporate governance mechanisms and arrangements that are associated with them.[84] Arguably there are other theories that can be found on the spectrum somewhere between these two dominant theories.

---

[83] For a good discussion of the power of companies, even though it is 18 years old, See Chapter 1 of John Parkinson's, *Corporate Power and Responsibility* (Oxford, Oxford University Press, 1993).

[84] See, S. Ayuso et al, 'Maximising Stakeholders' Interests: An Empirical Analysis of the Stakeholder Approach to Corporate Governance,' IESE Business School, University of Navarra, Working Paper No 670, January 2007 at 1.

These other theories are the stewardship, finance and political theories.[85] But they have attracted relatively little support and have rarely been articulated. Some scholars, and I tend to agree with them, see them merely as views advocated by splinter groups and they are rooted in either one of the two dominant theories.[86]

The crux of the debate is in relation to this question: for whose benefit do the managers of a company run the company? Under shareholder primacy, as the name suggests, the managers are to focus on the shareholders, and the managers are to maximise the interests of the shareholders ahead of any other interested parties who might have claims against the company. In contrast, under the stakeholder theory the managers are to consider the interests of all stakeholders (including the shareholders); the directors are not only to manage the company for the betterment of shareholders, but should balance the interests of a multitude of stakeholders. Many argue that these models are either not normatively desirable or workable or both, and each suffers from several shortcomings.

I should say that while there is a pronounced emphasis on legal issues, this study is intended to be trans-disciplinary for a number of reasons. Let me mention three. First, there have been insightful and scholarly contributions to the issues raised in relation to the area under consideration from writers in various disciplines. Second, the area under discussion benefits from a broad socio-legal approach for the company, as adverted to in the early parts of the Chapter, because it plays a critical function in the society in which we live and work. Third, it is not possible, for the most part, to deal with major issues affecting the company without taking into account the matters addressed by several disciplines. I merely mention some of the many disciplinary matters that are relevant, and why. Law is critical because besides the legal theory that has been written, there is legislation and case law that has addressed the objective of the company and this needs to be analysed and synthesised. Also, there are significant legal consequences flowing from the incorporation of a company. Finance and economics (I do not seek to amalgamate these disciplines, but for present purposes they can be discussed together) are crucial to all elements of commercial law and there has been a tradition from Coase, in particular, onwards for those versed in these disciplines to comment on the company

---

[85]   J. Kirkbride, S. Letza, X. Sun and C. Smallman, 'The Boundaries of Governance in the Post-modern World' (2008) 59 *Northern Ireland Legal Quarterly* 161 at 172.

[86]   S. Letza and X. Sun, 'Corporate Governance: Paradigms, Dilemmas and Beyond' (2002) 2 *Poznan University Economic Review* 43.

(or, often, the firm) and the fundamental theoretical elements related to it. Ethics scholars have, in recent years in particular, studied and commented on the company and the ethical issues that are relevant to a consideration of, especially, its power, responsibility, legitimacy and nature, and in any event ethical considerations affect (or should affect) all aspects of commercial life. Additionally, it is fair to say that ethical considerations are not an optional extra. Scholars in organisational behaviour have examined the functioning of companies and commented on a variety of matters that relate to the area under review. In particular many have developed aspects of the stakeholder theory.

To clarify, I should say that for this work I will refer to the corporate form as a company, in common with the British and Irish approach. American, Canadian and Australian readers, together with others, will be more familiar with the use of the word 'corporation.' Generally speaking, while there are esoteric historical reasons for differences in the meaning of the words 'company' and 'corporation,' I do not intend to make any distinction and in some works which I quote, the word 'corporation' has been used. On occasions I use the words interchangeably in my own commentary.

While the book does not intend to be restricted to particular jurisdictions or areas of the world, there is a focus on the law and practice in Anglo-American jurisdictions, namely those jurisdictions which have embraced UK and/or American law and practice. Such jurisdictions *include,* besides the UK and the US, Ireland, Australia, Canada and New Zealand. Other jurisdictions that have not embraced UK or US law and the common law system, have decided to adopt and adapt aspects of corporate governance that have been developed in either the UK or the US or both, such as provisions providing some protection for minority shareholders and the use of fiduciary duties of directors. Developing economies, in particular, have considered and either adopted or adapted a number of elements of approaches to corporate governance adopted in the Anglo-American system. While I tend to focus on companies that are founded in the Anglo-American tradition, I do not seek to limit my remarks only to those companies. I recognise that there are cultural, social, historical and political factors that mean that the approach, law and regulation in one country does not necessarily transplant well to another.[87]

---

[87]   See the various works that are based on the concept of 'path dependency'. For example, see what has become perhaps a classical work in the field of law: L. Bebchuk and M. Roe, 'A Theory of Path Dependence in Corporate Ownership and Governance' (1999) 52 *Stanford Law Review* 127.

6. THE FOCUS OF THE BOOK

As the two theories that I have mentioned above have so dominated the area, I will engage in a substantial, critical analysis of them. The dominance and popularity of these theories means that a considered and detailed examination of them is appropriate and warranted. The book then fixes on a new model, known as the entity maximisation and sustainability model ('EMS'). After laying out the essential aspects of the model and then, because EMS is focused on the company as an entity or enterprise, that is, the company is an institution in its own right, and the entity exists separately from those who invest in it, and continues to exist notwithstanding changes in the identity of the investors, the book will seek to justify reliance on the entity approach through an analysis of the theory and practice of the company from the perspective of various academic disciplines.

The rest of the book involves taking the EMS model and seeking to develop it into a full-blown model, with further and more detailed justification for its use, and consideration of any apparent problems that it produces. In particular, the book goes on: to ascertain if the model is able to be enforced and through what mechanism(s); to identify the investors in the company, their interests and roles and what benefits they will seek and receive from the company that adheres to EMS, and how conflicts between investors are to be addressed by the directors; to determine how the managers of a company are to act in employing the model; to assess the workability of the model; to explore the issue of distribution of company profits.

Chancellor William Allen, formerly Chancellor of the Delaware Court of Chancery opined in 1992, when writing extra-judicially,[88] that he did not think that there could be agreement in defining the purpose of the company. He is probably right, but nevertheless this book seeks to formulate a model that might attract further consideration, at least.

7. WHY ARE THE ISSUES IN THIS BOOK IMPORTANT?

The importance of the book lies first, and this has been noted already, in the fact that defining the objective of companies is regarded as the 'most

---

[88] W. Allen, 'Our Schizophrenic Conception of the Business Corporation' (1992) 14 *Cardozo Law Review* 261 at 280.

important theoretical and practical issue confronting us today'[89] and is the subject, directly or indirectly, of a substantial amount of literature in many disciplines, including law, finance, organisational behaviour, ethics and economics. It has been asserted recently that the need to resolve this issue has become increasingly important,[90] so it should not be shelved but subjected to further examination. Henry Hu has in the past claimed that the issue of the corporate objective is the most important in corporate finance and corporate law as it is omnipresent and should animate every decision a company makes,[91] and I do not think that anything has happened since Hu's statement to attenuate what he has said. One reason that this issue has not been resolved is that it is an exceptionally difficult one to resolve in a comprehensive fashion.[92] Second, a solid theoretical underpinning is needed for the company law that is developed by the legislature and the courts, something that so often has been missing in this area of the law, and a model which determines the objective would assist in this regard. The work also contributes to the area as it might enable scholars to assess companies and directors through a different lens. Until now there has been a tendency only either to focus on the two primary approaches mentioned above and discussed in detail in Chapters 2 and 3, or for scholars to take one of the approaches and introduce subtle changes to it. It is hoped that the outcome of the book would serve, amongst other things, as the basis for studying companies, provide insights to academics considering corporate behaviour, and act as a guide to firm behaviour.

Third, there is a need to articulate a clear objective so as to provide some guidance for directors in the carrying out of their functions and to shape the normative content of the roles of directors.[93]

Fourth, it is submitted that it is necessary to ascertain what should be the objective of the company before one formulates measures to ensure that there is adequate corporate governance and it helps us to formulate

---

[89] J. Walsh, 'Introduction to the "Corporate Objective Revisited" Exchange' (2004) 15 *Organization Science* 349 at 349.

[90] R. Colombo, 'Ownership, Limited: Reconciling Traditional and Progressive Corporate Law via an Aristotelian Understanding of Ownership' (2008) 34 *Journal of Corporation Law* 247 at 248.

[91] 'Buffet, Corporate Objectives, and the Nature of Sheep' (1997) 19 *Cardozo Law Review* 379 at 380.

[92] C. Brunner, 'The Enduring Ambivalence of Corporate Law' (2008) 59 *Alabama Law Review* 1385 at 1386.

[93] B. Choudhury, 'Serving Two Masters: Incorporate Social Responsibility into the Corporate Paradigm' (2009) 11 *University of Pennsylvania Journal of Business Law* 631 at 631.

corporate governance mechanisms. This last point is made more pertinent by Michael Jensen's assertion that at the very essence of the 'current global corporate governance debate is a remarkable division of opinion about the fundamental purpose of the corporation.'[94]

Fifth, as adverted to earlier, we must distinguish between objectives and responsibilities. It is submitted that it is not until we ascertain what the objective of the company is, that we can map out the responsibilities of the company. Most agree that companies have responsibilities, but there is significant debate about what they are and how far and in what direction they are to go.[95]

Sixth, I think that Elaine Sternberg is partially correct when she effectively states that the objective of a business will determine what is ethical.[96] Obviously, there will be things that are not ethical even if the actor has the objective in mind, and so I would annotate what the learned writer said by adding that the objective will determine to a large extent the ethics of a particular action.

Seventh, while a lot has been written about shareholder primacy and stakeholder theories, much of it has been from one perspective or the other, setting up the opposing theory as a straw man before demolishing it. The book seeks to examine the theories in depth and as objectively as possible.

Finally, and perhaps most importantly, the corporate objective may be seen as essential to the advancement of welfare in general.[97]

It was noted earlier in the Chapter that debate as to what should be the goal or purpose of a company has gone on for years. If that is the case why should we have another publication addressing the issue of the corporate objective? The fact that the debate is long-standing and, one might say, intense, is indicative of the importance of it, and that in itself is a fair reason for further study. Also, the fact that the debate is one that is long-standing should not pre-empt further study in the area, especially where publications, such as this book, do not involve re-hashing the arguments already propounded, but an extensive examination of the dominant theories and

---

[94]   'Value Maximisation, Stakeholder Theory, and the Corporate Objective Function' (2001) 14 *Journal of Applied Corporate Finance* 8 at 8.

[95]   For helpful discussions of corporate responsibility see, for instance, J. Brummer, *Corporate Responsibility and Legitimacy* (New York, Greenwood Press, 1991); J. Parkinson, *Corporate Power and Responsibility* (Oxford, Oxford University Press, 1993).

[96]   E. Sternberg, *Just Business* 2nd ed (Oxford, Oxford University Press, 2000) at 4.

[97]   W. Allen, 'Our Schizophrenic Conception of the Business Corporation' (1992) 14 *Cardozo Law Review* 261 at 265.

the development of a new approach to the issue. What this book is seeking to do, in the main, is to make a break from the situation that we have had for years, namely the polarisation of arguments around one or other of the two predominant theories (shareholder primacy theory and stakeholder theory) that provide for inconsistent conceptions.[98] At various points of time one or the other of the theories has been dominant, and from a historic point of view, we can see that dominance has run in cycles. While the lack of agreement concerning which of the two conceptions better sets out the corporate objective did not, for most of the first seven or eight decades of the last century,[99] generate really intense conflict, we have seen a significant development of conflict in the last 25–30 years.[100]

The fact that much of the debate has gravitated around the two dominant theories is exemplified in a paper where the authors only countenanced the two theories as providing possible purposes for the company.[101] The literature has generally focused on aspects of these theories whereas this book, after dealing with them in depth, seeks to move away from that and proposes a fresh approach, through the development of a new model, and to investigate its effects in a corporate setting. While there will be an examination of, and interaction with, existing theories (which fair and thorough scholarship would require), the focus of the book is not about re-working previous arguments. The new model that is posited in Chapter 4 represents taking the debate in a different direction. The outcomes of the book are not, it is submitted, merely going to lead to good or better arguments that will be cited by one side or the other side of the existing debate (shareholder primacy v stakeholder theory), but will lead to new thoughts on, and approaches to, how one is to address the issue at hand. While there has been

---

[98] Ibid at 264, 265.

[99] Ibid at 265.

[100] For example, see the exchange of arguments in the following set of articles: A. Sundram and A. Inkpen, 'The Corporate Objective Revisited' (2004) 15 *Organization Science* 350; R. E. Freeman, A. Wicks and B. Parmar, 'Stakeholder Theory and "The Corporate Objective Revisited"' (2004) 15 *Organization Science* 364; A. Sundaram and A. Inkpen, 'Stakeholder Theory and "The Corporate Objective Revisited"': A Reply' (2004) 15 *Organization Science* 370. Scholars' views have been deeply based on their individual preferences: A. Licht, 'The Maximands of Corporate Governance: A Theory of Values and Cognitive Style' (2004) 29 *Delaware Journal of Corporate Law* 649 at 719.

[101] T. Kochan and S. Rubinstein, 'Toward a Stakeholder Theory of the Firm: The Saturn Partnership' (2000) 11 *Organization Science* 367 at 367; S. Ayuso et al, 'Maximising Stakeholders' Interests: An Empirical Analysis of the Stakeholder Approach to Corporate Governance,' IESE Business School, University of Navarra, Working Paper No 670, January 2007 at 1.

significant debate surrounding the shareholder primacy and stakeholder theories, these predominant theories have not been developed as deeply as this book seeks to do and as deeply as the model that is proposed later. What we have had hitherto is scholars developing points and themes, attacking particular views, or focusing on a particular problem, but all within either a shareholder primacy or a stakeholder framework. The issue has generally been couched in terms of whether a company exists solely for the enhancement of the economic welfare of the shareholders or whether the company should embrace a wider approach and consider other values.[102] In the past proponents of both perspectives have been as bold as to claim victory for the theory which they favour. Henry Hansmann and Reinier Kraakman have done it for shareholder primacy,[103] and R. Edward Freeman, perhaps the 'father' of modern day stakeholder theory, has proclaimed the pre-eminence of stakeholderism,[104] but more recently it has been adroitly asserted that the normative debate is inconclusive.[105] It is acknowledged that this work will not end the debate, and it does not purport to do so. It is hoped that it will lead to further study and that there will be more of a focus on the corporate entity rather than on the groups who are interested in the company's management, actions and performance.

Historically there has been in most jurisdictions no legislative proclamation or unequivocal judicial statement[106] which provides directors with a clear answer as to what is the corporate objective. We have been left with essentially a debate based on lines of scholarly thought, and re-energised in light of the US corporate scandals of 2001 and 2002, namely between those scholars holding to shareholder primacy and those holding to stakeholder theory. The two approaches are based on radically different normative premises,[107] with little ground being given by the proponents of either

---

[102]   W. Allen, J. Jacobs and L. Strine, 'The Great Takeover Debate: A Meditation on Bridging the Conceptual Divide' (2002) 69 *University of Chicago Law Review* 1067 at 1067.

[103]   'The End of History for Corporate Law' (2001) 89 *Georgetown Law Journal* 439.

[104]   R. E. Freeman, 'The Politics of Stakeholder Theory: Some Future Directions' (1994) 4 *Business Ethics Quarterly* 409 at 413.

[105]   I. Lee, 'Corporate Law, Profit Maximization, and the "Responsible" Shareholder' (2004) 10 *Stanford Journal of Law Business and Finance* 31 at 42.

[106]   A. Keay, 'Enlightened shareholder value, the reform of the duties of company directors and the corporate objective' [2006] *Lloyds Maritime and Commercial Law Quarterly* 335 at 341–346.

[107]   D. Millon, 'New Game Plan or Business as Usual? A Critique of the Team Production Model of the Corporate Board' (2000) 86 *Virginia Law Review* 1001 at 1040–1042.

theory.[108] Notwithstanding the significant amount of commentary written in relation to both of the major models, little progress has been made in securing any common ground.

Clearly, the modern public company is a complex undertaking that consists of intertwined human and economic relationships and far more complex than that posited by the traditional shareholder primacy model.[109] The discovery of a new approach is justified by the fact, as we will see shortly, that the prevailing paradigms have patent problems, and were devised in old societal contexts. It is also justified by the fact that firms are clearly changing as commerce changes.[110]

There needs to be a consideration of the issue from a different perspective. It is submitted that what Daily, Dalton and Canella say in relation to corporate governance applies equally to determining the corporate objective:

> Researchers often embrace a research paradigm that fits a narrow conceptualisation of the entirety of corporate governance to the exclusion of alternative paradigms. Researchers are, on occasion, disinclined to embrace research that contradicts dominant governance models and theories (i.e. a preference for independent governance structures) or research that is critical of past research methodologies or findings. This will not move the field of corporate governance forward.[111]

Some years ago, in a broad study undertaken in relation to directors in the US, Jay Lorsch found that directors were not sure what the goal of a company should be, and they were rather troubled by the fact that

---

[108]   A good example of this is to be found in the series of articles published in volume 15 of *Organization Science* in 2004 where Anant Sundaram and Andrew Inkpen resolutely put forward the shareholder value approach, while R. Edward Freeman, Andrew Wicks and Bidhan Parmar responded on behalf of stakeholder theory, and then Sundaram and Inkpen provided a rejoinder. See 'The Corporate Objective Revisited' (2004) 15 *Organization Science* 350; Freeman, Wicks and Parmar, 'Stakeholder Theory and "The Corporate Objective Revisited"' (2004) 15 *Organization Science* 364; Sundaram and Inkpen, 'Stakeholder Theory and "The Corporate Objective Revisited"': A Reply' (2004) 15 *Organization Science* 370.

[109]   L. Mitchell, 'A Theoretical and Practical Framework for Enforcing Corporate Constituency Statutes' (1992) 70 *Texas Law Review* 579 at 630.

[110]   L. Zingales, 'In Search of New Foundations' (2000) 55 *Journal of Finance* 1623.

[111]   C.M. Daily, D.R. Dalton and A.C. Canella, 'Corporate Governance: Decades of Dialogue and Data' (2003) 28(3) *Academy of Management Review* 371 at 379.

there was no authoritative guidance on the issue.[112] It is submitted that ascertaining the ultimate objective is critical as all of the activity of a company should be able to be subsumed under the ultimate objective which, understandably, would be relatively broad. Within the parameters set by the objective the board of directors should have a wide discretion as to how they will run the company's affairs, and what commercial interests they should pursue on behalf of the company. Directors are called upon to be accountable for what they do, and while it is important to put in place mechanisms to require this, there has to be some objective against which this accountability is measured.[113]

Finally, the Company Law Review Steering Group, that reviewed UK company law at the end of the last century and the first year of this present one, referred to the ultimate objective[114] and ended up spending a reasonable amount of time considering it,[115] so this suggests that it is an important issue.

8.   THE THEORY OF THE COMPANY

A topic that has occupied the time of many academics in several disciplines, and particularly in law, finance, business ethics and organisational behaviour, and probably even more so than the subject of this book is what is broadly referred to as the theory of the company (or firm). This study involves asking what are companies (firms) and why do they exist?[116] It is not intended in this book to address these questions save in passing as they warrant a more detailed and focused treatment than can be devoted to them here. What must be said is that a lot of what has been written about companies and firms has in fact addressed these issues and not the subject of this book, and on occasions it is felt that writers have confused the issue of what is a company with what is the objective of the company. Nevertheless, significant aspects of this literature are relevant and worthy

---

[112]   J. W. Lorsch, *Pawns or Potentates* (Boston, Harvard Business School, 1989).

[113]   R. Monks and N. Minow, *Corporate Governance*, 4th ed (Chichester, John Wiley and Sons, 2008) at 27.

[114]   Company Law Review, *Modern Company Law For a Competitive Economy: The Strategic Framework* (London, DTI, 1999), at para 5.1.12.

[115]   Ibid at paras 5.1.1–5.1.47.

[116]   For instance, D. Rose, 'Teams, Firms and the Evolution of Profit Seeking Behavior' at 1, available at <http://papers.ssrn.com/paper.taf?abstract_id=224438> (last visited, 16 June 2009).

of mention. While this literature does not examine directly the objective of the company, arguably much of the material assumes that the objective of the company is to maximise profits. The renowned economics scholar, Harold Demsetz, states that: 'neoclassical theory uses maximization [of profits] to guide its deductions because this seems a sensible or desirable decision criteria.'[117] But he goes on to say that this criteria 'seems to spring willy-nilly from within the mind.'[118] As indicated earlier in the Chapter, the idea of stating that the objective is to make profits is rather glib as far as the ultimate object of the company is concerned.

It is worth noting at this point that a lot of debate has proceeded on the basis of whether the company is an entity or enterprise that is distinct from its members on the one hand or whether it is only an aggregate of individuals and merely a fiction or abstraction on the other. I will take up this matter in Chapter 4.

It is impossible to detail, or even identify, all of the theories of the company that have been articulated at one time or another. It is even more impossible to mention all of the various emanations that have been developed from the main theories. I shall restrict myself to theories proposed by three leading schools of thought. I caution that I intend only to outline the theories, as a discussion of the theory of the company is not the focus of the book. I say again, by way of emphasis, that I do not intend to address all iterations of the theories. I accept that not all scholars who find themselves in the camps to be discussed will hold exactly to the same views. I deal with the issue briefly and discuss the theories that I am about to consider as background to the focus of the book and to provide some context for later chapters. Clearly some of the work done in relation to the theories about to be mentioned has contributed to discerning what should be the objective of the company.

First, we will consider those theories proposed by the law and economics school. Any theoretical consideration of any aspect of corporate law warrants some reference to the work done by those in the law and economics school. It is not intended to indulge in a prolix discussion of the contribution of law and economics scholarship as the literature is voluminous. The discussion has to be framed in general terms and it is accepted that not all scholars hold to all of the views articulated here.

---

[117] H. Demsetz, 1996 and quoted in D. Rose, 'Teams, Firms and the Evolution of Profit Seeking Behavior' at 3, available at <http://papers.ssrn.com/paper.taf?abstract_id=224438> (last visited, 16 June 2009).

[118] D. Rose, 'Teams, Firms and the Evolution of Profit Seeking Behavior' at 3, available at <http://papers.ssrn.com/paper.taf?abstract_id=224438> (last visited, 16 June 2009).

The law and economics school takes the view that companies are private initiatives and not public institutions. The school has embraced economic theories of the company and legal theory has been generally eschewed.[119] This is notwithstanding the fact that even though it is 70 years since the seminal writings of Ronald Coase on the nature of the firm, no consensus has been reached.[120] Lawyers have adopted the terminology of economists even though economists and lawyers often use conflicting terms and expressions. Good examples of this are the terms 'contracts' and 'agent'. Economists have either given little attention or rejected the role of legal principles in defining the company/firm, and they have separated the legal fiction from the economic concept.[121] There are four primary theories adopted by law and economics scholarship. Probably the greatest number of scholars working in corporate law have embraced the contractarian approach,[122] and particularly that variant that has developed from the neo-classical model.[123] Generally law and economics theory presumes that individuals should be at liberty to live how they choose and make whatever agreements they see fit,[124] and be permitted to opt out of the application of legal rules,[125] so the paradigm is seen as individualistic and anti-regulatory. Law and economics scholars differ concerning the appropriate level of legal regulation that should exist, and restrict free bargaining between parties.[126] The majority of those holding

---

[119]   Some scholars have tried to address that state of affairs. For example, see E. Orts, 'Shirking and Shaking: A Legal Theory of the Firm' (1998) 16 *Yale Law and Policy Review* 265; M. Eisenberg, 'The Conception that the Corporation is a Nexus of Contracts, and the Dual Nature of the Firm' (1999) 24 *Journal of Corporation Law* 819.

[120]   S. Masten, 'A Legal Basis for the Firm' (1988) 4 *Journal of Law, Economics and Organisation* 181 at 181.

[121]   Ibid at 185.

[122]   'A Team Production Theory of Corporate Law' (1999) 85 *Virginia Law Review* 247 at 286.

[123]   The classic work on the subject is F.H. Easterbrook and D.R. Fischel, *The Economic Structure of Company Law* (Cambridge, Massachusetts, Harvard University Press, 1991).

[124]   D. Millon, 'New Directions in Corporate Law: Communitarians, Contractarians and Crisis in Corporate Law' (1993) 50 *Washington and Lee Law Review* 1373 at 1382.

[125]   For example, see S. Bainbridge, 'Community and Statism: A Conservative Contractarian Critique of Progressive Corporate Law Scholarship' (1997) 82 *Cornell Law Review* 856 at 860–861.

[126]   For perhaps an example of the extreme view, see L. Ribstein, 'The Mandatory Nature of the ALI Code' (1993) 60 *George Washington Law Review* 984.

to a contractarian approach adhere to the view that companies comprise a nexus of contracts,[127] although one notable contractarian, Stephen Bainbridge, prefers to see the company as having a nexus of contracts.[128] It is often asserted that the nexus of contracts model of the company is the dominant legal view of the company.[129] I should note that this form of contractarian thinking is often known as 'economic contractarianism'[130] because it was first developed by economists and financial scholars, and the law and economics school has subsequently run with it.[131] Economic thought analyses the company as a type of firm and ignores the concept of

---

[127]   G. Kelly and J. Parkinson, 'The Conceptual Foundations of the Company: a Pluralist Approach' in J. Parkinson, A. Gamble and G. Kelly (eds), *The Political Economy of the Company* (Oxford, Hart Publishing, 2000) at 115. The literature considering the nexus of contracts is too voluminous to cite. But see, for example, A. Alchian and H. Demsetz, 'Production, Information Costs and Economic Organizations' (1972) 62 *American Economic Review* 777; M. Jensen and W. Meckling, 'Theory of the Firm: Managerial Behaviour, Agency Costs, and Ownership Structure', (1976) 3 *Journal of Financial Economics* 305; E. Fama, 'Agency Problems and the Theory of the Firm' (1980) 88 *Journal of Political Economy* 228 at 290; F. Easterbrook and D. Fischel, 'The Corporate Contract' (1989) 89 *Columbia Law Review* 1416 at 1426–1427. Stephen Bainbridge has said that the nexus of contracts provides us with 'an educated guess' about the rule that most parties would embrace if they could bargain *ex ante* ('Community and Statism: A Conservative Contractarian Critique of Progressive Corporate Law Scholarship' (1997) 82 *Cornell Law Review* 856 at 869). The nexus of contracts approach is critiqued by W. Bratton Jr, in 'The "Nexus of Contracts Corporation": A Critical Appraisal' (1989) 74 *Cornell Law Review* 407 at 412, 446–465. For recent comments in the UK, see, for example, S. Deakin and A. Hughes, 'Economic Efficiency and the Proceduralisation of Company Law'(1999) 3 *Company Finance and Insolvency Law Review* 169 at 176–180; I. McNeil, 'Company Law Rules: An Assessment from the Perspective of Incomplete Contract Theory' (2001) 1 *Journal of Corporate Law Studies* 107.

[128]   S. Bainbridge, *The New Corporate Governance in Theory and Practice* (New York, Oxford University Press, 2008) at 24. The learned author sees the board of directors as the nexus: ibid at 34.

[129]   For example, see W. Allen, 'Contracts and Communities in Corporation Law' (1993) 50 *Washington and Lee Law Review* 1395 at 1399; M. Eisenberg, 'The Conception that the Corporation is a Nexus of Contracts, and the Dual Nature of the Firm' (1999) 24 *Journal of Corporation Law* 819; B. Sheedy, 'The Importance of Corporate Models, Economic and Jurisprudential Values and the Future of Corporate Law' (2004) 2 *De Paul Business and Commercial Law Journal* 463 at 464.

[130]   For example, see S. Bottomley, 'From Contractualism to Constitutionalism: A Framework for Corporate Governance' (1997) 19 *Sydney Law Review* 277 at 284.

[131]   For example, see J. Macey, 'Fiduciary Duties as Residual Claims: Obligations to Nonshareholder constituencies From a Theory of the Firm Perspective' (1998) 84 *Cornell Law Review* 1266.

the incorporation of a company as a separate legal entity. The company is seen as a mere fiction. Robert Hessen, for instance, sees the company as merely an extension of the partnership form of business vehicle.[132]

With nexus of contracts the company has been deconstructed, or, as William Bratton puts it, 'disaggregated,'[133] for it is a theory that provides that the company is to be seen as nothing more than a number of complex, private consensual transactions or contract-based relations, either express or implied, and they consist of many different kinds of relations that are worked out by those voluntarily associating in a company.[134] The parties involved in these contracts are regarded as rational economic actors, and include shareholders, managers, creditors, customers and employees, and it is accepted that each of these constituencies endeavour in their contracting to maximise their own positions, with the intention of producing concomitant benefits for themselves.[135] Referring to the relations as contracts is conceded to be incorrect from a legal perspective.[136] Economists tend to see contracts in terms of relationships featuring reciprocal expectations and behaviour,[137] whereas lawyers only refer to contracts where there is formal agreement consisting of the normal legal requirements, such as offer and acceptance. When referring to contracts in the context of this theory, contracts are seen as any voluntary social arrangement. They are regarded as indicating a person's intent. Often, like their economics colleagues, many lawyers refer to 'contracts' in a broad sense. Some authors refer to the relations as bargains to distinguish them from contracts in the legal sense. The nexus of contracts theory in relation to the firm was devised by economists[138] and embraced by economically inclined law aca-

---

[132]   *In Defense of the Corporation* (Stanford, Hoover Institution Press, 1979) at 17ff.

[133]   'The New Economic Theory of the Firm: Critical Perspectives from History' (1989) 41 *Stanford Law Review* 1471 and referred to by L. Johnson, 'Individual and Collective Sovereignty in the Corporate Enterprise' (1992) 92 *Columbia Law Review* 2215 at 2221.

[134]   F. Easterbrook and D. Fischel, 'The Corporate Contract' (1989) 89 *Columbia Law Review* 1416 at 1426. At p1428 the learned commentators give examples of some of the arrangements.

[135]   See, H. Butler, 'The Contractual Theory of the Corporation' (1989) 11 *George Mason University Law Review* 99; C. Riley, 'Understanding and Regulating the Corporation' (1995) 58 *Modern Law Review* 595 at 598.

[136]   See, M. Klausner, 'Corporations, Corporate Law and Networks of Contracts' (1995) 81 *Virginia Law Review* 757 at 759.

[137]   O. Hart, 'An Economist's Perspective on the Theory of the Firm' (1989) 89 *Columbia Law Review* 1757 at n30.

[138]   See R. Coase, 'The Nature of the Firm' (1937) 4 *Economica* 386 at 390–392; A. Alchian and H. Demsetz, 'Production, Information Costs, and Economic

demics.[139] In economic thought the firm, and remember that the company is regarded as a firm by economists, is a set of feasible production proposals which buys supplies and sells goods or services in spot markets.[140] Even though the concept is an economic construct, it is probably better viewed as a metaphor rather than economic reality.[141]

What is not clear with this theory is how scholars can say that the company makes promises in relation to the contracts that make up the nexus,[142] when the company is itself a nexus of contracts. For the company to make promises and contracts it would seem that the company would have to be a separate entity. But, as mentioned above, the company is regarded as a legal fiction that merely represents the contractual relations between the various actors that supply the inputs,[143] rather than being seen as a unit. This issue is taken up in Chapter 4.

While economic contractarianism is well employed in law circles there is a legal form of contractarianism. In some jurisdictions this is based on the statutory contract on which companies are said to be founded. By way of example, the contract is set out now for the UK in s.33 of the Companies Act 2006. It declares that the 'provisions of a company's constitution bind the company and its members to the same extent as if there were covenants on the part of the company and each member is to observe those provisions.' A similar provision has been in companies legislation since the Joint Stock Companies Act 1855, and it harks back to the days when members were actually required to sign the deed of settlement that established a company. It might be thought that the economic contractarian position is inconsistent with the legal contractarian approach. But lawyers

---

Organization' (1972) 62 *American Economic Review* 777 at 794; M. Jensen and W. Meckling, 'Theory of the Firm: Managerial Behaviour, Agency Costs, and Ownership Structure' (1976) 3 *Journal of Financial Economics* 305.

[139] See F.H. Easterbrook and D.R. Fischel, *The Economic Structure of Company Law* (Cambridge, Massachusetts, Harvard University Press, 1991) 37–39; W. Bratton Jr, 'The "Nexus of Contracts" Corporation: A Critical Appraisal' (1989) 74 *Cornell Law Review* 407.

[140] For example, see S. Bainbridge, 'Community and Statism: A Conservative Contractarian Critique of Progressive Corporate Law Scholarship' (1996) 82 *Cornell Law Review* 856.

[141] S. Bainbridge, 'The Board of Directors as Nexus of Contracts' (2002) 88 *Iowa Law Review* 1 at 11.

[142] For example, see J. Macey, *Corporate Governance* (Princeton, Princeton University Press, 2008) at 7.

[143] S. Bainbridge, 'Community and Statism: A Conservative Contractarian Critique of Progressive Corporate Law Scholarship' (1996) 82 *Cornell Law Review* 856.

have submitted that the two approaches can be considered together.[144] This is an issue that warrants significant examination and is too voluminous an issue to consider within the narrow parameters of this work, but it might be possible to say that the economic approach is a positive tool and not a normative one, that is, it is merely descriptive of what occurs in practice.[145] Furthermore, economic theories are concerned with the allocation of control rights and residual claims while legal theories concentrate on the legal significance of boundaries of firms, such as diminishing agency problems.[146]

A second theory is the agency theory. In this approach, management is seen as overseeing the process of 'voluntary negotiation, agreement and adjustment among the various actors who participate in the firm's activities.'[147] The directors are regarded as the agents of the shareholders.[148] The managers (executive directors) are employed by the board to run the company's business for the shareholders who do not have the time or ability to do so, and it is the shareholders who are best suited to guide and discipline managers in the carrying out of their powers and duties.[149] Costs, known as 'agency costs,'[150] will be incurred in monitoring the work of the directors, to ensure that they do not take value out of the company

---

[144]   For example, A. Belcher, 'Boundaries, Corporate Decision-Making and Responsibility' (2008) 58 *Northern Ireland Legal Quarterly* 211 at 215.

[145]   J. Macey, 'Fiduciary Duties as Residual Claims: Obligations to Nonshareholder Constituencies From a Theory of the Firm Perspective' (1998) 84 *Cornell Law Review* 1266 at 1272.

[146]   H. Hansmann, 'Ownership of the Firm' in L. Bebchuk (ed), *Corporate Law and Economic Analysis* (Cambridge, Cambridge University Press, 1990) at 283; E. Iaocobucci and G. Triantis, 'Economic and Legal Boundaries of Firms' (2007) 93 *Virginia Law Review* 515 at 517.

[147]   D. Millon, 'Theories of the Corporation' (1990) 193 *Duke Law Journal* 201 at 230.

[148]   It is arguable that the agency theory provides the basis for the predominant academic view of the company today: M. Gelter, 'The Dark Side of Shareholder Influence: Toward a Holdup Theory of Stakeholders in Comparative Corporate Governance,' Discussion Paper No 17, Harvard John Olin Fellow's Discussion Paper Series at 2 and available at <http://ssrn.com/abstract=1106008> (last visited, 16 August 2010).

[149]   J. Matheson and B. Olson, 'Corporate Law and the Longterm Shareholder Model of Corporate Governance' (1992) 76 *Minnesota Law Review* 1313 at 1328. But note the reservations, concerning the ability of shareholders to discipline directors, expressed in A. Keay, 'Company Directors Behaving Poorly: Disciplinary Options for Shareholders' [2007] *Journal of Business Law* 656.

[150]   These costs are those resulting from managers failing to act appropriately and the costs expended in monitoring and disciplining the managers in order to prevent them abusing their positions.

by shirking their responsibilities or acting opportunistically so as to benefit themselves, and one of the emphases of agency theory is to look at ways of reducing the amount of agency costs that are incurred. More will be said about this in Chapter 2 when we consider the shareholder primacy theory.

A third theory advocated by some is transaction cost theory, the roots of which may be traced to the work of the renowned economist Ronald Coase in the late 1930s.[151] Generally speaking Coase asserted that firms existed in order to reduce transaction costs. Such costs involved developing knowledge about, and negotiating terms of trade in, the marketplace. Rather than a number of individuals doing this separately, if there was only one, the firm, doing it, that would reduce costs. In corporate law transaction costs are reduced by the organisational design of the company, and this improves efficiency. [152] This work was subsequently developed by Oliver Williamson in order to put the theory advocated by Coase into operation,[153] and he said that the firm can be used to coordinate the trading process more efficiently than the market. Williamson submitted that the large company, and the conglomerate even more so, acts as a miniature capital market whereby executives relocate resources from underperforming areas to growth areas that are out-performing the market.[154] Williamson adopted a contractual approach, so in some respects there is a close relationship to the contractarian theory.[155]

Finally, as far as economic theories are concerned, other law and economics scholars hold to another theory that takes a property rights view of the company. Effectively this owes much to the work of Oliver Hart and his respective co-authors.[156] This approach argues that the ownership of property in the firm is fundamental, with Hart saying that 'the firm's

---

[151] 'The Nature of the Firm' (1937) 4 *Economica* 386.

[152] In corporate law transaction costs are reduced by the organisational design of the company: O.E. Williamson, 'Transactional-Cost Economics: The Governance of Contractual Relations' (1994) 21 *Journal of Law and Society* 168.

[153] See O. Williamson, 'The Vertical Integration of Market Production: Market Failure Considerations' (1971) 61 *American Economic Review* 112; 'Markets and Hierarchies: Some Elementary Considerations' (1973) 63 *American Economic Review* 316.

[154] J. Coffee, 'Shareholders v Managers: The Strain in the Corporate Web' (1986) 85 *Michigan Law Review* 1 at 31–32.

[155] O. Williamson, The Economic Institutions of Capitalism: Firms, Markets, Relational Contracting (1985) at 43–84 and referred to in E. Orts, 'Shirking and Shaking: A Legal Theory of the Firm' (1998) 16 *Yale Law and Policy Review* 265 at 290.

[156] For example, see the following: S. Grossman and O. Hart, 'The Costs and Benefits of Ownership: A Theory of Vertical and Lateral Integration' (1986) 94 *Journal of Political Economy* 691; O. Hart and J. Moore, 'Property Rights and the

non-human assets . . . represents the glue that holds the firm together.'[157] The firm is seen as a bundle of rights that is under common ownership.[158] The ownership of capital assets permits a person to be in a situation where he or she can organise production by 'purchasing' economic factors, such as the work input of employees,[159] and this ability to direct how assets are to be utilised will make a difference as far as outcomes are concerned.[160] In this context 'ownership' is seen as the right to exercise 'residual rights of control'.[161] Owners of assets that are used will not be able to control effectively all of the assets owned so they will need to delegate authority to others to exercise control rights. They may need to assign ownership so that the total transaction costs for all contributors are minimised.[162]

Many, but far from all, law and economics commentators take the view that the efficiency goal of maximising the company's value to investors is the principal function of corporate law.[163] Gillian Hadfield has described efficiency as '[t]he bedrock of gold that has carried economic analysis of law through three decades now.'[164]

Nature of the Firm' (1990) 98 *Journal of Political Economy* 1119; O. Hart, *Firms, Contracts and Financial Structure* (1995), Oxford, Oxford University Press.

[157]   O. Hart, *Firms, Contracts and Financial Structure* (1995) at 57 and quoted in E. Orts, 'Shirking and Shaking: A Legal Theory of the Firm' (1998) 16 *Yale Law and Policy Review* 265 at 295.

[158]   S. Grossman and O. Hart, 'The Costs and Benefits of Ownership: A Theory of Vertical and Lateral Integration' (1986) 94 *Journal of Political Economy* 691 at 693.

[159]   O. Hart and J. Moore, 'Property Rights and the Nature of the Firm' (1990) 98 *Journal of Political Economy* 1119 at 1120; O. Hart, *Firms, Contracts and Financial Structure* (1995) at 57 and referred to in E. Orts, 'Shirking and Shaking: A Legal Theory of the Firm' (1998) 16 *Yale Law and Policy Review* 265 at 296.

[160]   J. Armour and M. Whincop, 'The Property Foundations of Corporate Law' (2007) 27 *Oxford Journal of Legal Society* 429 at 437.

[161]   Ibid at 437.

[162]   H. Hansmann, 'Ownership of the Firm' in L. Bebchuk (ed), *Corporate Law and Economic Analysis* (Cambridge, Cambridge University Press, 1990) at 287.

[163]   For example, see B. Black and R. Kraackman, 'A Self-Enforcing Model of Corporate Law' (1996) 109 *Harvard Law Review* 1911 at 1921. Some law and economics scholars accept that other virtues besides efficiency are relevant and are to be taken into account (for example, see S. Bainbridge in 'Community and Statism: A Conservative Contractarian Critique of Progressive Corporate Law Scholarship' (1997) 82 *Cornell Law Review* 856 at 883). For examples of scholars in Britain who do not see efficiency as the only virtue, see S. Deakin and A. Hughes, 'Economics and Company Law Reform: a Fruitful Partnership' (1999) 20 *The Company Lawyer* 212 at 218; J. Armour, 'Share Capital and Creditor Protection: Efficient Rules for a Modern Company Law' (2000) 63 *Modern Law Review* 355 at 358.

[164]   'The Second Wave of Law and Economics: Learning to Surf' in Megan Richardson and Gillian Hadfield (eds), *The Second Wave in Law and Economics* (Sydney, Federation Press, 1999) at 56.

In contrast to the aggregation or nominalist approach adopted in relation to economic theories, there are several theories that are based on the company as a separate entity. These are often known as 'real entity theories'.[165] Some aspects of these will be discussed in some detail in Chapter 4, so the following consideration is brief. Suffice it to say the emphasis of these theories is on the company as an entity or enterprise.[166] Theorists also focus to some degree on the limited liability of the company and its virtual perpetual existence. Some argue that the company is a creation of human artifice, coming into being through the action of incorporation. Others, often referred to as 'natural entity' theorists, take the view that the company is a real personality that is *not created* by company law, but *recognised* by company law. That is, the law accepts the existence of the association and clothes it with legal personality. Still others, led by the German academic Gunther Teubner,[167]submit that the corporate personality is self-created on the basis that the company is a unit.[168] They rely on the autopoietic theory of the German sociologist, Niklas Luhmann, which applied to the organisational form.[169] The real entity theories are more commonly associated with continental Europe than the UK or the US. Under these theories any inputs received by the company, whether they be from shareholders, by way of share capital, supplies from suppliers or funds lent by creditors, are regarded as property owned by the company. The managers are not, in running the company and making decisions, acting as individuals but as organs of the corporate person. The legal rules that are applied to companies are respected and recognised, not only in practice, but in theory.

I should mention that an increasingly popular approach that also seeks to address the issue of what the company is, is the communitarian

---

[165] For a very readable and excellent discussion of the theories, see S. Worthington, 'Shares and Shareholders: Property, Power and Entitlement (Part 2) (2001) 22 *The Company Lawyer* 307 at 308–309.

[166] The so-called 'social contract model' and 'organic theory' both seem to fit, broadly speaking, within these general theories. See J. Brummer, *Corporate Responsibility and Legitimacy* (New York, Greenwood Press, 1991) at 56–58 and 65–67.

[167] See, for example, his work, 'Enterprise Corporatism: New Industrial Policy and the "Essence of the Legal Person"' (1988) 36 *American Journal of Comparative Law* 130.

[168] S. Worthington, 'Shares and Shareholders: Property, Power and Entitlement (Part 2) (2001) 22 *The Company Lawyer* 307 at 308.

[169] For a discussion of theory developed from aspects of his work, see T. Bakken and T. Hernes (eds), *Autopoietic Organisation Theory* (Copenhagen, Copenhagen Business School Press, 2002).

approach. This approach, more often referred to as the 'progressive' approach, at least by many of its advocates,[170] has some similarities to stakeholder theory as it argues that more than the interests of shareholders should be taken into account by the company in running its business.[171] It advocates the interests of other stakeholders, such as the employees and creditors,[172] being the subject of consideration. Just as those advocating stakeholder theory identify different people and groups whose interests should be considered by directors, progressives differ among themselves concerning the strength of the claims of various non-shareholder constituencies to warrant legal intervention.

Communiarianism has been applied in other fields of law and in the social sciences in general. The theory was devised by Amitai Etzioni.[173] It is only in more recent years that a group of scholars, largely located in the US,[174] have applied communitarian principles to corporate law. The communitarian school believes that large companies are public institu-

---

[170]   For example see L. Mitchell (ed), *Progressive Corporate Law* (Boulder, Westview Press, 1995). Mitchell himself rejects the use of the term 'communitarian' See, 'Trust. Contract. Process' in L. Mitchell (ed), *Progressive Corporate Law* (Boulder, Westview Press, 1995) 185 at 186–187). The appellation is challenged by some, such as Stephen Bainbridge in 'Community and Statism: A Conservative Contractarian Critique of Progressive Corporate Law Scholarship' (1997) 82 *Cornell Law Review* 856 at 856.

[171]   For example, Lawrence Mitchell criticises the whole notion of shareholder maximisation in corporate law ('A Theoretical and Practical Framework for Enforcing Corporate Constituency Statutes' (1992) 70 *Texas Law Review* 579 at 640). See D. Millon, 'Communitarianism in Corporate Law: Foundations and Law Reform Strategies' in L. Mitchell (ed), *Progressive Corporate Law* (Boulder, Westview Press, 1995), 1 at 7–9.

[172]   As to the latter, see A. Keay, 'A Theoretical Analysis of the Director's Duty to Consider Creditor Interests: The Progressive School's Approach' (2004) 4 *Journal of Corporate Law Studies* 307.

[173]   *The New Golden Rule: Community and Morality in a Democratic Society* (New York, Basic Books, 1996).

[174]   Some of the foremost have been Douglas Branson, William Bratton, Lyman Johnson, David Millon, and Lawrence Mitchell. For a brief consideration of the approach, see J. Dine, 'Companies and Regulations: Theories, Justifications and Policing' in D. Milman (ed), *Regulating Enterprise: Law and Business Organisations in the UK* (Oxford, Hart Publishing, 1999) at 295–296; *Company Law* (London, Sweet and Maxwell, 2001) at 27–30, where the learned commentator refers to it as 'the communitaire theory.' The pluralist approach that has been advocated in the UK by those such as John Parkinson (*Corporate Power and Responsibility* (Oxford, Clarendon Press, 1993) and (with Gavin Kelly), 'The Conceptual Foundations of the Company: A Pluralist Approach' (1998) 2 *Company Finance and Insolvency Law Review* 174) provides some similar views to progressive scholarship.

tions and not private ones. It perceives the company as 'a community of interdependence, mutual trust and reciprocal benefit.'[175] Communitarian theorists seek to focus on the fact that those involved in, and dealing with, companies are humans and corporate law should not be de-personalised.[176] In the communitarian assessment a greater array of social and political values are considered, and communitarians opine that whether the company is useful is measured by evaluating how it assists society in gaining a richer understanding of community by respecting human dignity and overall welfare.[177] Most communitarians are anti-contractarian in their view of the company. Rather than being concerned about the reduction of transaction costs, the progressives are concerned about the social effects of corporate activity.[178] Progressive scholars have rejected the idea that parties are able to protect themselves, and have posited the need for mandatory rules to provide adequate protection.[179] Many progressives have argued for respect, trust and fairness and other virtues to be considered when determining what shape corporate law should take.[180] In several ways this school has echoes of the views presented by Professor E. Merrick Dodd in the 1930s and 1940s, particularly in relation to his aforementioned debates with Adolf Berle, when Dodd argued that the company 'has a social service as well as a profit-making function.'[181]

---

[175] D. Millon, 'Communitarianism in Corporate Law: Foundations and Law Reform Strategies' in L. Mitchell (ed), *Progressive Corporate Law* (Boulder, Westview Press, 1995) at 10.

[176] For example, see L. Mitchell, 'Groundwork of the Metaphysics of Corporate Law' (1993) 50 *Washington and Lee Law Review* 1477 at 1479–1481. In another work ('The Death of Fiduciary Duty in Close Corporations' (1990) 138 *University of Pennsylvania Law Review* 1675 at 1675), the learned commentator states that 'The corporation is a human enterprise.'

[177] D. Sullivan and D. Conlon, 'Crisis and Transition in Corporate Governance Paradigms: The Role of the Chancery Court of Delaware' [1997] *Law and Society Review* 713 and referred to by J. Dine, 'Companies and Regulations: Theories, Justifications and Policing' in D. Milman (ed), *Regulating Enterprise: Law and Business Organisations in the UK* (Oxford, Hart Publishing, 1999) at 295.

[178] D. Millon, 'New Directions in Corporate Law: Communitarians, Contractarians and Crisis in Corporate Law' (1993) 50 *Washington and Lee Law Review* 1373 at 1379.

[179] D. Millon, 'Communitarianism in Corporate Law: Foundations and Law Reform Strategies' in L. Mitchell (ed), *Progressive Corporate Law* (Boulder, Westview Press, 1995) at 4.

[180] For example, L. Mitchell, 'Trust. Contract. Process' in L. Mitchell (ed), *Progressive Corporate Law* (Boulder, Westview Press, 1995) at 185.

[181] E M. Dodd, 'For Whom are Corporate Managers Trustees?' (1932) 45 *Harvard Law Review* 1145 at 1148.

The law and economics school's approach to corporate law is often subject to criticism by progressives when the latter are dealing with a particular issue. The law and economics approach is criticised for being too focused on self-interest.[182] While law and economics scholars have turned to finance theory and neoclassical economics,[183] the progressive school has embraced views from the humanities and social sciences. In this respect progressive law scholars have attacked the corporate focus on profit, and specifically the shareholder primacy theory.[184] In the progressive assessment of the company a greater array of social and political values are considered, and respect for human dignity and overall welfare is very important.[185] Progressives embrace a different normative world view compared to law and economics scholars, for the former emphasise the fact that people are part of a shared community who inherit the benefits, values and goals of the community, thus the cultural milieu in which people find themselves cannot be ignored.[186] It has been argued in the progressive literature,[187] inter alia, that companies are public institutions with public obligations and it is necessary to have mandatory rules to control what they and their managers do.[188]

The progressive approach differs from what is often seen as the usual stakeholder approach in that many of the advocates of the latter place some emphasis on efficiency and focus on the managers and their role. As

---

[182]   L. Mitchell, 'Groundwork of the Metaphysics of Corporate Law' (1993) 50 *Washington and Lee Law Review* 1477 at 1485.

[183]   For a critical discussion of mainstream, neoclassical theory of the firm, see, for example, O. Williamson, *The Mechanisms of Governance* (Oxford, Oxford University Press, 1996).

[184]   For example, see L. Mitchell (ed), *Progressive Corporate Law* (Boulder, Westview Press, 1995).

[185]   D. Sullivan and D. Conlon, 'Crisis and Transition in Corporate Governance Paradigms: The Role of the Chancery Court of Delaware' [1997] *Law and Society Review* 713 and referred to by J. Dine, 'Companies and Regulations: Theories, Justifications and Policing' in D. Milman (ed), *Regulating Enterprise: Law and Business Organisations in the UK* (Oxford, Hart Publishing, 1999) at 295.

[186]   D. Millon, 'New Directions in Corporate Law: Communitarians, Contractarians and Crisis in Corporate Law' (1993) 50 *Washington and Lee Law Review* 1373 at 1382.

[187]   Of course, just as with the law and economics school, not all progressives adhere to the same view on all matters.

[188]   For example, see D. Branson, 'The Death of Contractarianism and the Vindication of Structure and Authority in Corporate Governance and Corporate Law' in L. Mitchell (ed), *Progressive Corporate Law* (Boulder, Westview Press, 1995) at 93.

indicated, many progressives have a greater focus on fairness, although stakeholder advocates do not eschew such a value, as we will see in Chapter 3. Both progressives and stakeholder scholars do emphasise trust in the corporate environment. Many stakeholder scholars do employ an economic approach to numerous issues, while progressives generally do not. In the words of Douglas Branson, the progressive model 'focuses on sociological and moral phenomenon of the corporation as a community, in contrast to the individualistic and self-reliant group of economic actors.'[189]

Before completing this section of the Chapter some reference should be made to a more recent theory of the company. This is the team production theory formulated by Margaret Blair and Lynn Stout.[190] This is an approach which relies on micro-economic theory and behavioural economics.[191] The commentators build on work done by others on team production, notably Armen Alchian and Harold Demsetz,[192] on the one hand, and Bengt Holmstrom on the other.[193] Blair and Stout see the company as a team to which many constituencies contribute, including shareholders, managers and employees,[194] and they argue that this is what actually happens in a company, so they argue from a positivist approach. The argument is that the approach advocated solves the problem of organising production in teams. The commentators approve of the nexus of contracts approach, but would re-name it as 'a nexus of firm-specific investments.'[195] The main thrust of the Blair and Stout approach, after attacking the agency theory, is to nominate an independent board of directors as mediating hierarchs in monitoring inputs and outputs, with shareholders not having control rights. Blair and Stout seek to answer the following question: why are directors given so much discretion in public companies?

---

[189] 'Corporate Governance "Reform" and the New Corporate Social Responsibility' (2001) 62 *University of Pittsburgh Law Review* 605 at 639.

[190] The first article that set it out in detail was, 'A Team Production Theory of Corporate Law' (1999) 85 *Virginia Law Review* 247. Incipient aspects of the theory can be seen in Margret Blair's earlier book, *Ownership and Control* (Washington DC, The Brookings Institute, 1995).

[191] A. Kaufman and E. Englander, 'A Team Production Model of Corporate Governance' (2005) 19 *Academy of Management Executive* 9 at 12.

[192] 'Production, Information Costs and Economic Organizations' (1972) 62 *American Economic Review* 777.

[193] 'Moral Hazard in Teams' (1982) 13 *Bell Journal of Economics* 324. Also, see R. Marris, *The Economic Theory of 'Managerial' Capitalism* (New York, Free Press and McMillan, 1964) at 16; P. Doeringer and M. Piore, *Internal Labour Markets and Manpower Analysis* (Boston, D.C. Heath and Co, 1971) at 15–16.

[194] 'A Team Production Theory of Corporate Law' (1999) 85 *Virginia Law Review* 247 at 269.

[195] Ibid at 275.

They go on to say that the directors have ultimate power in both determining how company assets are to be used and in reconciling conflicts between the various interests of team members. The problem with this approach, and also a problem with the stakeholder approach, appears to be that it does not indicate how directors are to reconcile conflicting interests.

What a company is, is a matter for debate. Is it a production function, a legal entity, the aggregate of all individuals involved as shareholders in the company, or the managers and employees of the company?[196] The issue will be revisited in Chapter 4. What I would say at this point is that it is not easy to encapsulate in one theory all aspects of a company. I have great sympathy for Stephen Bottomley's view that it is not possible to devise 'a grand theory for all corporations in all contexts.'[197]

9.   THE STRUCTURE OF THE BOOK

The book commences in Chapters 2 and 3 with an analysis of the two dominant theories that have been posited for the ultimate objective of the company. While I wish to formulate a new approach it is necessary for thoroughness and context to consider these theories, and to consider them in some depth. Many pertinent issues relevant to the company and its objective have been raised in discussions of these theories and they warrant airing. Some need to be considered in the context of the model that I propose later in the book. These theories require examination because of the fact that many learned scholars from various disciplines have supported them. Their scholarship warrants consideration when seeking to propose a new approach. Following these Chapters on the dominant theories, Chapter 4 provides an introduction to the entity maximisation and sustainability model ('EMS') that I wish to formulate to explain what is believed to be the appropriate ultimate objective of the company. As this model is dependent on construing the company as an entity, the Chapter argues for the company being regarded as a legal entity. After doing this the book returns to articulate and provide justification for EMS. This is done by exploring various practical situations and important aspects of corporate life. In particular the remaining material explores matters such as how EMS could be enforced (Chapter 5), who are the investors and

---

[196]   G. Enderle and L. Tavis, 'A Balanced Concept of the Firm and the Measurement of Its Long-term Planning and Performance' (1998) 17 *Journal of Business Ethics* 1129 at 1131.

[197]   S. Bottomley, *The Constitutional Corporation* (Aldershot, Ashgate, 2007) at 17.

what role do they have (Chapter 6), how managers should act and how the law should deal with the fact that managers need to have broad discretion on the one hand, and yet need to be accountable, on the other hand (Chapter 7), and specifically how should directors deal with the issue of allocation of profits (Chapter 8). The final chapter, Chapter 9, provides a few conclusions and closing remarks.

2. Shareholder primacy

1. INTRODUCTION

As explained in the first Chapter, there are two major theories that have been proposed for dealing with the issue of the ultimate corporate objective. This Chapter seeks to articulate and analyse one of those, namely the shareholder primacy theory.[1] This theory is also known as 'shareholder value'[2] or 'shareholder wealth maximisation'.[3] It is a theory that is regarded as prevailing in Anglo-American law, and in other common law jurisdictions such as Australia, New Zealand and Canada. It has been said that the US and UK are liberal market economies that have features, such as a dispersed share ownership, more susceptibility to hostile takeovers and the existence of large institutional investors which are eager for quarterly improvements in the share price, and this tends to entrench shareholder primacy.[4]

The Chapter cannot possibly deal comprehensively with the shareholder primacy theory. Neither can it seek to interact with all of the literature that has been written on the subject. It is voluminous and has been written from the perspective of a number of different disciplines. The Chapter seeks to

---

[1] Scholars clearly see the approach as the company's purpose. For example, see L. Mitchell, 'Groundwork of the Metaphysics of Corporate Law' (1993) 50 *Washington and Lee Law Review* 1477 at 1485; L. Fairfax, 'The Rhetoric of Corporate Law: The Impact of Stakeholder Rhetoric on Corporate Norms' (2005) 21 *Journal of Corporation Law* 675 at 676; G. Crespi, 'Maximizing the Wealth of Fictional Shareholders: Which Fiction Should Directors Embrace?' (2007) 32 *Journal of Corporation Law* 381 at 383, 386 n15.

[2] The term 'shareholder value' was introduced in the 1980s by US consultants who were selling value-based management to companies already under stockmarket pressure to increase returns: K. Wiliams, 'From shareholder value to present-day capitalism' (2000) 29 *Economy and Society* 1 at 1.

[3] Stephen Bainbridge argues that shareholder primacy differs from shareholder wealth maximisation ('Director Primacy: The Means and Ends of Corporate Governance' (2003) 97 *Northwestern University Law Review* 547 at 574) but in this book the two are regarded as synonymous.

[4] R. Mitchell, A. O'Donnell and I.M. Ramsay, 'Shareholder Value and Employee Interests: Intersections Between Corporate Governance, Corporate Law and Labor Law' (2005) *Wisconsin International Law Journal* 417 at 420.

examine the main elements of the theory and the primary criticisms of it, and to assess the theory overall.

When the theory became prominent is not certain. David Millon states that shareholder primacy has been the orthodox assumption since the time of Adolf Berle and Gardiner Means,[5] when, due to their seminal work, *The Modern Corporation and Private Property*, and the individual writings of Berle, it gained momentum. Yet it would seem that the theory has been dominant at various points in history ever since the late 1800s, with one commentator stating that it was in the mid-nineteenth century when it blossomed.[6] Writing in 1931 Adolf Berle said that all powers given to management were exercisable for the benefit of all of the shareholders as their interest appeared.[7]

Shortly thereafter, E. Merrick Dodd said that it was the traditional view that directors managed a company for the private gain of the shareholders.[8] Nevertheless, from the 1930s until the 1970s it might be said that forms of stakeholder theory held sway in academia and practice. Notwithstanding this feature of this period, there was always some who took a shareholder primacy view, witness the comments of Nobel prize winner, Milton Friedman, when he said that the responsibility of managers was to make money for shareholders and not to engage in what we would now call corporate social responsibility.[9] While there were clearly times when the theory had impact, its prominence has been the greatest since the late 1970s.[10] This is when institutional investors began to support the employment of the theory,[11] and the time when the law and economics movement started to gain significant popularity and this movement generally embraced the theory, so wholeheartedly in fact that Jonathan Macey has said that any action by directors that was not consistent with

---

[5]   'New Directions in Corporate Law: Communitarians, Contractarians and the Crisis in Corporate Law' (1993) 50 *Washington and Lee Law Review* 1373 at 1374.

[6]   D.G. Smith, 'The Shareholder Primacy Norm' (1998) 23 *Journal of Corporation Law* 277 at 292.

[7]   'Corporate Powers as Powers in Trust' (1931) 44 *Harvard Law Review* 1049 at 1049.

[8]   'For Whom are Corporate Managers Trustees?' (1932) 45 *Harvard Law Review* 1145 at 1146–1147.

[9]   See, M. Friedman, 'The Social Responsibility of Business is to Increase its Profits' *New York Times*, 13 September 1970, Section 6 (Magazine) 32.

[10]   A. Rappaport, *Creating Shareholder Value* (New York, The Free Press, 1986) at 5.

[11]   W. Lazonick and M. O'Sullivan, 'Maximizing Shareholder Value: a New Ideology for Corporate Governance' (2000) 29 *Economy and Society* 13 at 16.

The corporate objective

shareholder wealth maximisation was regarded as 'corporate deviance.'[12] Margaret Blair has been of the view that in the 1980s the theory overtook a form of stakeholder theory.[13] It has been asserted that since the mid-1980s we have seen a much greater emphasis on shareholder value by directors not only in the US, but also in the UK.[14]

Whenever we actually determine that the shareholder primacy theory became more accepted, it is clear that it is now a dominant, if not *the* dominant theory in company law. This has been due, so it is said, to such things as the 'globalisation of capital markets, the rise of institutional investors, greater shareholder activism and the increasing importance of corporate governance issues.'[15] Even the UK's Combined Code, sanctioned by the Financial Reporting Council, provided, in the preamble to its 2008 version, that: 'Good governance should facilitate efficient, effective and entrepreneurial management that can deliver shareholder value over the longer term.'[16]

As we will see later there have been many who have criticised the theory, but notwithstanding that, the theory has proven to be resilient, perhaps because of the theory of path dependence.[17]

First, the Chapter sets out what the theory is, what is involved in maximising shareholder value, and this is followed by a consideration of the theoretical foundations of the theory. Then the Chapter explains the

[12] J. Macey, *Corporate Governance* (Princeton, Princeton University Press, 2008) at 2.
[13] M. Blair, 'For Whom Should Corporations Be Run?: An Economic Rational for Stakeholder Management' (1998) 31 *Long Range Planning* 195 at 195.
[14] M. Omran, P. Atrill and J. Pointon, 'Shareholders versus stakeholders: corporate mission statements and investor returns' (2002) 11 *Business Ethics: A European Review* 318 at 318. See The Company Law Review Steering Group, Department of Trade and Industry, *Modern Company Law for a Competitive Economy: The Strategic Framework* (1999) at para 5.1.24.
[15] M. Omran, P. Atrill and J. Pointon, 'Shareholders Versus Stakeholders: Corporate Mission Statements and Investor Returns' (2002) 11 *Business Ethics: A European Review* 318 at 318 and referring to R. Mills, *The Dynamics of Shareholder Value* (Lechlade, Mars Business Association, 1998) and N. Fera, 'Using Shareholder Value to Estimate Strategic Choice' (1997) 79 *Management Accounting* (USA) 47.
[16] Financial Reporting Council, *Combined Code on Corporate Governance*, June 2008, at para 1. In June 2010 a new version of the Code was published and paragraph 1 had changed to reflect the inclusion of s.172 of the Companies Act 2006 in UK law.
[17] S. Bottomley, *The Constitutional Corporation* (Ashgate, Aldershot, 2007) at 7. See L. Bebchuk and M. Roe, 'A Theory of Path Dependence in Corporate Ownership and Governance' (1999) 52 *Stanford Law Review* 127 for a discussion of path dependence.

leading arguments in favour of the theory. This is followed by an exposition of the arguments that have been mounted against the theory. The next part briefly considers the descriptive impact of the theory. Finally, I draw some conclusions.

2.   WHAT IS IT?

While this is a fundamental question, it is one that is not easily resolved.[18] As discussed above, there is no certainty as to when the theory rose to prominence. It is probably correct to say that the theory's dominance has fallen and risen ever since the 1800s, depending on economic and social conditions.[19] Certainly, one of the early manifestations of the theory is said to be found in the decision of the Michigan Supreme Court in the case of *Dodge v Ford Motor Corp*,[20] in 1919. This is an appropriate place to start. The Court said that a: 'business corporation is organized and carried on primarily for the profit of the stockholders . . . The discretion of the directors is to be exercised in the choice of means to attain that end . . .'[21] It must be said that it is probably possible to argue that the court was not against the company's consideration of the interests of stakeholders (Henry Ford as CEO of the Ford Motor Corp was concerned about the conditions of employees and that customers would be able to afford the company's cars), other than shareholders, but found against the company because the managers did not run the company as a business company, as required by the company's charter.[22]

Stephen Bainbridge has helpfully divided the theory into two limbs, namely: the objective of the company should be to maximise shareholder wealth; and shareholders should have ultimate control of the company.[23]

---

[18]   H. Hu, 'New Financial Products, the Modern Process of Financial Innovation and the Puzzle of Shareholder Welfare' (1991) 69 *Texas Law Review* 1273 at 1317.
[19]   T. Kochan and S. Rubinstein, 'Toward a Stakeholder Theory of the Firm: The Saturn Partnership' (2000) 11 *Organization Science* 367 at 368.
[20]   170 NW 668.
[21]   Ibid at 684.
[22]   S. Wallman, 'Understanding the Purpose of a Corporation: An Introduction' (1999) 24 *Journal of Corporation Law* 807 at 808. Also, it has been argued that the case only related to close corporations and not public companies: D.G. Smith, 'The Shareholder Primacy Norm' (1998) 23 *Journal of Corporation Law* 277 at 292.
[23]   'Director Primacy: The Means and Ends of Corporate Governance' (2003) 97 *Northwestern University Law Review* 547 at 573. Bainbridge actually rejects

The theory has been developed to the point where it now provides that directors are to manage the company in such a way as to ensure that the wealth of shareholders is maximised to the full.[24] Simply this means that the directors will endeavour to make as much money as they can for the shareholders. Effectively this can be seen to involve the directors protecting and enhancing the investment of shareholders in the company. Hence, in this theory managers only have economic goals and responsibilities. Managers have no other responsibilities besides these narrow ones, and so if there was a conflict between the interests of shareholders and non-shareholders the managers are only to be concerned with taking action that will benefit the former and produce wealth for them. The managers may do anything to enhance shareholder wealth provided that it is lawful.[25] Arguably the reason for this qualification is that failure to adhere to the law in any given area could generate risks which could prejudice the financial position of the shareholders ultimately.[26] 'Wealth' is able to be viewed as realised value and expressed in price terms. As Christos Pitelis explains: 'In a capitalist economy, value is created at the level of production by firms. It is then realised in exchange through the sale of commodities in markets for a profit.'[27]

While it was noted in Chapter 1 that large companies have a wide-ranging effect on many people in local, national and international communities, shareholder primacy, as the name suggests, is focused on shareholders; the expression was formulated to indicate the idea of shareholder pre-eminence when compared with other corporate constituencies.[28] The theory means that the principal sphere of the activities of the managers is defined by the obligation to shareholders, such that all other responsibilities are very much secondary or derivative.[29] But, while

---

the second limb, preferring to see directors having ultimate control. The author expands on his view in *The New Corporate Governance in Theory and Practice* (New York, Oxford University Press, 2008).

[24]   For instance, see M. Friedman, 'The Social Responsibility of Business is to Increase its Profits' *New York Times*, 13 September 1970, Section 6 (Magazine) 32 at 33.

[25]   M. Friedman, *Capitalism and Freedom* (Chicago, University of Chicago Press, 1962) at 133.

[26]   W. Cragg, 'Business Ethics and Stakeholder Theory' (2002) 12 *Business Ethics Quarterly* 113 at 125.

[27]   (Corporate) Governance, (Shareholder) Value and (Sustainable) Economic Performance' (2004) 12 *Corporate Governance: An International Review* 210 at 216.

[28]   L. Johnson and D. Millon, 'Missing the Point About State Takeover Statutes' (1989) 87 *Michigan Law Review* 846 at 848.

[29]   J. Brummer, *Corporate Responsibility and Legitimacy* (New York, Greenwood Press, 1991) at 103.

directors will not focus on non-shareholder constituencies, they might well take them into account[30] for if they do not it might impact on the maximising of shareholder wealth, for, inter alia, they may lose firm specific investments from stakeholders. An example of this is the resignation of employees who have particular and critical skills as far as the company's business is concerned. In dealing with this issue, James Brummer gives the example of paying company creditors. They are paid solely to ensure that the company survives and functions effectively,[31] because if they are not paid then they could withdraw critical funding that the company needs.

The Confederation of British Industry said in its evidence to the Hampel Committee on Corporate Governance that 'directors as a board are responsible for relations with stakeholders; but they are accountable to the shareholders.'[32] So the interests of non-shareholder stakeholders are only relevant to the extent that they contribute to achieving shareholder maximisation, and fostering better relations with stakeholders could lead to increased shareholder wealth; but it might be argued that they certainly cannot be ignored if a business is to develop, for in the long run the company cannot continuously prejudice stakeholders as that will eventually see the shareholders' interests damaged,[33] and particularly the company's reputation. Nevertheless, there might be times when the managers have to act in a way that prejudices some stakeholders in order to benefit shareholders.[34] On this point, finance theory provides, effectively, that a company should only allot resources to stakeholders to the point 'where the marginal dollar spent yields at least a dollar in return to the shareholders.'[35]

---

[30] This was expressly sanctioned by the Supreme Court of Canada in *BCE Inc v 1976 Debentureholders* 2008 SCC 69 at [82].

[31] J. Brummer, *Corporate Responsibility and Legitimacy* (New York, Greenwood Press, 1991) at 103.

[32] *Report of the Committee on Corporate Governance*, 1998 at para 1.17 and quoted in S. Wheeler, 'Fraser and the Politics of Corporate Governance' (1999) *Journal of Law and Society* 241 at 242.

[33] B. Black, 'Agents Watching Agents: The Promise of Institutional Investor Voice' (1992) 39 *University of California at Los Angeles Law Review* 811 at 863. See, M. Jensen, 'Value Maximisation, Stakeholder Theory, and the Corporate Objective Function' (2001) 7 *European Financial Management* 297 at 309.

[34] C. Bagley and K. Page, 'The Devil Made Me Do It: Replacing Corporate Directors' Veil of Secrecy with the Mantle of Stewardship' (1999) 36 *San Diego Law Review* 897 at 898.

[35] C.K. Prahalabad, 'Rethinking Shareholder Value' in D. Chew (ed), *Studies in International Corporate Finance and Governance Systems: A Comparison of the United States, Japan and Europe* (New York, Oxford University Press, 1997) and quoted in L. Mitchell, *Corporate Irresponsibility* (New Haven, Yale University Press, 2001) at 106.

Besides the positive obligation to do things that will maximise wealth, directors are to refrain from doing anything which might derogate from the wealth of shareholders.

As far as non-shareholder stakeholders are concerned, the theory assumes that these persons and groups who deal with, or are involved in, the company are granted rights through contracts and that satisfies their interests.

The fact that company managers will have to deal with stakeholders other than shareholders, has led the renowned finance theorist, Michael Jensen, to develop what he refers to as 'enlightened stakeholder theory' but it appears that apart from an emphasis on managing for the long term, it is very similar to shareholder primacy in direction and application. Jensen has said that 'the pursuit of shareholder value is the single "corporate objective function" which drives vital organisational and allocative efficiencies.'[36] The learned commentator has said that referring to the managers as undertaking 'value seeking' might be preferable to 'value maximising' as the latter might be said to be impossible in a complex world.[37]

It is probably true to say that the implementation of shareholder value is likely to lead to greater room for risk-taking on the part of directors.[38] Shareholders tend to favour more risk-taking by directors, and this will become greater the closer a company moves to financial instability, because the shareholders have little or nothing to lose (apart from their original capital) when financial instability hits. If the company fails through the risk-taking of the managers, then the shareholders will reason that they are no worse off, as the company was heading for liquidation anyway, but if the company succeeds as a result of taking the risk then they will benefit. In the circumstances outlined, it is potentially the creditors who stand to lose out. If the company collapses then they will not be fully paid what they are owed and if the company is successful the creditors will not get any more than what they are owed under the credit contract that they have with the company.[39] Managers are probably more

---

[36]   S. Deakin, 'The Coming Transformation of Shareholder Value' (2005) 13 *Corporate Governance: An International Review* 11 at 11 and referring to M. Jensen, 'Value Maximisation, Stakeholder Theory and the Corporate Objective Function' (2001) 14 *Journal of Applied Corporate Finance* 8.

[37]   Jensen, ibid at 11.

[38]   J. Macey, *Corporate Governance* (Princeton, Princeton University Press, 2008) at 36.

[39]   Directors are probably more likely to exercise a more conservative strategy where they are seeking to ensure that the company continues to exist: E. Orts, 'The

likely to exercise a more conservative strategy where they are seeking to ensure that the company continues to exist,[40] and they might seek to do this as their reputation in the labour market will be severely affected if the company collapses.

3. WHAT DOES IT INVOLVE?

3.1 Introduction

While the theory is the dominant view amongst many academics in the US, and the theory has apparent popularity in many common law jurisdictions, there is a lack of consensus concerning how the theory is accomplished.[41] What actually is meant by shareholder value? How is the theory accomplished?[42] What does shareholder value mean in the day-to-day operations of a company? Does it mean directing actions at maximising the share price? Does it mean that the managers, providing that they are acting within the law, are to maximise shareholder value, no matter what? The problem is that the expression 'shareholder value' and its alternative descriptor, 'shareholder value maximisation' is vague.[43] Many theorists seem to see shareholder wealth as equivalent to maximising company profit,[44] and this might be appropriate in a perfect market with rational and socially acceptable behaviour by all people across the globe. But this simply does not occur.[45]

In 1984 Coca-Cola had a shareholder value objective and to accomplish it, it stated that 'growth in annual earnings per share and increased return

---

Complexity and Legitimacy of Corporate Law' (1993) 50 *Washington and Lee Law Review* 1565 at 1588.

[40] E. Orts, 'The Complexity and Legitimacy of Corporate Law' (1993) 50 *Washington and Lee Law Review* 1565 at 1588.

[41] A. Rappaport, *Creating Shareholder Value* (New York, The Free Press, 1986) at 1.

[42] Ibid.

[43] C. Kirchner, 'Shareholder Value: A New Standard for Corporation Conduct' in K. Hopt and E. Vermeersch (eds), *Capital Markets and Corporation Law* (Oxford, Oxford University Press, 2003) at 343.

[44] The American Law Institute's *Principles of Corporate Governance* certainly do: Sec 2.01 (1994).

[45] M. Blair, 'Shareholder Value: A New Standard for Corporation Conduct' in K. Hopt and E. Vermeersch (eds), *Capital Markets and Corporation Law* (Oxford, Oxford University Press, 2003) at 348–349.

on equity are still the names of the game.'[46] At the same time another large US company that was committed to provide a superior return for shareholders stated in its annual report that shareholder value 'is created when a company generates free cash flow in excess of the shareholder's investment in the business.'[47] But, as we see below, other explanations of shareholder value have been given.

Very often the theory of shareholder value is said to entail, in simple terms, enhancing the value of the shares of the company, as discussed below, and increasing the dividends paid to shareholders.[48] Of course, there can be a variety of strategies employed to attain these goals, including the avoidance of costs where at all possible.

Anant Sundaram and Andrew Inkpen have said that shareholder value is superior as it 'is a single valued metric that is also observable and measurable.'[49] This is supported by many finance theorists, and it suggests that the shareholder value approach makes it all so much easier to implement. However, to say what the commentators say above does not take into account the fact that 'a single value . . . [does] not float free of decisions as to what strategies will count as enhancing shareholder value.'[50] Also, Henry Hu in an investigation of the meaning of shareholder primacy,[51] in the context of the development of new financial products and the process of financial innovation, concluded that shareholder value has never been certain. This assessment is consistent with the opinion of many that the objective of the theory is in fact unclear and ill-defined.[52]

---

[46] As quoted in A. Rappaport, *Creating Shareholder Value* (New York, The Free Press, 1986) at 1.

[47] Ibid.

[48] J. Brummer, *Corporate Responsibility and Legitimacy* (New York, Greenwood Press, 1991) at 20.

[49] A. Sundaram, and A. Inkpen, 'The Corporate Objective Revisited' (2004) 15 *Organization Science* 350 at 355.

[50] C. O'Kelly, 'History Begins: Shareholder Value, Accountability and the Virtuous State' (2009) 60 *Northern Ireland Legal Quarterly* 35 at 45.

[51] H. Hu, 'New Financial Products, the Modern Process of Financial Innovation and the Puzzle of Shareholder Welfare' (1991) 69 *Texas Law Review* 1273.

[52] M. Miller, 'The Informational Content of Dividends' in R. Dornbusch, S. Fischer, and J. Bossons, (eds), *Macroeconomics and Finance: Essays in Honor of Franco Modigliani*, (Cambridge, Massachusetts, MIT Press, 1987); C. Loderer, L. Roth, U. Waelchli, and P. Joerg, 'Shareholder Value: Principles, Declarations, and Actions' 22 April 2009, European Corporate Governance Institute Finance Working Paper No 95/2006 (revised), and accessible at <http://papers.ssrn.com/sol3/papers.cfm?abstract_id=690044> (last visited, 30 March 2010).

Of course, if that argument is correct then one can conclude that it is debatable whether shareholder value can actually be measured. Also, it is quite possible that if the theory is not certain then many managers will not understand what it means.

3.2   The Share Price

It has been said that shareholder primacy involves maximising the share value, and the value of a share is the present discounted value of the stream of dividends the share will pay in the indefinite future.[53] The strong version of the theory of efficient markets (efficient markets hypothesis) posits that the share price will take into account all of the information, public and private, available at a particular time about a company's performance and prospects, with the result that market capitalisation will indicate what a company is worth to the shareholders.[54] The semi-strong version states that the share price reflects all public information and the weak reading of the efficient markets hypothesis holds that the price simply changes in respect to the information about share price movements.[55] The share price is said to be a measure of a company's performance and the stock market is the only objective assessor of a management's performance.[56] So, some[57] will argue that the share price is a measure of whether the directors have fulfilled the corporate objective. There are many advantages, so it is argued, of relying on the share price. First, the price cannot be manipulated directly by management, certainly in the short run, and it embraces automatically the future effects of present actions, avoiding the

---

[53] E. Sternberg, *Just Business*, 2nd ed (Oxford, Oxford University Press, 2000) at 47; S. Bainbridge, 'The Importance of the Shareholder Wealth Maximization Standard,' *TCS Daily*, 7 February 2006, and accessible at <www.tcsdaily.com/article.aspx?id=020706G> (last visited, 7 July 2009).

[54] Sternberg, ibid at 47. Empirical evidence indicates that reported current earnings will affect share prices: J. Watts and J. Zimmerman, *Positive Accounting Theory* (Englewood Cliffs, Prentice-Hall, 1986) and referred to in J. Grinyer, A. Russell and D. Collision, 'Evidence of Managerial Short-termism in the UK' (1998) 9 *British Journal of Management* 13 at 15.

[55] E. Fama, 'Random Walks in Stock Market Prices' (1965) 21 *Financial Analysts Journal* 55.

[56] Given the instances of companies like Enron share price cannot be said to reflect necessarily the underlying value of a company's equity: M. Blair, 'Directors' Duties in a Post-Enron World: Why Language Matters' (2003) 38 *Wake Forest Law Review* 885 at 894.

[57] For example, M. van der Weide, 'Against Fiduciary Duties to Corporate Stakeholders' (1996) 21 *Delaware Journal of Corporate Law* 27 at 68–69.

short-term bias of one period of accounting.[58] In relation to this apparent advantage, Margaret Blair has asserted that managers might lie about accounting performance with the hope that the share price will increase.[59] Also, management is able to manipulate the price indirectly by doing things like delaying announcements. As far as the maximising of the share price is concerned, it is argued that that action harmonises the interests of both present and future shareholders as the value of the company in the future will be reflected in the share price.[60] The maximisation of the share value is said to permit the shareholder to secure the highest possible utility from the investment that is made in the company.[61]

A second perceived advantage of reliance on the share price is that it makes it easy to determine whether the directors are doing their job and the layperson can tell whether or not he or she is making money from the investment in the company.

Third, while accounting mechanisms are backward looking, focusing on share value is forward looking as it involves the market's best idea as to what is the value of the investments that a company has made and what is the value of investments to be arranged in the future.[62]

Many have focused on the share price. Yet recently Nicholas Hayek, the chairman of the Swatch Group, rejected the idea that the value of a company's shares is a standard of measurement of the value of a company.[63]

3.3 Metrics

There have been several attempts by management consultants to explain what shareholder value involves using value metrics.[64] The power of the

---

[58]   E. Sternberg, *Just Business*, 2nd ed (Oxford, Oxford University Press, 2000) at 47.

[59]   M. Blair, 'Directors' Duties in a Post-Enron World: Why Language Matters' (2003) 38 *Wake Forest Law Review* 885 at 904.

[60]   S. Wallman, 'Understanding the Purpose of a Corporation: An Introduction' (1999) 24 *Journal of Corporation Law* 807 at 808.

[61]   D. Mramor and A. Valentincic, 'When Maximising Shareholders' Wealth is Not the Only Choice' 2006, at 3, and available at <http://papers.ssrn.com/paper.taf?abstract_id=258269> (last visited, 24 July 2009).

[62]   M. Blair, 'Directors' Duties in a Post-Enron World: Why Language Matters' (2003) 38 *Wake Forest Law Review* 885 at 893.

[63]   Referred to in C. Loderer, L. Roth, U. Waelchli, and P. Joerg, 'Shareholder Value: Principles, Declarations, and Actions' 22 April 2009, ECGI – Finance Working Paper No 95/2005 at 2 and accessible at <http://papers.ssrn.com/sol3/papers.cfm?abstract_id=690044> (last visited, 30 March 2010).

[64]   See, J. Mouritsen, 'Driving Growth: Economic Value Added Versus Intellectual Capital' (1998) 9 (4) *Management Accounting Research* 461; J. Froud et

use of metrics is in the fact that they allow a ranking of performance.[65] It is not possible to deal with all of the different kinds of metrics that have been developed. What follows is a discussion in relation to some of the more popular ones. Some consultants have argued for one metric that can be used in relation to all companies, whilst other consultants contend that different metrics should apply to different sorts of companies. It has been contended that the shareholder value theory 'estimates the economic value of an investment [such as the company's shares, business strategies, mergers and acquisitions, and capital expenditures] by discounting forecasted cash flows by the cost of the capital.'[66] The cash flows are the basis for the returns to shareholders in the form of dividends and the increase in the value of shareholders' shares.[67] To ascertain shareholder value on this basis one ascertains the corporate/ market value of the company and deducts debt from it.[68] The corporate value of the company is the value of its equity and debt. Equity obviously covers the share capital of the company and debt includes what is owed to lenders and other elements such as unfunded pension liabilities of a company.[69] More precisely corporate/market value is the value of the company and consists of the present value of cash flow from operations in the relevant forecast period, the residual value representing the present value of the business relating to the period beyond the forecast period and the current value of marketable securities and other investments that are able to be converted into cash, and which are not required to operate the business.[70]

A well-used metric, known as EVA™,[71] involves 'a residual income measure which shows whether the firm in one year earns more than its weighted average cost of capital, that is ascertaining the net operating profits after tax, minus the required rate of return on capital employed.'[72]

---

al, 'Shareholder Value and Financialization: Consultancy Promises. Management Moves' (2000) 29 *Economy and Society* 80 for a critical discussion of the various approaches advocated.

[65] Froud, ibid at 82.

[66] A. Rappaport, *Creating Shareholder Value* (New York, The Free Press, 1986) at 12, 50.

[67] Ibid.

[68] Ibid at 51.

[69] Ibid.

[70] Ibid. The investments and their income are not included in cash flow.

[71] This stands for 'Economic Value Added' and was developed by the firm, Stern Stewart.

[72] J. Stern and D. Chew, *The Revolution in Corporate Finance*, 2nd ed (Malden, Massachusetts, Blackwell, 1992) at 34.

It has been said that this provides a clear directive 'to improve returns earned on existing capital, to invest in projects that earn returns above the cost of capital and to sell assets that are worth more to others.'[73] Another metric is SVA. This stands for shareholder value added.[74] It calculates whether there has been an accretion of shareholder value by determining 'net operating profit after tax . . . less a capital charge.' It 'can be enhanced by focusing on its four components: revenue and expenses . . . capital (value of assets), and cost of capital (adjusted for risk).'[75]

Others have sought to employ an approach that involves combining value metrics with other measures and techniques such as scorecards, identification of value drivers and value chain management in 'an approach which energizes a corporation to enhance shareholder wealth.'[76] Also, it has been asserted that in today's markets the sources of shareholder maximisation should not only include the net present value of profits, but also option value. This value represents the options companies have in relation to future developments.[77]

One of the problems with the use of metrics is that while there are similarities between various approaches, there are significant differences. Another issue is that the metrics used are often not understood and can be of little help to many.

3.4 Time Period

The theory does not state the time period in which the objective is to be achieved. It is not clear whether the theory involves short-term gains or long-term gains. It probably can cover both, although the emphasis in the

---

[73]   G. Milano and M. Schwartz, 'Need to delegate profitability? EVA™ Will Show You How', *Sunday Times* 27 September 1998 and quoted in J. Froud et al, 'Shareholder Value and Financialization: Consultancy Promises. Management Moves' (2000) 29 *Economy and Society* 80 at 83.

[74]   It was coined by the now defunct accounting firm, Arthur Andersen. See, Arthur Andersen *Shareholder Value Added* (London, Arthur Andersen, 1997).

[75]   Ibid at 5 and quoted in J. Froud et al, 'Shareholder Value and Financialization: Consultancy Promises. Management Moves' (2000) 29 *Economy and Society* 80 at 83.

[76]   For example, Price Waterhouse (undated), *Value Based Management: Energizing the Corporation to Create Shareholder Value* quoted in J. Froud et al, 'Shareholder Value and Financialization: Consultancy Promises. Management Moves' (2000) 29 *Economy and Society* 80 at 82.

[77]   R. Grant, 'Rescuing Shareholder Value Maximization' and accessible at: <http://www.viasarfatti25.unibocconi.eu/notizia.php?idArt=2131> (last visited, 30 March 2010).

past has certainly been on the short term,[78] and even quite recently Allen, Jacobs and Strine[79] referred to the long-term approach as being 'a weaker form' of wealth maximization. Clearly short-term and long-term strategies differ, so there is the problem of whether short-term or long-term horizons should be set.[80]

Short-termism has been defined as : 'foregoing economically worthwhile investments with longer-term benefits in order to increase reported earnings for the current period.'[81] This could mean scrimping on R & D (research and development), failing to renew plant and equipment or making employees redundant (even though they might need to hire more in the medium term. But it provides a short term boost at least). It has been said that to be strictly applying a short-term approach in this context would mean that the managers would be paying out to shareholders every amount earned as profit and with no consideration given to investing funds or expanding the company's market by reducing prices.[82]

The way that executive remuneration is formulated and the fact that directors often move on to other posts frequently do not contribute to an approach other than short term. In many cases executive directors are almost encouraged by their companies to focus on the short term. Their remuneration packages often involve significant stock options. It pays the directors to work to push up the share price as that will benefit them directly. Also, if executive directors look to the long term they may feel that they are not likely to gain the praise and the benefits from enriching the company as their tenure is usually not very long, and by the time that the company benefits from a long-term strategy they will not be in the job. In the recent past, some institutional investors in the Royal Bank of Scotland have indicated concern that the CEO of the Bank was being given an incentive with his remuneration package to push the share price up in the short term and that this would not be sustainable in the long term.[83] If maximising for long-term value, managers should aim to balance the

---

[78] D. Miles, *Testing for Short-Termism in the UK Stock Market* (London, Economics Division, Bank of England, 1992).

[79] 'The Great Takeover Debate: A Meditation on Bridging the Conceptual Divide' (2002) 69 *University of Chicago Law Review* 1067 at 1076.

[80] See H. Hu, 'Risk, Time and Fiduciary Principles in Corporate Investment' (1990) 38 *University of California at Los Angeles Law Review* 277.

[81] J. Grinyer, A. Russell and D. Collision, 'Evidence of Managerial Short-termism in the UK' (1998) 9 *British Journal of Management* 13 at 15.

[82] J. Heydon, 'Directors' Duties and the Company's Interests' in P. Finn (ed), *Equity and Commercial Relationships* (Sydney, Law Book Co, 1987) at 135.

[83] P. Hosking, 'RBS chief tries to defuse concern over pay' *The Times*, 2 July 2009.

seeking of opportunities to make profits now with opportunities to make profits in the future.

Managing for short-term gains does not appear to be as acceptable as it once was, and has come in for significant criticism over several years. For instance, focusing on producing short-term profits has been said to be unrealistic and fuelled the pressure to take on increased risk.[84] The former CEO of Railtrack, Steve Marshall, has asserted that the short-term approach leads to results that are proxy measures for shareholder value.[85]

Recently Michael Jensen has emphasised the need to manage for the long term,[86] saying that short-term maximisation is a way of destroying value,[87] and another commentator has suggested that leading scholars in economics and law have abandoned any focus on short-termism.[88] More will be said about this issue later in the Chapter.[89]

Historically, to overcome the problem of whether the short or the long term is in view, Chancellor William Allen, when Chancellor of the Delaware Court of Chancery, said extra-judicially that '[t]he law "papered over" the conflict in our conception of the corporation by invoking a murky distinction between long-term profit maximization and short-term profit maximization.'[90] Yet, the dichotomy between the short term and the long term has been underplayed. Commentators have said that the

---

[84] M. Lipton, T. Mirvis and J. Lorsch, 'The Proposed "Shareholder Bill of Rights Act of 2009"' Harvard Law School Forum on Corporate Governance and Financial Regulation (12 May 2009), and accessible at: <http://blogs.law.harvard.edu/corpgov/2009/05/12/the-proposed-%e2%80%9cshareholder-bill-of-rights-act-of-2009%e2%80%9d> (last visited, 2 April 2010).

[85] Referred to in Charted Institute of Management Accountants, 'Maximising Shareholder Value' 2004 and accessible at <http://www.cimaglobal.com/Documents/Thought_leadership_docs/MigratedDocsMarch2010/Resouces%20%28pdfs%29/Technical%20reports/Maximising%20shareholder%20value%20achieving%20clarity%20in%20decision-making.pdf> (last visited, 21 June 2010).

[86] M. Jensen, 'Value Maximisation, Stakeholder Theory and the Corporate Objective Function' (2001) 14 *Journal of Applied Corporate Finance* 8. In addition it is published in 'Value Maximisation, Stakeholder Theory, and the Corporate Objective Function' (2001) 7 *European Financial Management* 297. Also, see H. Hansmann and R. Kraakman, 'The End of History for Corporate Law' (2001) 89 *Georgetown Law Journal* 439 at 439; G. Dent, 'Corporate Governance: Still Broke, No Fix in Sight' (2006) 31 *Journal of Corporation Law* 39 at 57.

[87] M. Jensen, 'Value Maximisation, Stakeholder Theory and the Corporate Objective Function' (2001) 14 *Journal of Applied Corporate Finance* 8 at 16.

[88] E. Talley, 'On the Demise of Shareholder Primacy (Or, Murder on the James Trains Express)' (2002) 75 *Southern California Law Review* 1211 at 1214.

[89] Below at pp. 75–77, 82–83.

[90] W. Allen, 'Our Schizophrenic Conception of the Business Corporation' (1992) 14 *Cardozo Law Review* 261 at 273.

distinction between the short term and the long term is precluded by the assumption of market efficiency, 'whereby optimality in the long run is simply the result of a series of optimal short-run decisions,' although it has been acknowledged that the efficiency of markets has been subject to challenge.[91]

Steven Lydenberg has defined long-term investing as speculating: 'on the value of corporations to society and the environment, while simultaneously seeking to enhance that value at the company, industry and societal level.'[92] This approach questions the idea that share prices are proxies for societal value. As Allen White points out, high share prices might benefit shareholders in the short term, but this does not bear any relation to societal value in the long term.[93]

3.5 Shareholder Interests

It is not clear what shareholder value actually means as far as shareholders are concerned, for it can mean different things to different shareholders,[94] depending on what shareholders have as their expectations, investment goals, time-scales, the amount of risk they want to see taken, their resources, and their aims. For instance, some shareholders might have a short-investment strategy and others wish to embrace a longer term.[95] Although the focus of shareholder primacy has tended to be on short-term profits, courts have accepted arguments in favour of managers looking to the long term,[96] and as discussed above, there is greater focus

---

[91] A. Sundaram and A. Inkpen, 'The Corporate Objective Revisited' (2004) 15 *Organization Science* 350 at 358.

[92] *Corporations and the Public Interest: Guiding the Invisible Hand* (San Francisco, Berrett-Koehler, 2005) and quoted in A. White, 'What is Long-Term Wealth?' Business for Social Responsibility paper, September 2007 and accessible at <http://www.bsr.org/reports/bsr_awhite_long-term-wealth.pdf> (last visited, 8 July 2009) at 4.

[93] A. White, 'What is Long-Term Wealth?' Business for Social Responsibility paper, September 2007 and accessible at <http://www.bsr.org/reports/bsr_awhite_long-term-wealth.pdf> (last visited, 8 July 2009) at 4.

[94] C. Loderer, L. Roth, U. Waelchli, and P. Joerg, 'Shareholder Value: Principles, Declarations, and Actions' 22 April 2009, European Corporate Governance Institute Finance Working Paper No 95/2006 (revised), and accessible at <http://papers.ssrn.com/sol3/papers.cfm?abstract_id=690044> (last visited, 30 March 2010).

[95] Nevertheless, George Dent argues that most shareholders have the same goal, namely to maximise the value of their shares: 'The Essential Unity of Shareholders and the Myth of Investor Short-Termism' (2010) 35 *Delaware Journal of Corporate Law* 97 at 100, 105.

[96] For instance, see *Shlensky v Wrigley* 237 NE 2d 776 (Ill App Ct, 1968).

on the long term amongst shareholder primacists now than in the past. In many companies there are different kinds of shares and the interests and aspirations of the different shareholders may well diverge. Furthermore, are directors to aim to take action that will also benefit only the current shareholders, or should they also consider the interests of the future shareholders? If they are to consider the future shareholders, how do managers balance what they do between the interests of the current and future shareholders? Shareholders also have different investing approaches. Some shareholders in a company may only have shares in that company, while other shareholders may hold a diversified portfolio, with their investment spread around a number of companies. The shareholder value theory is, arguably, not sophisticated enough to allow for the fact that many investors are diversified and will have both the role of shareholder and bondholder in companies.[97] Because of the differences in shareholder interests, do the directors who implement shareholder value focus on what the majority of shareholders want? But how does one know what they want? The directors cannot keep running back to the shareholders' meeting to consult every time that a major decision has to be made.

3.6   Other Interests

It has been suggested that notwithstanding the apparent fixation on profits for shareholders, the theory does permit managers to consider non-financial matters.[98] It might be somewhat debatable how far such considerations can go. If an action will benefit a particular stakeholder group it might be regarded as pursuing shareholder value if the action will benefit shareholders directly or indirectly, but one would think that the benefit would have to be, ultimately, of a financial nature. This appears to be the general thrust of s.172(1) of the UK's Companies Act 2006 with its reliance on so-called 'enlightened shareholder value.'[99] In the course of promoting the success of the company for the benefit of shareholders the section states that directors have to have regard for other factors, such as the long-term consequences of directors' decisions, the interests of employees and the need to foster relations with its customers. This

---

[97]   T. Smith, 'The Efficient Norm for Corporate Law: A Neotraditional Interpretation of Fiduciary Duty' (1999) 98 *Michigan Law Review* 214 at 217.

[98]   S. Bottomley, *The Constitutional Corporation* (Aldershot, Ashgate, 2007) at 175.

[99]   See, A. Keay, 'Enlightened Shareholder Value, the Reform of the Duties of Company Directors and the Corporate Objective' [2006] *Lloyds Maritime and Commercial Law Quarterly* 335.

provision might be said to be in accordance with the view articulated in the late 1990s by the CEO of BAA, John Egan, that in order to provide for the long-term interests of shareholders one must satisfy and obtain the co-operation of all stakeholders in the company.[100] This approach has been labelled as a stakeholder approach,[101] but arguably it could equally be said to be invoking a shareholder value approach, although doing so in a realistic way.

It has been asserted that in today's markets the sources of shareholder maximisation should not only include the net present value of profits, but also option value. These represent the options companies have in relation to future developments.[102]

3.7 Summary

There appear to be a number of significant uncertainties surrounding the theory and its implementation. The theory has no distinct meaning and it tells us little about what managers should do. While agency theories and consultancy metrics have been devised around shareholder primacy, they do not enable managers to have a guide as to what they are actually to do.[103] Directors are left with little idea other than some general notion that they are to do their best for the shareholders. It has been said that shareholder value 'is not so much a precisely defined concept with a stable place in one discourse or politico-economic system, as a rhetoric which circulates widely and a thematic which can be variably invoked as cause, consequence or justification.'[104]

Finally in this section, it would seem fair to say that what is required to maximise shareholder wealth will very much depend on the financial situation and the company's individual circumstances, and thus this means that

---

[100] M. Omran, P. Atrill and J. Pointon, 'Shareholders Versus Stakeholders: Corporate Mission Statements and Investor Returns' (2002) 11 *Business Ethics: A European Review* 318 at 319. This approach is implicit in the statement from General Motors on its website at <http://www.gm.com/corporate/responsibility/reports/06/300_company/3_thirty/330.html> (last visited, 4 December 2009).

[101] Ibid.

[102] R. Grant, 'Rescuing Shareholder Value Maximization' and accessible at: <http://www.viasarfatti25.unibocconi.eu/notizia.php?idArt=2131> (last visited, 18 August 2010).

[103] R. Mitchell, A. O'Donnell and I.M. Ramsay, 'Shareholder Value and Employee Interests: Intersections Between Corporate Governance, Corporate Law and Labor Law' (2005) *Wisconsin International Law Journal* 417 at 429.

[104] J. Froud, et al, 'Shareholder Value and Financialization: Consultancy Promises. Management Moves' (2000) 29 *Economy and Society* 80 at 81.

it is not possible to lay down any form of precision as far as the theory is concerned.

4. WHY MAXIMISE SHAREHOLDER VALUE?

The answer to this question is discussed effectively in the forthcoming section titled, 'Arguments in Favour.' But there are probably a number of practical reasons for managers following this theory.[105] First, where managers hold a reasonably significant number of shares in the company, or hold options, there is an incentive to maximise shareholder wealth. Second, the remuneration of the managers is often linked to what shareholders get by way of returns on their investment. This is done to address the agency cost problem and to align the interests of managers with those of the shareholders. It is not unusual for managers to be promised bonuses over and above their salary if the company's performance leads to shareholder benefits, and often the benefits are linked to the performance of the share price. Third, there is always the threat of a takeover. Managers will endeavour to ensure that the shareholders are happy with their management, primarily by ensuring high share prices, and so they retain their shares and do not sell out to a corporate raider. Burton Malkiel has said that:

> A company that has been run by a management group whose major objective is *not* the well-being of shareholders will become a prime target for a take-over bid. The ever present threat of such a bid is likely to provide a powerful incentive for management to make the maximization of the shareholders' wealth a primary goal for the firm.[106]

If a takeover does transpire then the managers are likely to lose their posts.

Fourth, there is a competitive labour market for managers and if other companies see the shareholders of a manager's company benefiting they might seek to poach him or her. Conversely, if a manager's performance is not leading to shareholder benefits then the board or the general meeting might consider removing him or her and hiring someone else who can perform better. The following warning came from an editor of a finance

---

[105] The following reasons are based on A. Rappaport, *Creating Shareholder Value* (New York, The Free Press, 1986) at 7.

[106] 'Debt-Equity Combination of the Firm and the Cost of Capital' (1972) at 4 and quoted in R. Hessen, 'A New Concept of Corporations: A Contractual and Private Property Model' (1979) 30 *Hastings Law Journal* 1327 at 1346.

journal: 'Any management – no matter how powerful and independent – that flouts the financial objective of maximizing share value does so at its own peril.'[107]

Fifth, the theory is perceived as being coherent and that fact enables it to be explained and applied more easily by managers.[108]

Sixth, managers might well favour the theory as it arguably permits them to engage in activity that will produce short-term gains and defer costs to a later point of time.[109] Managers historically do not remain in post long enough for any disadvantages of this approach 'coming home to roost.'

A final point to make is that Jay Lorsch's research into what directors thought about their role (and this involved interviewing and surveying 80 directors in the US and Europe, although the majority were American) revealed that the general view of directors was that they had a legal obligation to maximise shareholder wealth.[110] This, of course, could be the most compelling reason for many directors as they would not want to be sued by the shareholders for breaching their duties.

5. THE BACKGROUND TO THE THEORETICAL FOUNDATIONS OF SHAREHOLDER PRIMACY

Shareholder primacy has been largely fostered as a leading principle of corporate law by the contractarian school in the US.[111] It was in the US in

---

[107] J. Treynor, 'The Financial Objective in the Widely Held Corporation' (1981) (March–April) *Financial Analysts Journal* at 69 and quoted in A. Rappaport, *Creating Shareholder Value* (New York, The Free Press, 1986) at 13.

[108] T. Smith, 'The Efficient Norm for Corporate Law: A Neotraditional Interpretation of Fiduciary Duty' (1999) 98 *Michigan Law Review* 214 at 230.

[109] M. Metzger and M. Phillips, 'Corporate Control, Business Ethics Instruction, and Intraorganizational Reality: A Review Essay' (1991) 29 *American Business Law Journal* 127 at 133.

[110] *Pawns or Potentates: The Reality of America's Corporate Boards* (Boston, Massachusetts, Harvard Business School Press, 1989) at 49.

[111] This is not to say that those who do not see themselves as contractarians do not agree with shareholder primacy. For some of the leading works on the principle, see J. Macey, 'An Economic Analysis of the Various Rationales for Making Shareholders the Exclusive Beneficiaries of Corporate Fiduciary Duties' (1991) 21 *Stetson Law Review* 23; S. Bainbridge, 'In Defense of the Shareholder Maximization Norm: A Reply to Professor Green' (1993) 50 *Washington and Lee Law Review* 1423; B. Black and R. Kraakman, 'A Self-Enforcing Model of Corporate Law' (1996) 109 *Harvard Law Review* 1911; D. Gordon Smith, 'The Shareholder Primacy Norm' (1998) 23 *Journal of Corporation Law* 277. It must be

the early 1930s that we find the genesis of the debate concerning the objective of a company. It all really started in earnest with the debates between Adolf Berle and E. Merrick Dodd, and was carried out in the literature published at the time.[112] Without going into great detail, Berle maintained, inter alia, that directors should not, as managers of companies, have any responsibilities other than to the shareholders of their companies, for whom money was to be made.[113] On the other hand, Dodd held that the public saw companies as economic institutions that have a social service role to play as well as making profits for shareholders, and that companies had responsibilities to the company's shareholders, employees, customers, and to the general public.[114] While the former conceded defeat eventually, the last half of the twentieth century has arguably been characterised as a time when many of Berle's views held sway, especially in the US. It might be said that this position has been attenuated somewhat by the introduction of constituency statutes in over 40 of the American states, an issue that is discussed later, in Chapter 4.[115] These statutes permit (one makes it mandatory) directors to take into account the interests of constituencies, other than shareholders, in the actions that they take. If there has been a weakening, and many would argue against that, it has been minimal, certainly amongst academic commentators, as the number of learned articles arguing for a shareholder maximisation approach attests.

The contractarian theorists, many of whom advocate a law and economics approach to law, focus on the contractual relationships that exist between persons involved in the affairs of the company, and, accordingly,

---

noted that some contractarians do not accept shareholder primacy: D.D. Prentice, 'The Contractual Theory of the Company and the Protection of Non-Shareholder Interests' in D. Feldman and F. Meisel, *Corporate and Commercial Law: Modern Developments* (London, Lloyds of London Press, 1996) at 121.

[112]   See A.A. Berle, 'Corporate Powers as Powers in Trust' (1931) 44 *Harvard Law Review* 1049; E.M. Dodd, 'For Whom are Corporate Managers Trustees?' (1932) 45 *Harvard Law Review* 1145; A.A. Berle, 'For Whom Managers are Trustees: A Note' (1932) 45 *Harvard Law Review* 1365. Also, see A.A. Berle and G. Means, *The Modern Corporation and Private Property* (New York, MacMillan, 1932); E.M. Dodd, 'Is Effective Enforcement of the Fiduciary Duties of Corporate Managers Practicable?' (1935) 2 *University of Chicago Law Review* 194.

[113]   A.A. Berle, 'Corporate Powers as Powers in Trust' (1931) 44 *Harvard Law Review* 1049. The view was put forward, in effect, in the earlier decision of *Dodge v Ford Motor Co* 170 NW 668 (1919) (Michigan).

[114]   E.M. Dodd, 'For Whom are Corporate Managers Trustees?' (1932) 45 *Harvard Law Review* 1145 at 1148.

[115]   Below at pp. 226–228. Also, see A. Keay, 'Moving Towards Stakeholderism? Constituency Statutes, Enlightened Shareholder Value and All That: Much Ado About Little?' (2011) 22 *European Business Law Review* 1.

hold to the principle of the sanctity of contract. Many contractarians adhere to the nexus of contracts approach to company law,[116] something that was discussed in Chapter 1. Although it is not an essential aspect of the contractarian approach,[117] contractarians generally[118] regard shareholder primacy as the focal point of their view of the public company.[119] The principle fills gaps in the corporate contract;[120] it establishes 'the substance of the corporate fiduciary duty'[121] that is owed by directors, namely that directors are required to act in such a way as to maximise the interests of the shareholders.

6.   THEORETICAL ARGUMENTS IN FAVOUR

Theorists will rely on different arguments for their support of the shareholder primacy theory, so it is not possible to identify a list of arguments

[116]   This idea is that the parties involved in these contracts are regarded as rational economic actors, and includes shareholders, managers, creditors and employees, and it is accepted that each of these constituencies endeavour in their contracting to maximise their own positions, with the intention of producing concomitant benefits for themselves. The literature considering the nexus of contracts is too voluminous to cite. But see, for example, M. Jensen and W. Meckling, 'Theory of the Firm' (1976) 3 *Journal of Financial Economics* 305 at 309–310; E. Fama, 'Agency Problems and the Theory of the Firm' (1980) 88 *Journal of Political Economy* 228 at 290; F. Easterbrook and D. Fischel, 'The Corporate Contract' (1989) 89 *Columbia Law Review* 1416 at 1426–1427; S. Deakin and A. Hughes, 'Economic Efficiency and the Proceduralisation of Company Law'(1999) 3 *Company Financial and Insolvency Law Review* 169 at 176–180; I. McNeil, 'Company Law Rules: An Assessment from the Perspective of Incomplete Contract Theory' (2001) 1 *Journal of Corporate Law Studies* 107.

[117]   I. Lee, 'Corporate Law, Profit Maximization and the "Responsible" Shareholder' (2005) 10 *Stanford Journal of Law, Business and Finance* 31 at 48.

[118]   Stephen Bainbridge would appear to be an exception as he emphasises director primacy: 'The Board of Directors as Nexus of Contracts' (2002) 88 *Iowa Law Review* 1; 'Director Primacy: The Means and Ends of Corporate Governance' (2003) 97 *Northwestern University Law Review* 547.

[119]   M. Bradley, C. Schipani, A. Sundaram and J. Walsh, 'The Purposes and Accountability of the Corporation in Contemporary Society: Corporate Governance at a Crossroads' (1999) 62 *Law and Contemporary Problems* 9 at 38.

[120]   F. Easterbrook and D. Fischel, *The Economic Structure of Company Law* (Cambridge, Massachusetts, Harvard University Press, 1991), at 90–93; J. Macey, and G. Miller, 'Corporate Stakeholders: A Contractual Perspective' (1993) 43 *University of Toronto Law Review* 401 at 404.

[121]   T. Smith, 'The Efficient Norm for Corporate Law: A Neotraditional Interpretation of Fiduciary Duty' (1999) 98 *Michigan Law Review* 214 at 217. A view with which Smith disagrees (ibid).

that are common to all scholars favouring this theory. Below I consider the leading arguments. The arguments are in no particular order of importance or strength. It is fair to say at the outset that most arguments are, in some way, informed by the value of efficiency, because it is argued that the principle is based on efficiency.[122] Also, there are clear overlaps between some arguments.

The preference for shareholder primacy is not a consequence of a 'philosophical predilection'[123] towards shareholders, but a concern that the business should be run for the benefit of the residual claimants, namely, the shareholders, while the company is solvent.[124] This is probably regarded as the primary argument in favour of the shareholder primacy approach. The residual claimants have the greatest stake in the outcome of the company,[125] as they will benefit if the company's fortunes increase, receiving healthy dividends, but they will lose out if the company hits hard times (with their claims being last in line if the company is liquidated), and they will value the right to control managers above any other stakeholders,[126] as they have an interest in every decision that is taken by a solvent firm.[127] Furthermore, shareholders have the greatest incentive to maximise profits and so they are the best group to make the directors accountable. As a result of this, it is asserted that the shareholders are the most appropriate group of constituents to decide on aspects of company

---

[122] Some empirical evidence suggests that shareholder wealth maximisation may not necessarily be efficient: J. Coffee, 'Shareholders Versus Managers: The Strain in the Corporate Web' (1986) 85 *Michigan Law Review* 1 at 91. Also, see E. Elhauge, 'Sacrificing Corporate Profits in the Public Interest' (2005) 80 *New York University Law Review* 733 at 776.

[123] M. van der Weide, 'Against Fiduciary Duties to Corporate Stakeholders' (1996) 21 *Delaware Journal of Corporate Law* 27 at 37.

[124] F. Easterbrook and D. Fischel, *The Economic Structure of Company Law* (Cambridge, Massachusetts, Harvard University Press, 1991) at 36–39.

[125] J. Macey, 'Fiduciary Duties as Residual Claims: Obligations to Nonshareholder Constituencies from a Theory of the Firm Perspective' (1999) 84 *Cornell Law Review* 1266 at 1267. This has been queried by several commentators, such as Margaret Blair (*Ownership and Control* (Washington DC, The Brookings Institute, 1995) at 229).

[126] M. van der Weide, 'Against Fiduciary Duties to Corporate Stakeholders' (1996) 21 *Delaware Journal of Corporation Law* 27 at 38; R. Gilson and M. Roe, 'Understanding the Japanese Keiretsu: Overlaps Between Corporate Governance and Industrial Organization' (1993) 102 *Yale Law Journal* 871 at 887.

[127] J. Macey and G. Miller, 'Corporate Stakeholders: A Contractual Perspective' (1993) 43 *University of Toronto Law Review* 401 at 408; F. Tung, 'The New Death of Contract: Creeping Corporate Fiduciary Duties for Creditors' (2008) 57 *Emory Law Journal* 809 at 819.

policy,[128] even though, as we will discuss in detail later, it is the board of directors that makes most of those decisions. Usually, shareholders can only respond in the affirmative or the negative to a motion; they cannot initiate fundamental changes or strategy.

Second, according to the prevailing agency theory,[129] directors are the agents of the shareholders and are employed to run the company's business for the shareholders who do not have the time or ability to do so, and it is the shareholders who are best suited to guide and discipline directors in the carrying out of their powers and duties.[130] The shareholders, who elected the managers, are regarded in a sense as the bosses of the managers.[131] It is said that if there is no shareholder primacy norm, the directors are able to engage in shirking or some opportunistic behaviour.[132] Costs, known as 'agency costs',[133] will be incurred in monitoring the work of the directors. In order to reduce the incidence of shirking and opportunism duties are owed to shareholders. Duties are also designed to protect the shareholders. The upshot is that shareholder primacy means that directors are fully accountable to shareholders for what they do in running the company's business.

The fact that derivative actions can be brought by a shareholder against the directors and others if they harm the company, is seen as a reason why

---

[128] J. Macey, *Corporate Governance* (Princeton, Princeton University Press, 2008) at 7. Also, see F. Easterbrook and D. Fischel, 'Voting in Corporate Law' (1983) 26 *Journal of Law and Economics* 395 at 403.

[129] This is based on a large number of works, but arguably the most influential are: M. Jensen and W. Meckling, 'Theory of the Firm: Managerial Behaviour, Agency Costs, and Ownership Structure' (1976) 3 *Journal of Financial Economics* 305; E. Fama, 'Agency Problems and the Theory of the Firm' (1980) 88 *Journal of Political Economy* 228; E. Fama and M. Jensen, 'Separation of Ownership and Control' (1983) 26 *Journal of Law and Economics* 301; F. Easterbrook and D. Fischel, *The Economic Structure of Company Law* (Cambridge, Massachusetts, Harvard University Press, 1991).

[130] J. Matheson and B. Olson, 'Corporate Law and the Longterm Shareholder Model of Corporate Governance' (1992) 76 *Minnesota Law Review* 1313 at 1328.

[131] T. Jones, 'Corporate Social Responsibility Revisited, Redefined' (1980) (Spring) *California Management Review* 59 at 61.

[132] In this work this concept, consistent with the way that it is used by Oliver Williamson (*The Economic Institution of Capitalism* (1985) at 47–49)), is employed to describe self-interested behaviour that includes features of guile, misrepresentation, deception or bad faith.

[133] These costs are those resulting from managers failing to act appropriately and the costs expended in monitoring and disciplining the managers in order to prevent them abusing their positions.

the directors must maximise shareholder wealth. If the directors do not do so, then shareholders can take action against them.

Third, it is more efficient if directors operate on the basis of maximising shareholder wealth, because the least cost is expended in doing this;[134] the directors can work more efficiently if they are focused only on one objective and the interests of one type of investor. If directors owed duties to various constituencies, then it would be impossible for directors to balance all of the divergent interests, with the result that directors will make poor decisions.[135] The work that managers do can, as a result, be monitored more efficiently and effectively than where they are required to consider the interests of a multitude of parties. This makes directors more accountable. Also, if directors were concerned about benefiting several constituencies then this would hamper the free-flowing allocation of resources.[136] In sum, it is argued that shareholder primacy is certain and easy to administer,[137] and enables courts to review managerial conduct with some rationality,[138] because the managers only have to concentrate on one goal.[139] In a nutshell, the approach is workable.

The fourth argument in favour of shareholder primacy is that it increases social wealth in general terms,[140] because of market mechanisms, as resources are allocated most efficiently. More specifically, all other

---

[134]   M. van der Weide, 'Against Fiduciary Duties to Corporate Stakeholders' (1996) 21 *Delaware Journal of Corporate Law* 27 at 56–57. T. Smith, 'The Efficient Norm for Corporate Law: A Neotraditional Interpretation of Fiduciary Duty' (1999) 98 *Michigan Law Review* 214, 215 questions whether the goal of shareholder maximisation is efficient.

[135]   The Committee on Corporate Law, 'Other Constituency Statutes: Potential for Confusion' (1990) 45 *Business Lawyer* 2253 at 2269.

[136]   J. Matheson and B. Olson, 'Corporate Law and the Longterm Shareholder Model of Corporate Governance' (1992) 76 *Minnesota Law Review* 1313 at 1346.

[137]   This is especially when compared with the stakeholder theory under which directors are to act with all stakeholder interests in view: M. van der Weide, 'Against Fiduciary Duties to Corporate Stakeholders' (1996) 21 *Delaware Journal of Corporate Law* 27 at 68.

[138]   M. van der Weide, 'Against Fiduciary Duties to Corporate Stakeholders' (1996) 21 *Delaware Journal of Corporate Law* 27 at 69; J. Plender, 'Giving People a Stake in the Future' (1998) 31 *Long Range Planning* 211 at 212.

[139]   M. Jensen, 'Value Maximisation, Stakeholder Theory, and the Corporate Objective Function' (2001) 7 *European Financial Management* 297 at 301; A. Sundaram, and A. Inkpen, 'The Corporate Objective Revisited' 15 *Organization Science* 350 at 353–355.

[140]   H. Hansmann and R. Kraakman, 'The End of History for Corporate Law' (2001) 89 *Georgetown Law Journal* 439 at 441; M. O'Sullivan, 'The Innovative Enterprise and Corporate Governance' (2000) 24 *Cambridge Journal of Economics* 393 at 395; J. Cohan, '"I didn't know" and "I was only doing my job": has corpo-

constituencies benefit from the directors being focused on maximising shareholder wealth, although it is hard to see all constituencies benefiting and one commentator restricts himself to saying 'many constituents benefiting.'[141] One study concluded that: 'Empirical evidence indicates that increasing shareholder value does not conflict with the long-run interests of other stakeholders. Wining companies seem to create relatively greater values for all stakeholders . . . Shareholders are the only stakeholders of a corporation who simultaneously maximize everyone's claim in maximizing their own.'[142] The UK's Company Law Review Steering Group, which was established to review UK company law, supported the idea of contributing to social wealth when it said in 1999 that: 'the ultimate objective of companies as currently enshrined in law – ie to generate maximum value for shareholders – is in principle the best means also of securing overall prosperity and welfare.'[143]

The assertion is made that whatever stakeholders sacrifice in a shareholder primacy paradigm, they will be compensated out of the enhanced arrangement for the shareholders in that, for example, employees will receive higher wages and lenders higher interest payments.[144] Some even suggest that the maximisation of share prices alone can benefit society.[145] Furthermore, the utilitarian argument is put forward in that when directors engage in activity that ensures that economic conditions for the company improve and thus benefit shareholders (such as lowering costs of production and increasing sales), society benefits as well.[146]

---

rate governance careered out of control?' (2002) 40 *Journal of Business Ethics* 275 at 291.

[141] J. MacIntosh, 'Designing an Efficient Fiduciary Law' (1993) 43 *University of Toronto Law Journal* 425 at 452.

[142] T. Copeland, T. Koller and J. Murrin, *Valuation, Measuring and Managing* (New York, John Wiley, 1995) at 22.

[143] Company Law Review, *Modern Company Law for a Competitive Economy: Strategic Framework* (London, DTI, 1999) at para 5.1.12.

[144] I. Lee, 'Efficiency and Ethics in the Debate About Shareholder Primacy' (2006) 31 *Delaware Journal of Corporate Law* 533 at 537–538.

[145] E. Brigham and M. Ehrhardt, *Financial Management: Theory and Practice,* 10th ed (Thomson Learning, South-Western, 2002) at 10 and referred to in C. Loderer, L. Roth, U. Waelchli, and P. Joerg, 'Shareholder Value: Principles, Declarations, and Actions' 22 April 2009, ECGI – Finance Working Paper No. 95/2005 at 3 and accessible at <http://papers.ssrn.com/sol3/papers.cfm?abstract_id=690044> (last visited, 30 March 2010); G. Dent, 'Corporate Governance: Still Broke, No Fix in Sight' (2006) 31 *Journal of Corporation Law* 39 at 51.

[146] K. Davis, 'The Case for and Against Business Assumption of Social Responsibilities' in A. Carroll (ed), *Managing Corporate Social Responsibility* (Boston, Massachusetts, Little, Brown and Company, 1977) at 40.

Fifth, the shareholders can be regarded as the owners of the assets of the company,[147] a view that was accepted by the UK's Cadbury Committee in its *Report on the Financial Aspects of Corporate Governance*.[148] As they are owners the shareholders should be able to have the assets managed in their favour; the managers owe the shareholders a special loyalty,[149] and that involves the managers owing the shareholders a fiduciary duty to manage the company in the interests of the shareholders.[150] If one owns something then one has control rights over it. This is put forward by economic thought which does not regard the company as an entity in its own right, and some have even said that this is a dominant view.[151]

Sixth, it is argued that the managers, when taking on the role of management, make a promise to shareholders that they will make decisions that will seek to maximise the shareholders' benefits.[152] This is allied to the point that companies participate in capital markets seeking investors and so when they get those investors the managers of the company should endeavour to work for shareholder benefits. From a perspective of economic reality, the shareholders are mainly concerned, in investing,

---

[147]   M. Friedman, 'The Social Responsibility of Business is to Increase its Profits' *New York Times*, 13 September 1970, Section 6 (Magazine) 32 at 33; R. Hessen, 'A New Concept of Corporations: A Contractual and Private Property Model' (1979) 30 *Hastings Law Journal* 1327 at 1330; E. Steinberg, 'The Responsible Shareholder' (1992) 1 *Business Ethics: A European Review* 192 at 192; M. van der Weide, 'Against Fiduciary Duties to Corporate Stakeholders' (1996) 21 *Delaware Journal of Corporate Law* 27 at 77.

[148]   London, Gee Publishing, 1992 at para 6.1.

[149]   R. Pilon, 'Capitalism and Rights: An Essay Toward Fine Tuning the Moral Foundations of the Free Society' (1982) (February) *Journal of Business Ethics* 29 at 31ff. Also, see for example, Committee on the Financial Aspects of Corporate Governance (Cadbury Report) (London, Gee Publishing, 1992) para 6.1; Confederation of British Industries, *Boards Without Tiers: A CBI Contribution to the Debate* (London, CBI, 1996) at 8.

[150]   It is certainly debatable whether shareholders, even as a group, are owed fiduciary duties. See, A. Keay, 'Enlightened Shareholder Value, the Reform of the Duties of Company Directors and the Corporate Objective' [2006] *Lloyds Maritime and Commercial Law Quarterly* 335 at 341–346. Certainly, save in very exceptional circumstances, shareholders are not individually owed any duties. For instance, see *Gething v Kilner* [1972] 1 WLR 337; [1972] 1 All ER 1166; *Re a Company* [1986] BCLC 382; *Glandon Pty Ltd v Strata Consolidated Pty Ltd* (1993) 11 ACSR 543 (NSWCA); *Brunninghausen v Glavanics* [1999] NSWCA 199; (1999) 17 ACLC 1247.

[151]   P. Selznik, 'Institutionalism: old and new' (1996) 41 *Administrative Science Quarterly* 270 at 271.

[152]   K. Goodpaster, 'Business Ethics and Stakeholder Analysis' (1991) 1 *Business Ethics Quarterly* 53 at 63. Also, see S. Bainbridge, *The New Corporate Governance in Theory and Practice* (New York, Oxford University Press, 2008) at 58.

to make a profit, that is, to benefit by way of dividends and a capital appreciation of their investment.[153]

Seventh, shareholders warrant being favoured by the managers as they are in a vulnerable position[154] compared with other constituencies who are able to protect themselves by the terms of the contracts that they make with the company, and obtain safeguards in the nature of governance rights,[155] while shareholders do not have this kind of protection; they have no guarantee of any return. Any attempt to write a contract between the shareholders and the managers would be otiose as it would be so incomplete given the various decisions which managers have to make in the course of managing the company, that it would not be worth making.[156] The assertion is made that the shareholders are, in many ways, at the mercy of the directors, for they have difficulty in monitoring the work of directors. Oliver Williamson put it this way when it comes to shareholders: 'the whole of their investment in the firm is potentially placed at hazard.'[157] Also, he states that the shareholders 'are the only constituency whose relation with the corporation does not come up for periodic renewal . . . all [other constituencies] have opportunities to renegotiate terms when contracts are renewed. Stockholders by contrast invest for the life of the firm . . .'[158] Shareholders' investment is not connected to any property, unlike other constituents, so it makes it difficult to obtain any safeguards.[159] So it is the shareholders' interest in the surplus,

---

[153] D. Greenwood, 'Fictional Shareholders: For Whom are Corporate Managers Trustees Revisited' (1996) 69 *Southern California Law Review* 1021 at 1023; M. Siems, 'Shareholders, Stakeholders and the "Ordoliberalism"' (2002) 13 *European Business Law Review* 147 at 147.

[154] H. Hansmann and R. Kraakman, 'The End of History for Corporate Law' (2001) 89 *Georgetown Law Journal* 439 at 449. See L. Zingales, 'Corporate Governance' in *The New Palgrave Dictionary of Economics and Law* (Basingstoke, Macmillan, 1997) at 501.

[155] G. Kelly and J. Parkinson, 'The Conceptual Foundations of the Company: a Pluralist Approach' in J. Parkinson, A. Gamble and G. Kelly (eds), *The Political Economy of the Company* (Oxford, Hart Publishing, 2000) at 118; J. Fisch, 'Measuring Efficiency in Corporate Law' (2006) 31 *Journal of Corporation Law* 637 at 667–668.

[156] F. Tung, 'The New Death of Contract: Creeping Corporate Fiduciary Duties for Creditors' (2008) 57 *Emory Law Journal* 809 at 813.

[157] *The Economic Institution of Capitalism* (New York, The Free Press, 1985) at 304.

[158] *The Economic Institution of Capitalism* (New York, The Free Press, 1985) at 304–305.

[159] J. Boatright, 'Fiduciary Duties and the Shareholder-Management Relation: Or, What's Special About Shareholders?' (1994) 4 *Business Ethics Quarterly* 393 at 395.

namely, in lay language, the amount remaining after paying off overheads in economic terms, selling products for more than the cost of the inputs, that is not specified and in need of protection.

Also, along similar lines, it is argued that non-shareholder stakeholders are protected by regulatory law, while shareholders are not.[160] Furthermore, unlike some groups, such as creditors, shareholders are not always able to diversify their exposure to losses sustained by their investments. Finally, shareholders are not, except in listed companies, always able to exit a company easily where they are not happy with the company's performance or management. Even if they are able to exit easily the fact is that the company's fortunes might be such that if they do exit then they will take a significant 'hit' when they do sell.

Eighth, as it would be an impossibly complex contract that detailed all of the decision-making obligations of directors to shareholders, as well as being inflexible and unable to adjust to developments in the commercial world, the shareholder primacy theory acts as a gap-filler, that is, it provides the substance of the managers' responsibility to the shareholders.[161]

7. THEORETICAL ARGUMENTS AGAINST, AND GENERAL CRITICISM

7.1 Introduction

It has been asserted in recent times that corporate governance debates have now been resolved in favour of the shareholder primacy model.[162] Ronald Gilson has even said that corporate law's only distinctive feature is as a means to increase shareholder value.[163] Even a robust critic of the theory, Larry Mitchell, has conceded that it is the watchword by which we live

---

[160]   A. Sundaram and A. Inkpen, 'The Corporate Objective Revisited' (2004) 15 *Organization Science* 350 at 355; M. Bradley, C. Schipani, A. Sundaram and J. Walsh, 'The Purposes and Accountability of the Corporation in Contemporary Society: Corporate Governance at a Crossroads' (1999) 62 *Law and Contemporary Problems* 9 at 24–29.

[161]   J. Fisch, 'Measuring Efficiency in Corporate Law: The Rule of Shareholder Primacy' December 2005, Fordham Law Legal Studies, Working Paper No 105 at p26 and available at <http://ssrn.com/abstract=878391> (last visited, 27 July 2009).

[162]   H. Hansmann and R. Kraakman, 'The End of History for Corporate Law' (2001) 89 *Georgetown Law Journal* 439.

[163]   'Separation and the Function of Corporation Law' (January 2005) Stanford Law and Economics Olin Working Paper No.307 and available at: http://ssrn.com/abstract=732832> (last visited, 18 August 2010).

today.[164] And another who does not favour the theory, Kent Greenfield, has acknowledged the pre-eminence of shareholder primacy.[165] However, these latter two scholars and many others have long taken issue with the theory, with some questioning its normative value.[166] Others, principally those adopting a communitarian, stakeholder or pluralist approach to corporate law,[167] have argued that directors should be required to consider the interests of others besides shareholders, namely those whom we can call contributors, stakeholders or constituents. While shareholder primacy appears to hold sway in legal, accounting and finance circles, this is not the case in relation to other disciplines, such as management and business ethics, which have embraced a wider perspective than shareholder primacy. Max Clarkson illustrates this when he states that: 'Managers are now accountable for fulfilling the firm's responsibility to its primary stakeholder groups.'[168] Some leading writers have even proclaimed boldly that

---

[164] *Corporate Irresponsibility* (New Haven, Yale University Press, 2001) at 4.

[165] K. Greenfield, 'New Principles for Corporate Law' (2005) 1 *Hastings Business Law Journal* 89 at 89.

[166] For example, see D. Millon, 'New Game Plan or Business as Usual? A Critique of the Team Production Model of the Corporate Board' (2000) 86 *Virginia Law Review* 1001 at 1001–1004; L. Stout, 'Bad and Not-So-Bad Arguments for Shareholder Primacy' (2002) 75 *South California Law Review* 1189 at 1191.

[167] For discussions of this approach to corporate law, see, for example, L. Mitchell (ed), *Progressive Corporate Law* (Boulder, Colorado, Westview Press, 1995); W. Bratton, 'The "Nexus of Contracts Corporation": A Critical Appraisal' (1989) 74 *Cornell Law Review* 407; L. Mitchell, 'The Fairness Rights of Bondholders' (1990) 65 *New York University Law Review* 1165; D. Millon, 'Theories of the Corporation' [1990] *Duke Law Journal* 201; L. Johnson, 'The Delaware Judiciary and the Meaning of Corporate Life and Corporate Law' (1990) 68 *Texas Law Review* 865. Works in the UK that have advocated this approach are: J. Dine, 'Companies and Regulations: Theories, Justifications and Policing' in D. Milman (ed), *Regulating Enterprise: Law and Business Organisations in the UK* (Oxford, Hart Publishing, 1999) at 295–296; J. Dine, *Company Law* (London, Sweet and Maxwell, 2001), 27–30; J. Parkinson, *Corporate Power and Responsibility* (Oxford, Clarendon Press, 1993); G. Kelly and J. Parkinson, 'The Conceptual Foundations of the Company: A Pluralist Approach' (1998) 2 *Company Financial and Insolvency Law Review* 174. Also, see W. Leung, 'The Inadequacy of Shareholder Primacy: A Proposed Corporate Regime that Recognizes Non-Shareholder Interests' (1997) 30 *Columbia Journal of Law and Social Problems* 589; G. Crespi, 'Rethinking Corporate Fiduciary Duties: The Inefficiency of the Shareholder Primacy Norm' (2002) 55 *Southern Methodist University Law Review* 141.

[168] M. Clarkson, 'A Stakeholder Framework for Analyzing and Evaluating Corporate Social Performance' (1995) 20 *Academy Management Review* 92 at 112.

stakeholder theory is generally so pre-eminent that shareholder primacy is dead.[169]

Those holding to a communitarian[170] view of the company object to the shareholder primacy principle on normative grounds,[171] arguing that directors should be obliged to run companies for the benefit of all potential stakeholders in companies, such as creditors, employees, suppliers, customers and the communities in which the company operates. This aligns with the view of communitarians that companies should serve broader social purposes than simply making money for shareholders. The company is seen not as an instrument of shareholders, but an instrument of society at large.[172] Communitarians embrace a normative world view that emphasises the fact that people are part of a shared community who inherit the benefits, values and goals of the community, thus the cultural milieu in which people find themselves cannot be ignored,[173] and the company is regarded as 'a community of interdependence, mutual trust and reciprocal benefit.'[174] A consequence of this view is that it is asserted that the interests of shareholders are not the only interests to be considered by directors when carrying out their functions, for there are other important constituencies that warrant consideration from directors.[175] The effect

---

[169]   For example, R. Edward Freeman: 'The Politics of Stakeholder Theory: Some Future Directions' (1994) 4 *Business Ethics Quarterly* 409 at 413.

[170]   Those arguing for a 'team production' approach to corporate law (the main scholars adopting this view are Margaret Blair and Lynn Stout in 'A Team Production Theory of Corporate Law' (1999) 85 *Virginia Law Review* 247; 'Director Accountability and the Mediating Role of the Corporate Board' (2001) 79 *Washington University Law Quarterly* 403.

[171]   For instance, see D. Millon, 'Redefining Corporate Law' (1991) 24 *Indiana Law Review* 223 at 227ff.

[172]   D. Schrader, 'The Corporation and Profits' (1987) 6 *Journal of Business Ethics* 589 at 594.

[173]   D. Millon, 'New Directions in Corporate Law: Communitarians, Contractarians and Crisis in Corporate Law' (1993) 50 *Washington and Lee Law Review* 1373 at 1382.

[174]   D. Millon, 'Communitarianism in Corporate Law: Foundations and Law Reform Strategies' in L. Mitchell (ed), *Progressive Corporate Law* (Boulder, Colorado, Westview Press, 1995) at 10.

[175]   For example, Lawrence Mitchell criticises the whole notion of shareholder maximisation in corporate law ('A Theoretical and Practical Framework for Enforcing Corporate Constituency Statutes' (1992) 70 *Texas Law Review* 579 at 640). See D. Millon, 'Communitarianism in Corporate Law: Foundations and Law Reform Strategies' in L. Mitchell (ed), *Progressive Corporate Law* (Boulder, Colorado, Westview Press, 1995) at 7–9. Progressives differ among themselves concerning the strength of the claims of various non-shareholder constituencies to warrant legal intervention.

of invoking a shareholder primacy approach is, arguably, to damage the incentives of non-shareholder stakeholders to make firm-specific investments in companies as they are aware that their investments will be subordinated to shareholder interests at all times,[176] therefore, communitarians have criticised it, with Lyman Johnson saying that 'a radically proshareholder vision of corporate endeavour [is] substantially out of line with prevailing social norms.'[177]

Other commentators, who specialise in ethics, organisational behaviour and other management disciplines, have also challenged shareholder value theory, and in doing so they have embraced a wider perspective. Such commentators propound what is called 'a stakeholder theory'.[178] This is discussed in detail in Chapter 3. Theorists embracing this approach take the view that directors have to balance the interests of different constituencies that make up the company. Clarkson illustrates this when he states that: 'Managers are now accountable for fulfilling the firm's responsibility to its primary stakeholder groups.'[179] Theorists adhering to this approach see the company as a set of relationships in which managers adopt an inclusive concern for all stakeholders, both internal stakeholders, such as employees, and external stakeholders, such as consumers. Unlike many communitarians who eschew economics and focus solely on ethics and fairness, stakeholder theory seeks to combine economics and ethics, and in doing so it has been said that it 'tames the harsher aspects of capitalism.'[180]

Below the Chapter adumbrates the principal arguments that are mounted against the shareholder primacy theory. There is some overlap between arguments. Before dealing with the arguments that are against

---

[176]   G. Kelly and J. Parkinson, 'The Conceptual Foundations of the Company: A Pluralist Approach' in J. Parkinson, A. Gamble and G. Kelly (eds), *The Political Economy of the Company*, (Oxford, Hart Publishing, 2000) at 131.

[177]   'The Delaware Judiciary and the Meaning of Corporate Life and Corporate Law' (1990) 68 *Texas Law Review* 865 at 934.

[178]   For instance, see R. E. Freeman, *Strategic Management: A Stakeholder Approach* (Boston, Massachusetts, Pitman/Ballinger, 1984); T. Clarke and S. Clegg, *Changing Paradigms: The Transformation of Management Knowledge for the 21st Century* (London, Harper Collins Business, 2000); T. Donaldson and L. Preston, 'The Stakeholder Theory of the Corporation: Concepts, Evidence, Implications' (1995) 20 *Academy of Management Review* 65.

[179]   M. Clarkson, 'A Stakeholder Framework for Analyzing and Evaluating Corporate Social Performance' (1995) 20 *Academy of Management Review* 92 at 112.

[180]   J. Plender, *A Stake in the Future: The Stakeholding Solution*, 1997, London: Nicholas Bradley Publishing, and quoted in Janice Dean, *Directing Public Companies: Company Law and the Stakeholder Society* (London, Cavendish, 2001), at 117.

the theory, in principle, I should mention that it has been suggested that shareholder primacy is not possible as it fails to take into account the fact that companies cannot convey value to shareholders easily as structural constraints related to products markets demand that any benefits made for capital as a result of saving in respect of labour costs frequently have to be passed on to customers in the form of reduced prices.[181] So, we might say that 'very often the shareholder primacy model does not work, even on its own terms.'[182]

7.2 Certainty?

One of the main selling points that is customarily given for the theory, and especially when compared with stakeholder theory, is that it is certain and clear. The shareholder primacy theory is regarded as far more pragmatic, on the basis that it provides for a clear criterion or metric for determining business success and it provides guidance for directors in the direction which they should take in managing the business of the company. But is that so? As touched upon briefly earlier in the Chapter,[183] there appear to be a number of significant uncertainties surrounding the theory and its implementation. First, advocates of the theory take some pride in the fact that the theory provides some certainty as far as the direction of management is concerned. But does it? As adverted to earlier,[184] the theory has no distinct meaning and it tells us little about what managers should do. Agency theories and consultancy metrics devised around shareholder primacy do not enable managers to have a guide as to what they are to do.[185] What does shareholder primacy mean in the day-to-day operations of a company? Does it mean directing actions at maximising the share price? It is not clear what managers should actually be doing. It might mean 'immediate revenue

---

[181] J. Froud, S. Johal and K. Williams, 'Financialisation and the Coupon Pool' (2002) 78 *Capital and Class* 119 and referred to in R. Mitchell, A. O'Donnell and I.M. Ramsay, 'Shareholder Value and Employee Interests: Intersections Between Corporate Governance, Corporate Law and Labor Law' (2005) *Wisconsin International Law Journal* 417 at 429, n32.

[182] S. Bottomley, *The Constitutional Corporation* (Aldershot, Ashgate, 2007) at 8.

[183] Above at p. 48–49.

[184] Above at p. 47–58.

[185] R. Mitchell, A. O'Donnell and I.M. Ramsay, 'Shareholder Value and Employee Interests: Intersections Between Corporate Governance, Corporate Law and Labor Law' (2005) *Wisconsin International Law Journal* 417 at 429.

or long range basic profitability of wealth-producing resources.'[186] Does it mean, providing that the directors are acting within the law, maximising shareholder value no matter what? That is, should they engage in massive downsizing or polluting the environment because preventative measures would be costly, if either of these actions will benefit the shareholders ultimately? It has been said that '[h]ard core advocates of the duty to profit maximize . . . argue that the law should allow and even require managers to violate the law when that is profit-maximizing, at least when the legal violation is not *malum in se*.'[187] The problem, so it is contended, is that the expression 'profit maximisation is vague, and shareholder value maximisation is not much better.'[188] Many American theorists seem to see shareholder wealth as equivalent to maximising company profit,[189] and this might be appropriate in a perfect market with rational and socially acceptable behaviour by all across the globe. But this does not occur.[190]

Henry Hu in a detailed investigation of the meaning of shareholder primacy,[191] in the context of the development of new financial products and the process of financial innovation, points out that there are three conflicting ways of understanding shareholder wealth maximization. The first way is what Hu calls 'the classic entity-oriented model.'[192] Essentially this is based on the notion that where the company's welfare is enhanced through earnings, the shareholders' interests are furthered.[193] He dismisses this approach on the basis, inter alia, that 'maximization of total corporate earnings or even earnings per share does not necessarily

---

[186] P. Drucker, 'Business Objectives and Survival Needs: Notes on a Discipline of Business Enterprise' (1958) 31 *Journal of Business* 81 at 82. For an instance of a court permitting a company to foster long-term benefits, see *Shlensky v Wrigley* 237 NE 2d 776 (Ill App Ct, 1968).

[187] E. Elhauge, 'Sacrificing Corporate Profits in the Public Interest' (2005) 80 *New York University Law Review* 733 at 756.

[188] C. Kirchner, 'Shareholder Value: A New Standard for Company Conduct' in K. Hopt and E. Vermeersch (eds), *Capital Markets and Company Law* (Oxford, Oxford University Press, 2003) at 343.

[189] The American Law Institute's *Principles of Corporate Governance* certainly do: Sec 2.01 (1994).

[190] M. Blair, 'Shareholder Value: A New Standard for Company Conduct' in K. Hopt and E. Vermeersch (eds), *Capital Markets and Company Law* (Oxford, Oxford University Press, 2003) at 348–349.

[191] H. Hu, 'New Financial Products, the Modern Process of Financial Innovation and the Puzzle of Shareholder Welfare' (1991) 69 *Texas Law Review* 1273.

[192] Ibid at 1277.

[193] Ibid at 1279.

maximize shareholder wealth.'[194] Second, we have, according to Hu, the '"pure" shareholder wealth maximization model.'[195] This provides that shareholder wealth is the direct aim of managers and not seen as a derivative of increasing corporate welfare. Under this approach there is no concern for the independent welfare of the company as an entity.[196] It would seem that this is the predominant explanation given for shareholder primacy, and Hu appears to concur.[197] He criticises this on the basis, inter alia, that this involves some concentration on the trading price of shares and that price can be far different from the price which rationally reflects the information about the company that is available.[198] In other words, there can be irrational factors that affect the pricing of shares. Also, there is always the problem of informational asymmetry which can lead to a pricing decision that is made without full knowledge of the facts. The third approach is what Hu calls, 'the "blissful" shareholder wealth maximization model,'[199] and it seeks to deal with the problems just adverted to by, instead of maximizing actual shareholder wealth, maximizing 'what stockholders' wealth would be if the stock market were perfectly omniscient and rational.'[200] Therefore, Hu concludes that all three understandings of maximising shareholder wealth fail to give managers useful guidance.[201]

The conclusion of many is that the objective of the theory is in fact unclear and ill-defined.[202] Of course, if that argument is correct then one can conclude that ascertaining whether the objective can be measured is debatable. Also, it is quite possible that many directors do not understand what is meant by it. As the theory does not provide any definition, even though it gives the connotation of an objective factor, it is malleable

---

[194] Ibid at 1280.
[195] Ibid at 1277.
[196] Ibid at 1282.
[197] Ibid at 1282–1283.
[198] Ibid at 1283.
[199] Ibid at 1277.
[200] Ibid at 1285.
[201] Ibid at 1312.
[202] Ibid at 1277; M. Miller, 'The Informational Content of Dividends' in R. Dornbusch, S. Fischer, and J. Bossons, (eds), *Macroeconomics and Finance: Essays in Honor of Franco Modigliani* (Cambridge, Massachusetts, MIT Press, 1987); C. Loderer, L. Roth, U. Waelchli, and P. Joerg, 'Shareholder Value: Principles, Declarations, and Actions' April 22, 2009, European Corporate Governance Institute Finance Working Paper No 95/2006 (revised), and accessible at <http://papers.ssrn.com/sol3/papers.cfm?abstract_id=690044> (last visited, 30 March 2010).

and can mean many different things, and can be used to support or challenge 'any management action by manipulating either the test of profit maximization or the "facts" to which the test is applied.'[203]

Ironically, one of the main criticisms that is espoused by advocates of shareholder value when it comes to a consideration of stakeholder theory is that the latter does not provide managers with any guidance as to how they should manage, with no aim being set, and in fact it could provide an opportunity for managers to shirk. Yet the same criticism could be levelled at shareholder primacy.

A second uncertainty relates to the fact that the theory does not state the time period in which the objective is to be achieved, a matter discussed earlier.[204] Does it involve the increase of shareholder value in the short or the long term?[205] Clearly short-term and long-term strategies differ, so there is the problem of whether short-term or long-term horizons should be set.[206] As I have indicated already, the favouring of long-term gains tends to be the position of many finance theorists today, but even the concept of the long term is not precise. How far in the future is the company aiming to make decisions for? Short term is difficult to assess, but it has been argued that the long term is even harder.[207] For some businesses which are established for one or two specific reasons, the next year is the long term and yet for more traditional businesses the long term will be further into the future.

As mentioned earlier the short-term approach seems to have been favoured in the past and still holds sway due, inter alia, to shareholder pressure. It could well be that managers favour the short term because they only have a temporary interest in the company, primarily limited to their time in the job. Managers get no or little benefit from planning for the long term as their successors will benefit from rents that come to the company, either financially or from kudos.[208] In fact planning for the

---

[203] G. Frug, 'The Ideology of Bureaucracy in American Law' (1984) 97 *Harvard Law Review* 1276 at 1311.

[204] Above at 52–55.

[205] H. Simon, 'Theories of Decision-Making in Economics and Behavioral Science' (1959) 49 *American Economic Review* 253 at 262. Stephen Bainbridge favours the latter and would prefer to see it referred to as 'wealth optimization': *Corporation Law and Economics* (New York, Foundation Press, 2002) at 21.

[206] See H. Hu, 'Risk, Time and Fiduciary Principles in Corporate Investment' (1990) 38 *University of California at Los Angeles Law Review* 277.

[207] E. Elhauge, 'Sacrificing Corporate Profits in the Public Interest' (2005) 80 *New York University Law Review* 733 at 756.

[208] F. Allen and D. Gale, *Comparing Financial Systems* (Cambridge, Massachusetts, MIT Press, 2000) at 382.

long term could in fact make today's managers not look so good as the share price might not increase as quickly as it might if short-term plans were implemented. The short-term approach, however, has been subjected to significant criticism over a long period. Focusing on producing short-term profits has been unrealistic and fuelled the pressure to take on increased risk.[209] Recently commentators have identified the problems for a company, and especially its survival, that short-term management creates. Some have identified, as a primary reason for the financial crisis of recent times, the short-termist pressure placed on directors as a result of the demands of shareholders for unsustainable ever-increasing earnings growth that was possible only by way of the shortcut of over-leverage and reduced investment, and the dangerous route of excessive risk. Such commentators have emphasised the fact that the stability and financial strength needed to endure economic cycles were sacrificed for immediate satisfaction.[210] Other commentators have said that:

> Short-termism is a disease that infects American business and distorts management and boardroom judgment. But it does not originate in the boardroom. [It] is bred in the trading rooms of the hedge funds and professional institutional investment managers who control more than 75% of the shares of most major

---

[209]   M. Lipton, T. Mirvis and J. Lorsch, 'The Proposed "Shareholder Bill of Rights Act of 2009"' Harvard Law School Forum on Corporate Governance and Financial Regulation (12 May 2009), and accessible at: <http://blogs.law.harvard.edu/corpgov/2009/05/12/the-proposed-%e2%80%9cshareholder-bill-of-rights-act-of-2009%e2%80%9d> (last visited, 24 July 2009).

[210]   M. Lipton, T. Mirvis and J. Lorsch, 'The Proposed "Shareholder Bill of Rights Act of 2009"' Harvard Law School Forum on Corporate Governance and Financial Regulation (12 May 2009), and accessible at: <http://blogs.law.harvard.edu/corpgov/2009/05/12/the-proposed-%e2%80%9cshareholder-bill-of-rights-act-of-2009%e2%80%9d> (last visited, 1 June 2010). Some support for this comes from the views of company officials interviewed in a small study of FTSE 350 companies in the UK: see, P. Taylor, 'Enlightened Shareholder Value and the Companies Act 2006' (unpublished PhD thesis, May 2010), Birkbeck College, University of London, at 179. The issue of immediate satisfaction is probably tied up with the fact that it had been said many years before the current crisis that the markets placed pressure on directors to meet their views of what results companies should be achieving. See C. Williams, 'A Tale of Two Trajectories' (2006) 75 *Fordham Law Review* 1629 at 1654–1655; N. Sharpe, 'Rethinking the Board Function in the Wake of the 2008 Financial Crisis' (2010) 5 *Journal of Business and Technology Law* 99 at 110–111. Also, see, J. Grinyer et al, 'Evidence of Managerial Short-termism in the UK' (1998) 9 *British Journal of Management* 13 at 14, 15; J. Graham et al, 'The Economic Implications of Corporate Financial Reporting' Duke University Research Paper, 11 January 2005 and accessible at <http://ssrn.com/abstract=491627> (last visited, 21 June 2010).

companies. Short-termist pressure bred by stockholder power demanded unsustainable ever-increasing (quarterly) earnings growth, possible only via the shortcut of over-leverage and reduced investment, and the dangerous route of excessive risk. Stability and financial strength to weather economic cycles were sacrificed for immediate satisfaction. That short-termist pressure, in the view of many observers, contributed significantly to the financial and economic crises we face today.[211]

There are clearly other instances of concern over the use of short-term measures, and that the long term should be taken into account by directors. The UK government has indicated this by requiring directors, under s.172(1) of the Companies Act 2006, to have regard for the long-term consequences of actions.

A third problem, following on from the first issue raised above, is that it is difficult for the courts to assess whether directors have in fact maximised profits.[212] The task of ascertaining whether the directors acted overall in such a way so as to maximise shareholder wealth is far from easy for experts let alone laypersons,[213] so it is difficult to assess whether directors are achieving the objective of the company. Hence, the idea that shareholder value is clear and, therefore, allows for more assessment of what directors do is illusory.[214]

Fourth, Gerald Frug asserts that the concept of shareholder primacy can be used to support or to attack any management action by manipulating either the test of maximisation or the facts to which the test is applied,[215] and so this again tends to derogate from the argument that the theory produces certainty.

Fifth, as Jonathan Macey notes, in general terms it is not possible to say with any certainty which actions are in the best interests of

---

[211] M. Lipton, T. Mirvis and J. Lorsch, 'The Proposed "Shareholder Bill of Rights Act of 2009"' Harvard Law School Forum on Corporate Governance and Financial Regulation (12 May 2009), and accessible at: <http://blogs.law.harvard.edu/corpgov/2009/05/12/the-proposed-%e2%80%9cshareholder-bill-of-rights-act-of-2009%e2%80%9d> (last visited, 24 July 2009).

[212] E. Elhauge, 'Sacrificing Corporate Profits in the Public Interest' (2005) 80 *New York University Law Review* 733 at 739.

[213] M. van der Weide, 'Against Fiduciary Duties to Corporate Stakeholders' (1996) 21 *Delaware Journal of Corporation Law* 27 at 69.

[214] It has been said that shareholder value entails companies focusing on high-value activities and diverse activities should be consolidated or divested: J. Bughlin and T. Copeland, 'The Virtuous Cycle of Shareholder Value Creation' (1997) 2 *The McKinsey Quarterly* 156.

[215] G. Frug, 'The Ideology of Bureaucracy in American Law' (1984) 97 *Harvard Law Review* 1276 at 1311.

shareholders and which are not,[216] especially when one takes into account the divergence in the shareholders of large public companies.

Sixth, earlier in the Chapter it was noted that shareholder primacy holds that while directors will not focus on non-shareholder constituencies, they might well take them into account for if they do not it might impact on the maximising of shareholder wealth, for, inter alia, they may lose firm specific investments that are contributed by stakeholders. What is not clear with this approach is how far managers are to go in taking stakeholder interests into account. Also, what if shareholder wealth can be fostered by both action A and action B to the same degree and action A will not affect stakeholder X, but would prejudice stakeholder Y, while action B will not affect stakeholder Y, but would prejudice stakeholder X. How do managers decide whether to take action A or action B?

A further problem, discussed earlier in the Chapter,[217] is that it is not clear what shareholder value maximisation actually means as far as shareholders are concerned, for it can mean different things to different shareholders.[218]

Finally, one other issue that follows on from the above discussion, and has not been broached thus far, is that in pursuing a particular kind of activity the directors might not be endearing themselves to some shareholder elements. If that is the case does that matter? Let us say that a number of shareholders firmly support specific environmental principles, and if the directors take the company down a path that involves production that will lead to an increase in dividends and an increase in share value, but will offend these shareholders' principles, can it be said that the shareholders' interests are being maximised? The response from the shareholder primacy school is probably that the directors are maximising shareholder interests as these interests must be seen as economic interests, and in any event disgruntled shareholders can exit if they do not like what is being done.

Notwithstanding this criticism many shareholder primacy adherents accept that the shareholder primacy theory is not without its uncertainty. The riposte is that the theory does not provide for as much ambiguity as other approaches. Jeffrey MacIntosh argues that : '[t]o tout the

---

[216] 'An Economic Analysis of the Various Rationales for Making Shareholders the Exclusive Beneficiaries of Corporate Fiduciary Duties' (1991) 21 *Stetson Law Review* 23 at 35.

[217] Above at pp. 55–56.

[218] C. Loderer, L. Roth, U. Waelchli and P. Joerg, 'Shareholder Value: Principles, Declarations, and Actions' April 22, 2009, European Corporate Governance Institute Finance Working Paper No 95/2006 (revised), and accessible at <http://papers.ssrn.com/sol3/papers.cfm?abstract_id=690044> (last visited, 30 March 2010).

uncertainty of the wealth maximization standard as a reason for rejecting it is to fall prey to the Nirvana Fallacy; imperfect solutions compete not with perfection, but with other imperfect solutions.'[219] This is an element of the argument that is put forward that the theory is admittedly second best, but according to law and economics scholars that is the best that we can hope for in an imperfect world.

7.3 Promises to Shareholders

It is argued that managers must act for shareholders as they have promised that they will maximise the shareholders' interests. Yet no such promise is ever made to shareholders, and no contract exists between the managers and the shareholders. As Ronald Green asks rhetorically: 'At what point do shareholders and managers ever freely enter into a relationship in which one party promises to perform specified services in return for payment or other consideration?'[220] The closest thing that comes to this in the UK is in relation to s.33 of the Companies Act 2006. Under this provision, the members and the company are bound to each other, but the company has not made any promise to maximise member interests. Shareholders can only fall back on the fact that they could expect that the directors would both conduct the business in such a way as to fulfil the goals set out in the constitution of the company,[221] and exercise their duties in a way that will promote the success of the company for the benefit of the members, as required by s.172 of the Companies Act 2006.

Tellingly, perhaps, the corporate constitution in the UK, Australia and elsewhere, and corporate charters in the US, do not appear to provide expressly that the company is to be managed so as to ensure there is shareholder primacy.[222]

7.4 Efficiency

It has been noted above that the theory relies on the argument that it fosters efficiency, particularly so as to produce social wealth. The

---

[219] J. MacIntosh, 'Designing an Efficient Fiduciary Law' (1993) 43 *University of Toronto Law Journal* 425 at 456.

[220] 'Shareholders as Stakeholders: Changing Metaphors of Corporate Governance' (1993) 50 *Washington and Lee Law Review* 1409 at 1413.

[221] S. Worthington, 'Shares and Shareholders: Property, Power and Entitlement (Part 2) (2001) 22 *The Company Lawyer* 307 at 311.

[222] L. Stout, 'Bad and Not-So-Bad Arguments for Shareholder Primacy' (2002) 75 *South California Law Review* 1189 at 1207.

argument is that it is just more efficient for the managers to run the business to benefit the shareholders. The shareholders have the leading incentive to monitor the directors' managing role and this will lead to increased benefits for all. This argument involves circular reasoning. First, it is said that the shareholders are entitled to have the company managed to foster their interests and it follows that they have an incentive to monitor, and they have this because they have the right to require the managers to favour their interests. Leaving that aside, the point is made by Sarah Worthington that one cannot say that the position of the shareholders will influence or constrain the directors to act efficiently to maximise social wealth, for directors might act inefficiently so that they only maximise shareholder value;[223] they cannot be compelled to foster social wealth.

It has been said that the theory is not efficient as it has often led to negative externalities (the practice of externalising costs and retaining benefits for shareholders) and unchecked social costs in that there has been harm to innocent third parties, poor products, high prices, and poor working conditions.[224] For instance, in a takeover scenario it is always possible that managers might, during the course of negotiations, extract side payments from the raider in exchange for attenuating stakeholder interests in the target company.[225] This side payment might simply be a promise to retain directors on the board following the finalisation of the takeover. It has been argued that stakeholders can attenuate the effect of externalities on them by protecting themselves through contract,[226] but not all stakeholders can do so *ex ante*, and many cannot do so *ex post*.

It has long been recognised, even by law and economics scholars who adhere to shareholder primacy, that because of things like bounded rationality, all contracts are incomplete and so it is not possible to guarantee that

---

[223] S. Worthington, 'Shares and Shareholders: Property, Power and Entitlement (Part 1) (2001) 22 *The Company Lawyer* 258 at 266.

[224] M. Velasquez, *Business Ethics: Concepts and Cases* (Englewood Cliffs, Prentice-Hall, 1982) at 149. Also, see J. Pichler, 'The Liberty Principle: A Basis for Management Ethics' (1983) (Winter) *Business and Professional Ethics Journal* 19 at 22; C. Bagley and K. Page, 'The Devil Made Me Do It: Replacing Corporate Directors' Veil of Secrecy with the Mantle of Stewardship' (1999) 36 *San Diego Law Review* 897 at 903.

[225] S. Bainbridge, 'In Defense of the Shareholder Maximization Norm: A Reply to Professor Green' (1993) 50 *Washington and Lee Law Review* 1423 at 1441.

[226] M. van der Weide, 'Against Fiduciary Duties to Corporate Stakeholders' (1996) 21 *Delaware Journal of Corporation Law* 27 at 69.

maximising shareholder interests will be efficient. To ensure efficiency the interests of non-shareholders would have to be considered.[227]

There are arguments to the effect that it is very difficult to secure evidence to support the claim that any particular economic system of corporate governance is more efficient than another.[228] It might be said that shareholder primacy is not a provision for efficiency, but rather it provides for a power relationship,[229] based on value judgments that are based on neutral forces.

Another concern is that there should not be an emphasis placed on efficiency in any event; there are other values, such as fairness, that warrant consideration.[230] The response to this might well be that in a competitive environment companies have no real choice but to focus on efficiency.[231] But it can be said that companies can seek to implement efficiency with other values in mind, so that efficiency is a means but not an end.

7.5 Right to Control

As mentioned above,[232] the theory is advocated on the basis that because the shareholders are owners they are entitled, therefore, to control company property. The argument goes along these lines: the shareholders control the assets of the company and it follows that they own them, and if they own them they are entitled to have the assets managed for their benefit. As has been pointed out, this involves circular reasoning.[233]

---

[227] M. Becht, P. Bolton and A. Roell, 'Corporate Governance and Control' Finance Working Paper No. 02/2002, European Corporate Governance Institute Working Papers in Finance, 31 October 2002 and last revised, 3 April 2006 at 9 and accessible at: <http://ssrn.com/abstract=343461> (last visited, 24 July 2009)

[228] R. Ball, 'What do we know about stock market "efficiency"'? unpublished paper, Managerial Economics Research Center, University of Rochester, 1989 and referred to in C. Kelly, 'History Begins: Shareholder Value, Accountability and the Virtuous State' (2009) 60 *Northern Ireland Law Quarterly* 35 at 45.

[229] A. Rebérioux, 'European Style of Corporate Governance at the Crossroads: The Role of Worker Involvement' (2002) 40 *Journal of Common Market Studies* 111 at 119.

[230] See A. Keay, 'Directors' Duties to Creditors: Contractarian Concerns Relating to Efficiency and Over-Protection of Creditors' (2003) 66 *Modern Law Review* 665 at 677–680.

[231] A. Sundaram and A. Inkpen, 'The Corporate Objective Revisited' (2004) 15 *Organization Science* 350 at 356.

[232] Above at p. 66.

[233] M. Blair, *Ownership and Control* (Washington DC, The Brookings Institute, 1995) at 27 and 224; S. Worthington, 'Shares and Shareholders: Property, Power and Entitlement (Part 1) (2001) 22 *The Company Lawyer* 258 at 265.

7.6 Myopic Management

It is argued that many managers manage for the short term not because
shareholders demand this approach, but because they perceive that the
theory of shareholder primacy constrains them to do so. Managers are
under pressure from the financial markets to engage in perverse behaviour that reduces the prospect of long-term benefits,[234] on the basis that
the markets take the view that 'the price of a share today reflects the
best estimate of the value of future profits and growth that will accrue to
that company,'[235] or are convinced that if they do not do so they will be
removed as a result of shareholder pressure, general meeting resolution or
a hostile takeover. This approach, so it is argued, harms the development
of the company and sacrifices long-term value.[236] In addition it is said that
the short-term strategy focuses on the share price and the stock market is
not an appropriate gauge of a company's performance for it is not able
to deal with uncertainty and frequently it fails to price assets correctly,[237]
and does not reflect the intrinsic value of the company. For instance,
the market undervalues plans where there will be long-term benefits.[238]
Undoubtedly, the share price can change as a consequence of guesses
about the behaviour of the market and not in response to a change in
fundamental values of companies.[239] The market may fail to indicate the
rational conclusion to be drawn from all of the available information.[240]
In response it might be said that a number of commentators emphasise the

---

[234] M. Blair, *Ownership and Control* (Washington DC, The Brookings
Institute, 1995) at 122.

[235] Ibid at 202.

[236] S. Letza, X. Sun and J. Kirkbridge, 'Shareholding Versus Stakeholding:
a Critical Review of Corporate Governance' (2004) 12 *Corporate Governance:
International Review* 242 at 249.

[237] C. Bagley and K. Page, 'The Devil Made Me Do It: Replacing Corporate
Directors' Veil of Secrecy with the Mantle of Stewardship' (1999) 36 *San Diego
Law Review* 897 at 920. For an argument to the contrary, see G. Dent, 'The
Essential Unity of Shareholders and the Myth of Investor Short-Termism' (2010)
35 *Delaware Journal of Corporate Law* 97.

[238] J. Parkinson, *Corporate Power and Responsibility* (Oxford, Clarendon
Press, 1993) at 92.

[239] R. Schiller, 'Do Stock Prices Move too Much to be Justified by Subsequent
Changes in Dividends?' in R. Schiller (ed), *Market Volatility* (Cambridge,
Massachusetts, MIT Press, 1989) and referred to in S. Letza, X. Sun and
J. Kirkbridge, 'Shareholding Versus Stakeholding: a Critical Review of Corporate
Governance' (2004) 12 *Corporate Governance: International Review* 242 at 249.

[240] H. Hu, 'New Financial Products, the Modern Process of Financial Innovation
and the Puzzle of Shareholder Welfare' (1991) 69 *Texas Law Review* 1273 at 1283.

long term now,[241] but having said that, there are theoretical models that suggest that even the long-term trading price of shares may fail to be equal to the true value.[242] While some will say that long term maximisation is consistent with the theory at hand, many would favour a concentration on short-term benefits to the point of being pre-occupied with it.[243]

As a consequence of managers becoming myopic in their view of developing the company, they may well sidestep the need to handle conflicts, and they may eschew issues of ethics as they get in the way of making short-term earnings.

7.7 Performance not Maximised

Some theorists argue that where managers implement the shareholder primacy approach the company's overall performance diminishes.[244] This is aligned with the view that if companies engage in corporate social responsibility, rather than merely following a shareholder-centric approach, then they will enhance the growth of the company.[245]

7.8 Shareholder Differences

Arguably the theory does not account for the fact shareholders' interests do diverge. Shareholders can be very different.[246] There is the distinction between those who are seeking long-term interests and those with short-term interests. Clearly short-term and long-term strategies differ,

---

[241] M. Jensen, 'Value Maximisation, Stakeholder Theory and the Corporate Objective Function' (2001) 14 *Journal of Applied Corporate Finance* 8; A. Sundaram and A. Inkpen, 'The Corporate Objective Revisited' (2004) 15 *Organization Science* 350 at 358; G. Dent, 'Corporate Governance: Still Broke, No Fix in Sight' (2006) 31 *Journal of Corporation Law* 39 at 57.

[242] H. Hu, 'New Financial Products, the Modern Process of Financial Innovation and the Puzzle of Shareholder Welfare' (1991) 69 *Texas Law Review* 1273 at 1285.

[243] See D. Millon, 'Why is Corporate Management Obsessed With Quarterly Earnings And What Should Be Done About It?' (2002) 70 *George Washington Law Review* 890.

[244] R.E. Freeman, *Strategic Management* (Boston, Pitman/Ballinger, 1984) at 65; G. Starling, The *Changing Environment of Business: A Managerial Approach* (Boston, Kent Publishing, 1980) at 224.

[245] There is some debate as to whether engaging in corporate social responsibility will be profitable for the business. See J. Brummer, *Corporate Responsibility and Legitimacy* (New York, Greenwood Press, 1991) at 128–132.

[246] See, S. Bainbridge, *The New Corporate Governance in Theory and Practice* (New York, Oxford University Press, 2008) at 50, 56.

and will have varying effects on shareholders. Orts gives the example of drastic cost-cutting which might achieve short-term results by improving the bottom line for a short while, but in the long-run this might deleteriously affect the company's business.[247] There are individual shareholders, who will have a different approach from many institutional shareholders. Companies have ordinary (or common as they are known in the US) shareholders and preferred shareholders. Some holding shares are focused on achieving capital appreciation from an increase in share value, while others are looking for dividend income.

Commentators have said that the theory fails to allow for the fact that many investors will follow modern portfolio techniques and diversify their risks, which can be done by investing across all capital assets in the financial markets. These techniques advocate investors having a portfolio that is constituted by various securities.[248] This kind of diversified approach will mean that investors are likely to be both shareholders and bondholders in companies.[249] Some shareholders might, either directly or indirectly, actually hold shares of competing companies, so their interests will probably diverge from other shareholders.[250] Those who are diversified are not going to have the same goals as those who are purely acting as shareholders, for the former will be looking for a more balanced approach to the making of investment decisions. Eric Orts has said that 'shareholders have different time and risk preferences that managers must somehow factor together, if they are to represent fairly the artificially unified interest of "the shareholders" in general.'[251]

Besides the issue of diversification we need to acknowledge that there are other important issues that produce shareholder differences. First, shareholders will have different approaches to risk[252] and have different

---

[247]   E. Orts, 'The Complexity and Legitimacy of Corporate Law' (1993) 50 *Washington and Lee Law Review* 1565 at 1592.

[248]   A. Kaufman and E. Englander, 'A Team Production Model of Corporate Governance' (2005) 19 *Academy of Management Executive* 9 at 16.

[249]   T. Smith, 'The Efficient Norm for Corporate Law: A Neotraditional Interpretation of Fiduciary Duty' (1999) 98 *Michigan Law Review* 214. Taking such action obviously reduces risk. Also, see M. Blair, *Ownership and Control* (Washington DC, The Brookings Institute, 1995) at 229.

[250]   H. Hu and B. Black, 'Hedge Funds, Insiders, and the Decoupling of Economic and Voting Ownership: Empty Voting and Hidden (Morphable) Ownership' (2007) 13 *Journal of Corporate Finance* 343.

[251]   'The Complexity and Legitimacy of Corporate Law' (1993) 50 *Washington and Lee Law Review* 1565 at 1591.

[252]   L. LoPucki, 'The Myth of the Residual Owner: An Empirical Study' (2004) 82 *Washington University Law Quarterly* 1341 at 1351–1352.

views as to what they want to get from their shareholding. Second, the shareholder group of any large company is not going to be an homogeneous group; they come in all shapes and sizes. Large shareholders, and particularly institutional investors, have interests that can diverge from those of minority shareholders,[253] and it may well be that managers will prefer the interests of the former over the latter as the former have more power and can possibly remove them. But, in most common law jurisdictions small investors do have protections like that provided by s.994 of the UK's Companies Act 2006 which enables a member to seek relief from a court where he or she has been unfairly prejudiced, but such provisions are not used frequently where public companies are concerned.

Third, clearly the interests of present and future shareholders might diverge in certain important respects.[254] The latter would, naturally, be more concerned about a long-term approach being employed.

Daniel Greenwood has long argued that shareholder primacy is wrongly based on some fictional shareholder (hypothetical) who is a rational economic actor, and the fact of the matter is that shareholders are to be regarded, in the main, as a 'large, fluid, changeable and changing market.'[255] The commentator opines that the shareholders, as envisaged in shareholder primacy theory, are a personification of their shares and only concerned about maximising the value of their shares.[256] The theory assumes that shareholders are always ready to act out of self-interest.[257] Further, the shareholders are not consulted about what they want save in very limited ways at general meetings. After saying this, it must be noted that in the US the law permits directors to consider the interests of a generic fictional shareholder, and this allows directors considerable discretion.[258]

---

[253] R. Miller, 'Ethical Challenges in Corporate-Shareholder and Investor Relations: Using the Value Exchange Model to Analyze and Respond' (1988) 7 *Journal of Business Ethics* 117 at 125; C. Loderer, L. Roth, U. Waelchli and P. Joerg, 'Shareholder Value: Principles, Declarations, and Actions' 22 April 2009, European Corporate Governance Institute Finance Working Paper No 95/2006 (revised), at 13, and accessible at: <http://papers.ssrn.com/sol3/papers.cfm?abstract_id=690044> (last visited, 30 March 2010).

[254] S. Schwarcz, 'Temporal Perspectives: Resolving the Conflict Between Current and Future Investors (2005) 89 *Minnesota Law Review* 1044.

[255] 'Fictional Shareholders: For Whom are Corporate Managers Trustees Revisited' (1996) 69 *Southern California Law Review* 1021 at 1026.

[256] Ibid at 1043.

[257] I. Lee, 'Corporate Law, Profit Maximization and the "Responsible" Shareholder' (2005) 10 *Stanford Journal of Law, Business and Finance* 31 at 46.

[258] D. Greenwood, 'Fictional Shareholders: For Whom are Corporate Managers Trustees Revisited' (1996) 69 *Southern California Law Review* 1021 at 1026.

Some might question whether shareholders who do not acquire shares from the company but simply buy shares in the market, contribute little if anything to the firm, and should not be entitled to be considered above all other stakeholders who contribute more to the company.[259] But can it be said that the shareholders do contribute something, for if they do not purchase the shares the share price would become depressed? Of course, it might be said that if A does not agree to buy the shares B will and if B does not then C will, and so on.

7.9   A Narrow Approach and Too Glib

It is asserted that while it might be acknowledged that shareholder primacy provides a convenient common metric, the theory is too narrow and glib in four respects. First, and most generally, shareholder primacy can be criticised for being narrow as it focuses on one single objective and that is unreasonable in a complex world and managers are bounded-ly rational.[260] Lyman Johnson has said that 'the meaning of corporate endeavour'[261] must involve the embracing of norms 'wider than the thin thread of shareholder primacy.'[262]

Second, the fact that the theory is effectively focused on making money and, more pointedly, in order to maximise the interests of the sharehold-ers, makes it narrow. It is not possible to reduce everything to a matter of profit, as it is argued that the theory does.[263] Too often the theory is reduced to the company's share price as an indication of the company's value and future prospects. Rather than relying on that as an indication of the performance of the company managers should be producing carefully developed strategic plans and forecasts.[264]

Third, the theory fails to consider values other than efficiency. The

---

[259]   C. Loderer, L. Roth, U. Waelchli and P. Joerg, 'Shareholder Value: Principles, Declarations, and Actions' April 22, 2009, European Corporate Governance Institute Finance Working Paper No 95/2006 (revised), at 19, and accessible at: <http://papers.ssrn.com/sol3/papers.cfm?abstract_id=690044> (last visited, 30 March 2010).

[260]   R.E. Freeman, A. Wicks and B. Parmar, 'Stakeholder Theory and "The Corporate Objective Revisited"' (2004) 15 *Organization Science* 364 at 366.

[261]   'The Delaware Judiciary and the Meaning of Corporate Life and Corporate Law' (1990) 68 *Texas Law Review* 866 at 873.

[262]   Ibid at 934.

[263]   D. Wood, 'Whom Should Business Serve?' (2002) 14 *Australian Journal of Corporate Law* 1 at 13.

[264]   M. Blair, 'Directors' Duties in a Post-Enron World: Why Language Matters' (2003) 38 *Wake Forest Law Review* 885 at 908.

concern is that the approach tends to ignore reality because more is at stake than the interests of shareholders when we are considering how companies should be run.[265] It is also true that directors have to deal on a regular basis with employees, creditors, local councillors and other community leaders, and government officers, and this may make it difficult for them to adhere strictly to shareholder primacy. To be practical they might have to compromise shareholder primacy to get the job done. Freeman et al assert that in the real world managers often work with stakeholder groups, such as customers and suppliers to test new products.[266] Additionally shareholder objectives tend to be seen in too simplistic and superficial a fashion.[267]

Fourth, the interests of shareholders are not the only interests that should be considered by directors when carrying out their functions, for there are other important constituencies that warrant consideration from directors.[268] Some, while accepting the fact that governance rights should attach to those who bear the residual risk of the company, take issue with the idea that the shareholders are the ones who bear the residual risk.[269] Even if there was one shareholder who held all of the shares in the company, he or she would not be the sole true residual claimant, for the welfare of many others would be affected by his or her decisions, at least *ex post*.[270] Many do argue that there are a significant number of persons, other than shareholders, who can be said to be residual claimants.

The fact that others besides shareholders bear residual risk is especially clear if one accepts the concept of a nexus of contracts, where there are surely many persons who constitute the nexus who can be said to be residual claimants. Margaret Blair notes that the idea that the shareholders receive

---

[265] W. Allen, J. Jacobs and L. Strine, 'The Great Takeover Debate: A Mediation on Bridging the Conceptual Divide' (2002) 69 *University of Chicago Law Review* 1067 at 1083.

[266] R.E. Freeman, A. Wicks and B. Parmar, 'Stakeholder Theory and "The Corporate Objective Revisited"' (2004) 15 *Organization Science* 364 at 368.

[267] R. Miller, 'Ethical Challenges in Corporate-Shareholder and Investor Relations: Using the Value Exchange Model to Analyze and Respond' (1988) 7 *Journal of Business Ethics* 117 at 126.

[268] For example, Larry Mitchell criticises the whole notion of shareholder maximisation in corporate law: 'A Theoretical and Practical Framework for Enforcing Corporate Constituency Statutes' (1992) 70 *Texas Law Review* 579 at 640.

[269] G. Kelly and J. Parkinson, 'The Conceptual Foundations of the Company: a Pluralist Approach' in J. Parkinson, A. Gamble and G. Kelly (eds), *The Political Economy of the Company* (Oxford, Hart Publishing, 2000) at 122; M. Blair and L. Stout, 'Director Accountability and the Mediating Role of the Corporate Board' (2001) 79 *Washington University Law Quarterly* 403 at 404.

[270] G. Garvey and P. Swan, 'The Economics of Corporate Governance: Beyond the Marshallian Firm' (1994) 1 *Journal of Corporate Finance* 139 at 140.

all of the returns and bear all of the risks of a company is a throwback to the nineteenth century when companies operated very differently.[271] Today, the shareholders are not necessarily the ones always most affected by a company's decisions.[272] The effect of invoking a shareholder primacy approach is, arguably, to damage the incentives of non-shareholder stakeholders to make firm-specific investments in companies[273] as they are aware that their investments will be subordinated to shareholder interests at all times.[274] As adverted to above, many stakeholders, such as creditors, managers, employees, suppliers, customers, and communities make firm-specific investments that tie their economic fortunes to the firm's fate.[275] Take the following examples. Employees invest firm-specific human capital in the company, and rely on the company's continuation as a safeguard for their pensions. This places them in a position where they are vulnerable to management caprice,[276] and if the company is liquidated they will lose their jobs based on their particular skills and, possibly, a part of their pensions. Suppliers might invest in highly specialised equipment and machinery so that they can supply a company with what it needs, and if the company withdraws its patronage, relocates or is liquidated, then the supplier is likely to lose out. Creditors might be entitled to share in corporate profits in lieu of a fixed rate of interest so if the company fails to make profits they lose out, as well as where the company is liquidated. The managers and other employees might be entitled to compensation based on performance rather than a fixed salary, so they are making firm-specific contributions. So, stakeholders other than shareholders can have a stake in a portion of a company's surplus through their contracts with the company.[277]

---

[271]   M. Blair, *Ownership and Control* (Washington DC, The Brookings Institute, 1995) at 232.

[272]   L. Zingales, 'In Search of New Foundations' (2000) 55 *Journal of Finance* 1623 at 1632; M. Blair and L. Stout, 'Specific Investment: Explaining Anomalies in Corporate Law' (2006) 31 *Journal of Corporation Law* 719 at 738.

[273]   These are investments which are difficult to recover once they have been committed to a particular venture.

[274]   G. Kelly and J. Parkinson, 'The Conceptual Foundations of the Company: A Pluralist Approach' in J. Parkinson, A. Gamble and G. Kelly (eds), *The Political Economy of the Company* (Oxford, Hart Publishing, 2000), 131.

[275]   M. Blair and L. Stout, 'Director Accountability and the Mediating Role of the Corporate Board' (2001) 79 *Washington University Law Quarterly* 403 at 418.

[276]   See M. O'Connor, 'The Human Capital Era' (1993) 78 *Cornell Law Review* 899, 905–917.

[277]   J. Fisch, 'Measuring Efficiency in Corporate Law: The Rule of Shareholder Primacy' December 2005, Fordham Law Legal Studies, Working Paper No 105 at p28 and available at: <http://ssrn.com/abstract=878391> (last visited, 27 July 2009).

Additionally, communities can be seriously affected by what companies do (for example, the town of Bhopal in India in December1984 when a disaster at a factory left many dead and others suffering long-term disability).

Of course, shareholders, compared with other contributors, usually have more of an opportunity to exit a public company. They can 'do the Wall Street Walk' and sell their shares on a stock exchange, whilst other stakeholders are not able to exit so easily. For example, suppliers might be bound under a long-term contract to keep supplying goods and/or services, lenders cannot withdraw capital advanced to the company and many employees cannot 'up sticks' and move jobs easily. Lyn Stout has suggested that the only time when shareholders are really treated as residual claimants is when the company enters bankruptcy.[278]

There are other actors besides the shareholders, who have incentives to ensure that the directors do act properly and in their best interests. For instance, lenders do this by sometimes including restrictive covenants in the loan contract with the company whereby directors are committed to do, or not to do, certain things.

If the shareholders were indeed the beneficiaries of all residual gain and the bearers of all residual risk then other actors who provided inputs to the company would have to be compensated by way of *complete* contracts which indicate what will happen in all circumstances. It is generally accepted that all contracts that are made by companies are incomplete for a number of reasons. Contracts are incomplete 'if performance of the actual terms of the agreement would leave gains from trade unrealised given the information available to the parties at the time performance takes place.'[279] The economics discipline has recognised the concept of incomplete contract, but it is something which has been developed predominantly by the law and economics literature.[280] The economic perspective of incomplete contracting is based on a simple idea that the human mind is a scarce resource.[281] As a scarce resource, the human mind

---

[278] L. Stout, 'Bad and Not-So-Bad Arguments for Shareholder Primacy' (2002) 75 *South California Law Review* 1189 at 1193.

[279] I. McNeil, 'Company Law Rules: An Assessment from the Perspective of Incomplete Contract Theory' (2001) 1 *Journal of Corporate Law Studies* 107 at 112 and referring to B. Holstrom and J. Tirole, 'The Theory of the Firm' in R. Schmalensee and R. Willig (eds), *Handbook of Industrial Economics* (1989).

[280] I. McNeil, 'Company Law Rules: An Assessment from the Perspective of Incomplete Contract Theory' (2001) 1 *Journal of Corporate Law Studies* 107 at 117.

[281] In other words, foresight is, at best, *imperfect*; information, at most, *incomplete*. See, for example, O. Hart and J. Moore, 'Foundations of Incomplete Contracts' (1999) 66 *Review of Economic Studies* 115.

is unable to gather, process, and understand an unlimited amount of information.[282]

7.10 Shareholder Impotence

Much is made of the fact that the shareholders will be motivated to monitor the managers so they should be the ones whose rights take centre stage. While much is made of the fact that the shareholders will be motivated to monitor the managers, many accept that shareholders do not have effective control of managers and so directors cannot be seen as being accountable to them,[283] and in fact Antoine Rebérioux concludes that shareholder primacy leads to less accountability.[284] Whilst in the early days of the joint stock company the company was seen in the same light as a partnership and shareholders could control the directors,[285] this eventually changed and now directors have broad powers of management which do not depend in the slightest on shareholder support. Admittedly, in recent times we have seen in the UK a number of examples of shareholder activism when board decisions and recommendations have been met with significant criticism at general meetings, and on occasions shareholders have organised themselves in order to have a director removed or, at least, place enough pressure on the board for the board to remove a director.[286] However, in the broad scheme of things it can be said that the shareholders' power is not all that substantial, notwithstanding the recent shareholder activism that has occurred.[287] For one reason it is difficult for shareholders to requisition the convening of an extraordinary meeting of shareholders to vote on a motion to remove. For another reason, company

---

[282] See, for example, K. Eggleston, E. Posner and R. Zeckhauser, 'The Design and Interpretation of Contracts: Why Complexity Matters' (2001) 95 *Northwestern University Law Review* 91.

[283] See, A. Keay, 'Company Directors Behaving Poorly: Disciplinary Options for Shareholders' [2007] *Journal of Business Law* 656.

[284] 'Does Shareholder Primacy Lead to a Decline in Managerial Accountability?' (2007) 31 *Cambridge Journal of Economics* 507 at 508.

[285] *Automatic Self-Cleansing Filter Syndicate Co Ltd v Cuninghame* [1906] 2 Ch 34.

[286] In November 2006, the chief executive officer of Deutsche Telekom, Kai-Uwe Ricke, resigned after intense pressure from investors (E. Judge, 'Under-fire leader quits Deutsche Telekom' *The Times*, November 13, 2006) as did the chief executive of LogicaCMG in May 2007 (D. Jordan, 'Shareholder forces Logica chief to resign' *The Times*, 28 May 2007).

[287] In some countries, such as the US, shareholders have less power than in the UK and so they are obviously less effective monitors.

wheels grind slowly and a movement to have a director removed takes time. To ameliorate their position shareholders generally have to arrange coalitions of their fellow members to get anywhere. The costs and effort involved in intervention and exercising 'voice' might lead shareholders to decide to choose 'exit' and sell their shares. Such a choice might be the most efficient outcome for individual shareholders.

Even institutional shareholders face heavy costs in engaging in activity designed to influence managers,[288] and may well be dissuaded from taking such action.[289] Well-known institutional shareholders, such as the California Public Employees Retirement System (CalPERS), that do take action may well be regarded as exceptions.[290] This conclusion might be supported by empirical evidence that was obtained in the mid-1990s, and which suggested that rarely do such investors put forward motions at general meetings of the shareholders.[291]

Sometimes the existence of derivative actions that can be brought by a shareholder against the directors and others if they harm the company, are seen as another reason why the directors must maximise shareholder wealth. But, in most jurisdictions derivative actions are not numerous, for besides the fact that a shareholder must obtain the permission of the courts to bring such an action,[292] it must be remembered that a claim will only be successful if the directors have injured the interests of the company as an entity, not the interests of the shareholders (although the two might well overlap).

The essential impotence of most shareholders means that the theory is not workable because directors are not always going to be held responsible if they shirk or if they act opportunistically and fail to foster shareholder maximisation. Even if it can be said that there is some shareholder control of directors, it will usually be vested in those with the largest shareholdings

---

[288]   G. Garvey and P. Swan, 'The Economics of Corporate Governance: Beyond the Marshallian Firm' (1994) 1 *Journal of Corporate Finance* 139 at 146.

[289]   B. Black and J. Coffee, 'Hail Brittania? Institutional Investor Behavior Under Limited Regulation' (1994) 92 *Michigan Law Review* 1999 at 2046.

[290]   G. Garvey and P. Swan, 'The Economics of Corporate Governance: Beyond the Marshallian Firm' (1994) 1 *Journal of Corporate Finance* 139 at 146. Compare the view of Stephen Bainbridge: 'Director Primacy: The Means and Ends of Corporate Governance' (2003) 97 *Northwestern University Law Review* 547 at 571.

[291]   B. Black, 'Shareholder Activism and Corporate Governance in the United States' Vol 3 *The New Palgrave Dictionary of Economics and Law* 459–460 at 462 (1998).

[292]   For instance, in the UK see ss.262 and 267 of the Companies Act 2008; in Australia, see s.237 of the Corporations Act 2001.

and the control therefore may not bring benefits to those with small hold-ings.[293] The fact is that to be in real control the shareholders would have to be able to make decisions that affect the benefits of other contributors to the company.[294] Arguably they cannot.

Another process that is often said to protect shareholders where share-holder primacy applies, is the market for corporate control. This is said to deter managers from failing to maximise shareholder wealth because if a company is run down, and below its potential, its share price will be depressed, and corporate raiders might see an opportunity to acquire the company at a good price and then run it efficiently to produce a profit. In such circumstances the shareholders will usually benefit because either they will sell their shares to the raider at a much better price compared with the listed price, or they remain in the company while the company's performance improves. The managers though will lose their jobs as the raider will usually replace them with its own nominees. But there has been theoretical argu-ment[295] and some empirical research[296] that denies the efficacious nature of the takeover in this regard. The use of the market for corporate control has also been questioned as an adequate device either for disciplining directors[297] or encouraging the directors to look after the interests of shareholders.[298]

So, shareholders cannot really monitor directors effectively. About the only thing that they can do is keep an eye on the share price, which is regarded as a crude instrument.[299]

---

[293]   There are several instances in recent years of institutional investors with large shareholdings exerting some control over the board. For example, see A. Keay, 'Company Directors Behaving Poorly: Disciplinary Options for Shareholders' [2007] *Journal of Business Law* 656 at 667–670.

[294]   L. Zingales, 'In Search of New Foundations' (2000) 55 *Journal of Finance* 1623 at 1632.

[295]   M. Lipton and S. Rosenblum, 'A New System of Corporate Governance: The Quinquenial Election of Directors' (1991) 58 *University of Chicago Law Review* 187 at 188; R. Booth, 'Stockholders, Stakeholders and Bagholders (or How Investor Diversification Affects Fiduciary Duty)' (1998) 53 *The Business Lawyer* 429 at 440. For a more recent view, see L. Bebchuk, 'The Myth of the Shareholder Franchise' (October 2005) and accessible at: <http://papers.ssrn.com/sol3/papers.cfm?abstract_id=829804>

[296]   J. Franks and C. Mayer, 'Hostile Takeovers in the UK and the Correction of Managerial Failure' (1996) 40 *Journal of Financial Economics* 163.

[297]   See I. Anabtawi, 'Some Skepticism About Increasing Shareholder Power' (2006) 53 *University of California at Los Angles Law Review* 561 at 568.

[298]   G. Garvey and P. Swan, 'The Economics of Corporate Governance: Beyond the Marshallian Firm' (1994) 1 *Journal of Corporate Finance* 139 at 145.

[299]   C. Brunner, 'The Enduring Ambivalence of Corporate Law' (2008) 59 *Alabama Law Review* 1385 at 1410.

The upshot of all of this is that directors enjoy a significant amount of discretion to pursue any agendas that they feel appropriate.[300]

7.11 The Shareholders are not so Special

One of the arguments in favour of shareholder primacy is that shareholders are to be regarded as special. We have already considered the issue of residual rights. It is said that shareholders are the ones who are most at risk. Yet other stakeholders are in risky positions. Unsecured creditors are not going to get paid in full if the company enters an insolvency regime, and it is quite likely that they will get nothing. Employees often have developed skills that are firm-specific and will not help them in seeking future employment if they are made redundant. Most stakeholders have some form of contract with the company that ties them to it.

The fact of the matter is that while shareholders are important, so are many contributors to the company. The shareholders are simply the ones who supply one element of the resources needed for the company to produce profits. Daniel Greenwood has argued that the idea that shareholders are to get dividends because they are entitled to residual returns is wrong, because no one is entitled to rents as a matter of course.[301] Also, while shareholders might have the right to vote at general meetings in relation to company affairs and, in some jurisdictions, to remove directors, these rights, and the position of the shareholders are not, as discussed earlier, very potent, and in fact other stakeholders have greater power in relation to the security, reputation and strength of the company and its managers. Some stakeholders might be able to take action that might indirectly lead to the replacement of the directors.[302]

Another aspect of the fact that the shareholders are not special might come from the nexus of contract concept. In this concept there is no notion of any of the actors having primacy, with all constituencies being on an equal footing,[303] and so nexus of contracts, so often relied on by law and economics scholars who advocate shareholder primacy, seems to be at odds with shareholder primacy. Nevertheless, Jonathan Macey

---

[300] M. Blair and L. Stout in 'A Team Production Theory of Corporate Law' (1999) 85 *Virginia Law Review* 247 at 252.

[301] 'The Dividend Puzzle: Are Shareholders Entitled to the Residual?' (2007) 32 *Journal of Corporation Law* 103.

[302] R.E. Freeman, *Strategic Management* (Boston, Pitman/Ballinger, 1984) at vi.

[303] F. Easterbrook and D. Fischel, 'Voting in Corporate Law' (1983) 26 *Journal of Law and Economics* 395 at 396.

argues that the participants in the corporate enterprise mutually agree that the non-shareholder constituents will subordinate their interests to those of the shareholders.[304] It is not clear how the commentator gets to this point. He assumes that in no situation would the non-shareholder constituents fail to agree to subordinate their interests to those of the shareholders, yet what indication of this do we have? It is submitted that one cannot make a general statement about what the non-shareholder constituents would agree to in all situations, even using hypothetical bargaining theory.

Luigi Zingales has posited that human capital has become the most important asset in today's firms and this warrants a fresh look at the foundations of the firm.[305] Certainly, this view means that we need to re-consider the idea that the shareholders are special, or at least more special than people such as the providers of critical human capital.

7.12 Failure to Enhance Social Wealth

Arguably shareholder primacy does not, contrary to the views of most shareholder primacy theorists, really increase social wealth.[306] According to several finance academics shareholder primacy produces a short-term focus and short-term earnings performance overshadows all else,[307] and this fails to maximise social wealth. All it does is merely benefit sharehold-ers, and only, perhaps, some of the shareholders at that. The shareholder primacy approach might in fact move managers to transfer value to share-holders away from other stakeholders, and at the latter's expense, instead of increasing overall value and making the wealth of the entity greater (the issue of externalising). A company might find that it is only able to

---

[304] 'Fiduciary Duties as Residual Claims Obligations to Nonshareholder Constituencies From a Theory of the Firm Perspective' (1998) 84 *Cornell Law Review* 1266 at 1272.

[305] 'In Search of New Foundations' (2000) 55 *Journal of Finance* 1623 at 1643.

[306] C. Loderer, L. Roth, U. Waelchli and P. Joerg, 'Shareholder Value: Principles, Declarations, and Actions' April 22, 2009, European Corporate Governance Institute Finance Working Paper No 95/2006 (revised), and accessible at <http://papers.ssrn.com/sol3/papers.cfm?abstract_id=690044> (last visited, 30 March 2010).

[307] S. Wallman, 'The Proper Interpretation of Corporate Constituency Statues and Formulation of Director Duties' (1991) 21 *Stetson Law Review* 163 at 176–177; M. Lipson and S. Rosenblum, 'A New System of Corporate Governance: The Quinquennial Election of Directors' (1991) 58 *University of Chicago Law Review* 187 at 205–215; M.E. van der Weide, 'Against Fiduciary Duties to Corporate Stakeholders' (1996) 21 *Delaware Journal of Corporate Law* 27 at 61.

enhance the benefits of shareholders through this action, for example closing down a factory and/or making some employees redundant in order to save on outgoings that can be transferred in the form of dividends to shareholders.[308] Finally on this point, while promoting shareholder value might lead indirectly to benefits for other investors, the promotion of this approach might lead to financial difficulty and that will adversely affect all other investors.

Claudio Loderer, Lukas Roth, Urs Waelchli, and Petra Joerg, demonstrate in a recent paper that economic theory, on which the theory prides itself, does not show that shareholder primacy is best for society as a whole.[309] The learned commentators deny the correctness of the point noted earlier that there is often a correlation between efficiency and social welfare. Loderer et al do not believe that increased efficiency can be seen necessarily as enhancing higher social welfare.[310]

Lastly, it has been argued that without some sort of mechanism to force shareholders to share gains with other stakeholders there is no benefit flowing to the latter.[311] Steven Wallman has argued that shareholder primacy can, in fact, lead to costs to society as a whole because of the increased costs to companies and the constituencies with whom companies do business as the latter might well assume that the company's managers could be forced to violate their trust and good faith in the course of maximising shareholder wealth.[312]

---

[308] Royal Dutch Shell axed jobs in July 2009 when the company sustained a loss of profits: D. Robertson, 'Shell cuts jobs as profits plunge 70%' *The Times*, 30 July 2009. Anglo-American followed suit shortly thereafter: D. Robertson, 'Anglo American cuts 15,000 jobs as profits dive' *The Times*, 31 July 2009. Shell again made a substantial number of workers redundant in October 2009 as a reaction to a drop in profits: C. Mortished, 'Shell to axe 5,000 jobs amid 73% profit fall' *The Times*, 29 October 2009.

[309] C. Loderer, L. Roth, U. Waelchli and P. Joerg, 'Shareholder Value: Principles, Declarations, and Actions' 22 April 2009, European Corporate Governance Institute – Finance Working Paper No 95/2005 at 6–8, and accessible at: <http://papers.ssrn.com/sol3/papers.cfm?abstract_id=690044> (last visited, 30 March 2010).

[310] Claudio Loderer, Lukas Roth, Urs Waelchli and Petra Joerg, 'Shareholder Value: Principles, Declarations, and Actions' April 22, 2009, European Corporate Governance Institute – Finance Working Paper No 95/2005 at 33, and accessible at: <http://papers.ssrn.com/sol3/papers.cfm?abstract_id=690044> (last visited, 30 March 2010).

[311] K. Greenfield, 'Saving the World With Corporate Law' (2008) 57 *Emory Law Journal* 947 at 967.

[312] S. Wallman, 'Understanding the Purpose of a Corporation: An Introduction' (1999) 24 *Journal of Corporation Law* 807 at 812.

7.13   Devoid of Moral Basis

Shareholder primacy has been criticised on the basis that there is no moral reason for the theory's implementation. The shareholders merely form one group amongst many who are affected by the company's actions,[313] so why should they be benefited in priority to others? Shareholder value is very narrow in focus and to such an extent that it is overly glib and fails to consider values other than efficiency. The emphasis on shareholder interests does not emanate from any moral reason, but from the desire to be efficient. There is no consideration of fairness, equality, justice etc. This means that it cannot 'do justice to the panoply of human activity that is value creation and trade, i.e., business.'[314] The concern is that the approach tends to ignore reality because more than the interests of shareholders are at stake when we are considering how companies should be run.[315] Take fairness for example. The ideals behind it would indicate that there should be a move away from shareholder primacy to ensure that companies do not impose externalities on stakeholders and society in general.[316]

While some have acknowledged the fact that shareholder primacy provides a convenient common metric, it is too simplistic to reduce everything to a matter of profit.[317] Many see the theory as cold and uncaring and totally omitting the human dimension that is critical to all facets of life, including business. Society values more than just maximisation of profit. It is concerned about how wealth is distributed, the creation of jobs, family time, the effect on the environment and so on.[318] But the theory ignores the human values of those who contribute to the operation of the company.[319]

---

[313]   D. Wood, 'Whom Should Business Serve?' (2002) 14 *Australian Journal of Corporate Law* 1 at 7.

[314]   R.E. Freeman, A. Wicks and B. Parmar, 'Stakeholder Theory and "The Corporate Objective Revisited"' (2004) 15 *Organization Science* 364 at 364.

[315]   W. Allen, J. Jacobs and L. Strine, 'The Great Takeover Debate: A Mediation on Bridging the Conceptual Divide' (2002) 69 *University of Chicago Law Review* 1067 at 1083.

[316]   B. Choudhury, 'Serving Two Masters: Incorporate Social Responsibility into the Corporate Paradigm' (2009) 11 *University of Pennsylvania Journal of Business Law* 631 at 655.

[317]   D. Wood, 'Whom Should Business Serve?' (2002) 14 *Australian Journal of Corporate Law* 1 at 13.

[318]   D. Greenwood, 'Markets and Democracy: The Illegitimacy of Corporate Law' (2005) 74 *University of Missouri at Kansas City Law Review* 41 at 50.

[319]   L. Mitchell, 'Groundwork of the Metaphysics of Corporate Law' (1993) 50 *Washington and Lee Law Review* 1477 at 1479.

It is asserted that making managers only fix on wealth maximisation for shareholders, and having no responsibility to other persons and groups permits managers to escape perceiving themselves as moral agents. The theory does not provide for any guidance for managers on moral or legal challenges which they encounter.[320] Managers may be able to use shareholder primacy as an answer to countless ethical dilemmas with which they may be confronted.

7.14 Ethical Issues

Notwithstanding the fact that adherents to the theory have argued that the theory itself is not unethical,[321] concerns over the ethical basis of the theory have been expressed. It has been said that the incentive remuneration schemes that are linked to share price performance, and which are often part of managers' employment contracts, may prejudice the ethical standing that managers should take.[322] Such schemes do tend to inculcate the idea of self-interest.[323] They also tend to encourage directors to engage in activity that will produce short-term gains as they will be remunerated for their work more quickly.[324] Robert Anthony put it this way when he stated that shareholder maximization required a manager:

> [T]o use every trick he can think of to keep wages and fringe benefits down, to extract the last possible dollar from the consumer, to sell as low quality merchandise as he can legally hoodwink the customer into buying, to use income solely for the benefits [sic] of the stockholder, to disclaim any responsibility in the community, to finagle the lowest possible price from his vendors regardless of its effect on them.[325]

---

[320] R.E. Freeman, A. Wicks and B. Parmar, 'Stakeholder Theory and "The Corporate Objective Revisited"' (2004) 15 *Organization Science* 364 at 367.

[321] E. Sternberg, *Just Business*, 2nd ed (Oxford, Oxford University Press, 2000).

[322] L. Dallas, 'A Preliminary Inquiry into the Responsibility of Corporations and their Directors and Officers for Corporate Climate: The Psychology of Enron's Demise' (2003) 35 *Rutgers Law Journal* 1.

[323] See, M. Blair, 'Directors' Duties in a Post-Enron World: Why Language Matters' (2003) 38 *Wake Forest Law Review* 885 at 907.

[324] See D. Walker, 'Boardroom Behaviours' Institute of Chartered Secretaries and Administrators, June 2009 at para 2.15.

[325] 'The Trouble with Profit Maximization' [1960] *Harvard Business Review* 126 at 132.

7.15   Encouraging Gambling

One of the problems that can result from a company adhering to share-holder primacy is that the directors might choose to follow wasteful investment policies where the company is close to defaulting on its debt obligations.[326] In such situations shareholders will prefer that directors not invest in certain projects with positive net present value because the net present value generated by these projects, though positive, will not produce sufficient benefits that will go to shareholders, who are junior to creditors when it comes to distribution of the company's receipts.[327] In such a situation the shareholders might prefer 'a bet the business' type of approach for they have nothing to lose. In fact even where a company is clearly solvent, embracing some of the risky opportunities that are pro-vided by capital markets will increase the expected value of shares, but it will decrease the value of other claims, 'thus decreasing the expected value of the sum of financial claims against the firm.'[328] The creditworthiness of the company might be damaged and this might devalue its debt, and put continued employment in jeopardy.[329]

7.16   Balancing is Needed

As we have seen, a major argument in favour of the theory is that man-agers can focus on one goal and that involves the interests of one group. Adherents to the theory argue that this makes it superior to stakeholder theory as with the latter theory directors are required to balance many interests, and that is impossible. Yet professionals regularly have to make decisions where there are conflicts and they end up having to engage in balancing interests. In many companies directors who practise

---

[326]   M. Jensen and W. Meckling, 'Theory of the Firm: Managerial Behaviour, Agency Costs, and Ownership Structure' (1976) 3 *Journal of Financial Economics* 305.

[327]   S.C. Myers 'Determinants of Corporate Borrowing' (1977) 5 *Journal of Financial Economics* 147. Also, see, R. Stulz and H. Johnson, 'An Analysis of Secured Debt' (1985) 14 *Journal of Financial Economics* 501; E. Berkovitch and E.H. Kim, 'Financial Contracting and Leverage-induced Over- and Underinvestment Incentives,' (1990) 45 *Journal of Finance* 765.

[328]   T. Smith, 'The Efficient Norm for Corporate Law: A Neotraditional Interpretation of Fiduciary Duty' (1999) 98 *Michigan Law Review* 214 at 220.

[329]   J. Fisch, 'Measuring Efficiency in Corporate Law: The Rule of Shareholder Primacy' December 2005, Fordham Law Legal Studies, Working Paper No 105 at p30 and available at <http://ssrn.com/abstract=878391> (last visited, 27 July 2009).

shareholder primacy have to engage in balancing as there are different classes of shareholders and their respective interests have to be balanced against one another. Shares come in different shapes and sizes, such as ordinary and preference, and it is incumbent on directors to balance the interests of different kinds of shareholders, so that they act fairly between them[330] as, on occasions, these different classes of shareholders have opposing interests.[331] Jonathan Macey and Geoffrey Miller point out[332] that some preferred shareholders may have interests that resemble those of fixed claimants, such as creditors, more than those associated with common shareholders. Some shareholders intend only to retain shares for a short term, while others are in for the long haul. Other shareholders hold a diversified portfolio, with their investment spread around a number of companies, and still others might have all their investment concentrated in the one company. The shareholder primacy theory does not allow for the fact that many investors are diversified and will be both shareholders and bondholders in companies.[333] As mentioned earlier, those in this situation are not going to have the same goals as those who are purely shareholders. Those who have diversified interests will be looking for a more balanced approach to the making of investment decisions. Notwithstanding this, no concerns are voiced about the stresses of decision-making for directors in undertaking a balancing of the interests of the various types of shareholders, nor is it argued that directors, in balancing interests, are too burdened.

7.17 Redundant

It has been argued that the shareholder primacy principle is not, in fact, relevant to business decisions today. It was introduced originally to resolve disputes among majority and minority shareholders in closely-held companies, well-illustrated in the celebrated American case of *Dodge v Ford Motor Co*.[334] There are two points to make in relation to this decision, which is so often relied on by shareholder primacists to support the

---

[330] *Mills v Mills* (1938) 60 CLR 150, 164; *Re BSB Holdings Ltd (No2)* [1996] 1 BCLC 155, 246–249.

[331] M. McDaniel, 'Bondholders and Stockholders' (1988) 13 *Journal of Corporation Law* 205 at 273; R.B. Campbell Jr, 'Corporate Fiduciary Principles for the Post-Contractarian Era' (1996) 23 *Florida State University Law Review* 561 at 593.

[332] 'Corporate Stakeholders: A Contractual Perspective' (1993) 43 *University of Toronto Law Review* 401 at 433.

[333] T. Smith, 'The Efficient Norm for Corporate Law: A Neotraditional Interpretation of Fiduciary Duty' (1999) 98 *Michigan Law Review* 214 at 217.

[334] 204 Mich 459; 170 NW 668.

theory. First, the court was not concerned that the managers had taken into account the interests of non-shareholding stakeholders, but that they had managed the company, in contravention of the company's charter, as a semi-charitable body and not as a business institution.[335] The company's charter clearly indicated that it was to be a profit-making organisation. Second, it is asserted that courts tended not to distinguish between closely-held and public companies until the middle of the last century.[336]

7.18 Shareholders are not Owners

As was noted earlier in the Chapter,[337] some theorists argue for share-holder primacy partly or wholly on the basis that the shareholders are the owners of the company and so their interests warrant being maximised in preference to anyone else's. But this view is not without significant criticism,[338] and this criticism is not of recent origin. As far back as 1962 Dow Votaw challenged it as a myth.[339] Even though shareholders might be seen as the owners of a company by many commentators,[340] this is generally not the case in the courts.[341] In the American case of *Kaufman v*

---

[335] At 683, 684.

[336] D.G. Smith, 'The Shareholder Primacy Norm' (1998) 23 *Journal of Corporation Law* 277 at 279.

[337] Above at p. 66.

[338] For example, M. Lipton and S. Rosenblum, 'A New System of Corporate Governance: The Quinquenial Election of Directors' (1991) 58 *University of Chicago Law Review* 187 at 195; P. Ireland, 'Capitalism Without the Capitalist: The Joint Stock Company Share and the Emergence of the Modern Doctrine of Separate Corporate Personality' (1996) 17 *Legal History* 40; S. Worthington, 'Shares and Shareholders: Property, Power and Entitlement (Part 1) (2001) 22 *The Company Lawyer* 258 and Part 2 (2001) 22 *The Company Lawyer* 307; L. Stout, 'The Mythical Benefits of Shareholder Control' (2007) 93 *Virginia Law Review* 789 at 804.

[339] 'The Mythology of Corporations' (1962) (Spring) *California Management Review* 58.

[340] R. Booth, 'Who Owns a Corporation and Who Cares?' (2001) 77 *Chicago-Kent Law Review* 147 at 147.

[341] Out of line with most authorities, Beach J of the Supreme Court of Victoria (in *Re Humes Ltd* (1987) 5 ACLC 64 at 67) said that the property of the company belonged to the shareholders. Earlier, in *Med. Comm. For Human Rights v SEC* (1970) 432 F 2d 659 at 662 the District of Columbia Circuit Court of Appeals indicated that shareholders were owners and, therefore, were entitled to control important decisions that affect them. Most recently, the Delaware Supreme Court said in *North American Catholic Education Programming Foundation Inc v Gheewalla* 930 A 2d 92 at 101 (2007)) that directors have the legal responsibility to manage the company for its shareholder owners.

Societe Internationale[342] Judge Reed said that a shareholder has no present interest in the property of a company that remained out of liquidation. Likewise, earlier in the case of *Short v Treasury Commissioners*[343] Lord Justice Evershed of the English Court of Appeal denied the ownership of the company by shareholders. Even earlier than that, the English case of *Bligh v Brent*[344] provided that shareholders had no proprietary interest in the company. Company law is unequivocal in holding that the company entity actually owns the assets of the company, and no one can own it, the entity, for it is a legal personality; people merely provide resources to it. This all follows from the seminal case of *Salomon v Salomon and Co Ltd*[345] generally approved in most common law jurisdictions.

From economic thought, some have criticised the view that the shareholders can be regarded as the owners of the company on the basis that it is not consistent with agency theory,[346] while others have perceived it as being inconsistent with the nexus of contracts theory, for with such a theory there is no firm that can be owned as the firm consists of various relational contracts and the shareholders merely supply one factor in the production process, namely the capital.[347] If the company were owned by the shareholders, there could not be a nexus of contracts.[348] Leaving aside these points, there is a legal reason for saying that the shareholders do not own the company. They own shares, which are items of property in their own right,[349] but this does not provide them with any interest in the company's assets or enable them to say that they own the company.[350] Also,

---

[342] 343 US156 at 166 (1952).

[343] [1948] 1 KB 116 at 122.

[344] (1837) 2 Y & C Ex 268.

[345] [1897] AC 22, HL.

[346] For example, see S. Bainbridge, 'Director Primacy: The Means and Ends of Corporate Governance' (2003) 97 *Northwestern University Law Review* 547 at 565. Also, see S. Bainbridge, *The New Corporate Governance in Theory and Practice* (New York, Oxford University Press, 2008) at 27, 32.

[347] See S. Deakin and G. Slinger, 'Hostile Takeover, Corporate Law and Theory of the Firm' (1997) 24 *Journal of Law and Society* 124 at 126; M. Eisenberg, 'The Conception That the Corporation is a Nexus of Contracts, and the Dual Nature of the Firm' (1999) 24 *Journal of Corporation Law* 819 at 825; D. Wood, 'Whom Should Business Serve?' (2002) 14 *Australian Journal of Corporate Law* 1 at 10.

[348] M. Eisenberg, 'The Conception That the Corporation is a Nexus of Contracts, and the Dual Nature of the Firm' (1999) 24 *Journal of Corporation Law* 819 at 825.

[349] S. Worthington, 'Shares and Shareholders: Property, Power and Entitlement (Part 1) (2001) 22 *The Company Lawyer* 258 at 259.

[350] In fact Alan Goldman views shareholders as gamblers: 'Business Ethics, Utilities and Moral Rights' (1980) 9 *Philosophy and Public Affairs* 260 at 284.

from an accounting perspective when a shareholder deposits money with a company, the money becomes the equity of the company.[351]

The notion that the shareholders of the company own the company goes back to the days of the early joint stock companies when they were, whether incorporated or not, perceived by the law as partnerships, and, of course, partners can be said to own a partnership. In these joint stock companies the shareholders had equitable ownership of the assets and they controlled the directors.[352] But things changed with the development of the company and the shareholders were regarded as having no direct interest in company assets, they were not entitled to the company's earnings, and they merely had the right to dividends and to transfer their shares.[353] By this time shares were seen as property in their own right, and not simply a bundle of contractual rights.[354] This also meant that the directors were no longer the agents of the shareholders.[355] The corporate concept divides property, namely a bundle of rights, into several lots. The shareholder when taking shares only acquires 'the right to receive some of the fruits of the use of property, a fractional residual right in corporate property and a very limited right of control.'[356]

The right that shareholders have to vote, to bring derivative proceedings and to receive a dividend all flow from being the holder of a share and not from owning the company. As Sheldon Leader has said: 'The judges have moved away from protecting the shareholders' property rights in the company, to a focus on protecting their property rights in their own shares.'[357] This is a matter that is discussed further in Chapter 4.

---

[351]   D. Li, 'The Nature of Corporate Residual Equity Under the Equity Concept' (1960) 35 *The Accounting Review* 258 at 261.

[352]   See *Isle of Wight Rly Co v Tahourdin* (1883) 25 Ch D 320 and referred to in S. Worthington, 'Shares and Shareholders: Property, Power and Entitlement (Part 1) (2001) 22 *The Company Lawyer* 258 at 260.

[353]   *Bligh v Brent* (1837) 2 Y & C Ex 268.

[354]   P. Ireland 'Capitalism Without the Capitalist: The Joint Stock Company Share and the Emergence of the Modern Doctrine of Separate Corporate Personality' (1996) 17 *Journal of Legal History* 41. Also, see S. Worthington, 'Shares and Shareholders: Property, Power and Entitlement (Part 1) (2001) 22 *The Company Lawyer* 258 at 259–261 for a useful discussion of the position of shares.

[355]   *Automatic Self-Cleansing Filter Syndicate Co Ltd v Cuninghame* [1906] 2 Ch 34.

[356]   D. Votaw, *Modern Corporations* (Englewood Cliffs, Prentice-Hall, 1965) at 96–97 and quoted in M. Blair, *Ownership and Control* (Washington DC, The Brookings Institute, 1995) at 224.

[357]   'Private Property and Corporate Governance Part I: Defining the Interests' in F. Patfield (ed), *Perspectives on Company Law: 1* (London, Kluwer Law International, 1995) at 94.

Margaret Blair has stated that even if one can say that shareholders are owners on the basis that they have property rights, the concept of 'property' is complex and it is difficult to say which of many control rights are given to shareholders.[358] Berle and Means said that there were three elements to the concept of private property, namely having an interest in an enterprise, having power over it and acting with respect to it.[359] Arguably the position in which shareholders find themselves does not meet all of these elements. Particularly, and as noted earlier, the shareholders even as a collective do not have the control to do what they wish to do, for they have effectively relinquished most of the powers of ownership.

Stephen Bainbridge regards the shareholders as 'nominally' those who 'own' the company.[360] He takes this view because the shareholders have no decision-making powers. UK shareholders arguably have more than their American counterparts, but not to the point that it makes a huge difference.[361] Jonathan Macey, a shareholder primacy advocate, accepts that shareholders do not own the company in any 'meaningful sense'.[362]

One economics commentator, Katsuhito Iwai,[363] has said that the shareholders do own the company, and the company owns the company assets. He distinguishes the company as a thing and a person. In its first role, it can be owned. In its second role it may own property.[364] I find this unconvincing. There is no basis for making the distinction. As stated earlier, the shareholders do own a share(s) in the company, but not the whole thing. In any event if the shareholders owned the company, then surely they would own the company assets.

The ethicist, John Boatright, argues that even if one accepts that shareholders do own the company, it does not necessarily mean that directors

---

[358] M. Blair, *Ownership and Control* (Washington DC, The Brookings Institute, 1995) at 226.

[359] A.A. Berle and G. Means, *The Modern Corporation and Private Property* (New York, MacMillan, 1932) and quoted in L. May, 'Corporate Property Rights' (1986) 5 *Journal of Business Ethics* 225 at 226.

[360] 'Competing Concepts of the Corporation (a.k.a. Criteria? Just Say No)' UCLA Law and Economics Research Paper Series, Research Paper No 05-1, 2005 at 13 and accessible at: <http://ssrn.com/abstract=646821> (last visited, 21 July 2009).

[361] A. Keay, 'Company Directors Behaving Poorly: Disciplinary Options for Shareholders' [2007] *Journal of Business Law* 656.

[362] 'An Economic Analysis of the Various Rationales for Making Shareholders the Exclusive Beneficiaries of Corporate Fiduciary Duties' (1991) 21 *Stetson Law Review* 23 at 26.

[363] 'Persons, Things and Corporations: The Corporate Personality Controversy and Comparative Corporate Governance' (1999) 47 *American Journal of Comparative Law* 583.

[364] Ibid at 592.

are under an obligation to manage the company for the sole benefit of the shareholders.[365] This, of course, leads to a wider discussion going back to the time of E. Merrick Dodd as to who are entitled to have their interests considered by corporate management.

It is possible to conclude that the ownership argument is the least persuasive of the arguments for shareholder primacy.[366] In fact, rather than seeing them as owners, Charles Handy embraced the appellation of 'punters at the races' for most shareholders in public companies.[367] Alan Goldman seems to agree with this sentiment as he describes shareholders as being akin to gamblers.[368]

7.19   Problems with the Agency Concept

When recounting the arguments in favour of the theory I mentioned the fact that the company's managers are seen, pursuant to the agency theory, and a point heavily relied on by many who advocate shareholder primacy, as agents of the shareholders, who are the principals, and consequently they must do their very best to enhance the principals' interests. But, the first thing to note is that the managers have no express contract with the shareholders, and arguably, no implied contract. The shareholder either buys shares from an existing shareholder, or from the company. In the first case it is not possible to imply a contract between the managers and the new shareholder, and, in the latter case, there is no real agreement beyond the prospectus.[369] Furthermore, there are UK,[370] US[371] and Australian[372]

---

[365]   'Fiduciary Duties and the Shareholder-Management Relation: Or, What's Special About Shareholders?' (1994) 4 *Business Ethics Quarterly* 393 at 395.

[366]   L. Stout, 'Bad and Not-So-Bad Arguments for Shareholder Primacy' (2002) 75 *South California Law Review* 1189; C. Kelly, 'History Begins: Shareholder Value, Accountability and the Virtuous State' (2009) 60 *Northern Ireland Legal Quarterly* 35 at 37.

[367]   'What is a Company For?'(1993) 1 *Corporate Governance: International Review* 14 at 15.

[368]   A. Goldman, 'Business Ethics: Profits, Utilities and Moral Rights' (1980) 9 *Philosophy and Public Affairs* 260 at 284.

[369]   J. Boatright, 'Fiduciary Duties and the Shareholder-Management Relation: Or, What's Special About Shareholders?' (1994) 4 *Business Ethics Quarterly* 393 at 397.

[370]   See, for example, *Lonrho Ltd v Shell Petroleum Co Ltd* [1980] 1 WLR 627 at 634 (HL).

[371]   See, for example, *United Teachers Associations Insurance Co v Mackeen and Bailey* 99 F 3d 645 at 650–651 (5th Cir, 1996).

[372]   See, for example, *Brunninghausen v Glavanics* [1999] NSWCA 199; (1999) 17 ACLC 1247 at [43].

cases that hold that directors owe their duties to the company. If there is no contract between the directors and the shareholders then there can be no agency. Even in 1984 Masahiko Aoki called the notion of agency in this context 'out-of-date'.[373] Boatright asserts that available evidence suggests that shareholders purchase shares with similar, if not the same, expectations to others making financial investments, such as bondholders.[374] A study by Larry Sonderquist and Robert Vecchio concluded that shareholders expect directors to consider a wide range of stakeholders when taking action.[375]

The next point is that legally speaking the managers are not the agents of the shareholders. First, the managers are employed by the company and not the shareholders. They make contracts on behalf of the corporate entity and bind that entity. Even if one can argue that the directors owe fiduciary duties to the shareholders as a group, and that is highly debatable,[376] there is nothing that suggests that fiduciary duties impose a demand that the company's business is to be run in a particular way,[377] and certainly not on the basis purely of shareholder maximisation. Second, the managers are not able to enter into any relationship that will modify the relations that the shareholders, personally, have with third parties. Third, principals are entitled to control their agents, but the managers and non-executive directors who make up the board are usually empowered to manage the company, and they cannot be ordered what to do by the shareholders in the general meeting, for the directors have the exclusive right to manage the company.[378] The directors are not agents of the shareholders, but agents of the company, as are the managers when acting alone or with others. Directors are clearly independent

---

[373] *The Co-operative Game Theory of the Firm* (Oxford, Clarendon Press, 1984) at 49.

[374] J. Boatright, 'Fiduciary Duties and the Shareholder-Management Relation: Or, What's Special About Shareholders?' (1994) 4 *Business Ethics Quarterly* 393 at 397.

[375] 'Reconciling Shareholders' Rights and Corporate Responsibility: New Guidelines for Management' [1978] *Duke Law Journal* 840.

[376] See, A. Keay, 'Enlightened Shareholder Value, the Reform of the Duties of Company Directors and the Corporate Objective' [2006] *Lloyds Maritime and Commercial Law Quarterly* 335 at 341–346.

[377] R. Marens and A. Wicks, 'Getting Real: Stakeholder Theory, Managerial Practice and the General Irrelevance of Fiduciary Duties Owed to Shareholders' (1999) 9 *Business Ethics Quarterly* 273 at 277.

[378] *Automatic Self-Cleansing Filter Syndicate Co Ltd v Cuninghame* [1906] 2 Ch 34. Also, see *Salmon v Quin & Axtens Ltd* [1900] AC 442.

of the shareholders. As the managers work for the company, at best the responsibilities owed to shareholders are only indirect.[379]

7.20   Shareholders and Vulnerability

It is questionable whether the argument that shareholders are more vulnerable than other constituencies, because the latter are able to protect themselves by the terms of the contracts that they make while shareholders do not have this kind of protection, is able to be sustained. This might be the case with some groups within some constituencies, such as powerful creditors like banks, but many do not obtain protection for a number of reasons, such as lack of bargaining power, ignorance or insufficient funds to pay necessary costs (e.g. legal costs). In the real world it is infrequent to find contractual arrangements made by equals. In many contracts there is a 'take it leave it approach' with little or no room for negotiation, and with the result that costs are imposed on third parties with whom the company does business.[380] Stakeholders, when making contracts, often suffer from informational asymmetry in that the managers of companies know far more, particularly about the performance and systems of the company, than the stakeholders. It has been said that shareholders have to rely on trust and not contract,[381] but that is effectively the case with many stakeholders. Stakeholders can enter into contracts with the company, but they often rely on the good faith of the directors in carrying out the terms of the contract. Several scholars have reported the fact that contracts involving stakeholders are not complete and not perfectly priced,[382] and so it can be submitted that contracts are unable to protect non-shareholders. Consequently, shareholders are not so disadvantaged vis à vis other stakeholders as is often asserted.

It was reported in 2002 that about 70 per cent of UK listed shares were held by institutional investors,[383] and the portion held by such investors

---

[379]   D. Millon, 'Theories of the Corporation' [1995] *Duke Law Journal* 201 at 218.

[380]   F. Easterbrook and D. Fischel, 'Antitrust Suits by Targets of Tender Offers' (1982) 80 *Michigan Law Review* 1155 at 1156.

[381]   J. Macey, *Corporate Governance* (Princeton, Princeton University Press, 2008) at vi.

[382]   J. Fisch, 'Measuring Efficiency in Corporate Law: The Rule of Shareholder Primacy' December 2005, Fordham Law Legal Studies, Working Paper No 105 at p29 and available at <http://ssrn.com/abstract=878391> (last visited, 27 July 2009).

[383]   J. Armour, B. Cheffins and D. Skeel, 'Corporate Ownership Structure and the Evolution of Bankruptcy Law: Lessons from the United Kingdom' (2002) 55 *Vanderbilt Law Review* 1699 at 1750.

in the US has increased to the point of being 66 per cent.[384] So, a large portion of Anglo-American companies have their shares held by institutional investors and it could be argued that these shareholders do not warrant any special protection given the resources that they have and the power that they wield.

Shareholders are able to vote at meetings on motions put before them and vote on the election of directors. Also, they have the power in many jurisdictions to remove a director.[385] Shareholders can always exit from the company by selling their shares (in the words of Eric Orts: 'exit the firm in an electronic flash'[386]), even though it might be at a loss, whereas constituents cannot bale out or, if they can, like employees on monthly contracts, they may do so at personal risk. Lenders cannot recall the principal that they have lent (save where there is a breach of a covenant in the agreement), employees cannot always resign and move to another employer without huge upheaval involving some financial costs, and communities certainly cannot move.[387] Shareholders do have the right to bring a derivative claim against the directors and others (albeit in some jurisdictions subject to obtaining court permission).[388] They also are entitled, in many jurisdictions, to institute proceedings under unfair prejudice or oppression provisions in companies legislation, such as s.994 of the UK Companies Act 2006.[389] In fact it might be argued that shareholders are in fact overly protected as they lose nothing but their investment in the company if the company enters liquidation.

Furthermore, the argument that non-shareholder stakeholders are also safeguarded by regulatory law is too broad an assertion. Many laws are of limited or no benefit to stakeholders. Take s.214 of the Insolvency Act 1986, which outlaws wrongful trading. It is seen by some as protecting

---

[384] C. Brancato and S. Rabimov, *The Conference Board*, 2008, Institutional Investment Report 6, 9, 20 and referred to in V. Ho, '"Enlightened Shareholder Value": Corporate Governance Beyond the Shareholder-Stakeholder Divide' abstract accessible at <http:ssrn.com/abstract=1476116> (last visited, on 10 December 2009).

[385] This power is provided in the UK by s.168 of the Companies Act 2006. But, see A. Keay, 'Company Directors Behaving Poorly: Disciplinary Options for Shareholders' [2007] *Journal of Business Law* 656.

[386] 'Shirking and Sharking: A Legal Theory of the Firm' (1998) 16 *Yale Law and Policy Review* 265 at 311.

[387] J. Boatright, 'Fiduciary Duties and the Shareholder-Management Relation: Or, What's Special About Shareholders?' (1994) 4 *Business Ethics Quarterly* 393 at 396.

[388] Part 11 of the Companies Act 2006.

[389] This is discussed in Chapter 4 at p. 235.

creditors, but few successful actions have been brought during the life of this provision, and, in any event, they can only be brought by liquidators and not the creditors.[390]

It is argued by some commentators, even where there have been collapses of companies that have practised shareholder value, such as Enron, that stakeholders like employees benefited from the approach as they took stock benefits and received payments as a result, but shareholders do not get anything because they only receive any repayment of capital if the company is solvent.[391] This overlooks the fact that shareholders received healthy dividends whilst the company was prosperous,[392] and these cannot be clawed back by a liquidator unless the payments were not made out of profits.

The issue of vulnerability needs to be considered in light of the fact that many, if not most, shareholders will not invest in only one or two companies. They will diversify their investments, so that they will have shares in a number of companies and they will be bondholders in relation to other companies.

It might be argued that it is not shareholders who absorb the risk. Rather, as we have seen, they engage in externalising and transfer risk to other constituencies, notably employees who are often made redundant to lessen the reduction of the dividends to be paid to shareholders.[393]

7.21   Gap-filling

As noted under the heading of '6. Theoretical Arguments in Favour' it was pointed out that contractarians generally say that the idea of

---

[390]   See A. Keay, *Company Directors' Responsibilities to Creditors* (Abingdon, Routledge/Cavendish, 2007) at 81–150.

[391]   A. Sundaram and A. Inkpen, 'The Corporate Objective Revisited' (2004) 15 *Organization Science* 350 at 358.

[392]   This is particularly pertinent to shareholders of banks that have been baled out by the UK taxpayer. They received huge dividends in the later part of the 1990s and the first years of this century. For example the Royal Bank of Scotland paid out a final dividend of 17% in 2005, 22% in 2006 and 23% in 2007 <http://www.investors.rbs.com/our_performance/dividend.cfm> (last visited, 7 June 2010). Also see the position of the Bank of New York Meillon which slashed its dividend payable in 2009 by 63% (Ben Steverman, 'The Ever-Shrinking Bank Dividend' *Blomberg Businessweek*, 21 April 2009 and accessible at <http://www.businessweek.com/investing/insights/blog/archives/2009/04/the_ever-shrink.html> (last visited, 7 June 2010).

[393]   L. Johnson, 'Individual and Collective Sovereignty in the Corporate Enterprise' (1992) 92 *Columbia Law Review* 2215 at 2224.

shareholder primacy can be seen as the correct gap-filling term for the corporate contract, but Thomas Smith has argued that this is wrong.[394] He maintains that, in employing hypothetical bargaining analysis, rational investors would not agree to shareholder primacy as the appropriate gap-filling rule. He asserts that companies are always in the vicinity of insolvency as they are only one decision away from collapse so managers should not be managing for shareholder wealth maximisation, but for broader considerations.

8. THE EMPLOYMENT OF THE THEORY

Clearly many have asserted that shareholder primacy is practised across the board in the UK and the US and in other nations titled, rather erroneously, as Anglo-Saxon. While this book is focused primarily on normative issues, it is worth briefly analysing whether the theory is implemented in the places just mentioned. Is it widely employed?

The results of research suggest that there is conflicting evidence as to whether companies are in fact embracing shareholder value as their corporate objective. In a large study conducted in the late 1980s including interviews of 80 directors, most of whom were American, Jay Lorsch found that the main focus of directors when making decisions was on the interests of shareholders.[395] Later, in a study in the mid-1990s by Masaru Yoshimori involving Japanese and western companies, it was found that in the UK 71 per cent of managers took the view that the interests of shareholders should be given the first priority.[396] In a more recent Australian study, which invoked a stakeholder salience approach,[397] it was found that only 44 per cent of managers ranked shareholders as their top priority,[398]

---

[394] T. Smith, 'The Efficient Norm for Corporate Law: A Neotraditional Interpretation of Fiduciary Duty' (1999) 98 *Michigan Law Review* 214 at 217.

[395] *Pawns or Potentates: The Reality of America's Corporate Boards* (Boston, Massachusetts, Harvard Business School Press, 1989) at 38.

[396] 'Whose Company is it? The Concept of Corporations in Japan and the West' (1995) 28 *Long Range Planning* 33 at 34. Also, see F. Allen and D. Gale, *Comparing Financial Systems* (Cambridge, Massachusetts, MIT Press, 2000) at 111.

[397] This approach is perhaps most associated with R. Mitchell, B. Agle and D. Wood, 'Toward a Theory of Stakeholder Identification Salience: Defining the Principle of Who and What Really Counts?' (1997) 22 *Academy of Management Review* 853.

[398] M. Jones, S. Marshall, R. Mitchell and I.M. Ramsay, 'Company Directors' Views Regarding Stakeholders,' Research Report, Faculty of Law, University

although overall the shareholders were seen by managers as the most important of all stakeholders.[399]

Loderer et al reported from their study involving consideration of the websites of a wide range of public companies based in several countries, and a survey of chairmen of Swiss companies, that publicly few managers see shareholder value maximisation as an objective; in fact shareholder value is often not mentioned as one of the aims of directors, and if it is it certainly is not the highest priority.[400] While this might be expected of companies in civil law countries, interestingly the commentators found that the situation is very similar in relation to companies in Anglo-American jurisdictions.[401]

Schrader records that empirical studies of firms suggest that executives do regularly sacrifice profits for other considerations.[402] Justice Heydon of the Australian High Court, many years before his elevation to the bench, asserted that 'businessmen in their daily talk reveal that they are constantly considering, without impropriety, interests other than those of the shareholders.'[403] Einer Elhauge has argued that the maximisation of profits has never been an enforceable duty on directors, as they have always enjoyed discretion in relation to how they run the company.[404] The chairman of the US company, Standard Oil, stated, in 1946, that the business of companies should be carried on 'in such a way as to maintain

---

of Melbourne and accessible at <http://cclsr.law.unimelb.edu.au/go/centre-activities/research/research-reports-and-research-papers/index/cfm> (last visited, 13 July 2009). Also, see M. Anderson et al, 'Shareholder Primacy and Directors' Duties: An Australian Perspective' (2008) 8 *Journal of Corporate Law Studies* 161 at 166.

[399] M. Anderson et al, 'Shareholder Primacy and Directors' Duties: An Australian Perspective' (2008) 8 *Journal of Corporate Law Studies* 161 at 188.

[400] C. Loderer, L. Roth, U. Waelchli, and P. Joerg, 'Shareholder Value: Principles, Declarations, and Actions' 22 April 2009, European Corporate Governance Institute Finance Working Paper No 95/2006 (revised), and accessible at <http://papers.ssrn.com/sol3/papers.cfm?abstract_id=690044> (last visited, 30 March 2010).

[401] Ibid.

[402] D. Schrader, 'The Corporation and Profits' (1987) 6 *Journal of Business Ethics* 589 at 591.

[403] J.D. Heydon, 'Directors' Duties and the Company's Interests' in P. Finn (ed), *Equity and Commercial Relationships* (Sydney, Law Book Co, 1987) at 134–135.

[404] E. Elhauge, 'Sacrificing Corporate Profits in the Public Interest' (2005) 80 *New York University Law Review* 733 at 738. The learned professor argues this on the basis that if the discretion were taken away one would destroy the business judgment rule that is so critical to corporate law in the United States.

an equitable and working balance among the claims of the various directly interested groups – stockholders, employees, customers and the public at large,'[405] although this statement was made during a period where a form of stakeholderism prevailed.[406] In the 1920s Owen Young, the President of General Electric said that he acknowledged that he had an obligation to the stockholders to pay a fair rate of return, but he said that he also had an obligation to labour, customers and the public.[407] Far more recently, a corporate reputation survey of Fortune 500 companies (the largest listed companies in the US) found that satisfying the interests of one stakeholder does not automatically mean that this is at the expense of other stakeholders.[408] This is supported by empirical evidence, obtained in a study by the *Financial Times* of Europe's most respected companies, which found that chief executive officers were of the view that one of the features of a good company was the ability to ensure that there was a balancing of the interests of stakeholder groups.[409] Chancellor William Allen of the Delaware Chancery Court has said that the dominant view among leaders for the past 50 years has been that no single constituency's interests should exclude the interests of other constituencies from the fair consideration of the board.[410] Some might regard the following opinion as reflective of business life:

> By definition the leader of a coalition of constituencies, the most important of which are the long-term investors of human and financial capital – the primary risk-takers. In pursuit of a defined corporate mission, the CEO must necessarily gain and maintain the full commitment of *all* constituencies to the common objective, and in the process strike a balance among the competing interests and rewards to each constituency . . .[411] (emphasis in original)

---

[405] Quoted in M. Blair, *Ownership and Control* (Washington DC, The Brookings Institute, 1995) at 212. It is also quoted in N. Craig Smith, *Morality and the Market* (London, Routledge, 1990) at 65 and referred to in J. Parkinson, *Corporate Power and Responsibility* (Oxford, Oxford University Press, 1993) at 494, although the date given in the latter is 1950.

[406] See Chapter 3.

[407] E.M. Dodd, 'For Whom are Corporate Managers Trustees?' (1932) 45 *Harvard Law Review* 1145 at 1154.

[408] L. Preston and H. Sapienza, 'Stakeholder Management and Corporate Performance' (1990) 19 *Journal of Behavioral Economics* 361.

[409] Referred to in E. Scholes and D. Clutterbuck, 'Communication with Stakeholders: An Integrated Approach' (1998) 31 *Long Range Planning* 227 at 230.

[410] 'Our Schizophrenic Conception of the Business Corporation' (1992) 14 *Cardozo Law Review* 261 at 271.

[411] G. Donaldson, 'The Corporate Restructuring of the 1980s – and its Impact for the 1990s' (1994) 6 *Journal of Applied Corporate Finance* 55 at 65.

However, there are clear instances of express support for shareholder value maximisation amongst directors. Many managers say, in effect, that they are bound to act so as to maximise shareholder wealth. The Confederation of British Industry said in its evidence to the Hampel Committee on Corporate Governance that 'directors as a board are responsible for relations with stakeholders; but they are accountable to the shareholders.'[412] Writing in 1991, Lord Hanson of Hanson Plc said that the directors' primary responsibility is to the increase of shareholder value.[413] More recently, in 2006, the chairman of NTL, the cable company, said that: 'We always look to maximise shareholder value.'[414] At about the same time, the chief executive officer of Nestle, Peter Brabeck-Letmathe, advocated shareholder value in a speech at the London Business School.[415] Shell appears to adhere to shareholder primacy for very recently, notwithstanding a large fall in profits, it boosted the dollar value of the dividend by five per cent, but axed 5000 jobs.[416] One quite recent study reports that managers appear to be ready to go to great lengths to ensure that they do not have to reduce dividends and will sell assets, make employees redundant, raise external funds etc rather than cutting dividends.[417] Furthermore, when it comes to consideration of the company's objective, shareholder primacy is often the only theory that is set out in texts and certainly in all those written by law and economics scholars. Undoubtedly there is substance in what Stephen Bottomley states when he takes the view that the theory 'exercises a powerful grip on the mind-set of corporate managers and officers.'[418]

---

[412] *Report of the Committee on Corporate Governance*, 1998 at para 1.17 and quoted in S. Wheeler, 'Fraser and the Politics of Corporate Governance' (1999) *Journal of Law and Society* 241 at 242.

[413] 'Shareholder Value: Touchstone of Managerial Capitalism' (1991) *Harvard Business Review* 141 at 142 (November–December).

[414] E. Judge, 'NTL open to offer as customers drop off' *The Times*, 9 August 2006.

[415] 'Creating Shareholder Value and Corporate Responsibility: Competing Goals?' 2006, and referred to in C. Kelly, 'History Begins: Shareholder Value, Accountability and the Virtuous State' (2009) 60 *Northern Ireland Legal Quarterly* 35 at 41.

[416] C. Mortished, 'Shell to axe 5,000 jobs amid 73% profit fall' *The Times*, 29 October 2009.

[417] N. Daniel, D. Denis and L. Naveen, 'Do Firms Manage Earnings to Meet Dividend Thresholds?' (2008) 45 *Journal of Accounting and Economics* 2 at 2 and referring to A. Brav, J. Graham, C. Harvey and R. Michaely, ' Payout Policy in the 21st Century' (2005) 77 *Journal of Financial Economics* 483. Also, see J. Lintner, 'Distribution of Incomes of Corporations Among Dividends, Retained Earnings, and Taxes' (1956) 46 *American Economic Review* 97.

[418] *The Constitutional Corporation* (Aldershot, Ashgate, 2007) at 8.

9.   CONCLUSION

At the end of the last century D. Gordon Smith asserted in a very well-regarded piece that the shareholder primacy theory 'was one of the most overrated doctrines in corporate law.'[419] Notwithstanding the fact that the theory has been subjected to a number of concerted challenges, there is little doubt that it has shown its resilience. Many managers say, in effect, that they are bound to act so as to maximise shareholder wealth. The theory undoubtedly has some strong points, such as the focus on a single objective which can facilitate more certain management. Nevertheless, significant arguments have been made, successfully it is arguable, against the theory on a number of scores, and it clearly has some major short-comings, such as the fact that it does not produce as much certainty for managers as we are led to believe. It is rather disturbing that there has been so little consideration of how such an influential theory in corporate life, is applied in commercial terms. In addition to the above, its foundations are of questionable worth. The problem is not so much in finding weak-nesses in shareholder primacy, it is replacing the theory with something else. Stakeholder theory is the obvious answer, and that is considered in the next Chapter.

---

[419]   D.G. Smith, 'The Shareholder Primacy Norm' (1998) 23 *Journal of Corporation Law* 277 at 323.

3. Stakeholder theory

1. INTRODUCTION

We now come to the second dominant theory concerning the objective of the company, namely the stakeholder theory (also known as the 'stakeholder model,' 'stakeholder framework' or 'stakeholder management'[1]). This approach operates widely in many continental European and East Asian countries. The prime examples are usually said to be Germany and Japan.

Clearly there are more than just shareholders who contribute to a company. There are others who are affected by the actions of the company. Should the shareholders or non-shareholders with interests in the company or both have their interests taken into account when constructing a normative objective for the company? There are scholars who refer to persons and groups who contribute to the company as stakeholders,[2] constituencies or even contributors. Others count people or groups affected, or potentially affected by the company as stakeholders. For this Chapter I will refer to such people and groups as stakeholders, in order to be consistent with the majority of the literature dealing with the theory, but in later Chapters I prefer to refer to some of them, at least, as investors. Some of these stakeholders do not have contractual protection nor do they have protection afforded by fiduciary duties, and it is argued that their interests deserve consideration by directors when they are managing the affairs of the company. As far as public companies are concerned it has been contended that their affairs are of such broad public concern,

---

[1] R.E. Freeman, *Strategic Management: A Stakeholder Approach* (Boston, Pitman/Ballinger, 1984) at 25. Some regard the last descriptor to be outdated: J. Andriof, B. Hunter, S. Waddock and S. Rahman, 'Introduction' in J. Andriof, B. Hunter, S. Waddock and S. Rahman (eds), *Unfolding Stakeholder Thinking* (Sheffield, Greenleaf Publishing, 2002) at 9.

[2] The term 'stakeholder' is said to have its genesis in a 1963 Stanford Research Institute memorandum where it was used to refer to 'those groups without whose support the organization would cease to exist': R.E. Freeman and D. Reed, 'Stockholders and Stakeholders: A New Perspective on Corporate Governance' (1983) 25 *California Management Review* 88 at 89.

and affect the lives and interests of so many, that they can no longer be managed solely for the benefit of shareholders.[3]

There are several approaches to the objective of the company that may be classified as stakeholder in orientation. Of particular note are the communitarian (or progressive) and pluralist theories that have become popular in corporate law in the past 20 years. Reference will be made to them in places, but the focus of the Chapter is on what is termed 'stakeholder theory'. This might suggest that there is one form of the theory, but that is not correct. This is not unusual with any theory, and shareholder primacy is an example. It has actually been suggested that there is a genre of stakeholder theories, and not one basic theory.[4] What I intend to do here is to discuss the main aspects of stakeholder theory to which most scholars would adhere, but emitting the disclaimer that the Chapter does not purport to cover all possible views that might or might not be said to be influential in the development of stakeholder theory.[5] There have been many variations of certain points that might be seen as critical to the theory. The following statement goes some way to explaining the situation: 'The result [of the literature in the field] is a baffling exchange of stakeholder interpretations and aims that often have little in common and serve to mystify rather than clarify the intellectual terrain, rendering practical applications implausible if not impossible.'[6]

One reason for the greater focus on stakeholder theory is globalisation; companies are now competing globally for success and as a result of such increased competition, the need to attract suppliers and customers and maintain them has become more evident.[7] Furthermore globalisation has played a key role in emphasising the need to recognise stakeholders as an influential force in the modern day company.[8] Some commentators

---

[3] R. Karmel, 'Implications of the Stakeholder Model' (1993) 61 *George Washington Law Review* 1156 at 1171–1175; L. Johnson and D. Millon, 'Corporate Takeovers and Corporate Law: Who's in Control?' (1993) 61 *George Washington Law Review* 1177 at 1197–1207.

[4] R. E. Freeman, 'The Politics of Stakeholder Theory: Some Future Directions' (1994) 4 *Business Ethics Quarterly* 409.

[5] For a discussion, see M. Huse and D. Eide, 'Stakeholder Management and the Avoidance of Corporate Control' (1996) 35 *Business and Society* 211.

[6] C. Stoney and D. Winstanley, 'Stakeholding: Confusion or Utopia? Mapping the Conceptual Terrain' (2001) 38 *Journal of Management Studies* 603 at 604.

[7] E. Scholes and D. Clutterbuck, 'Communication with Stakeholders: An Integrated Approach' (1998) 31 *Long Range Planning* 227.

[8] A. Hillman and G. Keim, 'Shareholder Value, Stakeholder Management and Social Issues: What's The Bottom Line?' (2001) 22 *Strategic Management Journal* 125 at 125.

also point to the rise of the sophisticated customer and the empowered employee as having caused the stakeholder theory to become more dominant within companies.[9] Finally, society today has become more aware of the influence that companies have on the community,[10] and the general public is more ethically tuned into the impact that actions can have on the environment and individual communities.[11]

This chapter begins with an explanation of the stakeholder theory followed by consideration of the rationale that has been given for it. It then considers the arguments that are made in its favour. This is followed by a part of the Chapter that discusses the primary arguments that are mounted against the theory. As with shareholder primacy, the Chapter is not able to deal with all of the issues that relate to stakeholder theory, nor is it able to do justice to all of the literature written; it is voluminous. As adverted to above, those who would place themselves in the stakeholder group vary in thinking, so what is considered here are only what can be regarded as the views held by the majority of scholars and practitioners of the theory. Stakeholding is a broad concept. The theory also continues to develop as scholars seek to address issues which they feel have not been explicated sufficiently, or at all. This is often done to combat the influence of shareholder primacy.

2.   WHAT IS THE THEORY?

Stakeholder theory is clearly a theory that purports to provide us with an account of the purpose of the company.[12] It is a theory of organisational management and ethics that has been evolving as more and more scholars address aspects of it and confront weaknesses in the theory. Before articulating the basic theory we should note that there are three (some might say four) aspects of the theory: normative, descriptive and instrumental. The normative is an explanation, on a moral basis, of how those who are able to be classified as stakeholders should be treated, and it holds that

---

[9]   Ibid.

[10]   E. Scholes and D. Clutterbuck, 'Communication with Stakeholders: An Integrated Approach' (1998) 31 *Long Range Planning* 227 at 228.

[11]   For example, there was great concern in 2006 across the world when it was alleged that the sports brand 'Nike' was using sweat-shop working conditions in the manufacturing of their goods <http://news.bbc.co.uk/1/hi/programmes/panorama/archive/970385.stm> (last visited, 4 April 2010).

[12]   B. Lantry, 'Stakeholders and the Moral Responsibilities of Business' (1994) 4 *Business Ethics Quarterly* 431 at 431.

stakeholders should be seen as 'ends' and not 'means'. Stakeholders are inherently valuable to the company and as a result they should be treated as such in the management of the affairs of the company.[13] It is a legitimacy claim and at its heart is a clear disagreement with shareholder primacy.[14] The descriptive aspect is that the theory is used to explain specific corporate behaviour. The instrumental aspect provides a framework for examining the links between the practice of stakeholder management and a company's performance, and is concerned with looking at how stakeholderism can improve a company's efficiency and success. There is some support amongst commentators for a fourth aspect of the stakeholder theory, and that is the convergent approach. It is a combination of the normative and instrumental aspects.[15]

Undoubtedly, the central core of the theory is normative.[16] The Chapter focuses on the normative, but there is some discussion of some issues that are relevant to the instrumental aspect. This latter aspect tends to provide an approach that is closer to the Anglo-American idea of private ownership in corporate governance, but while it does not advocate moving away from ownership rights it does assert that emphasis should not be on the sole ownership of shareholders as other stakeholders can claim ownership rights.[17] Perhaps the comment of Andrew Campbell that, 'I support stakeholder theory not from some left wing reason of equity, but because I believe it to be fundamental to understanding how to make money in business'[18] is somewhat indicative of some who would take an instrumental approach.

Stakeholding notes that shareholders are merely one of many competing and diverse groups that have an interest in the affairs of a company. A stakeholder approach in general terms is premised on the notion that

---

[13]   S. Reynolds, F. Schultz and D. Hekman, 'Stakeholder Theory and Managerial Decision-Making: Constraints and Implications of Balancing Stakeholder Interests' (2006) 64 *Journal of Business Ethics* 285 at 293.

[14]   B. Van de Ven, 'Human Rights as a Normative Basis for Stakeholder Legitimacy' (2005) 5 *Corporate Governance* 48 at 51.

[15]   T. Jones and A. Wicks, 'Convergent Stakeholder Theory' (1999) 24 *Academy of Management Review* 206.

[16]   T. Donaldson and L. Preston, 'The Stakeholder Theory for the Corporation: Concepts, Evidence, Implications' (1995) 20 *Academy Management Review* 65 at 74.

[17]   S. Letza, X. Sun and J. Kirkbride, 'Shareholding and Stakeholding: a Critical Review of Corporate Governance' (2004) 12 *Corporate Governance: An International Review* 242 at 251.

[18]   'Stakeholders, the Case in Favour' (1997) 30 *Long Range Planning* 446 at 446.

inclusion from a social, economic and political perspective is valuable, and the theory focuses on fostering the full potential of all contributors. The ideal in stakeholderism is that 'all parties work together for a common goal and obtain shared benefits, "opting in" to the business's project,'[19] and all those who contribute critical resources to the company should benefit. So, rather than the company working to create value for shareholders (the company is separate from the shareholders), the theory adheres to the idea that the company works towards creation of value for all stakeholders. Furthermore, it is fundamental to stakeholding that organisations are to be managed for the benefit of, and accountable to, all stakeholders.[20] Stakeholding sees the purpose of the company as providing a vehicle to serve in such a way as to co-ordinate the interests of stakeholders.[21] Stakeholders do not have identical interests, but they do have many common interests.[22] The theory is concerned about the damage that externalities can have on participants in the corporate enterprise.[23] Externalising is the practice of managers externalising costs and retaining benefits for shareholders.[24]

Under this theory it is advocated, in broad terms, that the duty of managers of companies is to create optimal value for all social actors who might be regarded as parties who can affect or are affected by a company's decisions.[25] The argument is that those that are able to affect or be

---

[19]   J. Dean, *Directing Public Companies* (London, Cavendish, 2001) at 94.

[20]   W. Hutton, *The State We're In* (London, Jonathan Cape, 1995).

[21]   W. Evan and R.E. Freeman, 'A Stakeholder Theory of the Modern Corporation' in T. Beauchamp and N. Bowie (eds), *Ethical Theory and Business* (Englewood Cliffs, Prentice Hall, 1974) and referred to in C. Metcalfe, 'The Stakeholder Corporation' (1998) 7 *Business Ethics: A European Review* 30 at 30.

[22]   B. Ford, 'In Whose Interest: An Examination of the Duties of Directors and Officers in Control Contests' (1994) 26 *Arizona State Law Journal* 91 at 101.

[23]   Anon, 'Principles of Stakeholder Management' (2002) 12 *Business Ethics Quarterly* 257 at 258.

[24]   It is argued by some shareholder primacy theorists that departing from shareholder primacy to ensure no externalities would add to agency costs and reduce social wealth: I. Lee, 'Efficiency and Ethics in the Debate About Shareholder Primacy' (2006) 31 *Delaware Journal of Corporate Law* 533 at 539.

[25]   R.E. Freeman, *Strategic Management: a Stakeholder Approach* (Boston, Pitman/Ballinger, 1984). Some would restrict this more than Freeman. For instance, Margaret Blair (*Ownership and Control* (Washington DC, The Brookings Institute, 1995)) in the mid-1990s (she has subsequently embraced team production) limited the number of those social actors who made specific investments in the company (something that she continues to hold to under the team production approach: M. Blair and L. Stout in 'A Team Production Theory of Corporate Law' (1999) 85 *Virginia Law Review* 247).

affected by the company are stakeholders and all stakeholders play a vital role in the success of the company enterprise and they have a right to be regarded as an end and not a means to an end (that is they are not used just to benefit the company in the long run, but their benefits are an end for the company).[26] As a consequence it is necessary for the managers to balance the interests of all (some might restrict it to 'main'[27]) stakeholders in coming to any decisions with the aim of making the company a place where stakeholder interests can be maximised in due course.[28] The theory sees the role of directors as one involving their acting as mediators between the various stakeholders.[29] This is tied up with their obligation to engage in balancing the interests of the stakeholders. Balancing involves 'assessing, weighing and addressing the competing claims of those who have a stake in the actions of the organization . . .,'[30] and it is a critical element in stakeholderism. In undertaking balancing it must be noted by managers that while all stakeholders might be regarded as equal, not all claims and interests of stakeholders are equal or relevant in any given situation. The facts will be determinative, and the outcome of managers' decision-making and who gets what from company outputs is based on a meritocracy, namely what did stakeholders contribute to the enterprise.[31] Managers should engage with stakeholders in mutual respect and ascertain what they are saying, so that there is not one-sided management.[32]

The people who have a stake in the company are generally seen as *including* its: customers, suppliers, creditors, shareholders, lenders, employees, the tax authorities and the local communities. The rights of these groups must be taken into account, and, further, the groups must participate, in

---

[26] R.E. Freeman, *Strategic Management: a Stakeholder Approach* (Boston, Pitman/Ballinger, 1984) at 97.

[27] For example, J. Plender, 'Giving People a Stake in the Future' (1998) 31 *Long Range Planning* 211 at 214.

[28] R.E. Freeman and R. Phillips, 'Stakeholder Theory: A Libertarian Defense' (2002) 12 *Business Ethics Quarterly* 331 at 333.

[29] R. Karmel, 'Implications of the Stakeholder Model' (1993) 61 *George Washington Law Review* 1156 at 1157.

[30] S. Reynolds, F. Schultz and D. Hekman, 'Stakeholder Theory and Managerial Decision-Making: Constraints and Implications of Balancing Stakeholder Interests' (2006) 64 *Journal of Business Ethics* 285 at 286.

[31] R. Phillips, E. Freeman and A. Wicks, 'What Stakeholder Theory is not' (2003) 13 *Business Ethics Quarterly* 488.

[32] J. Andriof, B. Hunter, S. Waddock and S. Rahman, 'Introduction' in J. Andriof, B. Hunter, S. Waddock and S. Rahman (eds), *Unfolding Stakeholder Thinking* (Sheffield, Greenleaf Publishing, 2002) at 9.

some sense, in decisions that substantially affect their welfare.[33] Not only must all stakeholder interests be taken into account, the theory does not endorse any prioritisation of interests of stakeholders in relation to one another. Any inequality between stakeholders would only be acceptable if the action causing it improved the situation of the stakeholder(s) most in need.[34] Managers are obliged to deal transparently and honestly with all stakeholders,[35] and to ask: what will stakeholders feel about the decision that we are contemplating? They then have to consider which stakeholders warrant or require attention and which of them do not?[36]

The notion of stakeholder involves people or groups being seen as having a stake in the company. A stake 'is an asserted or real interest, claim or right, whether legal or moral, or an ownership share in an undertaking.'[37] It is where someone has something that is at risk due to company action.[38]

The idea of 'stakeholder' connotes legitimacy and so it is legitimate for managers to spend time and resources on those who are able to be classed as stakeholders.[39] William Evan and R. Edward Freeman have sought to extend acknowledgment of who are stakeholders to people and groups who have morally valid claims on the company, thus covering a wider spread than those who have been recognised previously.[40] The critical thing is that the company must 'manage its relationships with its specific

---

[33] W. Evan and R.E. Freeman, 'A Stakeholder Theory of the Modern Corporation: Kantian Capitalism' in T. Beauchamp and N. Bowie (eds), *Ethical Theory and Business* (Englewood Cliffs, NJ, Prentice-Hall, 1988) at 103.

[34] R.E. Freeman, 'The Politics of Stakeholder Theory: Some Future Directions' (1994) 4 *Business Ethics Quarterly* 409 at 415.

[35] Anon, 'Principles of Stakeholder Management' (2002) 12 *Business Ethics Quarterly* 257 at 259. How managers should act is set out on page 260 of the article and the principles reproduce those contained in The Clarkson Centre for Business Ethics, *Principles of Stakeholder Management* (Toronto, University of Toronto Press, 1999).

[36] R. Mitchell, B. Agle and D. Wood, 'Toward a Theory of Stakeholder Identification and Salience: Defining the Principle of Who and What Really Counts' (1997) 22 *Academy of Management Review* 853 at 855.

[37] L. Ryan, 'The Evolution of Stakeholder Management: Challenges and Potential Conflicts' (1990) 3 *International Journal of Value Based Management* 105 at 108.

[38] Anon, 'Principles of Stakeholder Management' (2002) 12 *Business Ethics Quarterly* 257 at 258.

[39] R.E. Freeman, *Strategic Management: a Stakeholder Approach* (Boston, Pitman/Ballinger, 1984) at 45.

[40] B. Lantry, 'Stakeholders and the Moral Responsibilities of Business' (1994) 4 *Business Ethics Quarterly* 431 at 432.

stakeholder groups in an action-oriented way.'[41] This involves directors being aware of the effect of their decisions on stakeholder groups.[42] It is trite to say, but as indicated above, no stakeholder has primacy. Stakeholder theory appeals to many people because it has been said to be a matter of 'taming' the 'harsher aspects of capitalism.'[43] The theory asserts that there is more to business than just making money, and it seeks to ensure that the vision of managers is broadened.[44] In her study of the documents of Fortune 100 companies in the United States Lisa Fairfax found that all but two companies included stakeholder rhetoric,[45] and it might be concluded from this that companies do this to offset the negative feelings that come from pursuing the maximisation of shareholder wealth, especially in difficult financial times. Stakeholder theory has portrayed the image of being able to right the wrongs that have been caused by the perceived worst excesses of shareholder primacy in the management of companies such as Enron and WorldCom. It has become 'the vocabulary and methodology for doing this because it is seen as being capable of satisfaction by the construction of a passive notion of social responsibility.'[46]

As with shareholder primacy, it is probably correct to say that the theory's dominance has fallen and risen ever since the 1800s, depending on economic and social conditions. As one might expect, the theory has not been consistently the same throughout corporate history. Perhaps stakeholder ideas can be traced back to J. Maurice Clark in an article in 1916,[47] and it would seem that the first writer to develop the stakeholder idea, but who did not use the term, was Mary Parker Follett in 1918.[48] While it is possible to see this theory in some incipient form in the work

---

[41]   R.E. Freeman, *Strategic Management: a Stakeholder Approach* (Boston, Pitman/Ballinger, 1984) at 53.

[42]   Ibid at 196.

[43]   J. Plender, *The Stakeholding Solution* (London, Nicholas Brealey, 1997) referred to in J. Dean, *Directing Public Companies* (London, Cavendish, 2001) at 117.

[44]   E. Orts and A. Strudler, 'The Ethical and Environmental Limits of Stakeholder Theory' (2002) 12 *Business Ethics Quarterly* 215 at 216.

[45]   L. Fairfax, 'The Rhetoric of Corporate Law: The Impact of Stakeholder Rhetoric on Corporate Norms' (2005) 21 *Journal of Corporation Law* 675 at 677–678.

[46]   S. Wheeler, 'Works Councils: Towards Stakeholding?' (1997) 24 *Journal of Law and Society* 44 at 49.

[47]   'The Changing Basis of Economic Responsibility' (1916) 24 *Journal of Political Economy* 203.

[48]   J. Post, L. Preston and S. Sachs, *Redefining the Corporation – Stakeholder Management and Organizational Wealth* (Stanford, Stanford Business Books, 2002) at 18.

of E. Merrick Dodd in the early 1930s, and a form of it (referred to as the 'benign managerial model'[49]) was applied by academics like Edward Mason[50] and Carl Kaysen[51] in the 1950s as well as being practised by many successful American companies (who made reference to their adopting a 'stakeholder management' approach) in the period from the 1930s to the 1950s,[52] the development of the theory is usually traced to R. Edward Freeman and particularly his influential book, *Strategic Management: A Stakeholder Approach* in 1984.[53] Of course, stakeholder theory in broader social terms has been invoked by several theorists for a great number of years, and one can trace it back to work of a German social theorist, Johannes Althusius, in the seventeenth century,[54] and incipient forms of stakeholder theory have existed since the advent of industrialism.[55] In the early 1980s Freeman called for a re-think about business organisations, arguing that economic theories that had been pre-eminent in the 1970s, and argued for before that period, were outdated.[56] Notwithstanding the fact that many years have now passed, we have yet to see a robust and workable theory of stakeholderism formulated, something on which critics often focus, and an issue to which we will return later.

Freeman's view, when he wrote his seminal book in 1984, was that there are more than just shareholders who contribute to a company, and they can be referred to as stakeholders[57] or constituencies. Some of these

---

[49] By John Parkinson in 'Models of the Company and the Employment Relationship' (2003) 41 *British Journal of Industrial Relations* 481 at 493.

[50] 'The Apologetics of Managerialism' (1958) 31 *Journal of Business* 1.

[51] 'The Social Significance of the Modern Corporation' (1957) 47 *American Economic Review* 311.

[52] See L. Preston, 'Stakeholder Management and Corporate Performance' (199) 19 *Journal of Behavioral Economics* 361 at 362. John Hendry describes this period as marked by 'industrial managerialism': 'Missing the Target: Normative Stakeholder Theory and the Corporate Governance Debate' (2001) 11 *Business Ethics Quarterly* 159 at 160.

[53] Boston, Pitman/Ballinger, 1984.

[54] E. Orts, 'A North American Legal Perspective on Stakeholder Management Theory' in F. MacMillan Patfield (ed), *Perspectives on Company Law: 2* (London, Kluwer, 1997) at 170.

[55] J. Clarke, 'The Stakeholder Corporation: A Business Philosophy for the Information Age' (1998) 31 *Long Range Planning* 182 at 186.

[56] Thus, the theory was a response to the shareholder primacy theory: R. Phillips, 'Stakeholder Theory and a Principle of Fairness' (1997) 7 *Business Ethics Quarterly* 51 at 52.

[57] The term 'stakeholder' is to have its genesis in a 1963 Stanford Research Institute memorandum where it was used to refer to 'those groups without whose support the organization would cease to exist': R.E. Freeman and D. Reed,

stakeholders do not have contractual protection and their interests deserve consideration by directors in how they manage the company and what decisions they make. So, stakeholder theory rejects the idea of maximising a single objective, as one gets with shareholder primacy, where the focus is all on maximising shareholder wealth. As a normative thesis stakeholder theory holds to the legitimacy of the claims on the company that many different groups and people have and this justifies its implementation.[58] In other words, this theory is premised on the idea that in addition to shareholders other groups have claims on the property of companies as they contribute to its capital.[59] As part of this, Freeman has said that it is necessary for a company to identify those who are its stakeholders.[60]

Identifying who are a company's stakeholders is not a straightforward issue; identification has been a rather vexed issue. There are a number of approaches adopted in determining who are stakeholders, and there were 28 different definitions of 'stakeholder' proposed between 1963 and 1995.[61] A leading advocate of stakeholder theory, Max Clarkson, adopted a narrow definition of stakeholders as those who 'bear some form of risk as a result of having invested some form of capital, human or financial, something of value, in a firm.'[62] The approach taken by Clarkson has been endorsed by a substantial number of commentators.[63] Many commentators have distinguished between primary (inside or internal) stakeholders, on the one hand, and secondary (outside or external) stakeholders, on the other, with the former being focused on. Primary stakeholders are seen as those who have a formal, official or contractual relationship with the

---

'Stockholders and Stakeholders: A New Perspective on Corporate Governance' (1983) 25 *California Management Review* 88 at 89.

[58] See T. Donaldson and L. Preston, 'The Stakeholder Theory for the Corporation: Concepts, Evidence, Implications' (1995) 20 *Academy Management Review* 65 at 66–67.

[59] R. Karmel, 'Implications of the Stakeholder Model' (1993) 61 *George Washington Law Review* 1156 at 1171.

[60] R.E. Freeman, *Strategic Management: a Stakeholder Approach* (Boston, Pitman/Ballinger, 1984) at 54 and 196.

[61] R. Mitchell, B. Agle and D. Wood, 'Toward a Theory of Stakeholder Identification and Salience: Defining the Principle of Who and What Really Counts' (1997) 22 *Academy Management Review* 853.

[62] M. Clarkson, 'A Risk Based Model of Stakeholder Theory,' Proceedings of the Second Toronto Conference on Stakeholder Theory, Centre for Corporate Social Performance, University of Toronto, 1994 at 5 and quoted in A. Hillman and G. Klein, 'Shareholder Value, Stakeholder Management and Social Issue. What's the Bottom Line? (2001) 22 *Strategic Management Journal* 125.

[63] For example, E. Orts and A. Strudler, 'The Ethical and Environmental Limits of Stakeholder Theory' (2002) 12 *Business Ethics Quarterly* 215.

company, and without whom the company could not function as a going concern, and many stakeholder theorists have said that there are five internal or primary stakeholders, namely financiers, customers, suppliers, employees, and shareholders, and some might also add communities. These stakeholders will have priority at different times and they will have to be kept contented. They are clearly the kind of stakeholders which Clarkson had in mind. There is a fair degree of interdependence between the company and these stakeholders. Secondary stakeholders are those who have not negotiated with the company, such as the community and the media, but who can have influence and who can affect the company; their interests might on occasions lead to the need for companies to refrain from a particular course of action.[64] Some deny that such are stakeholders as they are not involved, arguably, in value exchanges with the company,[65] while others deny them standing as stakeholders as they have no financial interest in the company.[66] Often it is said that there are six external or secondary stakeholders: governments, environmentalists, NGOs, critics, the media and others.[67]

Archie Carroll divides stakeholders into three categories, namely ones who: have ownership; have a right or claim on the company (and this could be legal or moral); assert an interest in the outcome of the company's business.[68] Some theorists distinguish those who merely influence the company from those who are truly stakeholders.[69] The following are usually identified by most writers and accepted by most scholars as being stakeholders: employees, shareholders, suppliers, financial institutions and lenders, general creditors, customers, the local community, local and national governments, and the environment. Of course, several people might possess a number of overlapping interests and might be both primary and secondary stakeholders. For instance, employees might hold

---

[64]   J. Dean, *Directing Public Companies* (London, Cavendish, 2001) at 99, 103.

[65]   For example, see R. Miller, 'Ethical Challenges in Corporate-Shareholder Investor Relations: Using the Value Exchange Model to Analyze and Respond' (1988) 7 *Journal of Business Ethics* 117 at 121.

[66]   E. Orts and A. Strudler, 'The Ethical and Environmental Limits of Stakeholder Theory' (2002) 12 *Business Ethics Quarterly* 215.

[67]   Y. Fassin, 'The Stakeholder Model Refined' (2009) 84 *Journal of Business Ethics* 113 at 115.

[68]   *Business and Society: Ethics and Stakeholder Management* (Cincinnati, South-Western, 1989) at 56–57.

[69]   T. Donaldson and L. Preston, 'The Stakeholder Theory for the Corporation: Concepts, Evidence, Implications' (1995) 20 *Academy Management Review* 65 at 86.

shares in their company, buy products from their company and live in the community where the company's factory/office is located.

Unlike shareholder primacy which focuses on efficiency, stakeholder theory embraces a number of other values, whilst not, necessarily, rejecting efficiency. The value of trust is an important element in this theory. It is critical that the company secures the trust and, hence, co-operation of its main stakeholder groups in particular.[70] The existence of trust means that there is no need for elaborate contracts to be formulated. As Janice Dean states: 'the decision to trust, in business as elsewhere centres on interpersonal expectations, the willingness to accept temporary vulnerability and optimism about one's partner's behaviour.'[71] Stakeholder theorists will argue that trust can lead to enhanced reputation. It also means that if action that might be contrary to a stakeholder's interests is contemplated, the managers need to explain the thinking behind the action and what are the consequences. The emphasis of the theory on values such as trust means that the involvement of stakeholders cannot be priced.

It has been said that there should be provision for rules in companies that ensure the relations between stakeholders are governed by justice and these rules must be endorsed by the stakeholders.[72] Some have taken this view further and argued that there should be a board of directors that is representative of the stakeholders in a company,[73] so, not only shareholders should get to vote for the directors. Kent Greenfield asserts that the best way for a board to engage in decision-making is to have all important stakeholders represented on it. The learned commentator acknowledges that this mechanism presents difficulties but argues that employees, the communities in which the company employs a significant portion of its workers, long-term business partners and creditors could all be represented.[74] We shall return to this later. On the subject of directors, in such a system as stakeholding the directors are perceived as trustees of the stakeholders' interests, and they are to have a focus on the

---

[70]   C. Handy, *The Hungry Spirit* (London, Hutchinson and Co, 1997) at 181.

[71]   J. Dean, *Directing Public Companies* (London, Cavendish, 2001) at 107.

[72]   N. Bowie, 'A Kantian Theory of Capitalism' (1998) 8 *Business Ethics Quarterly* 37 at 47.

[73]   For example, K. Greenfield, 'Saving the World With Corporate Law' (2008) 57 *Emory Law Journal* 947 at 978; F. Post, 'A Response to "The Social Responsibility of Corporate Management: A Classical Critique"' (2003) 18 *Mid-American Journal of Business* 25 at 32. This issue is discussed briefly in Chapter 5.

[74]   'Reclaiming Corporate Law in a New Gilded Age' (2008) 2 *Harvard Law and Policy Review* 1 at 24.

long-term future of the company,[75] while they act as stewards of all that they manage.

In an attempt to have the theory taken seriously, Dean has suggested the following as an appropriate legislative provision that allows for stakeholding:

> A director of a public limited company shall in all his/her conduct and decision making so act as to advance the development of the company in the interests of its customers, its employees and its shareholders and with proper regard for the effect of its operations on the environment and on the community. The interests to which a director of a public company should give due consideration include:
> - The provision for customers of safe and effective goods and services of good quality at fair prices
> - The provision for employees of fair remuneration and secure work with reasonable opportunity for their interests to be heard within the company and for their promotion and development of skills
> - The provision for shareholders of fair returns to remunerate past investment and encourage future investment in the company
> - The provision for key business associates including suppliers of goods and services of secure relationships and ongoing co-operation where such connections offer advantages to both parties
> - The provision for the community of programmes to monitor and mini-mise the environmental impact of the company's operations and advance responsible conduct towards the company's neighbours.[76]

Aspects of what Dean proposes can be seen in s.172 of the UK's Companies Act 2006.[77]

According to some theorists, the theory is founded on fairness, in that it provides that those who provide resources to the company are entitled to a return on their contributions.[78] Robert Phillips puts it this way:

---

[75]   J. Plender, 'Giving People a Stake in the Future' (1998) 31 *Long Range Planning* 211 at 215.

[76]   J. Dean, *Directing Public Companies* (London, Cavendish, 2001) at 138

[77]   For a discussion of which, see, for example, A. Keay, 'Enlightened Shareholder Value, the Reform of the Duties of Corporation Directors and the Corporate Objective' [2006] *Lloyds Maritime and Commercial Law Quarterly* 335; S. Kiarie, 'At Crossroads: Shareholder Value, Stakeholder Value and Enlightened Shareholder Value: Which Road Should the United Kingdom Take?' (2006) 17 *International Corporation and Commercial Law Review* 329; A. Keay, *Directors' Duties* (Bristol, Jordan Publishing, 2009), Chapter 6; A. Keay, 'Moving Towards Stakeholderism? Constituency Statutes, Enlightened Shareholder Value and All That: Much Ado About Little?' (2011) 22 *European Business Law Review* 1.

[78]   C. Metcalfe, 'The Stakeholder Corporation, (1998) 7 *Business Ethics: A European Review* 30 at 32.

Whenever persons or groups of persons voluntarily accept the benefits of a mutually beneficial scheme of co-operation requiring sacrifice or contribution on the parts of the participants and there exists the possibility of free-riding, obligations of fairness are created among the participants in the co-operative scheme in proportion to the benefits accepted.[79]

Phillips argues that commercial transactions are able to be encompassed by the concept of co-operative schemes and he also takes the view that consent is not necessary for a person to be regarded as a stakeholder.[80] He opines that the fairness principle is able to take business relations and reconceptualise them as co-operative rather than adversarial.[81] This approach, he argues, is likely to enable a resolution to a conflict situation between stakeholders to be sought.

Other scholars rely on different moral bases for the theory. For example, Evan and Freeman base their views on Kantian philosophical foundations, with some reliance on social contract theory.[82] This is discussed later. They also argue that stakeholders giving careful consideration in a rational fashion behind a Rawlsian veil of ignorance would adopt principles of fair contracting that would produce management for all stakeholders.[83] Another scholar, Antonio Argandona, argues that the theory can be based on the concept of the common good.[84] The common good involves establishing the conditions that enable those linked with a company to achieve their personal goals.[85] Thomas Donaldson and Lee Preston suggest a base that is built upon property rights and posit the idea that stakeholder rights can compete with those of shareholders.[86] Yet another basis given is that

---

[79] 'Stakeholder Theory and a Principle of Fairness' (1997) 7 *Business Ethics Quarterly* 51 at 57.

[80] Ibid at 59.

[81] Ibid at 64.

[82] W. Evan and R.E. Freeman, 'A Stakeholder Theory of the Modern Corporation: Kantian Capitalism' in T. Beauchamp and N. Bowie (eds), *Ethical Theory and Business* (Englewood Cliffs, NJ, Prentice-Hall, 1988).

[83] R.E. Freeman and W. Evan, 'Corporate Governance: A Stakeholder Interpretation' (1990) 19 *Journal of Behavioral Economics* 337. This is critiqued by J. Child and A. Marcoux in 'Freeman and Evan: Stakeholder Theory in the Original Position' (1999) 9 *Business Ethics Quarterly* 207.

[84] 'The Stakeholder Theory and the Common Good' (1998) 17 *Journal of Business Ethics* 1093.

[85] A. Argandona, 'The Stakeholder Theory and the Common Good' (1998) 17 *Journal of Business Ethics* 1093 at 1097.

[86] 'The Stakeholder Theory for the Corporation: Concepts, Evidence, Implications' (1995) 20 *Academy Management Review* 65. The learned authors do not develop the view.

failure by managers to consider stakeholders would be a breach of the latter's human rights.[87] This justification obviously only applies to those who can be regarded as primary stakeholders and who have a formal, official or contractual relationship with the company.

Unlike shareholder value, and the communitarian movement, both of which separate the economic and the ethical, stakeholder theory embraces both, with the theory being used as a basis for translating business ethics to management practice and strategy.[88] The separation provided for under shareholder primacy, together with a focus on a single objective, means that shareholder value provides a narrow approach that cannot 'do justice to the panoply of human activity that is value creation and trade, i.e., business.'[89] The relationship between economics and ethics has always been ambiguous[90] and stakeholder theory seeks to bring the two together.[91] Some stakeholder theorists even embrace a form of agency theory, with stakeholders being regarded as principals.[92] Also, while the nexus of contracts metaphor for the company is often associated with the shareholder primacy theory, some of those holding to stakeholder theory accept such a metaphor on the basis that all corporate constituents are part of the nexus and all are on an equal footing.[93] However, some groups who are generally thought of as stakeholders in most companies, such as suppliers and customers, are arguably not regarded as part of the company in this theory.[94]

Under the theory, companies should be prepared to make disclosures to stakeholders where appropriate and the latter should be encouraged by

---

[87]   B. Van der Veer 'Human Rights as a Normative Basis for Stakeholder Legitimacy' (2005) 5 *Corporate Governance: International Review* 48.

[88]   Y. Fassin, 'The Stakeholder Model Refined' (2009) 84 *Journal of Business Ethics* 113 at 113.

[89]   R.E. Freeman, A. Wicks and B. Parmar, 'Stakeholder Theory and "The Corporate Objective Revisited"' (2004) 15 *Organization Science* 364 at 364.

[90]   J. Hendry, 'Missing the Target: Normative Stakeholder Theory and the Corporate Governance Debate' (2001) 11 *Business Ethics Quarterly* 159 at 161.

[91]   Interestingly, Elaine Sternberg, a shareholder primacy supporter also purports to bring them together: E. Sternberg, *Just Business*, 2nd ed (Oxford, Oxford University Press, 2000).

[92]   C. Hill and T. Jones, 'Stakeholder-Agency Theory' (1992) 19 *The Journal of Management Studies* 131.

[93]   For example, see M. Eisenberg, 'The Conception That the Corporation is a Nexus of Contracts, and the Dual Nature of the Firm' (1999) 24 *Journal of Corporation Law* 819 at 833.

[94]   L. Zingales, 'In Search of New Foundations' (2000) 55 *Journal of Finance* 1623 at 1634.

the former to be involved in the life of the company.[95] While so often the emphasis is on the relationship between stakeholders and the company (represented by the managers), theorists do emphasise also the fact that stakeholders do interact with one another.

As mentioned a little earlier, the theory is concerned with those who have a voice in the decision-making process in companies in addition to the results of that process,[96] so some theorists have argued for the need for institutional representation, namely places on the board of directors for the various stakeholders,[97] something which has been high on the pluralist theory's agenda. While employee representation is usually associated with corporate systems where there are two-tier boards of directors, it has been pointed out that Denmark, Sweden and Luxembourg all have employee representatives on one-tier boards of directors.[98]

Finally, while few theorists come to terms with how they see the nature of the company, as they are more concerned with what the company does, it might be said that many would agree with Ayuso et al that it is 'a public association constituted through political and legal processes as a social entity for the pursuing of collective goals with public obligations.'[99]

3. THE RATIONALE FOR, AND ARGUMENTS IN FAVOUR OF, THE THEORY

Some take the view that shareholder primacy in fact damages the interests of non-shareholding stakeholders and this forms the basis for a legitimate claim that these stakeholders warrant some consideration and protection

---

[95]   J. Dean, *Directing Public Companies* (London, Cavendish, 2001), at 101

[96]   R.E. Freeman, *Strategic Management: a Stakeholder Approach* (Boston, Pitman/Ballinger, 1984) at 196; R. Phillips, E. Freeman and A. Wicks, 'What Stakeholder Theory is not' (2003) 13 *Business Ethics Quarterly* 487.

[97]   W. Evan and R. E. Freeman, 'A Stakeholder Theory of the Modern Corporation: Kantian Capitalism' in T. Beauchamp and N. Bowie (eds), *Ethical Theory and Business* (Englewood Cliffs, Prentice-Hall, 1988); K. Greenfield, 'Reclaiming Corporate Law in a New Gilded Age' (2008) 2 *Harvard Law and Policy Review* 1 at 24.

[98]   F. Allen, E. Carletti, and R. Marquez, 'Stakeholder Capitalism, Corporate Governance and Firm Value,' August 4, 2007, Working Paper, University of Pennsylvania, at 6, and accessible at: <http://knowledge.wharton.upenn.edu/papers/1344.pdf> (last visited, 3 August 2009).

[99]   S. Ayuso et al, 'Maximising Stakeholders' Interests: An Empirical Analysis of the Stakeholder Approach to Corporate Governance,' IESE Business School, University of Navarra, Working Paper No 670, January 2007 at 3.

in the management of a company's affairs.[100] But, theorists provide other
rationales for stakeholding. Perhaps one of the classic statements is made
by Freeman and his co-authors when they express the rationale behind the
theory in this way:

> Business is about putting together a deal so that suppliers, customers, employ-
> ees, communities, managers and shareholders all win continuously over time.
> In short, at some level, stakeholder interests have to be joint – they must
> be traveling in the same direction – or else there will be exit, and a new
> collaboration formed.[101]

There are two points here. First, a company needs a number of contributors to ensure that it thrives and survives. If directors do not consider
other stakeholders then these people and groups will have no commitment
to the company and this might lead to withdrawal of their investment or
their unwillingness to support the company when it is in need. All of this
could affect the performance and wealth of the company, thereby failing
to enhance social wealth.

The second point is that it is the best deal for everyone if the company
is run in such a manner that as much value for stakeholders as possible is
created.[102] Shareholder value advocates say similar things, but get there
via a different route. The stakeholder theory school seems to argue that
it is clearly more reasonable and beneficial to take into account all stakeholders rather than pursue shareholder primacy. It is argued that for a
company to thrive it must: produce competitive returns for shareholders;
satisfy customers in order to produce profits; recruit and motivate excellent employees; build successful relationships with suppliers.[103] It has been
asserted that stakeholding is the instrument through which efficiency,
profitability, competition and economic success can be promoted on the
basis that if one removed cohesion among stakeholders it would not be

---

[100]   D. Millon, 'Communitarianism in Corporate Law: Foundations and
Law Reform Strategies' in L. Mitchell (ed), *Progressive Corporate Law* (Boulder,
Colorado, Westview Press, 1995) at 3.

[101]   R.E. Freeman, A. Wicks and B. Parmar, 'Stakeholder Theory and "The
Corporate Objective Revisited"' (2004) 15 *Organization Science* 364 at 365
and referring to S. Venkataraman, 'Stakeholder Value Equilibration and the
Entrepreneurial Process' in R. E. Freeman and S. Venkataraman (eds), *The
Ruffin Series No 3: Ethics and Entrepreneurship* (Charlottesville, Philosophy
Documentation Center, 2002), at 45.

[102]   R. E. Freeman, A. Wicks and B. Parmar, 'Stakeholder Theory and "The
Corporate Objective Revisited"' (2004) 15 *Organization Science* 364 at 365.

[103]   J. Dean, *Directing Public Companies* (London, Cavendish, 2001) at 251.

possible for companies to be competitive.[104] The huge mining company, BHP Billiton, has acknowledged this and states that it seeks a competitive advantage by exploring new ways of approaching and engaging in relationships with its key stakeholders.[105]

The theory provides that if the interests of stakeholders in general are catered for and such stakeholders are shown loyalty, then the shareholders will benefit more than if shareholder maximisation were practised because the company would benefit and it would also produce greater social wealth.[106] However, many shareholder primacy theorists will argue that shareholders' interests have to be first priority or else the company will not prosper. The fact of the matter is that it is probably a matter of the degree to which stakeholder interests are taken into account, and what happens when there is a conflict between shareholder interests and the interests of other stakeholders. Shareholder primacy would say that the former are automatically to be preferred, while stakeholder theory would probably say that it all depends on a number of factors and would depend on balancing. Dean states that '[i]f the board had to consider the interests of all relevant stakeholders and the standards expected of directors were more clearly defined in law, the position would become simpler overall.'[107] The reason she gives for this is that it will enhance the company's reputation and lead others to feel that the company operates on principles and can be trusted. All of this would, Dean asserts, benefit everyone involved.[108] If stakeholders' interests are taken into account by managers in running the company, and stakeholders are going to be rewarded, it is likely that they will be more ready 'to go the extra mile' in their dealings with the company.[109] Employees might devote more time and care to their labour, suppliers might be ready to deliver smaller quantities of goods when to do so might be of

---

[104] A. Campbell, 'Stakeholders, the Case in Favour' (1997) 30 *Long Range Planning* 446 at 446.

[105] BHP Billiton, *Submission 13*, p1 to the Australian Joint Parliamentary Committee on Corporations and Financial Services, *Corporate Responsibility: Managing Risk and Creating Value*, June 2006 para 4.46 and accessible at <http://www.aph.gov.au/senate/committee/corporations_ctte/completed_inquiries/2004-07/corporate_responsibility/report/index.htm> (last visited, 16 December 2009) and referred to at para 3.18 of the report.

[106] K. Greenfield, 'Saving the World With Corporate Law' (2008) 57 *Emory Law Journal* 947 at 975.

[107] J. Dean, *Directing Public Companies* (London, Cavendish, 2001) at 108

[108] Ibid.

[109] J. Plender, 'Giving People a Stake in the Future' (1998) 31 *Long Range Planning* 211 at 215.

marginal economic benefit to them, and customers will remain loyal through difficult times.

Besides relying on the need to keep stakeholders involved in companies, Freeman and Philips have argued for the theory on the basis that stakeholders deserve protection as they have property rights in the company to which they have contributed. For instance, suppliers have property in what they supply to the company.[110] The argument is that stakeholder groups besides shareholders have a claim on the company's property and profits as they contributed to the capital of the company;[111] they have risked their investment in the company. The point is often made that stakeholders make firm specific investments in the company. For instance, employees may make investments in companies such as undergoing specialised training that might not be able to be used elsewhere, and suppliers might acquire specialised machinery to enable them to supply the company with particular kinds of products and this machinery could not be used on any other contracts that they have or hope to obtain in the future.

Leaving aside any notion of property rights, it is often argued that stakeholders warrant protection on other grounds. It was noted in Chapter 2 that non-shareholder constituencies are said to be protected by contract, but the riposte to that was that most stakeholders are unable to negotiate on an even footing. So, a normative foundation for providing protection for stakeholders is that it makes sure that the legitimate expectations of such people that are above and beyond the terms of any contract are fulfilled.[112] When stakeholders get involved with a company then it might be argued that this elicits an implied promise that the directors will consider the interests of the stakeholders. This is a form of social contract approach to the issue.

It is argued, from an efficiency viewpoint, that as managers do not generally have any real personal association and ties with shareholders, yet they do have with many of those who can be regarded as stakeholders,[113]

---

[110] R. E. Freeman and R. Phillips, 'Stakeholder Theory: A Libertarian Defense' (2002) 12 *Business Ethics Quarterly* 331 at 338.

[111] R. Karmel, 'Implications of the Stakeholder Model' (1993) 61 *George Washington Law Review* 1156 at 1171.

[112] W. Leung, 'The Inadequacy of Shareholder Primacy: A Proposed Corporate Regime that Recognizes Non-Shareholder Interests' (1997) 30 *Columbia Journal of Law and Social Problems* 589 at 622.

[113] E.M. Dodd, 'Is Effective Enforcement of the Fiduciary Duties of Corporate Managers Practicable?' (1935) 2 *University of Chicago Law Review* 194 at 202–203.

they can do a better job if they practise stakeholderism. The managers regularly deal with: employees in relation to how to get the job done and negotiating working conditions; suppliers concerning things like the state of the goods delivered and the non-delivery of goods ordered; customers who complain about the goods that the corporation markets; local communities about what the company is doing or not doing as a corporate citizen. If managers practise stakeholder theory they can really take into account what is said to them by stakeholders and, in many cases, demonstrate that they are considering the interests of the stakeholders. Consequently, managers gain respect and trust in the eyes of stakeholders and, importantly for the company, they can do their job better and more efficiently.

It has been said that the running of the modern company leads to interdependencies involving many groups for whom the company should have a legitimate concern.[114] If the reasonable expectations of such groups are not met then the long-term profitability of the company will suffer, and the theory is concerned about the long term. Taking into account all stakeholders' interests recognises the interdependence of parties involved in companies and is likely to pre-empt selfish competition between constituents.[115] Where conflict between stakeholders cannot be avoided, then managers are to embrace actions that will at least compensate stakeholders for any loss suffered.[116]

It has been noted already that the stakeholder theory rejects the idea of maximising a single objective. As a normative thesis the theory holds to the legitimacy of the claims on the company that many different groups and people have and this justifies its implementation.[117] It has been asserted that: '[T]he economic and social purpose of the corporation is to create and distribute wealth and value to all its primary stakeholder groups, without favoring one group at the expense of others.'[118]

---

[114] R. Karmel, 'Implications of the Stakeholder Model' (1993) 61 *George Washington Law Review* 1156 at 1169.

[115] L. Mitchell, 'A Theoretical and Practical Framework for Enforcing Corporate Constituency Statutes' (1992) 70 *Texas Law Review* 579 at 641–643.

[116] D. Millon, 'Communitarianism in Corporate Law: Foundations and Law Reform Strategies' in L. Mitchell (ed), *Progressive Corporate Law* (Boulder, Colorado, Westview Press, 1995) at 12.

[117] See T. Donaldson and L. Preston, 'The Stakeholder Theory for the Corporation: Concepts, Evidence, Implications' (1995) 20 *Academy Management Review* 65 at 66–67.

[118] M. Clarkson, 'A Stakeholder Framework for Analyzing and Evaluating Corporate Social Performance' (1995) 20 *Academy Management Review* 92 at 112.

In comparison with shareholder primacy, no grouping has prima facie priority over another,[119] for no group warrants priority over any other groups.[120] Donaldson and Preston have said that 'each group of stakeholders merits consideration for its own sake and not merely because of its ability to further the interests of some group, such as shareowners.'[121] Unlike in shareholder primacy, where stakeholders are treated as means, the theory provides that stakeholders should be treated as ends. The adherents to this theory have advocated concepts of individual autonomy and fairness to all members of society.[122] The theory holds to equality of all stakeholders in that they all have intrinsic value and all are entitled morally to be considered in the management of the company's affairs and to be considered simultaneously,[123] and, according to some, even if they do not advance the interests of shareholders.[124] The rights of these groups must be assured, and, further, the groups must participate, in some sense, in decisions that substantially affect their welfare.[125] The moral basis is that a duty is imposed on all organisations in relation to all individuals involved with them. Failure to do so would be a breach of human rights irrespective of who was the stakeholder prejudiced.[126] This ties in with the arguments of the communitarian (or progressive) school that stakeholders who are not shareholders are entitled to consideration being shown to them because they are owed more than what they have bargained for.

---

[119]   T. Donaldson and L. Preston, 'The Stakeholder Theory for the Corporation: Concepts, Evidence, Implications' (1995) 20 *Academy Management Review* 65.

[120]   M. Omran, P. Atrill and J. Pointon, 'Shareholders Versus Stakeholders: Corporate Mission Statements And Investor Returns' (2002) 11 *Business Ethics: A European Review* 318 at 318.

[121]   T. Donaldson and L. Preston, 'The Stakeholder Theory for the Corporation: Concepts, Evidence, Implications' (1995) 20 *Academy Management Review* 65 at 67.

[122]   For example, J. Boatright, 'Fiduciary Duties and the Shareholder-Management Relation: Or, What's So Special About Shareholders?' (1994) 4 *Business Ethics Quarterly* 393.

[123]   R. Mitchell, 'Toward a Theory of Stakeholder Identification and Salience: Defining the Principle of Who and What Really Counts' (1997) 22 *Academy Management Review* 853 at 862.

[124]   R. Marens and A. Wicks, 'Getting Real: Stakeholder Theory, Managerial Practice and the General Irrelevance of Fiduciary Duties Owed to Shareholders' (1999) 9 *Business Ethics Quarterly* 273 at 274.

[125]   W. Evan and R.E. Freeman, 'A Stakeholder Theory of the Modern Corporation: Kantian Capitalism' in T. Beauchamp and N. Bowie (eds), *Ethical Theory and Business* (Englewood Cliffs, Prentice-Hall, 1988) at 103.

    Phillips, E. Freeman and A. Wicks, 'What Stakeholder Theory is not' *Business Ethics Quarterly* 494.

It asserts that those involved in a company owe each other respect and support.[127]

As mentioned earlier, emphasis in stakeholder theory is placed on trust, and a number of stakeholders have to rely on trust and virtually nothing else. The advantage of trustworthiness for the company is that it can lead to an enhanced reputation. If there is trust between companies and their stakeholders, it is argued that it can reduce costs as stakeholders do not have to monitor the company and its affairs so much, or at all; they can trust the managers to do their job properly.

Many of the arguments in favour of the theory are economic or economic related, but stakeholding also has a moral basis in that it provides for how moral agents should treat each other. This reflects, according to some, a deontological or duty foundation whereby persons should respect others. Some look to the writings of the philosopher, Immanuel Kant, in this regard, and say that the idea of respecting others (as equals) and seeing all groups as having intrinsic worth, leads to us seeing people not as means to ends, but ends in themselves.[128] Hence, they should not be seen as ways of making profits for shareholders. Another moral basis is that distributive justice entitles stakeholders to a share of the corporate earnings as they have contributed to the creation of the earnings and they had legitimate expectations that they would share in earnings when they made their contributions.

The discussion in the last paragraph is taken further on the basis that many stakeholders must rely on fair treatment as they are not able to obtain protection for a number of reasons, such as lack of bargaining power, ignorance or insufficient funds to pay necessary costs (e.g. legal costs). In a real world it is infrequent that there are contractual arrangements made by equals. In many contracts there is a 'take it leave it approach' with the result that costs are imposed on third parties with whom the company does business.[129] Several scholars have reported the fact that contracts involving stakeholders are not complete and not perfectly priced.[130] This is due to a number of factors, including the fact that

---

[127] D. Millon, 'Communitarianism in Corporate Law: Foundations and Law Reform Strategies' in L. Mitchell (ed), *Progressive Corporate Law* (Boulder, Colorado, Westview Press, 1995) at 4.

[128] K. Gibson, 'The Moral Basis of Stakeholder Theory' (2000) 26 *Journal of Business Ethics* 245 at 248. Also, see T. Donaldson and L. Preston, 'The Stakeholder Theory for the Corporation: Concepts, Evidence, Implications' (1995) 20 *Academy Management Review* 65 at 67.

[129] F. Easterbrook and D. Fischel, 'Antitrust Suits by Targets of Tender Offers' (1982) 80 *Michigan Law Review* 1155 at 1156.

[130] J. Fisch, 'Measuring Efficiency in Corporate Law: The Rule of Shareholder Primacy' December 2005, Fordham Law Legal Studies, Working Paper No 105

stakeholders, like all people, are subject to bounded rationality: people are rational rather than hyper-rational. As Professor Dale Tauke has said:

> The ability of contracting parties to enter into complete contingent claims contracts in the face of complex and uncertain contingencies is limited by the bounded rationality of the parties – the limits of the human mind in comprehending and solving complex problems.[131]

It could be said that stakeholder theory is consistent with the fact that the world has become more and more complex and as a result the affairs and decisions of companies affect or are affected by an increasing number of people and groups. An example is environmental issues, which until more recent times have not been regularly or widely seen as being of major concern to companies. Stakeholder theorists will often say that their theory takes in the complexity of the world, whereas shareholder primacy is far too glib.

Undoubtedly this model has a lot of attraction. It emphasises values that are endearing. Trust and fairness are prime examples. The model also seeks to embrace both economics and ethics, which have been elements that have been difficult to balance. The focus on stakeholders has, as we have noted, several advantages, but there are drawbacks and a number of concerns have been raised in relation to the theory and we now turn to examine them.

4. CONCERNS WITH, AND ARGUMENTS AGAINST, THE THEORY

Some leading writers have proclaimed boldly that stakeholder theory is generally so pre-eminent that shareholder primacy is dead.[132] Yet, while the stakeholder theory has spread rapidly as far as its influence and application,[133] there are many criticisms of the theory in the literature.

---

at p29 and available at <http://ssrn.com/abstract=878391> (last visited, 27 July 2009).

[131]   Dale B. Tauke, 'Should Bondholders Have More Fun? A Reexamination of the Debate Over Corporate Bondholder's Rights' [1989] *Columbia Business Law Review* 1 at 15, n28.

[132]   For example, R.E. Freeman, 'The Politics of Stakeholder Theory: Some Future Directions' (1994) 4 *Business Ethics Quarterly* 409 at 413.

[133]   P. Ireland, 'Corporate Governance, Stakeholding, and the Company: generate Capitalism' (1996) 23 *Journal of Law and Society* 287

In general terms the theory has been said to be 'naive, superficial and unrealistic.'[134] One of the principal critics has said that the theory is 'deeply dangerous and wholly unjustified'[135] on the basis that it 'undermines private property, denies agents' duties to principals, and destroys wealth.'[136] It has even been said that it does not have the status of a theory but it is merely a research tradition,[137] or a framework, and the literature dealing with stakeholder theory has tended to focus on justifying the approach, rather than developing a systematic theory.[138]

This Part of the Chapter seeks to identify and examine the concerns that have been expressed about the stakeholder theory as well as analysing the primary arguments that have been raised against the theory by critics. A number of the concerns considered and arguments put forward against the theory can be said to overlap, but it is helpful for purposes of exposition and clarity to try and classify arguments under particular headings.

4.1 Lack of Solid Normative Foundations

The point has been made that stakeholder theory has failed to refer to normative foundations as a justification for it.[139] It fails to provide a normative base to enable one to ascertain who can be a stakeholder and what weight ought to be given to each stakeholder.[140] The consequence is that it is often argued that there is no basis for a manager to prefer stakeholderism to other moral approaches in running the company.

---

[134] C. Stoney and D. Winstanley, 'Stakeholder Confusion or Utopia? Mapping the Conceptual Terrain' (2001) 38 *Journal of Management Studies* 600 at 606.

[135] E. Sternberg, 'The Defects of Stakeholder Theory' (1997) 5 *Corporate Governance: An International Review* 3 at 6.

[136] Ibid at 9.

[137] L. Trevino and G. Weaver, 'The Stakeholder Research Tradition: Converging Theorists – not Convergent Theory' (1999) 24 *Academy of Management Review* 222.

[138] S. Learmount, 'Theorizing Corporate Governance: New Organizational Alternatives' (2003) 14 *Journal of Interdisciplinary Economics* 159.

[139] T. Donaldson, *The Ethics of International Business* (New York, Oxford University Press, 1989) at 45. See, A. Argandona, 'The Stakeholder Theory and the Common Good' (1998) 17 *Journal of Business Ethics* 1093; F. Lépineux, 'Stakeholder Theory, Society and Social Cohesion' (2005) 5 *Corporate Governance: An International Review* 99 at 99; S. Wheeler, *Corporations and the Third Way* (Oxford, Hart Publishing, 2002) at 6.

[140] T. Donaldson and T. Dunfee, 'Toward a Unified Conception of Business Ethics: Integrative Social Contracts Theory (1994) 19 *Academy of Management Review* 252.

This problem arises because explanations of the philosophical bases of the theory have differed with the various apologists for the theory. As discussed earlier, Robert Phillips has sought to build a foundation using the principle of fairness,[141] while Evan and Freeman[142] have employed Kantian principles. Kant had espoused the view that humans are to: 'act in such a way that you always treat humanity, whether in your own person or in the person of any other, never simply as a means, but always at the same time as an end.'[143] A criticism of the employment of this view is that the Kantian approach provides that humans as rational moral agents are to be regarded as ends in themselves, but the stakeholder theory generally identifies non-persons, such as the environment as a stakeholder,[144] so this basis for the theory does not work for it.

4.2   Lack of Clarity

In general terms one of the major criticisms has been that the concepts underpinning stakeholder theory are confusing.[145] Even zealous stakeholder theorists have said that the theory suffers from vagueness, ambiguity and breadth.[146] James Humber is of the view that the theory appears to be a collage and its elements are at odds with one another, so it has no systematic coherence.[147] Goyder says that in adopting stakeholderism in lieu of shareholder primacy one is sacrificing clarity for blancmange,[148] presumably because blancmange is difficult to get hold of. One of the major problems

---

[141]   'Stakeholder Theory and a Principle of Fairness' (1997) 7 *Business Ethics Quarterly* 51.

[142]   Freeman has asserted that no normative foundational justification is necessary: 'Ending the So-called "Friedman-Freeman" Debate' in B. Agle, T. Donaldson, R. E. Freeman, M. Jensen, R. Mitchell and D. Wood, 'Dialogue: Towards Superior Stakeholder Theory' (2008) 18 *Business Ethics Quarterly* 153 at 161.

[143]   I. Kant, 'Groundwork of the Metaphysic of Morals' translated in H.J. Paton, *The Moral Law* (Hutchinson, 1948) at 91.

[144]   E. Steinberg, 'The Defects of Stakeholder Theory' (1997) 5 *Corporate Governance: An International Review* at 3 at 6.

[145]   For instance, see C. Stoney and D. Winstanley, 'Stakeholder Confusion or Utopia? Mapping the Conceptual Terrain' (2001) 38 *Journal of Management Studies* 600; F. Lepineux, 'Stakeholder Theory, Society and Social Cohesion' (2005) 5 *Corporate Governance: An International Review* 99.

[146]   R. Phillips, E. Freeman and A. Wicks, 'What Stakeholder Theory is Not' (2003) 13 *Business Ethics Quarterly* 479.

[147]   'Beyond Stockholders and Stakeholders: A Plea for Moral Autonomy' (2002) 36 *Journal of Business Ethics* 207 at 215.

[148]   M. Goyder, *Living Tomorrow's Company* (Hampshire, Gower, 1998) at 3.

that the theory faces is that it is not always clearly articulated. It has been said that stakeholding is 'a slippery creature . . . used by different people to mean widely different things which happen to suit their arguments.'[149]

Many proposals have been propounded but they have tended to rely on 'a serious mismatch of variables which are mixed and correlated almost indiscriminately with a set of stakeholder-related performance variables that are not theoretically linked.'[150] Another reason that is given is that 'most work in this field appears to be preoccupied with justifying a stakeholder approach to the firm rather than the construction of a systematic theory to describe more adequately contemporary organizational practices.'[151] Further confusion might come from the fact that the theory provides that it is morally correct for companies to be managed for stakeholders means that it is inconsistent with the relativism of the theory.[152]

First and foremost, stakeholder theory has been a difficult concept to define.[153] There has been difficulty in identifying and defining stakeholders,[154] and there has been a variety of signals emitted on how stakeholders can be identified.[155] In fact the number of stakeholders can be very significant. One of the main difficulties for the theory, and acknowledged by stakeholder theorists themselves,[156] has been in identifying and

---

[149] M. V. Weyer, 'Ideal World' (1996) *Management Today*, September, 35 at 35.

[150] D.J. Wood and R.E. Jones, 'Stakeholder Mismatching: a Theoretical Problem in Empirical Research on Corporate Social Performance' (1995) 3(3) *The International Journal of Organizational Analysis* 229 at 231.

[151] S. Learmount, 'Theorizing Corporate Governance: New Organizational Alternative' ESRC Centre for Business Research, University of Cambridge, Working Paper No 237, June 2002 at p10.

[152] J. Humber, 'Beyond Stockholders and Stakeholders: A Plea for Moral Autonomy' (2002) 36 *Journal of Business Ethics* 207 at 215.

[153] M. Omran, P. Atrill and J. Pointon, 'Shareholders Versus Stakeholders: Corporate Mission Statements and Investor Returns' (2002) 11 *Business Ethics: A European Review* 318 at 318.

[154] R. E. Mitchell and his co-authors in 'Toward a Theory of Stakeholder Identification and Salience: Defining the Principle of Who and What Really Counts' (1997) 22 *Academy Management Review* 853 at 858 identify 27 definitions for stakeholders. This has also been a problem with the various constituency statutes in the United States: W. Leung, 'The Inadequacy of Shareholder Primacy: A Proposed Corporate Regime that Recognizes Non-Shareholder Interests' (1997) 30 *Columbia Journal of Law and Social Problems* 589 at 618.

[155] R. Mitchell, B. Agle and D. Wood, 'Toward a Theory of Stakeholder Identification and Salience: Defining the Principle of Who and What Really Counts' (1997) 22 *Academy Management Review* 853 at 853.

[156] For instance, R. Phillips, 'Stakeholder Legitimacy' (2003) 13 *Business Ethics Quarterly* 25 at 25.

defining who are, in fact, stakeholders.[157] This is critical as it is the first step in applying the theory.[158]

Notwithstanding the volume of the literature in the field the concept of stakeholder is seen as vague and blurred.[159] Definitions have varied from the narrow to the very broad. It is easier to broaden the concept, but when that is done the theory becomes more and more meaningless, and, therefore, useless.[160] Simon Deakin and Alan Hughes have said that if the theory is so wide as to embrace interests of a broader range of people and groups, such as potential consumers and the interests of society then the theory risks being regarded as irrelevant.[161]

Probably the first articulation of the concept of the stakeholder was provided in an internal memorandum at the Stanford Research Institute in 1963,[162] which said that stakeholders were 'those groups without whose support the organization would cease to exist.' This tended to be narrow and the groups covered by the term were seen as shareholders, employees, customers, suppliers, lenders and society.[163] Freeman built on this and in 1984 he felt that stakeholder should denote those who make a difference and he ended up defining stakeholders as 'any group or individual who can affect or is affected by the achievement of the organization's objectives.'[164] This broadens the category of stakeholders to include governments and environmental groups etc, while in the past employees have tended to be the focus of those wanting a broader perspective in management. The criticism often voiced is that managers are given no basis or method for identifying who are stakeholders.[165] Furthermore, some stakeholders are regarded as more important than others, but there is no guidance to deter-

[157]   R. E. Mitchell, B. Agle and D. Wood in 'Toward a Theory of Stakeholder Identification and Salience: Defining the Principle of Who and What Really Counts' (1997) 22 *Academy Management Review* 853 at 858 identify 27 definitions of stakeholders.
[158]   Y. Fassin, 'The Stakeholder Model Refined' (2009) 84 *Journal of Business Ethics* 113 at 125.
[159]   See, E. Orts and A. Strudler, 'The Ethical and Environmental Limits of Stakeholder Theory' (2002) 12 *Business Ethics Quarterly* 215 at 215 and the articles referred to at note 1.
[160]   Ibid at 218.
[161]   'Comparative Corporate Governance: An Interdisciplinary Agenda' (1997) 24 *Journal of Law and Society* 1 at 4.
[162]   Referred to by Freeman in his book, *Strategic Management: A Stakeholder Approach* (Boston, Pitman/Ballinger,1984) at 31.
[163]   Ibid at 32.
[164]   Ibid at 246.
[165]   J. Humber, 'Beyond Stockholders and Stakeholders: A Plea for Moral Autonomy' (2002) 36 *Journal of Business Ethics* 207 at 211.

mine who is the more important.[166] And as Wai Leung has said: 'there is no easy way to delineate the stakeholder class.'[167] There are a huge number of potential stakeholders and the problem for a board is to determine how they are to address the needs of divergent groups.[168]

The stakeholder case has probably been harmed by the fact that Freeman included terrorist groups as stakeholders in some companies (on the basis that they can affect how companies are run).[169] Many have sought to distance the theory from this approach. Some commentators have said that one must distinguish between those who influence the company and those who are true stakeholders. Some investors are in both categories. But the media, for instance, is in the first category only.[170] As mentioned earlier, other commentators distinguish between primary or inside stakeholders, on the one hand, and secondary or outside stakeholders, on the other, with the former being the focus of attention. Primary stakeholders are seen as those who have a formal, official or contractual relationship with the company.[171] John Parkinson said that stakeholders included those who entered a long-term relationship with the company and hold legitimate expectations of mutual gain from the continuing relationship.[172] Al Khafaji has said that stakeholders are groups to whom the company is responsible.[173] Other commentators have introduced other ways of defining and differentiating stakeholders. Robert Phillips referred to normative, derivative and dormant stakeholders.[174] Normative are those to whom the company owes a moral obligation, while derivative stakeholders are ones who can either damage or benefit the company, and no moral obligation is owed to them. Dormant stakeholders are groups such as terrorists who may affect the company at some time.

---

[166] A. Sundaram and A. Inkpen, 'The Corporate Objective Revisited' 15 *Organization Science* 350 at 352.

[167] W. Leung, 'The Inadequacy of Shareholder Primacy: A Proposed Corporate Regime that Recognizes Non-Shareholder Interests' (1997) 30 *Columbia Journal of Law and Social Problems* 589 at 622.

[168] Ibid at 621.

[169] R. E. Freeman, *Strategic Management: A Stakeholder Approach* (Boston, Pitman/Ballinger, 1984) at 53.

[170] T. Donaldson and L. Preston, 'The Stakeholder Theory for the Corporation: Concepts, Evidence, Implications' (1995) 20 *Academy Management Review* 65 at 86.

[171] A. Carroll, *Business and Society* (Cincinnati, South-Western Publishing, 1993) at 62.

[172] 'Company Law and Stakeholder Governance' in G. Kelly, D. Kelly and A. Gamble (eds), *Stakeholder Capitalism* (Basingstoke, Macmillan, 1997) at 149–150.

[173] A. Al Khafaji, *A Stakeholder Approach to Corporate Governance: Managing in a Dynamic Environment* (Westport, Quorum Books, 1989) at 36.

[174] 'Stakeholder Legitimacy' (2003) 13 *Business Ethics Quarterly* 25.

The main distinction as far as stakeholders are concerned is between those without whom the company cannot function, and those who can affect or be affected by the company,[175] the latter being the classical and managerial approach, while the former was more of a legal view. The classical approach is far broader and, given the way that trade has developed, it could encompass just about anyone.[176] Technically, it is not just the actors who have contact with the company that could be included under this approach. Parties who deal with those who contract with the company could be said to be stakeholders. For example, a company, X supplies bolts to Y. Y is a company that supplies engine parts to carmaker, Z. X could be regarded as a stakeholder in Z. Certainly if Y lost its business with Z, X would be affected significantly, yet X and Z have no direct relationship. Stakeholders of a company have their own subset of stakeholders[177] and so the net grows ever wider.

In recent research Yves Fassin found in excess of 100 stakeholders groups and sub-groups identified in the literature.[178] Elaine Sternberg has said that:

> [G]iven the increasing internalisation of modern life and the global connections made possible by improved transportation, telecommunications and computing power, those affected (at least distantly or indirectly) by any given organisation, and thus counting as its stakeholders include virtually everyone, everything, everywhere.[179]

Whilst Sternberg might be said to be using hyperbole, the general point has, with respect, some merit.

Andrew Campbell, a stakeholder theorist, has effectively said that one cannot identify stakeholders in the abstract; it will depend on the company's purpose.[180] The commentator has noted that most companies will have four active stakeholders, namely the shareholders, employees,

---

[175]   Y. Fassin, 'The Stakeholder Model Refined' (2009) 84 *Journal of Business Ethics* 113 at 117.

[176]   C. Metcalfe, 'The Stakeholder Corporation' (1998) 7 *Business Ethics: A European Review* 30.

[177]   R. Phillips, 'Stakeholder Legitimacy' (2003) 13 *Business Ethics Quarterly* 25.

[178]   Y. Fassin, 'The Stakeholder Model Refined' (2009) 84 *Journal of Business Ethics* 113 at 120.

[179]   'Stakeholder Theory: The Defective State It's In' in *Stakeholding and its Critics* (London, Institute of Economic Affairs, 1997) and quoted in C. Metcalfe, 'The Stakeholder Corporation' (1998) 7 *Business Ethics: A European Review* 30 at 32.

[180]   A. Campbell, 'Stakeholders, the Case in Favour' (1997) 30 *Long Range Planning* 446 at 448.

suppliers and customers.[181] These clearly fit within the primary category. Also, they are clearly interdependent, one of the main tenets of the theory. Some stakeholders though are not able to be said to be part of any interdependence. In this light one thinks of pressure groups and terrorists, where there is no real relationship with the company and other stakeholders, as is presumed with the concept of interdependence in this context. According to a study done by Fassin, there is unanimity amongst commentators in respect of only three stakeholders, namely, financiers, employees and customers.[182] It is assumed that shareholders are not included because the research Fassin conducted did not concentrate solely on companies, but took into account other forms of business.

An added problem, once one has identified who are stakeholders, is the fact that some stakeholder groups are large and not homogenous, and they will have different interests. This creates further difficulties, as we will see shortly, for directors seeking to balance interests.

A way of responding to the criticism here might be to follow a suggestion by John Parkinson that 'stakeholder' should be restricted to people and groups who enter long-term co-operative relationships with the company.[183] This has the advantage of permitting the managers to know who the stakeholders of the company are and to move away from reliance on legal rights and to develop trust.

It has not been determined, and maybe it is not possible to do so, the nature and extent of the responsibility that directors have to each stakeholder. Likewise, John Argenti has pointed out, correctly according to Campbell, that it is not clear what stakeholders should expect to get out of a company with which they are involved.[184] The response to that is that this cannot be outlined in general, as it is a matter for the board to specify this and to convey it to the stakeholders.[185] As far as the earnings of the company are concerned it is said that, again, there is no indication what groups will receive any benefits. Shareholder primacy theorists indicate that they are concerned that directors, because they have no objective guidelines, will act in a self-interested fashion.

---

[181]   Ibid.
[182]   Y. Fassin, 'The Stakeholder Model Refined' (2009) 84 *Journal of Business Ethics* 113 at 120.
[183]   'Company Law and Stakeholder Governance' in G. Kelly, D. Kelly and A. Gamble (eds), *Stakeholder Capitalism* (Basingstoke, Macmillan Press, 1997) at 149.
[184]   A. Campbell, 'Stakeholders , the Case in Favour' (1997) 30 *Long Range Planning* 446 at 446.
[185]   Ibid at 448.

4.3   Problem of Balancing

As discussed earlier, the theory presupposes the fact that directors will, when making decisions and running the company, balance the interests of all stakeholders. This is necessary as stakeholders will often have conflicting interests. Balancing is a critical aspect of the theory. The idea of balancing interests appears to be an attractive and reasonable way of dealing with constituencies with conflicting interests. But in fact stakeholder management involves, in the words of adherents to the theory, 'a neverending task of balancing and integrating multiple relationships and multiple objectives.'[186] Thus the primary argument that is mounted against the stakeholder approach is that the requirement that directors have to balance the interests of all stakeholders means they are faced with an impossible task.[187] Even Evan and Freeman have said that the task of the managers is akin to that encountered by King Solomon.[188] Also, the process of balancing might lead directors to opportunism, namely, benefiting themselves at the expense of others, or shirking, that is, failing to do their job well, because directors end up accountable to no one.

There are several problems which directors encounter in engaging in balancing. As we have seen, potentially there are a huge number of stakeholders. The first problem for managers is ascertaining who are stakeholders to be considered by managers in a fair balancing of interests and claims. The second is to determine how the directors are to address the needs of divergent groups.[189] Directors are not always aware of what stakeholders themselves will consider as a benefit to them, and this is exacerbated by the fact that in practice, within a stakeholder group, there may well be different views and attitudes.[190] How can managers know what stakeholders consider

---

[186]   R.E. Freeman and J. McVea, 'A Stakeholder Approach to Strategic Management' in M. Hitt, R.E. Freeman and J. Harrison (eds), *Handbook of Strategic Management* (Oxford, Blackwell Publishing, 2001) at 194.

[187]   The difficulty of doing so is demonstrated in B. Shenfield, *Company Boards* (London, George Allen and Unwin, 1971), Chapter 7.

[188]   W. Evan and R.E. Freeman, 'A Stakeholder Theory of the Modern Corporation' in T. Beauchamp and N. Bowie (eds), *Ethical Theory and Business* (Englewood Cliffs, Prentice Hall, 1974) at 314.

[189]   W. Leung, 'The Inadequacy of Shareholder Primacy: A Proposed Corporate Regime that Recognizes Non-Shareholder Interests' (1997) 30 *Columbia Journal of Law and Social Problems* 589 at 621.

[190]   S. Letza, X. Sun and J. Kirkbride, 'Shareholding and Stakeholding: a Critical Review of Corporate Governance' (2004) 12 *Corporate Governance: An International Review* 242 at 255.

as a benefit or what is in their interests?[191] As mentioned above, groups are not marked by homogeneity and so this creates further difficulties for directors seeking to balance. The board may have to balance within groups. Take creditors as an example. Companies might have all or any of the following creditors: secured creditors, suppliers with a retention of title clause in supply contracts, general trade creditors, suppliers under long-term contracts, landlords, holders of unexpired intellectual property licences, employees (owed back pay), tax authorities, tort victims with claims, and customers who have paid deposits for goods or services to be supplied by the company in the future. There is, for instance, likely to be a significant difference between the interests of a bank creditor with a charge (lien in the US) over company assets compared with an unsecured trade creditor. In considering creditor interests what does a director do if the interests of different groups do not accord? There is going to be conflict, and this internecine conflict can be as difficult to resolve as the group versus group conflict.

Returning to the problem of a lack of homogeneity in the same group, we can note that often members of the group might not have the same interests. For instance, let us take the broad grouping of trade creditors. These creditors are generally treated in the same way by the law, and certainly they are when it comes to a liquidation of an insolvent company. This group might include, at one extreme, large companies that supply significant quantities of goods to the company, and, at the other end of the spectrum, self-employed tradespersons, like plumbers, who do the occasional job for the company when it is necessary. The former type of creditors might have a turnover of many millions of dollars/pounds/euro/yen per annum and are likely to be more willing to accept the directors embracing ventures and actions that involve a greater amount of risk, as large company suppliers are probably not so reliant as the tradespersons, whose turnover is likely to be only in the region of thousands of dollars/pounds/euro/yen, on being paid the debt owed. While the large company can, in effect, gamble with its debt, tradespersons probably cannot. The latter would prefer to be assured of receiving, say half of what is owed, rather than seeing company funds used in such a way that *might* lead to full payment of the debt, but could just as likely lead to no funds being left to pay creditors on liquidation. In contrast, the large company supplier might be ready to approve of a gamble because if it does not get paid it can still survive.

Stakeholder theorists assert that companies need to engage with stakeholders to ascertain their interests and needs, but the practical concern

---

[191] E. Steinberg, 'The Defects of Stakeholder Theory' (1997) 5 *Corporate Governance: An International Review* at 3 at 4.

that can be voiced is: how is this to be done, especially as managers are probably not going to be aware of the existence of some stakeholders when the stakeholding category is defined widely? Also, as mentioned earlier, how can managers know what stakeholders consider as a benefit or what is in their interests?[192]

A third issue is: what does balancing actually entail? Does it mean embracing compromise or taking such action that enables the interests of stakeholders to coincide?[193] The former might not be acceptable to many and leave some disenchanted, and the latter does not appear to be possible for the most part. In this respect a concern for directors is to know the basis on which they are to balance interests. How do directors deal with the case where several constituencies are deserving, but it is impossible to favour them all, certainly equally? One particular problem identified by many scholars is that it is often not possible to advance the interests of non-shareholder stakeholders in conjunction with those of the share-holders.[194] There is no specification given to managers, or even guidance, permitting them to identify the values relied on in stakeholding and there is no indication how these are to inform their decision-making.[195] There are no standards devised for assigning relative weight to the interests of the constituencies involved and no criteria for solving problems.[196] Effectively, directors are presented with 'standardless discretion'.[197] This is emphasised somewhat by Ronald Mitchell et al who stated that the extent to which priority is given by managers to particular stakeholders whose claims are in conflict with others cannot be explained by the stakeholder framework, as complex issues are involved.[198] Michael Jensen has stated, in the context of directors having to consider all interests and to balance

---

[192]   Ibid.

[193]   B. Shenfield, *Company Boards* (London, George Allen and Unwin Ltd, 1971) at 149.

[194]   See sources referred to in A. Licht, 'The Maximands of Corporate Governance: A Theory of Values and Cognitive Style' (2004) 29 *Delaware Journal of Corporate Law* 649 at 686ff.

[195]   A. Sundaram and A. Inkpen, 'The Corporate Objective Revisited' (2004) 15 *Organization Science* 350 at 353; M. Jensen, 'Value Maximisation, Stakeholder Theory, and the Corporate Objective Function' (2001) 7 *European Financial Management* 297 at 305.

[196]   T. Donaldson, *The Ethics of International Business* (New York, Oxford University Press, 1989) at 45.

[197]   L. Mitchell, 'A Theoretical and Practical Framework for Enforcing Corporate Constituency Statutes' (1992) 70 *Texas Law Review* 579 at 589

[198]   R. Mitchell, B. Agle and D. Wood, 'Toward a Theory of Stakeholder Identification and Salience: Defining the Principle of Who and What Really Counts' (1997) 22 *Academy Management Review* 853 at 854.

them that '[i]t is logically impossible to maximise in more than one dimension at the same time.'[199] His concern is that there is no objective on which a manager can focus, thus leading to confusion.[200] In response to Jensen's criticism of the theory as one that is confusing for managers, Amir Licht takes the view that Jensen is depicting managers as being unable to handle more than one task, namely, to 'walk and chew gum at the same time.'[201] But in all fairness to Jensen there is little guidance, as we have seen, and even experienced managers might ask where they should start in balancing interests when difficult decisions have to be made.

John Parkinson's view on this point is that:

> There seems no reason in principle why management performance cannot be effectively evaluated by reference to multiple standards. What is required is an independent process of review that is capable of discriminating between management actions that result from incompetence or the pursuit of self-interest on the one hand, and those motivated by attempts to accommodate the legitimate interests of affected parties on the other.[202]

However, the response from shareholder primacists would probably be that directors might be able to muddy the waters in such a way as to leave someone reviewing their actions, possibly a judge, not being able to say that the directors have not attempted to benefit at least one stakeholder.

The lack of direction is further exemplified by what the Supreme Court of Canada said in the case of *BCE Inc v 1976 Debentureholders*.[203] It said that there is no principle that one set of interests should prevail over another. Then the Court said that which set prevails depends on the situation that is before the directors, and they have to use their business judgment. Again, no guidance whatsoever is provided, especially concerning what weight is to be given to particular interests. Some scholars would say that it is not possible for judges to be involved in passing judgment on what directors have done, in using their commercial judgment, as judges

---

[199]   M. Jensen, 'Value Maximisation, Stakeholder Theory, and the Corporate Objective Function' (2001) 7 *European Financial Management* 297 at 300–301.

[200]   Ibid at 301

[201]   'The Maximands of Corporate Governance: A Theory of Values and Cognitive Style' (2004) 29 *Delaware Journal of Corporate Law* 649 at 731.

[202]   'Models of the Company and the Employment Relationship' (2003) 41 *British Journal of Industrial Relations* 481 at 499 and referring to J. Kay and A. Silberston, 'Corporate Governance' (1995) *National Institute Economic Review* 84 at 93–95.

[203]   [2008] SCC 69 at [84].

lack, inter alia, competence, but my view is that that is an overly restricted opinion of the calibre of modern common law judges, many of whom specialise in commercial and/or corporate law.[204]

It is argued that arriving at a set of values that accounts for the concerns across a heterogeneous group of stakeholders requires managers to fulfil unrealistic expectations.[205] Furthermore, as mentioned above, it is contended by many scholars that it is not in fact possible to advance the interests of non-shareholder stakeholders in conjunction with those of the shareholders.[206] Balancing is made difficult by the fact that as contracts are incomplete it means that the constituencies of a company will usually have conflicting claims and each constituency will be subject to the opportunistic actions of other constituencies.[207] This complicates any decisions that the directors are to make in balancing interests. The challenge for stakeholder theory is to specify how managers are to balance between stakeholders. A critical element for the theory is the need to satisfy legitimate expectations, but a vague requirement to ensure that legitimate expectations are taken into account does not provide any guidance whatsoever, but leaves managers confused.[208]

Even with the best will in the world and acting in good faith, it would be very difficult for directors to know what are the best interests of individual stakeholders. This is exacerbated by the fact that stakeholders will continually change and the expectations of existing ones could be revised. Added to this is the fact that as a long-term approach is championed by stakeholder theory, managers are required to look not only to present interests, but to the future. This is not an easy task and particularly when

---

[204]   For instance, see the discussion on this point in A. Keay, 'The Ultimate Objective of the Public Company and the Enforcement of the Entity Maximisation and Sustainability Model' (2010) 10 *Journal of Corporate Law Studies* 35 at 65–71. A good example of judges who specialise are the judges of the Companies Court in the Chancery Division of the High Court of Judicature in England. Another is the eminent judges of the Chancery Court in the State of Delaware. This is discussed further in Chapter 5: below at pp. 267–274.

[205]   A. Sundaram and A. Inkpen, 'The Corporate Objective Revisited' (2004) 15 *Organization Science* 350 at 353.

[206]   A. Licht, 'The Maximands of Corporate Governance: A Theory of Values and Cognitive Style' (2004) 29 *Delaware Journal of Corporate Law* 649 at 686ff

[207]   M. Blair and L. Stout, 'A Team Production Theory of Corporate Law' (1999) 85 *Virginia Law Review* 247 at 276–287. The answer according to the learned commentators (pursuant to what they call 'the team production theory') is that the board must make the ultimate decisions in reconciling competing interests and disputes (ibid at 276–277).

[208]   M. Jensen, 'Value Maximisation, Stakeholder Theory, and the Corporate Objective Function' (2001) 7 *European Financial Management* 297 at 301.

one accepts that stakeholders themselves are likely not to be able to articulate their interests, and certainly not their future interests.[209]

The fact is that during the life of a company some stakeholders will be more important to a company than others. If this is so, are directors to take this into account in balancing interests? If they do then they might be subject to claims of unethical conduct, but if they do not then they might hamper the success of the company. Of course, the more stakeholder groups there are in a company, the more difficult it is, potentially, for directors to take all interests into account in what they propose to do. The danger is that in some circumstances the directors are in a 'no win situation' and might feel that the preferable thing to do is nothing. Kenneth Goodpaster is concerned that the stakeholder approach is likely to push: 'decision-making towards paralysis because of the dilemmas posed by divided loyalties and, in the final analysis, represents nothing less than the conversion of the modern private corporation into a public institution . . .'[210] Ultimately this could prejudice all stakeholders.

As noted earlier, it is quite possible that a person can be a constituent of more than one stakeholder group, for instance an employee might be a customer, and the theory fails to determine in which capacity he or she is to be included in the managers' balancing calculation.[211] Members of the same group might not agree on what is a benefit for that group,[212] so how are managers to make a determination? Further, directors have the dual responsibility of deciding who is a stakeholder and then implementing their decision, which does permit them room to manoeuvre for their own benefit.

It might be argued that the need to engage in balancing can exacerbate the transaction costs of companies, although on the other side stakeholder theorists might say that the trust engendered between companies and their stakeholders can reduce costs, as, for example, stakeholders have to do less monitoring.

One specific concern that writers[213] have with balancing is where the managers are identified as stakeholders, for it is the managers who

---

[209] S. Berns and P. Barron, *Company Law and Governance: An Australian Perspective* (Melbourne, Oxford University Press, 1998) at 149.

[210] 'Business Ethics and Stakeholder Analysis' in M. Clarkson (ed), *The Corporation and its Stakeholders: Classic and Contemporary Readings* (Toronto, University of Toronto Press, 1998) at 115.

[211] E. Steinberg, 'The Defects of Stakeholder Theory' (1997) 5 *Corporate Governance: An International Review* at 3 at 4.

[212] Ibid at 5.

[213] For instance, P. Coelho, J. McClure and J. Spry, 'The Social Responsibility of Management: A Reprise' (2003) 18 *Mid-American Journal of Business* 51 at 53.

will usually be required to do the balancing. If they have a stakeholder role, are they then not judges in their own cause? But many will regard managers as a mediating body between the stakeholder groups, rather than stakeholders per se.[214]

While balancing seems meritorious, in practice it would be very difficult for a director, in many situations, to know what to do. The main problem is that balancing is a fairly nebulous idea unless there is a goal that has been set for the balancing exercise. To what end is the balancing to be directed? To be effective any balancing must be done in the context of achieving an aim. The problem is that: '[a]dvocates of traditional stakeholder theory . . . hand managers a theory that makes purposeful decisions impossible. And, with no way to keep score, stakeholder theory forces managers to be unaccountable for the very actions through which they were to be evaluated.'[215]

Another leading argument against the theory, and based on the notion that directors have to consider many interests, is something to which I have adverted already, namely, that directors are given licence to do whatever they like, and that state of affairs is likely to lead to directors, as rational actors, engaging in either or both of two kinds of behaviour. The first is opportunistic activity, namely directors taking the opportunity to benefit themselves at the expense of others. The second is shirking, namely not devoting their best efforts to the tasks at hand. These kinds of activity are possible because directors end up accountable to no one (known as the 'too many masters' problem). 'A manager who is told to serve two masters (a little for the equity holders, a little for the community) has been freed of both and is answerable to neither . . . Agency costs rise and social wealth falls.'[216] It is likely that: '[a]ll but the most egregious self-serving managerial behaviour will doubtless serve the interests of *some*

---

[214] L. Mitchell, 'A Critical Look at Corporate Governance' (1992) 45 *Vanderbilt Law Review* 1263 at 1272; S. Bainbridge, 'Director Primacy: The Means and Ends of Corporate Governance' (2003) 97 *Northwestern University Law Review* 547. Also, see R. Colombo, 'Ownership, Limited: Reconciling Traditional and Progressive Corporate Law via an Aristotelian Understanding of Ownership' (2008) 34 *Journal of Corporation Law* 247 at 249.

[215] L. Donaldson, 'The Stakeholder Revolution and the Clarkson Principles' (2002) 12 *Business Ethics Quarterly* 107 and quoted in F. Robins, 'Why Corporate Social Responsibility Should be Popularised but not Imposed' (2007) 8 *Corporate Governance: An International Review* 330 at 333.

[216] F. Easterbrook and D. Fischel, *The Economic Structure of Company Law* (Cambridge, Massachusetts, Harvard University Press, 1991) at 38. Also, see M. Jensen, 'Value Maximisation, Stakeholder Theory, and the Corporate Objective Function' (2001) 7 *European Financial Management* 297 at 305.

stakeholder constituencies and work against the interests of others,'[217] and hence directors can mount a credible defence in relation to what they have done and play off one group against another. They can say that after balancing interests they made a decision to benefit stakeholders X and Y, and this decision just happened to benefit or protect themselves. It is difficult to impugn the decision. Oliver Hart says that requiring managers to consider the interests of all constituencies 'is essentially vacuous, because it allows management to justify almost any action on the grounds that it benefits some group.'[218] In such a system the directors are arguably given too much of an unfettered discretion that cannot be monitored. Managers can effectively do whatever they wish. The concern is that directors will simply pay lip-service to the need to consider the interests of stakeholders, and then make the decision that they want, possibly based on self-interest.[219] There is the general point that directors should not be permitted to decide what to do with company assets and its business based on caprice because they should be accountable for what they do with other people's property. While it has been said that managers will be more accountable and subjected to greater monitoring if they have to take into account all stakeholders,[220] it makes sense to say that if they have a responsibility to a lot of stakeholders they virtually become accountable to no one.[221] So one of the problems is to ascertain how one can make directors sufficiently accountable.

The riposte from the stakeholder adherents might be that the view expressed in the last paragraph is a cynical way of viewing things and that managers as professionals will be concerned to retain their reputation and integrity and will refrain from acting opportunistically or shirking.

---

[217] 'Balancing Act' in J. DesJardins and J. McCall (eds), *Contemporary Issues in Business Ethics*, 4th ed (Wadsworth, 2000) at 97.

[218] O. Hart, 'An Economist's View of Fiduciary Duty' (1993) 43 *University of Toronto Law Journal* 299 at 303.

[219] The UK Government said that in meeting their duty under s.172 of the Companies Act 2006 directors must not merely pay lip-service to the factors set out in the provision (these include taking into account the interests of employees and fostering relationships with suppliers, and are set out in full in the text following n236 below): Explanatory Notes to the Companies Act 2006, at para 328. But neither the government in the Notes nor the section itself provides any guidance on how the directors will be judged.

[220] K. Greenfield, 'A New Era for Corporate Law' *Summit on the Future of the Corporation*, Paper No 2, November 2007, 19 at 23 and accessible at: <http://www.corporation2020.org/pdfs/SummitPaperSeries.pdf> (last visited, 17 July 2009).

[221] M. Blair, *Ownership and Control* (Washington DC, The Brookings Institute, 1995) at 225.

Stakeholderism states that the trustworthiness of the directors must be relied on. And Margaret Blair and Lynn Stout, amongst others, point out there is ample evidence from behavioural theory of people acting altruistically and sacrificing selfish interests to achieve a result that benefits others and is consistent with ethical behaviour. Under the stewardship theory, embraced by many favouring stakeholder theory or something akin to it, there is a focus on directors' need for achievement, responsibility, recognition, altruism and respect for authority, and as a result they can be seen not as opportunistic actors, necessarily, but as good stewards who will act in the best interests of the stakeholders. Stakeholderism asserts that directors will have a moral obligation to stakeholders and will use their powers ethically.[222]

The issue really comes down to a philosophical debate. The shareholder primacy school says that you cannot trust directors because human nature is such that they will want to seek benefits at every possible turn (and you must have tight monitoring measures in place), whereas the stakeholder theory school, and others, asserts that while there will be some improper actions by directors, generally they will be fair, can be trusted and will act in good faith, making them good stewards of the company. The latter view asserts that directors have other motives beyond self-interest, including professionalism, satisfaction in performing well, respect for authority etc.

Another concern is that in the United States and some other jurisdictions, such as Australia,[223] directors are protected by the business judgment rule. In the US the business judgments of directors are only reviewed in extraordinary circumstances,[224] because of the business judgment rule, which might be regarded as US corporate law's central doctrine.[225] The rule takes the focus of the court from whether the director made the correct decision to whether the director adhered to adequate and appropriate processes that led to the decision. Consequently, it is said to provide a 'safe harbour' for directors. So, American directors are entitled to rely

---

[222] S. Sharma, 'Managerial Interpretations and Organizational Context as Predictors of Corporate Choice of Environmental Strategy' (2000) 43 *Academy of Management Journal* 581; J. Aragon-Correa, F. Matias-Resch and M. Senise-Barrio, 'Managerial Discretion and Corporate Commitment to the Natural Environment' (2003) 57 *Journal of Business Research* 964; C. Cennamo, P. Berrone and L. Gomez-Mejia, 'Does Stakeholder Management have a Dark Side?' (2009) 89 *Journal of Business Ethics* 491 at 492.

[223] s.180(2) of the Corporations Act 2001.

[224] D. Rosenberg, 'Galactic Stupidity and the Business Judgment Rule' (2006–07) 32 *Journal of Corporation Law* 301 at 301–302.

[225] S. Bainbridge, *Corporation Law and Economics* (New York, Foundation Press, 2002) at 241.

on the business judgment rule if they can establish in relation to the particular judgment in question that: they exercised a business judgment (including a decision to refrain from taking any action); the judgment was made in good faith for a proper purpose; they do not have a material personal interest in the subject matter of the judgment, so that there is no conflict of interest; they informed themselves about the subject matter of the judgment to the extent that they reasonably believed to be appropriate;[226] and they rationally believe that the judgment is in the best interests of the company.[227] The presumption[228] is that the director has acted properly and it is the job of the plaintiff/claimant to rebut this presumption. If the plaintiff/claimant can do so, then the director has to establish the fairness of the transaction that is impugned.[229]

The rule pervades every aspect of corporate law in the US.[230] It is designed to preserve directors' discretion and to protect the directors from courts using hindsight to find them liable. The rule provides, in a nutshell, that courts will not substitute their business judgment for that of the informed, reasonable director who acts bona fide in the best interests of the company,[231] and an action will fail even if the claimant can demonstrate that the action of the directors has caused loss to the company unless the director's actions do not meet the aforementioned qualities.[232] So, an American director cannot be held liable if he or she makes a bad

---

[226] See *Cede and Co v Technicolor Inc* (1993) 634 A 2d 345 (Delaware) for a case where the directors were held not to have informed themselves appropriately.

[227] American Law Institute, *Principles of Corporate Governance and Structure: Restatement and Recommendations*, 1982 at s.4.01. See, for example, *Aronson v Lewis* (1984) 473 A 2d 805; *Parnes v Bally Entertainment Corp* (1999) 722 A 2d 1243 (Delaware). Also, see S. Bainbridge, *Corporation Law and Economics* (New York, Foundation Press, 2002) at 270–283.

[228] Stephen Bainbridge argues that it is really an assumption and not a presumption in the evidentiary sense of 'presumption' (*Corporation Law and Economics*, (New York, Foundation Press, 2002) at 269–270).

[229] L. Johnson 'The Modest Business Judgment Rule' (2000) 55 *Business Lawyer* 625 at 628.

[230] S. Bainbridge, 'Director Primacy: The Means and Ends of Corporate Governance' (2003) 97 *Northwestern University Law Review* 547 at 601.

[231] For instance, see *Moran v Household International Inc* (1983) 500 A 2d 1346 at 1356 (Delaware); *Aronson v Lewis* (1984) 473 A 2d 805 at 812 (Delaware); *Spiegel v Buntrock* 571 A 2d 767 at 774 (1990) (Delaware); R. Cieri, P. Sullivan, and H. Lennox, 'The Fiduciary Duties of Directors of Financially Troubled Companies' (1994) 3 *Journal of Bankruptcy Law and Practice* 405 at 408.

[232] See, D. Millon, 'Why is Corporate Management Obsessed with Quarterly Earnings and What Should be Done About it?' (2002) 70 *George Washington Law Review* 890 at 917.

judgment, or a decision which he or she makes is unsuccessful,[233] provided the above factors can be established on his or her behalf. In the context of our discussion, it means that in the US if a director has acted in good faith then it will not matter whose interests have been enhanced.

While the business judgment rule[234] does not apply in the UK,[235] a derivation of it arguably applies. The courts do not second guess what directors have done. In fact UK judges have consistently refrained from reviewing business judgments made by directors,[236] and thus they have protected directors from the use of judicial hindsight. In the UK a director is required under s.172 of the Companies Act 2006 to act in the way that he considers, in good faith, would be most likely to promote the success of their company for the benefit of the members as a whole and in doing so he is to have regard for:

(a) the likely consequences of any decision in the long term;
(b) the interests of the company's employees;
(c) the need to foster the company's business relationships with suppliers, customers and others;
(d) the impact of the company's operations on the community and the environment;
(e) the desirability of the company maintaining a reputation for high standards of business conduct; and
(f) the need to act fairly between the members of the company.

The fact of the matter is that while the provision seems to be stakeholder-oriented, it is up to the directors and not the courts to decide what benefits the shareholders and which of the factors listed, if any, should

---

[233] *Joy v North* (1983) 692 F 2d 880 at 885.

[234] For example, see *In re Healthco International Inc* (1997) 208 BR 288 at 306 (Massachusetts). Also, see American Law Institute, *Principles of Corporate Governance and Structure: Restatement and Recommendations*, 1982; M. Eisenberg, 'The Duty of Care and the Business Judgement Rule in American Corporate Law' (1997) 2 *Company Financial and Insolvency Law Review* 185.

[235] The Law Commission in its 1999 Report on 'Company Directors: Regulating Conflicts of Interest and Formulating a Statement of Duties' (No 261) thought that such a rule was not necessary (Pt 5). The CLRSG agreed: Company Law Review, *Modern Company Law for a Competitive Economy*: Developing the Framework (London, DTI, 2000) at paras. 3.69–3.70. The CLRSG felt that such a rule would add complexity and would be unfair as it would be overly harsh in some cases and give too much leeway in others.

[236] R. Reed, 'Company Directors – Collective or Functional Responsibility' (2006) 27 *The Company Lawyer* 170 at 170.

affect what he or she decides to do, provided that the directors act in good faith.[237] Except for cases of really bad behaviour, it is very difficult to demonstrate that the directors have breached their duty of good faith.[238] It is very difficult, in most cases, to impugn the actions of someone who is able to state clearly that he or she believed that what was done was for the company's best. Directors will normally assert that their motives were pure, and they are likely to be able to convince themselves after the event of these pure motives. Courts are going to be rather reluctant to decline to accept written or oral evidence given by directors concerning their motives, and especially because alleging improper motives is relatively serious.[239]

Another major problem is enforcing any breach of directorial responsibilities. Does one give the power to anyone to bring legal proceedings? Are legal proceedings appropriate? Derivative proceedings will not help most stakeholders as the only ones who can bring such proceedings are the shareholders and they are not likely to be inclined to take action (which opens them up to the possibility of a costs order) as they will not be benefiting save where they are members of other stakeholder groups. This is an issue which is discussed in brief towards the end of the Chapter and then in some depth in Chapter 5.

Before closing this part of the Chapter we must acknowledge the fact that there are responses to the concern over the issue of balancing conflicting interests. First, it might be said that it is part and parcel of being a director. Some management specialists have even said that managing competing interests is a primary function of management.[240] The fact that the

---

[237] See, A. Keay, 'Enlightened Shareholder Value, the Reform of the Duties of Corporation Directors and the Corporate Objective' [2006] *Lloyds Maritime and Commercial Law Quarterly* 335; A. Keay, *Directors' Duties* (Bristol, Jordan Publishing, 2009), Chapter 6; A. Keay, 'Moving Towards Stakeholderism? Constituency Statutes, Enlightened Shareholder Value and All That: Much Ado About Little?' (2011) 22 *European Business Law Review* 1.

[238] P. Davies, *Gower and Davies' Principles of Company Law*, 7th ed (London, Sweet and Maxwell, 2003) at 389. This is also acknowledged by Richard Nolan in 'The Legal Control of Directors' Conflicts of Interest in the United Kingdom: Non-Executive Directors Following the Higgs Report' (2005) 6 *Theoretical Inquiries in Law* 413 at 424.

[239] R. Hollington, *Shareholders' Rights,* 5th ed (London, Sweet and Maxwell, 2007) at 51.

[240] H. Ansoff, *Implanting Strategic Management* (Englewood Cliffs, Prentice Hall, 1984) and referred to in J. Harrison and R. Freeman, 'Stakeholders, Social Responsibility and Performance: Empirical Evidence and Theoretical Perspectives' (1999) 42 *Academy of Management Journal* 479 at 479. Management commentators have asserted that directors are in effect to act as referees between

balancing of diverse interests is within directors' abilities and skills is something that has been recognised as far back as 1973 by a UK Department
of Trade and Industry Report,[241] and by some American courts.[242] It has
been contended that it is not unmanageable or unreasonable for persons
occupying positions like directors, to make allocative decisions. Directors
have been classified as fiduciaries and society regularly requires those who
are fiduciaries to make decisions that require a balancing of interests and
factors and which can be quite difficult.[243] Proponents of the view might
point to another kind of fiduciary, the trustee. Trustees have to make
investment decisions sometimes with various categories of beneficiaries
in mind. This can involve weighing up risk in a similar manner to that
required by a director under a duty to consider creditor interests when his
or her company is in financial difficulty.[244] It usually involves the steering
of a middle course.

Second, although balancing might be demanding, there is evidence
that directors are often seeking to balance interests in the decisions which
they make.[245] A corporate reputation survey of Fortune 500 companies
(the largest listed companies in the United States) found that satisfying
the interests of one stakeholder does not automatically mean that this is
at the expense of other stakeholders.[246] It might be concluded that if the
interests of creditors are considered then it does not necessarily mean that
shareholders' interests will be prejudiced. It has been found empirically, in

---

two stakeholder groups (M. Aoki, *The Co-operative Game Theory of the Firm*
(Oxford, Oxford University Press, 1984) and referred to in T. Donaldson and L.
Preston, 'The Stakeholder Theory of the Corporation Concepts, Evidence, and
Implications' (1995) 20 *The Academy of Management Review* 65 at 86).

[241]   *Company Law Reform*, Cmnd. 5391 at [55]–[59].

[242]   For example, *Unocal Corporation v Mesa Petroleum Corporation* 493 A 2d
946 (1985).

[243]   R. Campbell Jr, 'Corporate Fiduciary Principles for the Post-Contractarian
Era' (1996) 23 *Florida State University Law Review* 561 at 593.

[244]   It might be asserted, with some merit, that directors and trustees are
regarded differently in a number of ways. For example, a trustee is not permitted to engage in the same amount of risk-taking as directors, whose role is partly
entrepreneurial. See A. Keay, *Directors' Duties* (Bristol, Jordan Publishing, 2009)
at 18–21.

[245]   It has been noted that directors do already consider the interests of
various constituents: *Report of the Committee on Corporate Governance* (chair, Sir
Ronald Hampel) (1998) and referred to by J. Dine, 'Implementation of European
Initiatives in the UK: The Role of Fiduciary Duties' (1999) 3 *Company Financial
and Insolvency Law Review* 218 at 223.

[246]   L. Preston and H. Sapienza, 'Stakeholder Management and Corporate
Performance' (1990) 19 *Journal of Behavioral Economics* 361.

a study of UK private water companies, that the requirement that directors must consider customer interests as well as those of shareholders, can result in 'mutual benefits for different stakeholder groups with apparently conflicting economic interests.'[247] For instance, in taking into account creditor interests by reviewing all available material information relating to the financial standing of the company before embarking on any actions, shareholders might well benefit in that the company might be spared from pursuing an inappropriate strategy.

Third, even with shareholder primacy it is necessary for directors to engage in some balancing. As discussed in Chapter 2,[248] shares come in different shapes and sizes and companies often have different kinds of shares, such as ordinary and preference, and it is incumbent on directors to balance the interests of different kinds of shareholders, so that they act fairly between them[249] as, on occasions, these different classes of shareholders have opposing interests.[250]

4.4 Unworkable

The problem that exists when there is a large and apparently untrammelled stakeholder grouping is that the concept becomes unworkable. There are a huge number of potential stakeholders and the problem for a board is to determine how they are to address the needs of divergent groups.[251]

It has always been perceived that one of the strengths of the shareholder primacy position, and certainly when compared with stakeholder theory, has been that it provides greater certainty and it is workable. In fact often one of the main arguments against the stakeholder theory is that it has problems when it comes to application – it is indecisive and imprecise.

---

[247] S. Ogden and R. Watson, 'Corporate Performance and Stakeholder Management: Balancing Shareholder and Customer Interests in the UK Privatized Water Industry' (1999) 42 *Academy of Management Journal* 526 at 536.

[248] Above at 84–85.

[249] *Mills v Mills* (1938) 60 CLR 150 at 164; *Re BSB Holdings Ltd (No2)* [1996] 1 BCLC 155 at 246–249.

[250] M. McDaniel, 'Bondholders and Stockholders' (1988) 13 *Journal of Corporation Law* 205 at 273; R. Campbell Jr, 'Corporate Fiduciary Principles for the Post-Contractarian Era' (1996) 23 *Florida State University Law Review* 561 at 593; R. de R Barondes, 'Fiduciary Duties of Officers and Directors of Distressed Corporations' (1998) 7 *George Mason Law Review* 45 at 78.

[251] W. Leung, 'The Inadequacy of Shareholder Primacy: A Proposed Corporate Regime that Recognizes Non-Shareholder Interests' (1997) 30 *Columbia Journal of Law and Social Problems* 589 at 621.

Elaine Sternberg has said that the 'essential principle of stakeholder theory that corporations are accountable to *all* their stakeholders' is something that is 'unworkable.' [252] On the other hand, the shareholder primacy theory is regarded as far more pragmatic, on the basis that the latter provides for a clear criterion or metric for determining business success and it provides guidance for directors in the direction which they should take in managing the business of the company. The previous Chapter questioned that premise. It was argued that shareholder primacy is not as workable as is often thought. Nevertheless, stakeholder theory suffers from its own problems in relation to being workable.

The Hampel Report, delivered in 1998 as part of the development of a corporate governance code in the UK, stated that having directors' duties defined in:

> [T]erms of the stakeholders would mean identifying all the various stakeholder groups; and deciding the extent and nature of the directors' responsibility to each. The result would be that the directors were not effectively accountable to anyone since there would be no clear yardstick by which to judge their performance. This is a recipe neither for good governance nor for corporate success.[253]

The approach of stakeholderism is to incorporate values as a critical aspect of the strategic management process, but the riposte from shareholder value advocates is: how do managers identify these values and how are they to inform decision-making?[254] They argue that arriving at a set of values that accounts for the concerns across a heterogeneous group of stakeholders requires managers to fulfil unrealistic expectations.[255]

The UK's Company Law Review Steering Group was against stakeholder theory (it referred to it as 'pluralism'[256]) because:

> [I]n particular that this would impose a distributive economic role on directors in allocating the benefits and burdens of management of the company's resources; that this role would be uncontrolled if left to directors in the form of a power or discretion; and that a similarly broad role would be imposed

---

[252]   E. Sternberg, 'The Defects of Stakeholder Theory' (1997) 5 *Corporate Governance: An International Review* 3 at 6.

[253]   *Final Report of the Committee on Corporate Governance* (Hampel Report), 1998 at para 1.17.

[254]   A. Sundaram and A. Inkpen, 'The Corporate Objective Revisited' (2004) 15 *Organization Science* 350 at 353.

[255]   Ibid.

[256]   Arguably pluralism differs in some respects from stakeholder theory. Janice Dean states that the former implies diversity and conflict while the latter emphasises inclusivity: *Directing Public Companies* (London, Cavendish, 2001) at 93.

on the judges if the new arrangement took the form of an enforceable obliga-tion conferring rights on all the interested parties to argue for their interests in court.[257]

Frederick, Davis and Post have proposed several stages in conduct-ing stakeholder analysis, namely: mapping stakeholder relationships; mapping stakeholder coalitions; assessing the nature of each stakeholder interest; assessing the nature of each stakeholder's power; constructing a matrix of stakeholder priorities; and monitoring shifting coalitions.[258] This is an extremely complicated and time-consuming enterprise which is, arguably, not a possible approach which managers can adopt.

The theory provides that directors are to be accountable to all stake-holders, but that is not possible. What happens with large companies with many stakeholders is that the managers become accountable to no one.[259] As we have seen earlier, managers are able to defend allegations that they have failed to act properly by asserting that they have sought to balance some or all of the stakeholder interests.

As mentioned earlier, many stakeholder theorists argue that stakehold-ers should be represented on the board of directors, thereby providing, inter alia, procedural justice.[260] It has often been said that, as in companies in some European states and elsewhere, employees should have director representatives or works councils. It might be argued that this works. But how could one possibly have some form of representation from all stakeholders? Assuming one can determine who are the stakeholders in the company, a difficult task as already noted, there are likely to be too many stakeholder groups, even if one applies the narrow approach to the definition of stakeholder, for them all to be represented. Back in the 1970s a critic of companies, Ralph Nader (and his co-authors) recognised the fact that it seemed to be 'impossible to design a general "interest group" formula which will assure all affected constituencies of large industrial corporations will be represented . . .'[261] In European companies where

---

[257] Company Law Review, *Modern Company Law for a Competitive Economy*: Developing the Framework (London, DTI, 2000) at para 2.12.

[258] W. Frederick, K. Davis and J. Post, *Business and Society* (New York, McGraw-Hill, 1988) and referred to in G. Vinten, 'Shareholder v Stakeholder – is there a governance dilemma?' (2001) 9 *Corporate Governance: An International Review* 36 at 41.

[259] E. Steinberg, 'The Defects of Stakeholder Theory' (1997) 5 *Corporate Governance: An International Review* at 3 at 4.

[260] For instance, P. Phillips, R. E. Freeman and W. Wicks, 'What Stakeholder is Not' (2003) 13 *Business Ethics Quarterly* 479.

[261] *Taming the Giant Corporation*, 1976, at 124 and quoted in D. G. Smith, 'The Dystopian Potential of Corporate Law' (2008) 56 *Emory Law Journal* 985.

representation occurs, many of the companies have a two-tier board system, and representation is on the supervisory board. This board can be large and does not have to be so wieldy and flexible like the management board or the one-tier board employed elsewhere, and most notably in Anglo-American jurisdictions.

4.5   Stakeholders are Protected by Contract and/or Regulation

This was a matter raised in the last Chapter in the course of discussing shareholder primacy. Shareholder primacy scholars argue that non-shareholder stakeholders, such as creditors and employees are, unlike shareholders, adequately protected, for the most part, by contract and/or statutory provisions.[262] For instance, it is contended that stakeholders can provide in the terms of their contracts that they make with the company that they are granted safeguards in the nature of governance rights.[263] All of this leads to the argument that if directors are required to take the interests of such constituencies into account the constituencies are receiving very special preferential treatment, or 'having a second bite of the cherry.' Critics compare this to shareholders who have no such benefits.

Stakeholder theorists will usually take issue with the general assertion that constituencies are able to protect themselves by the terms of the contracts that they make. It is acknowledged that some groups are able to enter into contracts that provide them with protection, and powerful creditors like banks are usually cited as examples, but the contention is made that many constituencies do not obtain protection for a number of reasons, such as lack of bargaining power and ignorance or insufficient funds to pay necessary costs (e.g. legal costs). In the real world it is infrequent to find contractual arrangements made by equals. In many contracts there is a 'take it leave it approach' with little or no room for negotiation, and with the result that costs are imposed on third parties with whom the company does business.[264] Stakeholder adherents point to the fact that when making contracts, stakeholders often suffer from informational asymmetry in that the managers of companies know far

---

[262]   H. Hansmann and R. Kraakman, 'The End of History for Corporate Law' (2001) 89 *Georgetown Law Journal* 439 at 442.

[263]   G. Kelly and J. Parkinson, 'The Conceptual Foundations of the Corporation: a Pluralist Approach' in J. Parkinson, A. Gamble and G. Kelly (eds), *The Political Economy of the Corporation* (Oxford, Hart Publishing, 2000) at 118.

[264]   F. Easterbrook and D. Fischel, 'Antitrust Suits by Targets of Tender Offers' (1982) 80 *Michigan Law Review* 1155 at 1156.

more than they do, particularly about the performance and systems of the company. Several scholars have reported the fact that contracts involving stakeholders are not complete and not perfectly priced.[265]

In like fashion stakeholder theorists will submit that the argument that non-shareholding stakeholders are also safeguarded by regulatory law is too broad an assertion. Many laws are of limited or no benefit to stakeholders. Even if they are, stakeholders have to take the initiative to inform regulatory authorities, or take legal action themselves. This involves a time and/or cost factor that might dissuade them from taking action.

4.6 Enforcement

Adolf Berle observed that if one abandons the focus on shareholder primacy there needs to be a clear and reasonably enforceable scheme of responsibilities to someone else.[266] Clearly, enforcing the stakeholder approach has, as recognised as far back as the 1930s,[267] significant problems in implementation. Berle was of the view that running companies for many constituencies was attractive, but he could not determine how it could be done. That is why he regarded shareholder primacy as the way forward, as it could help to control the managers. Even E. Merrick Dodd, who wrote in opposition to Berle's views, acknowledged[268] that there were significant problems in implementation of a stakeholder approach to corporate governance.

Another major problem is enforcing any breach of a stakeholder approach. Do you give the power to anyone who is a stakeholder to bring proceedings? Are legal proceedings appropriate? The leading problem in this area is that the breach will usually be perpetrated by one or more directors. It is trite law that only the company can enforce any harm done to it. As the directors manage the company and usually have the power to decide whether or not legal proceedings should be initiated on the part of the company, if they have breached their duties they are unlikely to sanction proceeding against themselves. In most Anglo-American jurisdictions

---

[265] J. Fisch, 'Measuring Efficiency in Corporate Law: The Rule of Shareholder Primacy' December 2005, Fordham Law Legal Studies, Working Paper No 105 at p28 and available at: <http://ssrn.com/abstract=878391> (last visited, 27 July 2009).

[266] A. Berle, 'For Whom Corporate Managers Are Trustees: A Note' (1932) 45 *Harvard Law Review* 1365 at 1367.

[267] E.M. Dodd, 'Is Effective Enforcement of the Fiduciary Duties of Corporate Managers Practicable?' (1934) 2 *University of Chicago Law Review* 194 at 199.

[268] Ibid.

there is legislative[269] and/or judicial authority[270] that permits shareholders to take what are known as derivative proceedings against the directors and/or other miscreants who have damaged their company in order to obtain a judgment in favour of the company. But, derivative proceedings will not help most stakeholders as the only ones who can bring such proceedings, for the most part,[271] are the shareholders and they are not likely to be inclined to take action (which opens them up to a costs order) where stakeholders have been hurt by directorial action as they will not be benefiting save where they are members of other stakeholder groups. Shareholders as rational economic actors will only be ready to embark on litigation involving derivative proceedings if there is some benefit for them in due course.

In more recent times Janice Dean, in her defence of stakeholding, acknowledged that if stakeholding is to be implemented then there has to be a power to protect stakeholder expectations.[272] As discussed more in Chapter 5, Dean appears to think that permitting stakeholders the right to bring proceedings based on the unfair prejudice ground under s.994 of the Companies Act 2006 (formerly, s.459 of the Companies Act 1985) is the most promising for stakeholders.[273] The defence that would be available is that the directors had properly examined all the relevant options with appropriate reference to stakeholder interests.

John Parkinson recognised the enforcement problem when he said that placing a duty on directors to balance conflicting interests would:

> [P]resent the courts with a near-impossible task . . . not only would the court need to assess the likely impact on each group of a contested business policy, in both the short and the long term, but also it would have to evaluate the policy

---

[269]   For example, see UK (Pt. 11 of the Companies Act 2006), Canada (s.239 of the Canada Business Corporations Act 1985), Australia (Pt. 2F1A of the Corporations Act 2001), Singapore (s.216A of the Companies Act), New Zealand (s.165 of the Companies Act 1993), Hong Kong (s.168BC of the Companies Ordinance).

[270]   For example, in the US, see *Kusner v First Pa Corp*, 395 F. Supp. 276 at 280–83 (ED Pa 1975); *Dorfman v Chem Bank,* 56 FRD 363 at 364 (SDNY 1972).

[271]   Examples of exceptions are Canada and Singapore. Section 238(d) of the Canada Business Corporations Act 1985 includes amongst those who may make applications, 'any other person who, in the discretion of a court, is a proper person to make an application.' In a similar vein, s.216A(1)(c) of the Singaporean Companies Act provides that the range of persons who can apply for a derivative action includes 'any other person who, in the discretion of the Court, is a proper person.' For discussion of this issue, see Chapter 5.

[272]   J. Dean, *Directing Public Companies* (London, Cavendish, 2001) at 176.

[273]   Ibid at 177.

in accordance with a theory which stipulated when one set of interests should prevail over the others.[274]

Even if there were proceedings that could be taken by a stakeholder, it would be hard to assess if the interests of some stakeholders have been prejudiced, and then it may well be difficult to quantify the extent of the loss,[275] so any proceedings could, arguably only lead to an award for the company.

It is clearly difficult to formulate a set of rules that are able to be enforced by the courts.

4.7 Responsibilities and Objectives

The stakeholder theory often confuses responsibilities and objectives. Yet, responsibilities and objectives are, as argued in Chapter 1, to be distinguished.[276] It is necessary to identify the corporate objective before deciding what responsibilities might exist. Stakeholder theory tends to be used to support corporate social responsibility (CSR). But this is not the only theory that might favour CSR, for other theories could be used to support CSR.

4.8 Wrong View on Accountability

Elaine Sternberg argues[277] that the stakeholder theory is confused when it comes to the issue of accountability. She asserts that a company cannot be accountable to all people, groups or things that are related in some way, even if obscurely, and also while it may be said that a company should

---

[274] *Corporate Power and Responsibility* (Oxford, Clarendon Press, 1993) at 86.

[275] Gregory Crespi has attempted to explain how a court might go about determining whether a stakeholder had been injured by the decision-making of the directors, and, if so, to what extent ('Redefining the Fiduciary Duties of Corporate Directors in Accordance with the Team Production Model of Corporate Governance' (2002–03) 16 *Creighton Law Review* 623 at 637–639). But, with respect, the process with which a court would be faced, if the learned commentator's explanation were applied, is extremely complex. Crespi seemed to acknowledge this problem later in the article in which his views were asserted as he states that any obligation on a director in relation to stakeholder interests would have to be an aspirational norm rather than a legal directive (at 641).

[276] See I. Ansoff, *Corporate Strategy* (New York, McGraw-Hill, 1965).

[277] E. Sternberg, *Just Business*, 2nd ed (Oxford, Oxford University Press, 2000) at 50.

respond to so-called stakeholders such as employees or suppliers, this does not mean that it is accountable to them, except where there is some contractual (or legislative) provision requiring it in some form or another. Further, those whose co-operation is sought by a company cannot expect the company to account to them. If they are not content with what the managers are doing then they have the option of withdrawing their co-operation.[278] One response to that might be that some stakeholders will not be in a position to withdraw their involvement in the company. For instance, employees whose skills are inextricably related to what the company does and are not easily transferable elsewhere, and suppliers who are bound to provide goods and/or services for a prescribed period of time.

4.9   Fairness

The value of fairness is often highlighted as an element of stakeholder theory. But, it is argued by some that if non-shareholder stakeholders are favoured when they do not have contractual rights to warrant such favour being shown, then this involves an unfair and illegitimate transfer of value, and it comes at the expense of the shareholders.[279] Employing stakeholder theory ignores the free choice that was made to set up the company;[280] the shareholders engineered the establishment of the company and they expected the company to be their investment. When contracting, scholars have argued that stakeholders are able to 'price up' their provision of resources and so protect themselves while shareholders cannot do so.

It has also been argued that stakeholders are not as vulnerable as they are often made out to be, and so taking into account their interests means that they are unfairly advantaged. It is asserted that non-shareholding stakeholders do not invest all of their resources in the company at the one time, but incrementally, so if their expectations are not met or the bargain they struck is not honoured then they can withdraw their investment without substantial loss.[281]

---

[278]   E. Steinberg, 'The Defects of Stakeholder Theory' (1997) 5 *Corporate Governance: An International Review* at 3 at 7.

[279]   D. Millon, 'Communitarianism in Corporate Law: Foundations and Law Reform Strategies' in L. Mitchell (ed), *Progressive Corporate Law* (Boulder, Colorado, Westview Press, 1995) at 4.

[280]   T. Fort, 'The Corporation as Mediating Institution: An Efficacious Synthesis of Stakeholder Theory and Corporate Constituency Statutes' (1998) 73 *Notre Dame Law Review* 173 at 187.

[281]   A. Marcoux, 'A Fiduciary Argument Against Stakeholder Theory' (2003) 13 *Business Ethics Quarterly* 1 at 17.

Another issue of fairness is relevant, namely that companies who wish to engage in stakeholderism are not able to treat all stakeholders equally, and this is acknowledged by stakeholder theory. There will have to be, on occasions, partiality shown. It might be said that this, therefore, constitutes unfairness, given that many maintain that stakeholder theory is based on Kantian notions of equality.

It is possible that managers could, in purporting to implement stakeholder theory, choose to favour constituencies which have the best bargaining strength or political clout, and thus doing so would clearly breach the application of the value of fairness.

4.10 Legitimacy

We have seen that the theory posits that stakeholders are legitimate recipients of benefits from the company. However, there are doubts as to what are the conceptual grounds for asserting this. John Parkinson stated that: 'No single allocation of governance rights can be said to follow from the analyses that underpin stakeholder conceptions of the company.'[282]

4.11 Politicisation

It is argued that the stakeholder theory politicises the company as it enables special interests to place pressure on managers so they obtain benefits. In the same vein it permits managers to make decisions pursuant to their own personal views and to use resources for their own ends. This, it is argued, will reduce social wealth.[283]

4.12 Inefficient

It is argued that if those (the shareholders) who do not receive the marginal gains from the company's endeavour are not influencing decision-making, the company's wealth will not be maximised and, therefore, those involved in the company will not benefit.[284] The reason for this is that if the interest of stakeholders, such as creditors and employees, are to be taken into account then the directors will have to enter into only those

---

[282] J. Parkinson, 'Models of the Company and the Employment Relationship' (2003) 41 *British Journal of Industrial Relations* 481 at 495.

[283] M. Jensen, 'Value Maximisation, Stakeholder Theory, and the Corporate Objective Function' (2001) 7 *European Financial Management* 297 at 306.

[284] F. Easterbrook and D. Fischel, *The Economic Structure of Company Law* (Cambridge, Massachusetts, Harvard University Press, 1991), at 69.

ventures which will satisfy these interests. It is likely that these sorts of ventures will generally be of low risk as it is not in the interests of creditors and employees that the company embarks on actions that might produce huge benefits, but are of high risk.[285] This is because most non-shareholding stakeholders will not benefit from any great successes of the company, but will lose significantly if the risky action fails and the company becomes insolvent. For instance, the creditors will not be repaid the full amount owed, and employees will lose their jobs (unless the company or its business can be rescued). It might be contended that limiting the company to low risk activity could stifle the company's opportunities for higher returns and this produces inefficiency.

4.13   Vagueness in Promises

As mentioned earlier, some assert that directors are obliged to consider stakeholder interests to fulfil implied promises made to stakeholders. This assertion suffers from the same or similar problems discussed in relation to shareholder primacy theory (in Chapter 2). No such promise is ever made to stakeholders, and no contract exists between the managers and the stakeholders; any contracts are between the company and the stakeholder. And certainly there is no indication as to the substance of the promise. For many stakeholders it would be impossible to establish what directors are to do in relation to their interests and what interests they are to consider and favour. Take the community for instance. As Eugene Schlossberger has stated: 'the ways in which a company should be sensitive to the needs of its community are complex, flexible, subtle and changing characteristics ill-suited to a contract.'[286]

Rather than relying on particular promises some theorists rely upon the fact that managers should consider stakeholder interests out of benevolence.[287] This does not appear to be a reason for not implementing shareholder primacy, with, perhaps, some sensitivity to the needs of society

---

[285]   Shareholders at times may support the taking of excessive risk at the direct expense of other stakeholders, particularly creditors, in the hope of realising higher returns, and in the process running the risk of betting the company away (i.e. the asset substitution problem). See, M. Jensen and W. Meckling, 'Theory of the Firm: Managerial Behaviour, Agency Costs, and Capital Structure' (1976) 3 *Journal of Financial Economics* 305. Also, see C. Smith and J. Warner, 'On Financial Contracting – An Analysis of Bond Covenants' (1979) 7 *Journal of Financial Economics* 117 at 119.

[286]   'A New Model of Business: A Dual-Investor Theory' (1994) 4 *Business Ethics Quarterly* 459 at 463.

[287]   Ibid at 462.

being seen as a responsibility, but certainly not an objective of business. Again the theory mixes responsibility and objective.

5.   THE EMPLOYMENT OF THE THEORY

Whilst this book involves, primarily, a normative study, it might be helpful just to mention briefly what the descriptive situation is. Some would say that the stakeholder theory has been prejudiced by the implementation of shareholder value and this has been done through hostile takeovers, down-sizing, mergers and aligning executive pay to share values,[288] and it is, as we have seen, difficult to apply. Therefore, is it employed at all in Anglo-American jurisdictions?

There are some indications that stakeholder theory has been effectively applied in business. As far back as the 1920s Owen Young, the President of General Electric said that he acknowledged that he had an obligation to the stockholders to pay a fair rate of return, but he said that he also had an obligation to labour, customers and the public.[289] Later the chairman of the US company, Standard Oil, stated, in 1946, that the business of companies should be carried on 'in such a way as to maintain an equitable and working balance among the claims of the various directly interested groups – stockholders, employees, customers and the public at large.'[290] As indicated earlier, it is possible to find numerous references to the implementation of a form of stakeholder theory during the period from the 1920s to the 1960s. What about more recent times? A corporate reputation survey of Fortune 500 companies (the largest listed companies in the US) in the late 1980s found that satisfying the interests of one stakeholder does not automatically mean that this is at the expense of other stakeholders.[291] This is supported by empirical evidence, obtained in a study by the *Financial Times* of Europe's most respected companies, which found that chief executive officers were of

---

[288]   W. Beaver, 'Is the Stakeholder Model Dead?' (1999) 42 *Business Horizons* 3.

[289]   E. M. Dodd, 'For Whom are Corporate Managers Trustees?' (1932) 45 *Harvard Law Review* 1145 at 1154.

[290]   Quoted in M. Blair, *Ownership and Control* (Washington DC, The Brookings Institute, 1995) at 212. It is also quoted in N. Craig Smith, *Morality and the Market* (London, Routledge, 1990) at 65 and referred to in J. Parkinson, *Corporate Power and Responsibility* (Oxford, Oxford University Press, 1993) at 494, although the date given in the latter is 1950.

[291]   L. Preston and H. Sapienza, 'Stakeholder Management and Corporate Performance' (1990) 19 *Journal of Behavioral Economics* 361.

the view that one of the features of a good company was the ability to ensure that there was a balancing of the interests of stakeholder groups.[292] Former Chancellor William Allen of the Delaware Chancery Court in the US has said, extra-judicially, that the dominant view among leaders for the past 50 years has been that no single constituency's interests should exclude the interests of other constituencies from the fair consideration of the board.[293]

In a study conducted recently in Australia directors were asked by way of survey about their views of, and attitudes towards, stakeholders, and it was found that a majority (55 per cent) of directors said that they felt that they ought to balance the interests of stakeholders.[294]

Generally, apart from acknowledging the fact that creditors' interests need to be taken into account when the company is in financial difficulties (in the vicinity of insolvency in the US), courts in many jurisdictions reject any suggestions that interests wider than those of shareholders have to be taken into account by managers.[295] Although it must be noted that in the past seven years two critically important decisions of the Canadian Supreme Court have unequivocally rejected shareholder primacy, and while neither of these Canadian decisions stated that directors must consider stakeholder interests, they have permitted directors to do so. In *Peoples' Department Stores v Wise*[296] the Court said that directors had a duty to act in the best interests of the corporation and that 'best interests of the corporation' meant acting to maximise the value of the corporation. Justices Major and Deschamps went on to say that:

> We accept as an accurate statement of law that in determining whether they are acting with a view to the best interests of the corporation it may be legitimate, given all the circumstances of a given case, for the board of directors to consider, *inter alia*, the interests of the shareholders, employees, suppliers, creditors, consumers, governments and the environment . . . At all time, directors and officers owe their fiduciary duties to the corporation. The interests of the

---

[292]   Referred to in E. Scholes and D. Clutterbuck, 'Communication with Stakeholders: An Integrated Approach' (1998) 31 *Long Range Planning* 227 at 230.

[293]   'Our Schizophrenic Conception of the Business Corporation' (1992) 14 *Cardozo Law Review* 261 at 271.

[294]   S. Marshall and I. M. Ramsay, 'Shareholders and Directors' Duties: Law, Theory and Evidence,' Centre for Corporate Law and Securities Regulation, University of Melbourne, 2009, at 35 and accessible at: <http://cclsr.law.unimelb. edu.au/go/centre-activities/research/research-reports-and-research-papers/index. cfm> (last visited, 25 August 2009).

[295]   In the US and UK managers may have regard to stakeholder interests, but are not compelled to.

[296]   [2004] SCC 68; (2004) 244 DLR (4th) 564.

corporation are not to be confused with the interests of the creditors or those of any other stakeholders.[297]

The Court expressly stated that 'the best interests of the corporation' should be read not simply as 'the best interests of the shareholders.'[298] In the later case of *BCE Inc v 1976 Debentureholders*[299] the Court affirmed the fact that the directors may take into account the impact of decisions on non-shareholding stakeholders.[300]

It is asserted that some companies, such as Motorola and 3M, do run companies on a stakeholder basis.[301] In a study of the documents of Fortune 100 companies in the United States Lisa Fairfax found that all but two included commentary that indicated concern for stakeholder interests.[302] She has stated it is possible to see a shift in the greater employment of stakeholder rhetoric in the documents and communications of US companies.[303] Fairfax concluded from her study that companies feel obliged to pay attention to the concerns of groups and issues that are not related to shareholder profit,[304] and that companies do put into practice what they say they will do.[305]

The literature dealing with stakeholder theory continues to grow and more and more scholars appear to be persuaded that the theory is developing in strength in Anglo-American jurisdictions. The greater amount of social reporting that occurs[306] and the greater importance of human capital to companies[307] in Anglo-American jurisdictions, have, it has been

---

[297]   Ibid at [42]–[43].

[298]   Ibid at [42].

[299]   [2008] SCC 69.

[300]   Ibid at [39].

[301]   R. E. Freeman, A.Wicks and B. Parmar, 'Stakeholder Theory and "The Corporate Objective Revisited"' (2004) 15 *Organization Science* 364 at 365.

[302]   'Easier Said Than Done? A Corporate Law Theory for Actualizing Social Responsibility Rhetoric' (2007) 59 *Florida Law Review* 771 at 773.

[303]   L. Fairfax, 'The Rhetoric of Corporate Law: The Impact of Rhetoric on Corporate Norms' (2006) 31 *Journal of Corporation Law* 875; L. Fairfax, 'Easier Said Than Done? A Corporate Law Theory for Actualizing Social Responsibility Rhetoric' (2007) 59 *Florida Law Review* 771.

[304]   L. Fairfax, 'Easier Said Than Done? A Corporate Law Theory for Actualizing Social Responsibility Rhetoric' (2007) 59 *Florida Law Review* 771 at 775.

[305]   Ibid at 776.

[306]   S. Thomsen, 'The Convergence of Corporate Governance Systems and European and Anglo-American Standards' (2003) 4 *European Business Organization Law Review* 31.

[307]   S. Jacoby, 'Corporate Governance in Comparative Perspective: Prospects for Convergence' (2002) 22 *Comparative Labour Law and Policy Journal* 5.

suggested, moved these jurisdictions closer to the stakeholder position. Other commentators have questioned that conclusion.[308]

The above is only a soupçon of the influences of stakeholderism on practice, but it does show that aspects of it are applied, although not permitting us to conclude, especially in Anglo-American jurisdictions, that stakeholder theory is dominant or that it is operating in an undiluted form.

6. CONCLUSION

Stakeholder theory purports to bring economics and ethics together and to ensure that the interests of all stakeholders are taken into account by managers when deciding what action should be taken by the company. Importantly stakeholders are not to be seen as the means by which managers maximise the wealth of shareholders; considering stakeholder interests and benefiting such groups should be seen as an end in itself.

One of the major disagreements between the two leading theories seeking to determine the corporate objective relates to the issue of whether the managers can or cannot be trusted. Can they be trusted to seek the betterment of the stakeholders notwithstanding a lack of certainty in how they are to operate? The stakeholder theory relies on the professionalism and trustworthiness of the directors, while the shareholder primacy theory does not accept this as a relevant element as it assumes that directors will act opportunistically or shirk. It might actually be argued that implementation is a problem for stakeholder theory even leaving director opportunism and shirking aside. Directors who want to act honourably and properly would have difficulty knowing what to do in some situations. For instance, what if a course of action will benefit constituencies A, B and C, but not D and E? Another equally efficient course of action will benefit constituencies A, D and E, but not B and C. What do the directors do in such a case? How do the directors decide which of the two actions should be taken? They cannot benefit all groups and they have no real guidance as to which action they should take. Should they, therefore, take no action at all? Conceivably inertia could damage all constituencies.

The stakeholder model has a lot of attractions to many groups and people. It emphasises good values like trust and fairness (because the

---

[308] For example, see A. Keay, 'Moving Towards Stakeholderism? Constituency Statutes, Enlightened Shareholder Value and All That: Much Ado About Little?' (2011) 22 *European Business Law Review* 1.

employees are often a company's principal assets and the community is critical as the place where the company operates, so fairness dictates that their interests should be considered), but it has significant problems in implementation, which were recognised as far back as the 1930s.[309] Adolf Berle was of the view that running companies for many constituencies was appealing, but could not determine how it could be done. That is why he regarded shareholder primacy the way forward, as it could help to control managers.

The fact is that stakeholder theory has a lot of adherents and continues to have a significant amount of influence outside of stakeholder oriented jurisdictions, but as with many models it has substantial difficulties. Chief amongst these are: its failure to define who are stakeholders of a company; an inability to explain critical aspects of the theory, such as how directors are to balance the interests of stakeholders; its lack of clarity; a failure to articulate how the theory would work; the fact that it struggles to provide a normative basis; and it has not laid down a convincing answer to how the theory can be enforced. Arguably shareholder primacy is not as attractive from a normative perspective, although it might be regarded as more pragmatic and workable. While stakeholder theory has attractions, normatively speaking, it is not practical, and it has been argued[310] that stakeholder theory, while solving the problem of shareholder opportunism,[311] leads to a more serious problem of stakeholder opportunism, which can cause companies to pay a higher cost for public equity capital,[312] because investors are concerned about protecting their investment from rent-seeking by stakeholders.

So, there are significant points that favour the idea that directors should balance the interests of all stakeholders. However, it is submitted that they are outweighed by the many problems that are caused by endeavouring to strike a balance between interests. Clearly, most commentators, whatever view they take, accept that the balancing of stakeholder interests is a tricky

---

[309]   E.M. Dodd, 'Is Effective Enforcement of the Fiduciary Duties of Corporate Managers Practicable?' (1934) 2 *University of Chicago Law Review* 194 at 199.

[310]   L. Ribstein, 'Accountability and Responsibility in Corporate Governance' (2006) 81 *Notre Dame Law Review* 1431 at 1440.

[311]   That is shareholders choosing to take excessive risk at the direct expense of creditors in the hope of realising higher returns, and in the process running the risk of betting the company away (i.e. the asset substitution problem). See, M. Jensen and W. Meckling, 'Theory of the Firm: Managerial Behaviour, Agency Costs, and Capital Structure' (1976) 3 *Journal of Financial Economics* 305.

[312]   D. G. Smith, 'The Dystopian Potential of Corporate Law' (2008) 56 *Emory Law Journal* 785.

issue. It means that directors have to solve what some commentators see as impossible conflicts of interests.[313]

We have now ascertained that there are significant problems with both shareholder primacy and its main alternative, stakeholder theory. Consequently, we must look for some other approach. The next Chapter seeks to provide one.

---

[313] There are many American commentators who take this view. For example, J. Macey, 'An Economic Analysis of the Various Rationales for Making Shareholders the Exclusive Beneficiaries of Corporate Fiduciary Duties' (1991) 21 *Stetson Law Review* 23 at 31; V. Jelisavcic, 'A Safe Harbour Proposal to Define the Limits of Directors' Fiduciary Duty to Creditors in the "Vicinity of Insolvency"' (1992) 17 *Journal of Corporation Law* 145 at 148; N. Beveridge, 'Does a Corporation's Board of Directors Owe a Fiduciary Duty to its Creditors?' (1994) 25 *St Mary"s Law Journal* 589 at 621. This view gains some support from the Ontario High Court of Justice in *Royal Bank of Canada v First Pioneer Investments Ltd* (1980) 20 OR (2d) 352.

4. An entity maximisation and sustainability model

1. INTRODUCTION

Thus far the book has concentrated on examining the two dominant theories put forward for dealing with the issue of the corporate objective. While weaknesses have been identified most frequently in shareholder primacy by stakeholder theorists and weaknesses have been found in stakeholder theory by shareholder primacy advocates, leading to a significant polarisation in the consideration of the issue of the corporate objective, it is submitted that many of the weaknesses suggested in relation to each model are legitimate. Jonathan Macey has said[1] that no company can sustain the abstract goal of shareholder wealth maximisation or the broad stakeholder model. The former is unachievable given management's control, power and relationship to constituents other than shareholders. Similarly, given the fact that shareholders provide the capital required to keep the company going, the sustained application of the stakeholder model is precluded. Arguably, shareholder primacy is not attractive from a normative perspective, although it might be regarded as pragmatic and workable. It is argued that it provides for more certainty than stakeholder theory, but, although often overlooked, it does suffer from many uncertainties, as identified and discussed in Chapter 2. While stakeholder theory has attractions, normatively speaking, because, inter alia, it embraces values of trust and fairness, it is difficult to see how it can be applied effectively in practice.

Rather than seeking to modify either of these models it is felt that it is better to seek a new model. Consequently, in this Chapter I seek to formulate a new theory. A case for the need for a new model was made in Chapter 1 and further developed in examining the two predominant models that have been advocated, in Chapters 2 and 3. I do not intend to repeat what I have said earlier. The balance of the Chapter purports to

---

[1] 'Convergence in Corporate Governance' (1999) 84 *Cornell Law Review* 1166 at 1172.

explain the theory. Following Chapters will then add flesh to the material discussed in this Chapter as well as seeking to attempt to address some of the difficult issues that might be thrown up by implementing this model in practice.

The Chapter begins with a brief and general explanation of the new model. It is followed by an extensive discussion of the company as an entity. This discussion includes a consideration of much of the literature that has sought to examine the entity concept, and it is necessary given the focus of the model. Besides considering the theoretical literature on the nature of the company as an entity, this part of the Chapter refers to the doctrinal position that exists as well as drawing on the approach taken in the accounting discipline. After this discussion the Chapter returns to provide further consideration of the new model being posited, and it seeks to explain it and its consequences in greater detail, with some emphasis on trying to deal with hard cases that might be identified.

2.   A NEW MODEL

To ensure there is no confusion with stakeholder theory in this Chapter and following Chapters, those people and groups who have interests in the company will be referred to as investors. The term is often used to describe shareholders alone, but it is submitted that it is an appropriate term to be used for others, as people other than shareholders invest capital in companies. Creditors invest their money when they give credit, employees their skill and time, local governments invest in services, and so on. More will be said about these investors in Chapter 6.

Generally the emphasis of the literature has been on the issue: for whom should managers run the business or in whose interests should directors act? The general approaches, as already discussed, have been that the business is to be managed either for the shareholders in particular or for the stakeholders in general. However, this suggests a focus on people or groups rather than on an objective. It is too loaded a question to ask for whom the business should be run. Once we focus on groups, partisan interests come to the fore. Of course, one cannot dismiss concern for such groups, but once one begins to ask the question posed above, it becomes difficult for a model outside of the two major ones discussed to emerge.

The model that is being proposed here, the entity maximisation and sustainability Model (EMS) has two elements to it. First, putting it simply, there is a commitment to maximise the wealth of the entity. Management should seek to develop the total wealth-creating potential of the enterprise that they oversee.[2] The second part is to sustain the company as a going concern, that is, to ensure its survival;[3] that it will remain as a going concern.

An important aspect of the model is that there is focus on the company as an entity or enterprise, that is: 'an institution in its own right.'[4] The model assumes that the company has interests that are independent of any investor or group of investors who affect the company or are affected by it. The model might be thought to steer a course somewhere between the individualism of shareholder primacy and the collectivism of stakeholder theory.[5]

The corporate objective under this model is not the attainment of the public good. However, it is argued that seeking to meet the objective set out pursuant to this model will undoubtedly benefit the public good as the enhancement of the entity will result in benefits to the company's investors who are integral members of society, and whose good fortune from their involvement with the company can be transmitted into benefits for others not related to, or associated with, the company.

As EMS aims for the long term this will generally be fairer and benefit more investors, for some investors' interests are not satisfied short term. If a company aims to develop itself and to have a long existence, many shareholders are more ready to make long-term commitments to the business because if there is a risk of a sudden liquidation shareholders are more likely to make short-term and smaller investments in a company.[6] With such an approach the directors do not have to worry about fluctuations in the share price over a short term.

There are several attractive aspects to this model. First, investors are protected in that managers are not to foster the interests of any one investor or a particular group of investors, and this promotes fairness and

---

[2]   See M. Blair, *Ownership and Control* (Washington DC, The Brookings Institute, 1995) at 239.

[3]   The French Vienot Report in 1995 stated something that is similar (MEDEF-AFEP, Report 1 at 8) and referred to in E. Pichet, 'Enlightened Shareholder Value: Whose Interests Should be Served by the Supports of Corporate Governance' at 16 (accessible at <http://ssrn.com/abstract=1262879> (last visited, 15 December 2009).

[4]   W. Suojanen, 'Accounting Theory and the Large Corporation' (1954) 29 *The Accounting Review* 391 at 392.

[5]   Steering such a course is advocated in S. Wheeler, *Corporations and the Third Way* (Oxford, Hart Publishing, 2002) at 33, although the learned author takes things in a different direction.

[6]   K. Iwai, 'Persons, Things and Corporations: The Corporate Personality Controversy and Comparative Corporate Governance' (1999) 47 *American Journal of Comparative Law* 583 at 590.

decency. Second, this approach fosters maximum utilisation of assets. Directors are expected to refrain from mismanaging assets and as the focus is on the maximisation of the entity's wealth it is possible for assets to be used more efficiently. Third, the model attenuates the view that capitalism is harsh, because directors do not have to maximise the interests of shareholders at all costs, and they can also take into account, in their decision-making, issues other than economic ones. Fourth, it might be argued that when investing in a company, investors, besides expecting their rights to be respected, would expect their investment to be used to maximise company wealth;[7] that is how they will gain benefits.

This model is company focused, and while the company owes something to each of its investors, it is owned by nobody[8] and it is not a composite of all of the individual products of each co-operating resource;[9] it is an end in itself, and it is not an instrument of anyone but a living and developing enterprise[10] that is autonomous[11] and has a life of its own. The decision of the English Court of Appeal in *Short v Treasury Commissioners*[12] accords with this when it was said by Evershed LJ that the shareholders were not the owners of a company. His Lordship said that: 'Shareholders are not in the eyes of the law, part owners of the undertaking. The undertaking is something different from the totality of its shareholding.' As a result, EMS turns on the company being regarded as a distinct legal entity. The fact of the matter is that the entity exists separately from those who invest

---

[7] See R. Campbell Jr, 'Corporate Fiduciary Principles for the Post-Contractarian Era' (1996) 23 *Florida State University Law Review* 561 at 591–592.

[8] C. Handy, 'What is a Company For? (1993) 1 *Corporate Governance: An International Review* 14 at 16.

[9] This was acknowledged as far back as 1972 and mentioned in the classic work on team production: A. Alchian and H. Demsetz, 'Production, Information Costs and Economic Organizations' (1972) 62 *American Economic Review* 777 at 781–783. It would be impossible to find a single way of aggregating the interests of all stakeholders over time: S. Marshall and I. Ramsay, 'Stakeholders and Directors' Duties: Law, Theory and Evidence,' Centre for Corporate Law and Securities Regulation, University of Melbourne, 2009, at 15 and accessible at: <http://cclsr.law.unimelb.edu.au/go/centre-activities/research/research-reports-and-research-papers/index.cfm> (last visited, 25 August 2009).

[10] C. Handy, 'What is a Company For? (1993) 1 *Corporate Governance: An International Review* 14 at 17.

[11] This is the vision of the company in France: M. Vienot, 'Rapport sur le Conseil d'Administration des Societes Cotees' (1995) 8 *Revue de Droit des Affaires Internationales* 935 and referred to in A. Alcouffe and C. Alcouffe, 'Control and Executive Compensation in Large French Companies' (1997) 24 *Journal of Law and Society* 85 at 91.

[12] [1948] 1 KB 116 at 122.

in it, and continues to exist notwithstanding changes in the identity of the investors.[13] This is consistent with the view of the company articulated by Margaret Blair and Lynn Stout in their team production approach.[14] They said that once the shareholders have formed a corporation and selected a board, they have 'created a new and separate entity that takes on a life of its own and could, potentially, act against their interests.'[15] In effect EMS deals with the question of what is a company for, by answering 'for itself'.[16]

It is appropriate to consider the concept of the entity before explaining the model in any further detail given the fact that the entity approach is critical to EMS.

3.   THE CONCEPT OF THE ENTITY

3.1   Introduction

While it is not intended to embark on a detailed discussion of the nature of the company and the concept of the entity, because EMS is based on the entity concept it is not possible to refrain from some consideration of the nature of the company. However, I am conscious of the fact that the issue is a significant one that has been subject directly or indirectly to a substantial amount of comment and I cannot do justice to it with broader concerns in mind in this book.

The issue of the nature of the company is something over which there has been and still is significant uncertainty. As Stephen Bottomley points out, when considering the issue of the nature of a company:

> We are presented with a disjointed collection of rules in which the concept of the corporation is sometimes reduced to as a mere legal device (the corporation categorised as a legal person for liability purposes), but at other times is described by reference to the decisions of majority voters at a general meeting or 'the interests of the members as a whole,' or as an entity with interests that transcend the immediate concerns of its present members and directors.[17]

---

[13]   W. Suojanen, 'Accounting Theory and the Large Corporation' (1954) 29 *The Accounting Review* 391 at 393.

[14]   'A Team Production Theory of Corporate Law' (1999) 85 *Virginia Law Review* 247 at 251.

[15]   Ibid at 277.

[16]   C. Handy, *The Empty Raincoat: Making Sense of the Future* (Arrow Business Books, 1994) at 143.

[17]   S. Bottomley, *The Constitutional Corporation* (Aldershot, Ashgate, 2007) at 30–31.

The first point to note is the fact that EMS treats the entity as an actor, which is responsible for what is done in its name. In this interpretation the company can lead a life of its own.[18] A company is:

> [A] legal concept which, through the conferment of separate legal personality, provides legal recognition of bodies of persons as distinctive holders of rights under a collective name, having distinct legal consequences. This is not simply a matter of form and fiction.[19] (footnote omitted)

3.2 The Corporate Entity

3.2.1 The theory

The entity is an organisation that is separate from all those associated with it, including the members, and has legal standing and personality. It has its own purposes, rights and duties and is responsible for what it does, through its directors and agents. The company is not a fiction. It is an independent body that is self-sufficient and self-renewing,[20] and it acts in competition with other companies, firms and people.[21] Under this approach the organisation is very much the key to our experience of the company.[22] The life of the organisation is not simply the sum of all of the actions, rights and obligations of the individuals who are involved in the company;[23] it constitutes more than its changing parts.[24] The company

---

[18] M. Blair and L. Stout, 'A Team Production Theory of Corporate Law' (1999) 85 *Virginia Law Review* 247 at 277.

[19] J. Farrar, 'Frankenstein Incorporated or Fools Parliament? Revisiting the Concept of the Corporation in Corporate Governance' (1998) 10 *Bond Law Review* 142 at 142 and referring to *The Case of Sutton Hospital* (1613) 10 Coke Rep 1 at 32.

[20] M. Horwitz, '*Santa Clara* Revisited: The Development of Corporate Theory' (1985) 88 *West Virginia Law Review* 173 at 218.

[21] E. Orts, 'Shirking and Sharking: A Legal Theory of the Firm' (1998) 14 *Yale Law and Policy Review* 265 at 283.

[22] W. Bratton, 'The Economic Structure of the Post-Contractual Corporation' (1992) 87 *Northwestern University Law Review* 180 at 209. Also, see M. Blair, 'The Neglected Benefits of the Corporate Form: Entity Status and the Separation of Asset Ownership from Control' in A. Grandori (ed), *Corporate Governance and Firm Organization: Microfoundations and Structural Forms* (New York, Oxford University Press, 2004) at 45.

[23] P. Selznick, 'The Moral Commonwealth: Social Theory and the Promise of Community' (1992) at 242 and referred to in S. Bottomley, *The Constitutional Corporation* (Ashgate, Aldershot, 2007) at 31.

[24] P. Blumberg, 'The Corporate Personality in American Law: A Summary Review' (1990) 38 *American Journal of Comparative Law* 49. Also, see L. Hobhouse, *The Metaphysical Theory of the State: A Criticism* (1951) at 6

has its own characteristics that do not belong to its members.[25] The fact is that an organisation like a company can produce effects that are its true properties and not those of the people who are its members. These effects occur 'because of the way that people behave *together*, not just as aggregate effects of their separate behaviours.'[26](emphasis in original). The company's autonomy emerges as an effect of social action of the human parts.[27] That a company is entitled to use its profits to develop its operations etc and to maximise its wealth is itself evidence of the fact that it enjoys autonomy. The company in this way is to be contrasted with the unincorporated company which was popular in the nineteenth century and which involved a mere collection of individuals who constituted the company.[28] The company is individual entities in the form of shareholders unified into a single collective entity.[29] The corporate form developed because of its unique ability to promote and protect interests not only of shareholders but all kinds of investors whose investment was predicated on the continued existence and financial survival of the company, and all of this was possible because a separate entity was created that was separate from all investors.[30] The company can, for instance, own property in its name, make contracts, and take and defend legal proceedings. The fruit of any contract or legal proceedings is not for benefit of the shareholders, although they may receive something by way of dividend, but initially for the company itself. The interests of the shareholders and the interests of the company

---

and referred to by M. Phillips, 'Reappraising the Real Entity Theory of the Corporation' (1994) 21 *Florida State University Law Review* 1061 at 1114.

[25] Hobhouse, ibid at 27 referred to in Phillips, ibid at 1115.

[26] M. Keeley, *A Social-Contract Theory of Organizations* (Notre Dame, Indiana, Notre Dame University Press, 1988) at 230.

[27] K. Iwai, 'Persons, Things and Corporations: The Corporate Personality Controversy and Comparative Corporate Governance' (1999) 47 *American Journal of Comparative Law* 583 at 616. Also, see G. Teubner, 'Enterprise Corporatism: New Industrial Policy and the "Essence" of the Legal Person' (1988) 36 *American Journal of Comparative Law* 130.

[28] F.B. Palmer, *Company Law*, 21st ed (London, Sweet and Maxwell, 1968) at 134 and referred to in P. Ireland, I. Grigg-Spall and D. Kelly, 'The Conceptual Foundations of Modern Company Law' (1987) 14 *Journal of Law and Society* 149 at 150.

[29] V. Chassagnon, 'The Network-Firm as a Single Entity: Beyond the Aggregate of Distinct Legal Entities' and available at <http://ssrn.com/abstract=1386962> (last visited, 6 November 2009).

[30] M. Blair, 'The Neglected Benefits of the Corporate Form: Entity Status and the Separation of Asset Ownership from Control' in A. Grandori (ed), *Corporate Governance and Firm Organization: Microfoundations and Structural Forms* (New York, Oxford University Press, 2004).

can diverge. Also, as Sarah Worthington points out, the law recognises a distinction between corporate actions that lead to corporate liability and personal acts (of directors and shareholders) leading to personal liability, and she draws the conclusion that 'the company cannot realistically be regarded simply as shorthand for the shareholders; real entity theory recognises the legal realities associated with the company's position.'[31] The single entity, the company, submerges the interests, rights and liabilities of the shareholders who 'make up' the entity. The company is an institution as its existence and limits are defined and administered by an exogenous authority.[32] This was recognised by Lord Robertson in the UK House of Lords' decision in *British Equitable Assurance Company Ltd v Baily*.[33] Blair and Stout have asserted that the personality of the company is a key aspect of the corporate form, and it might be the most important characteristic in distinguishing it from other business vehicles such as partnerships and sole proprietorships.[34] The upshot is that the company is a real entity.

Of course, this general approach to the company is taken in many countries in continental Europe and Japan. In these jurisdictions the company is seen as an end in itself, something argued for in this book, although in Europe and Japan the interests of stakeholders intervene in a more direct way than is envisaged by EMS, with a greater focus on balancing the interests of the stakeholders.

There are different approaches propounded by those theorists advocating a real entity theory. What appears to be common to these approaches is that companies are real (not fictions), naturally occurring beings with features that their human members do not have.[35] Perhaps the most prominent approach has been the natural entity theory or organic theory,[36] which holds that the entity is not created by incorporation, but is merely

---

[31] 'Shares and Shareholders: Property, Power and Entitlement (Part 2)' (2001) 22 *The Company Lawyer* 307 at 309.

[32] S. Masten, 'A Legal Basis for the Firm' (1988) 4 *Journal of Law, Economics and Organization* 181 at 184.

[33] [1905] AC 35 at 39.

[34] M. Blair and L. Stout, 'Specific Investments and Corporate Law' (2006) 31 *Journal of Corporation Law* 719 at 729.

[35] A. Machen, 'Corporate Personality' (1911) 24 *Harvard Law Review* 253 at 262; M. Phillips, 'Reappraising the Real Entity Theory of the Corporation' (1994) 21 *Florida State University Law Review* 1061 at 1062, 1068.

[36] For some theorists taking this view, the term is interchangeable with 'real entity theory.' For example, see R. Harris, 'The Transplantation of the Legal Discourse on Corporate Personality Theories: From German Codification to British Political Pluralism and American Big Business' (2006) 63 *Washington and Lee Law Review* 1421.

recognised by that act.[37] The company is not a fiction but a non-reducible real entity,[38] and it is 'a group-person' with 'a group-will'. It is a living organism and a real person. The theory recognised the company's origin in the natural activities of individuals and it possessed powers given to it by its shareholders. Dicey said that 'whenever men act in concert for a common purpose, they tend to create a body which, from no fiction of law, but from the very nature of things, differs from the individuals of whom it is constituted.'[39]

A second approach was championed by Arthur Machen, and it posited that the entity is not a rational being, as the previous view would hold, and it has no will.[40] He argued that while the corporate personality was a fiction, 'the entity which is personified is no fiction.'[41] Machen took the view that this approach provided two critical propositions, namely that the corporation is an entity distinct from those who compose it, and the entity is a person.[42]

Another approach is that contended for by Gunther Teubner. It is based on autopoesis, which holds that the company is self-created as it is able to be described as a unit, and it has an independent existence.[43] In taking this approach Teubner builds on the work of Nicklas Luhmann.[44] Teubner states that: 'The internal dynamics of the legal person's substratum can be better understood by viewing the substratum as an autonomous communicative process, with actual people simply being treated as

---

[37]   This was made popular by the work of Otto Gierke, *Political Theories of the Middle Ages* (Cambridge, Cambridge University Press, 1900) (translated by F. Maitland). But there were writers taking the same view in ignorance of this work: J. Davis, 'The Nature of Corporations' (1897) 12 *Political Science Quarterly* 173. Also, see W. Brown, 'The Personality of the Corporation and the State' (1905) 21 *Law Quarterly Review* 365 at 370.

[38]   D. Gindis, 'From Fictions and Aggregates to Real Entities in the Theory of the Firm' (2009) 5 *Journal of Institutional Economics* 25 at 26.

[39]   A. Dicey, *Lectures on the Relation Between Law and Public Opinion in England during the Nineteenth Century* (London, Macmillan, 1905) at 154.

[40]   'Corporate Personality' (1911) 24 *Harvard Law Review* 253 at 265.

[41]   Ibid at 266.

[42]   Ibid at 258.

[43]   For example, see G. Teubner, *Law as an Autopoietic System* (Oxford, Blackwells, 1993); G. Teubner, 'Enterprise Corporatism: New Industrial Policy and the "Essence" of the Legal Person' (1988) 36 *American Journal of Comparative Law* 130. For a relatively recent work on autopoesis in general, see, T. Bakken and T. Hernes (eds), *Autopoietic Organization Theory* (Copenhagen, Copenhagen Business School Press, 2002).

[44]   For example, see N. Luhmann, *Social Systems* (Stanford, Stanford University Press, 1995).

part of the process's environment.'[45] Teubner argues that the autopoetic social system was a 'system of actions/communications that reproduces itself by constantly producing from the network of its elements new communications/actions as elements.'[46] According to Teubner, the company is real as it is a fiction that takes on structural effect and 'orients social actions by binding them collectively.'[47] The corporate entity is defined by the decisions that it makes and these decisions lead to further decisions, and this enables the entity to survive.[48] Teubner argues that there is no basis for any of the investors having the right to paramountcy. Rather the 'distribution of control rights within the firm is . . . governed by considerations of efficiency oriented towards the interests of the "corporate actor," which does not coincide with the interests of any participants.'[49] In French and German law a company is not a fiction or a convenience, but is part of a social reality.[50]

In any event real entity theory differs from fiction theory that provides that incorporation creates a company. As far as fiction theory is concerned it holds that the law cannot create an entity, but just recognises its existence. Under fiction theory a company cannot exist just because a certificate of incorporation is issued. Berle argued that the corporate entity takes its being from the reality of the underlying enterprise that is formed. It is this enterprise that is the true entity and because of this it is not the incorporation formalities that lead to the entity existing.[51]

David Gindis[52] takes the view that there are three generations of entity theorists. The first is the organic approach, as mentioned above. The second is the approach identified with Machen. The third generation focused, according to Gindis, on the effect of the entity view and not on essential definitions. The view of Berle falls into this camp. It also encompasses the approach adopted by Blair and Stout in their team production theory and their individual writings.

---

[45] 'Enterprise Corporatism: New Industrial Policy and the "Essence" of the Legal Person' (1988) 36 *American Journal of Comparative Law* 130 at 135.

[46] Ibid at 136.

[47] Ibid at 138.

[48] G. Teubner, *Law as an Autopoietic System* (Oxford, Blackwells, 1993) at 134.

[49] Ibid at 140.

[50] P. Nobel, 'Social Responsibility of Corporations' (1999) 84 *Cornell Law Review* 1255 at 1259.

[51] A. Berle, 'The Theory of Enterprise Entity' (1947) 47 *Columbia Law Review* 343 at 344, 358.

[52] D. Gindis, 'From Fictions and Aggregates to Real Entities in the Theory of the Firm' (2009) 5 *Journal of Institutional Economics* 25 at 32–35.

The view taken in this book is that the corporate entity is real and more than, and different from, the sum of its parts. The entity is created by the will of the members who come together to form it and have a common purpose. The entity is independent from, but dependent on, its members. All in all, the identity of the company entity and perpetual existence 'allow us to speak of collective capabilities, firm competitiveness, reputation, and so on, as emergent properties and causal powers of the firm.'[53]

3.2.2 Law and practice

While this is primarily a normative study, it is important to note that there is descriptive support for the entity concept. We have seen in the courts in the UK, the US and other jurisdictions references to companies as entities.[54] The entity theory better fits the law to the facts of the corporate world.[55] It also explains why shareholders can be members of the company, on the one hand, and yet bring legal proceedings against it, on the other. The company remains the same even when the identity of the shareholders and managers changes completely. A company established in the early twentieth century, and still existing today, has a completely different group of managers and shareholders, yet in a legal sense it is the same company. Also, the members of, say, a large company like BP are different today than they were a week or so ago, due to the large numbers of shares that are traded.

The case of *Lee v Lee's Air Farming Ltd*[56] is somewhat instructive. In this case there was a company, the archetypal 'one man company,' where Lee was the governing director and controlling shareholder. Lee was also appointed by the company (a crop-dusting contractor) as its chief pilot (and, therefore, an employee). Lee was killed while flying for the company and his wife claimed workers' compensation from the company's insurer. The insurer rejected the claim as it was of the view, inter alia, that Lee and the company were the same. Importantly, the Judicial Committee of the Privy Council differentiated Lee from the company and it said that Lee was, in his pilot capacity, contracted to the company. It went on to say: 'That relationship came about because the deceased as one legal person was willing to work for and to make a contract with the company which was another legal entity.'[57]

---

[53] Ibid at 41.
[54] See, G. Mark, 'The Personification of the Business Corporation in American Law' (1987) 54 *University of Chicago Law Review* 1441 at 1465.
[55] Ibid at 1470.
[56] [1961] AC 12.
[57] Ibid at 25.

In the classic UK case of *Salomon v Salomon and Co Ltd* [58] Lord
Halsbury LC said that:

> [O]nce the company is legally incorporated it must be treated like any other
> independent person with its rights and liabilities appropriate to itself, and that
> the motives of those who took part in the promotion of the company are abso-
> lutely irrelevant in discussing what those rights and liabilities are.[59]

His Lordship went on to say that the judges in the lower courts were
not certain whether to treat the company as a real thing. His Lordship
said that: 'If it was a real thing; if it had a legal existence, and if consequently the law attributed to it certain rights and liabilities . . . it is impossible to deny the validity of the transaction into which it has entered.'[60]
In the same case, Lord MacNaughton said that the company is at law a
different person altogether from the subscribers to the memorandum of
association.[61]

More recent case law acknowledges the entity principle. We have already
seen this in *Lee v Lee's Air Farming Ltd.* In *Re Halt Garages (1964) Ltd*[62]
Oliver J noted that several English cases had accepted the notion that the
directors could be required to work towards the success of the corporate
entity. Lord Denning MR said in *Wallersteiner v Moir (No 2)*[63]:

> It is a fundamental principle of our law that a company is a legal person,
> with its own corporate identity, separate and distinct from the directors or
> shareholders, and with its own property rights and interests to which alone it
> is entitled.[64]

The Supreme Court of New South Wales in *Darvall v North Sydney
Brick & Tile Co Ltd* [65] said that it was quite proper to have regard to the
interests of the company as a commercial entity, separate from the members.[66] The English Court of Appeal in *Fulham Football Club Ltd v Cabra
Estates plc*[67] appeared to adopt a similar approach when it stated that 'the
duties owed by the directors are to the company and the company is more

---

[58] [1897] AC 22.
[59] Ibid at 30.
[60] Ibid at 33.
[61] Ibid at 51.
[62] [1982] 3 All ER 1016 at 1035.
[63] [1975] QB 373.
[64] Ibid at 390.
[65] (1988) 6 ACLC 154 at 176.
[66] But see, *Re Humes Ltd* (1987) 5 ACLC 64 at 67.
[67] [1994] 1 BCLC 363 at 379.

than just the sum total of its members.' In *Peoples' Department Stores v Wise*[68] the Supreme Court of Canada, said that directors had a duty to act in the best interests of the corporation and that the phrase 'the best interests of the corporation' meant acting to maximise the value of the corporation. In the Scottish case of *Dawson International Plc* v. *Coats Paton Plc (No.1)*,[69] it was stated that the directors were, in conducting the affairs of the company and discharging their duties, to consider the interests of the company; they did not owe duties to the shareholders.[70] Other courts in the UK,[71] the US,[72] Canada[73] and Australia,[74] for example, have held that directors owe their duties *to the company*. Besides that fact, legislation in the UK[75] now clearly states that directors owe their duties to the company. This should surely mean the corporate entity.

In the US, the Delaware Chancery Court in *Credit Lyonnais Bank Nederland NV v Pathe Communications Corp*[76] also accepted the notion of the entity, referring to it as 'the corporate enterprise.' In that case, Chancellor Allen said that the board 'had an obligation to the community of interest that sustained the corporation, to exercise judgment in an informed, good faith effort to maximize the corporation's long-term wealth creating capacity.'[77] This was followed up in the same court in *Guttman v Huang*[78] in 2003 with the court saying that provided that he or she is fair to the corporation as an entity a director is able to engage in a self-dealing transaction.

The virtual abolition of the ultra vires doctrine in many common law jurisdictions in the past 20 years or so also speaks of the concept of

---

[68]   [2004] SCC 68; (2004) 244 DLR (4th) 564. Its approach was broadly accepted by the later Supreme Court case of *BCE Inc v 1976 Debentureholders* [2008] SCC 69.

[69]   1988 SLT 854; [1989] BCLC 233.

[70]   Ibid at 860; 241.

[71]   See, for example, *Lonrho Ltd v Shell Petroleum Co Ltd* [1980] 1 WLR 627 at 634 (HL).

[72]   See, for example, *United States v Byrum* 408 US 125 at 138 (1972); *United Teachers Associations Insurance Co v Mackeen and Bailey* 99 F 3d 645 at 650–651 (5th Cir, 1996).

[73]   *Peoples' Department Stores v Wise* [2004] SCC 68; (2004) 244 DLR (4th) 564; *BCE Inc v 1976 Debentureholders* [2008] SCC 69.

[74]   See, for example, *Brunninghausen v Glavanics* [1999] NSWCA 199; (1999) 17 ACLC 1247 at [43] (New South Wales Court of Appeal).

[75]   s.170(1) of the Companies Act 2006.

[76]   1991 WL 277613; 1991 Del Ch LEXIS 215; reprinted in (1992) 17 *Delaware Journal of Corporate Law* 1099 (Delaware Chancery Court).

[77]   See n. 55.

[78]   823 A 2d 492 at 502 (Del Ch Ct, 2003).

separate entity. Many pieces of legislation specify now that companies are not limited in their capacity to do things, no matter what the incorporators state in the company's constitution or charter.[79] The situation in the US is consistent with this latter development. The model Model Business Corporations Act provides companies with 'the same powers of an individual to do all things necessary or convenient to carry out its business and affairs.'[80]

A specific instance demonstrates the approach taken here. It is trite law that no one but the company is entitled to initiate proceedings to right a wrong done to it.[81] Even though derivative actions can now be brought by shareholders in most jurisdictions, either under legislation[82] or common law,[83] provided that there is court approval in most situations, the law regards the company as the victim. Such proceedings may be brought to serve the interests of the company as a whole, and not the shareholders' interests (at least not directly). Any financial benefits from the action go into the company's coffers. The existence of derivative actions might be said to be consistent with the acceptance of the entity theory and, even, entity maximisation.[84] Writers like Michael Whincop, who endorse the economic theory of the company to which we will refer shortly, have to go to extreme lengths to repudiate this, and do so by interpreting the exceptions to the rule in *Foss v Harbottle* as limits on majority rule.[85] In relation to this rule Lord Denning in *Wallersteiner v Moir (No 2)*[86] said that if a company is:

> [D]efrauded by a wrongdoer, the company itself is the one person to sue for the damage. Such is the rule in *Foss v. Harbottle* (1843) 2 Hare 461. The rule is easy

---

[79]   For instance, see s.39 of the Companies Act 2006 (UK).

[80]   s.3.02.

[81]   In English law this is encapsulated in the case of *Foss v Harbottle* (1843) 2 Hare 461.

[82]   For instance, see the UK (Part 11 of the Companies Act 2006); Canada (s.239 of the Canada Business Corporations Act 1985), Australia (Part 2F1A of the Corporations Act 2001), Singapore (s.216A of the Companies Act), New Zealand (s.165 of the Companies Act 1993), Hong Kong (s.168BC of the Companies Ordinance).

[83]   In the US, see *Kusner v First Pa Corp* 395 F Supp 276 at 280–83 (ED Pa 1975); *Dorfman v Chem. Bank* 56 FRD. 363 at 364 (SDNY 1972).

[84]   R. Campbell Jr, 'Corporate Fiduciary Principles for the Post-Contractarian Era' (1996) 23 *Florida State University Law Review* 561 at 589.

[85]   M. Whincop, 'Overcoming Corporate Law: Instrumentalism, Pragmatism and the Separate Legal Entity Concept' (1997) 15 *Company and Securities Law Journal* 411 at 424.

[86]   [1975] QB 373.

enough to apply when the company is defrauded by outsiders. The company itself is the only person who can sue. Likewise, when it is defrauded by insiders of a minor kind, once again the company is the only person who can sue. But suppose it is defrauded by insiders who control its affairs – by directors who hold a majority of the shares – who then can sue for damages? Those directors are themselves the wrongdoers. If a board meeting is held, they will not authorise the proceedings to be taken by the company against themselves. If a general meeting is called, they will vote down any suggestion that the company should sue them themselves. Yet the company is the one person who is damnified. It is the one person who should sue.[87]

Besides the case law, one can find recognition of the corporate entity, in the way we have been considering it, in the comments of the UK's Company Law Review Steering Group ('CLRSG') which, interestingly, said that shareholder wealth maximisation was the objective of the company.[88] The CLRSG talked about the business relationships which companies have as important intangible assets of *the company*.[89] It then went on to say that the state of directors' duties at common law are often regarded as leading to directors having 'an undue focus on the short term and the narrow interests of members at the expense of what is in a broader and a longer term sense the best interests of *the enterprise* . . .' (my emphasis).[90]

The concept of the entity has undoubtedly developed from the early days of the modern company law era. The deed of settlement company in the eighteenth and early part of the nineteenth centuries was really a glorified partnership,[91] and hence the company was not an entity separate from its members. The Joint Stock Companies Act 1844 regularised the position of the company and it was granted corporate status, but the legislation presumed that there was an existing association of individuals.[92] The situation was perpetuated by the Joint Stock Companies Act 1856, but things changed with the enactment of the Companies Act 1862. This development and its consequence are well articulated by Ireland, Grigg-Spall and Kelly.[93]

---

[87]   Ibid at 390.

[88]   Company Law Review, *Modern Company Law for a Competitive Economy*: Strategic Framework (London, DTI, 1999) at para 5.1.17.

[89]   Ibid at para 5.1.10.

[90]   Ibid at para 5.1.17.

[91]   M. Lobban, 'Corporate Identity and Limited Liability in France and England 1825–67' (1996) 25 *Anglo-American Law Review* 397 at 401.

[92]   R. Grantham, 'The Limited Liability of Company Directors' [2007] *Lloyds Maritime and Commercial Law Quarterly* 362 at 369.

[93]   P. Ireland, I. Grigg-Spall and D. Kelly, 'The Conceptual Foundations of Modern Company Law' (1987) 14 *Journal of Law and Society* 149 at 150. Also, see L.S. Sealy, 'The Director as Trustee' [1967] *Cambridge Law Journal* 83 at 89–90.

They explain that there was in the UK a subtle, but critical, distinction made in the Companies Act 1862, when compared with its 1856 predecessor. The earlier piece of legislation provided in section 3 that 'Seven or more persons . . . may . . . form *themselves into* an incorporated company.'[94] This suggested that the newly formed company was made up of the creators. Yet, the corresponding provision in the 1862 Act omitted the words 'themselves into'. So, the indication is that people no longer formed themselves into companies. Rather 'a company was made *by* them but not of them.'[95] This suggests that companies are separate from the members. Ireland et al point out that today a company is normally referred to by the use of the pronoun, 'it,' thus 'confirming its depersonalised, reified status,'[96] whereas during the nineteenth century and prior to the 1862 Act both incorporated and unincorporated companies were individually referred to as 'they'.[97]

In the modern world where the idea of ownership without control prevails in large public companies, the notion of entity sits better with the fact that shareholders of large companies are not actively involved in the company's business; they are merely investors,[98] as are others, such as creditors. The *Principles of Corporate Governance* that has been published by the Organisation for Economic Co-operation and Development seems to accept the fact that the company is an entity.[99]

Finally, accountants employ the entity concept. They utilise what is known as the entity theory of accounting, the essence of which involves recognising that creditors as well as shareholders contribute resources to the company and the company exists as a separate entity apart from those groups.[100] Assets and liabilities belong to the company,[101] and in

---

[94]   This is the emphasis of the authors.

[95]   P. Ireland, I. Grigg-Spall and D. Kelly, 'The Conceptual Foundations of Modern Company Law' (1987) 14 *Journal of Law and Society* 149 at 150. The emphasis is that of the authors.

[96]   Ibid at 150.

[97]   Ibid. The commentators take the view that it is not incorporation that is the source of the principle of separate personality, but the historical processes that lead to the company share emerging as a form of fictitious money capital (at 160).

[98]   D. Millon, 'The Ambiguous Significance of Corporate Personhood', Washington and Lee University, School of Law, Working Paper No 01-6, January 2001 at 8–9.

[99]   OECD Publications, 2004 at 46.

[100]   See, R. Sprouse, 'The Significance of the Concept of the Corporation in Accounting Analyses' (1957) 32 *The Accounting Review* 369.

[101]   R. Schroeder, M. Clark and J. McCathey, *Accounting Theory and Analysis*, 7th ed (New York, John Wiley, 2001) at 444. Also, see R. Scott, '"Owners" Equity: The Anachronistic Element' (1979) 54 *The Accounting Review*

accounting terms the company is an entity and a going concern that is autonomous and separate from shareholders and all other stakeholders.[102]

3.2.3 The criticism

Notwithstanding the above, there has been a significant amount of criticism of the entity concept of the company.[103] For some the theory was said to be 'medieval, mystical, unrealistic and romantic.'[104] Those favouring economic analysis of law tend to assert, in furthering their methodological individualism, the fact that the company is an aggregation of persons[105] and they take the view that the company is an abstraction; it is a sum of its human and, sometimes non-human parts.[106] Robert Hessen saw the company as a shorthand symbol.[107] Where the company is an aggregate one cannot, so the argument goes, distinguish in any real sense between the rights of the company and those humans that constitute it.[108] But, if one reduces the company to no more than its constituent parts, it also means that we humans can be reduced simply to a load of chemicals.[109] Just as one loses the big picture by reducing a human to a selection of

---

750; Y. Biondi, 'Accounting and the Economic Nature of the Firm as an Entity' in Y. Biondi, A. Canziani and T. Kirat (eds), *The Firm as an Entity* (Abingdon, Routledge, 2007).

[102] Y. Biondi, A. Canziani and T. Kirat (eds), *The Firm as an Entity* (Abingdon, Routledge, 2007) at 17.

[103] For example, see M. Radin, 'The Endless Problem of Corporate Personality' (1932) 32 *Columbia Law Review* 643; F. Cohen, 'Transcendental Nonsense and the Functional Approach' (1935) 35 *Columbia Law Review* 809.

[104] M. Phillips, 'Reappraising the Real Entity Theory of the Corporation' (1994) 21 *Florida State University Law Review* 1061 at 1099, and referring to M. Radin, 'The Endless Problem of Corporate Personality' (1932) 32 *Columbia Law Review* 643 at 649.

[105] The academic forebears of these scholars are Ihering in Germany, de Vareilles-Sommières in France and Schwabe in Switzerland: A. Machen, 'Corporate Personality' (1911) 24 *Harvard Law Review* 253 at 257

[106] M. Phillips, 'Reappraising the Real Entity Theory of the Corporation' (1994) 21 *Florida State University Law Review* 1061 at 1066.

[107] 'A New Concept of Corporations: A Contractual and Private Property Model' (1979) 30 *The Hastings Law Journal* 1327 at 1336. This approach is not new. It was in existence in the nineteenth century. See W.J. Brown, 'The Personality of the Corporation and the State' (1905) 21 *Law Quarterly Review* 365 at 370.

[108] M. Metzger and D. Dalton, 'Seeing the Elephant: An Organizational Perspective on Corporate Moral Agency' (1996) 33 *American Business Law Journal* 489 at 497.

[109] D. Greenwood, 'Introduction to the Metaphors of Corporate Law' (2005) 4 *Seattle Journal for Social Justice* 1 at 15.

chemicals, one does the same with a company by seeing it as made up of a group of people.[110] One loses sight of the bigger picture.

Whincop regarded the company as 'a pragmatic compromise'.[111] One of the problems with the aggregate approach is that if new members join the company then the attributes of the company cannot be the same as they were before the entry of the new people.[112] Just as the entry of a new partner to a partnership sees the creation of new partnership, the entry of new members to a company would, on this view, see a new firm created. In some ways a closely-held company can be seen as an aggregate of individuals carrying on business together because the shareholders usually have far more involvement than do shareholders in public companies, but even so, not one individual or a group of them can do certain things, such as making contracts save through the company itself or holding property as the company, unless they have authority under the company's constitution or pursuant to a board resolution, and the membership may well not remain the same for the life of the company.

Ross Grantham has said that the company is merely a device that enables the law to distinguish between the rights of individuals involved in the company as individuals from the rights of those individuals in a different collective capacity.[113] But that seems to be making shareholders schizophrenic. Shareholders who are individuals have rights, and that is the end of the story.

Frank Easterbrook and Daniel Fischel scoff at the notion that the company is an entity in its own right.[114] They see the concept of 'the personhood of the company as a matter of convenience rather than a reality.'[115] The company is not real according to these commentators.[116]

---

[110]   D. Gindis, 'Some Building Blocks for a Theory of the Firm as a Real Entity' in Y. Biondi, A. Canziani and T. Kirat (eds), *The Firm as an Entity* (Abingdon, Routledge, 2007) at 278.

[111]   'The Political Economy of Corporate Law Reform in Australia' (1999) 27 *Federal Law Review* 77

[112]   M. Phillips, 'Reappraising the Real Entity Theory of the Corporation' (1994) 21 *Florida State University Law Review* 1061 at 1108. This did not appear to worry Armen Alchian who saw the entry of new members as leading to a new firm: 'Specificity, Specialization and Coalitions' (1984) 140 *Journal of Institutional and Theoretical Economics* 34 at 47.

[113]   R. Grantham, 'The Limited Liability of Company Directors' [2007] *Lloyds Maritime and Commercial Law Quarterly* 362 at 369.

[114]   F. Easterbrook and D. Fischel *'The Economic Structure of Corporate Law* (Cambridge, Massachusetts, Harvard University Press, 1991) at 12.

[115]   Ibid.

[116]   Ibid at 89.

Others, such as, Michael Jensen and William Meckling deny that a company has its own goals and intentions.[117] On the aggregate view the company is merely regarded as involving actions by individuals and the only aim is to maximise the benefits of the shareholders. The company is regarded by some as a mirage,[118] but if that is so, it makes it difficult to explain why many companies spend large amounts of money in merging and de-merging.[119]

Advocates of the approach just outlined, generally subscribe to the view that the company is a nexus of contracts,[120] whereby the company is seen in economic rather than legal terms.[121] The firm is not regarded as existing as a separate entity – it is just a shorthand notation for the set of contracts.[122] The firm, as it is often referred to, is merely the sum of the contracts that constitute it and the firm cannot be worth more than the sum of the contracts.[123] The nexus of contracts paradigm asserts that the idea of the company being a person is an empty fiction and is to be rejected.[124] The problem with this view is that if the company is merely

---

[117] 'Theory of the Firm' (1976) 3 *Journal of Financial Economics* 305.

[118] O. Hart, 'An Economist's Perspective on the Theory of the Firm' (1989) 89 *Columbia Law Review* 1757 at 1764.

[119] J. Moore, 'The Firm as a Collection of Assets' (1992) 36 *European Economic Review* 493 at 494.

[120] This idea is that the parties involved in these contracts are regarded as rational economic actors, and includes shareholders, managers, creditors and employees, and it is accepted that each of these constituencies endeavour in their contracting to maximise their own positions, with the intention of producing concomitant benefits for themselves. The literature considering the nexus of contracts is too voluminous to cite. But see, for example, M. Jensen and W. Meckling, 'Theory of the Firm' (1976) 3 *Journal of Financial Economics* 305 at 309–310; E. Fama, 'Agency Problems and the Theory of the Firm' (1980) 88 *Journal of Political Economy* 228 at 290; F. Easterbrook and D. Fischel, 'The Corporate Contract' (1989) 89 *Columbia Law Review* 1416 at 1426–1427; S. Deakin and A. Hughes, 'Economic Efficiency and the Proceduralisation of Company Law'(1999) 3 *Company Financial and Insolvency Law Review* 169 at 176–180; I. McNeil, 'Company Law Rules: An Assessment from the Perspective of Incomplete Contract Theory' (2001) 1 *Journal of Corporate Law Studies* 107.

[121] S. Bainbridge, 'Director Primacy in Corporate Takeovers: Preliminary Reflections' (2002) 55 *Stanford Law Review* 791 at 799.

[122] L. Zingales, 'In Search of New Foundations' (2000) 55 *Journal of Finance* 1623 at 1631.

[123] According to Luigi Zingales, some definitions of the nexus only include explicit contracts, while others embrace implicit contracts as well: ibid at 1634.

[124] Although, often law and economics scholars do accept the entity concept when explaining the company in legal terms. For example, see S. Bainbridge, *Corporation Law and Economics* (New York, Foundation Press, 2002) at 7.

a matter of convenience for arranging the affairs of individuals, how is it that a shareholder can sue the company or even be said to own it? Further, how can contracts be made with a company if the company entity does not exist and the company is really a nexus of contacts, made up of a number of constituencies? Yet it is the case that the shareholders can actually make legally enforceable contracts with the company entity. This was well demonstrated, above, in the case of *Lee v Lee's Airfarming Ltd.* [125]

Another concern is that in the nexus approach it is not just humans who make up the firm, but 'the utility maximizing rational actors of economic theory.'[126] These can include non-humans which seems to contradict aspects of aggregate theory. How can non-humans be members of the parts whose sum equals the firm?

A further problem with the nexus concept is that it is not clear where the firm begins and ends,[127] for there appear to be no precise limits to it. An illustration given by Blair and Stout is thought-provoking.[128] They ask whether an executive director who makes a contract with General Motors is 'in' the firm at that point? What if a small company makes a contract with General Motors to supply car parts? The commentators ask in relation to this latter situation: are GM and the supplier one single company?

Whincop explains that the nexus metaphor is not a 'simulacrum of truth' but a 'paradigm in which research is conducted.'[129] If this is correct the problem is that the nexus idea strays past its boundaries. Those arguing for an explanation of the company in economic terms tend to want to 'have their cake and eat it.' They wish to deny the personhood of the company and see the company as merely an aggregation of individuals in some circumstances, and at other times, particularly when it comes to liability issues and in other situations where it is pragmatically attractive, to invoke the separate personhood of the company; shareholders and managers cannot be liable for the contracts and other actions of the company. Many of the writings of aggregate proponents assume that there is a company entity and that it, itself, can prosper or fail; there is

---

[125] [1961] AC 12.
[126] M. Phillips, 'Corporate Moral Personhood and Three Conceptions of the Corporation' (1992) 2 *Business Ethics Quarterly* 435 at 439.
[127] M. Blair and L. Stout, 'Specific Investments and Corporate Law' (2006) 31 *Journal of Corporation Law* 719 at 739.
[128] Ibid.
[129] M. Whincop, 'Overcoming Corporate Law: Instrumentalism, Pragmatism and the Separate Legal Entity Concept' (1997) 15 *Company and Securities Law Journal* 411 at 412.

often a reference to 'the organisation' or 'the company' etc, but there is no indication what this means.

All will agree that a company is not human. But if a company is a collection or aggregation of humans, as law and economics posits, one would think that one could not deny the humanness of the company?[130] Also, if a company was the sum of its human parts it could not act without the agreement of all shareholders.[131] The fact of the matter is that the courts clearly say that the company is not to be confused with the shareholders. This latter point accords with the fact, as discussed in Chapter 2,[132] that the people who are supposed to 'own' the company have very limited control over it, under company law, particularly in the US. Finally, the problem that is presented with the contractarian model of the company, embraced in aggregate theory, is that it is unable:

> to deal with the relationship between the company and other entities because it does not provide any unambiguous conceptual vehicle by which the company may be disaggregated from its shareholders . . . It is extremely difficult to provide an adequate conceptual foundation for the ability of the company itself to enter into a variety of external relationships and to be held accountable for its conduct in those relationships.[133]

Of course, the nexus of contract theory is based on economic analysis rather than legal analysis, but even accepting that point, we cannot deny the legal and the fact that the theory does not fit either law or accounting practice, discussed above.[134]

Law and economics scholars are not the only ones to eschew the notion of the company entity when considering in whose interests the directors should act. John Parkinson, who was a strong supporter of the pluralist approach to company law, said, in his excellent book on corporate power and responsibility, that there can be no emphasis on benefiting the company. He said:

---

[130] C. Bruner, 'The Enduring Ambivalence of Corporate Law' (2008) 59 *Alabama Law Review* 1385 at 1389.

[131] M. Phillips, 'Reappraising the Real Entity Theory of the Corporation' (1994) 21 *Florida State University Law Review* 1061 at 1083.

[132] Above at 90–92.

[133] S. Berns and P. Baron, *Company Law and Governance: An Australian Perspective* (Melbourne, Oxford University Press, 1998) at 143–144.

[134] Paddy Ireland argues that nexus of contracts tries to take us back to the early nineteenth century and before the time when we got general limited liability and other aspects of company law: 'Property and Contract in Contemporary Corporate Theory' (2003) 23 *Legal Studies* 453 at 474.

A requirement to benefit an artificial entity, *as an end in itself*, would be irrational futile, since a non-real entity is incapable of experiencing well-being. Indeed, it is doubtful that an inanimate entity can meaningfully be said to have interests . . . and the enterprise's purpose can be understood only in terms of serving human interests or objectives. The correct position is thus that the corporate entity is a vehicle for benefiting the interests of a specified group or groups. (footnotes omitted)[135]

I would respectfully disagree, as companies can clearly have interests. For instance, companies have been said to be able to seek protection of their interests and rights under the Human Rights Act 1998 (this incorporates the European Convention on Human Rights into UK law). It was held by the English Court of Appeal in *R v Broadcasting Standards Commission*[136] that a company can have its privacy infringed and could complain about that fact under the Broadcasting Act 1996. The Court of Appeal in *Huntingdon Life Sciences v Curtin*[137] said that a company could be the subject of harassment.[138] In the United States the Fourteenth Amendment of the American Constitution, which 'has proven to be the wellspring' of many of the individual rights of American citizens,[139] has been applied to corporations. A company's property cannot be taken from it without the due process of the law.[140] Companies will have interests that continue as the number and identity of investors in the company changes. All of this manifests the fact that the company has moved to the point of having a form that is equivalent to the nature and status of a natural person.[141] The judgment of the court in *Dawson International Plc v. Coats Paton Plc (No.1)*,[142] to which reference has already been made, appears, as Parkinson acknowledges,[143] to accept a separate entity interest. In that case Lord Cullen said:

---

[135]   J. Parkinson, *Corporate Power and Responsibility* (Oxford, Oxford University Press 1993) at 76–77.

[136]   [2001] QB 885; [2000] 3 WLR 1327; [2001] BCC 432.

[137]   [1998] Env LR D9, CA.

[138]   The case was distinguished in *Daiichi Pharmaceuticals UK Ltd and others v Stop Huntingdon Animal Cruelty* [2003] EWHC 2337; [2004] 1 WLR 1503.

[139]   L. Mitchell, *Corporate Irresponsibility* (New Haven, Yale University Press, 2001) at 42.

[140]   R. Monks and N. Minnow, *Corporate Governance*, 4th ed (Chichester, John Wiley, 2008) at 14.

[141]   J. Nesteruk, 'Persons, Property and the Corporation: A Proposal for a New Paradigm' (1990) 39 *DePaul Law Review* 543 at 551.

[142]   1988 SLT 854; [1989] BCLC 233.

[143]   J. Parkinson, *Corporate Power and Responsibility* (Oxford, Oxford University Press, 1993) at 78, n21.

At the outset I do not accept as a general proposition that a company can have no interest in the change of identity of its shareholders on a take-over. It appears to me that there will be cases in which its agents, the directors, will see the take-over of its shares by a particular bidder as beneficial to the company. For example, it may provide the opportunity for integrating operations or obtaining additional resources. In other cases the directors will see a particular bid as not in the best interests of the company.[144]

My argument is that for the purposes of the corporate objective directors are to work to enhance the benefit of the entity, but I must add that in doing so natural people will ultimately and necessarily benefit, that is, the investors' interests will be fostered.

The objection that is sometimes voiced is that the entity concept requires the company to be reified.[145] The worry that is often raised is that it is a mechanism 'for making something that is in fact complex seem simple, and that can be dangerous.'[146] Nevertheless it has been accepted as a useful mechanism, even by its critics,[147] and the latter have acknowledged that it would be difficult to communicate in an effective way without the use of reification.[148] The law does not appear to have a problem with reification,[149] and there seems no reason why it cannot be employed provided that it is used subject to caveats. It is worth noting that adherents to the fiction concept of the company and who support the nexus of contracts metaphor, and who are some of the most fervent critics of the entity theory on the basis that it relies on reification, in fact acknowledge that saying that the company is a nexus of contracts involves engaging in reification.[150]

---

[144]   [1989] BCLC 233 at 242–243.

[145]   For example, see F. Easterbrook and D. Fischel, *The Economic Structure of Corporate Law* (Cambridge, Massachusetts, Harvard University Press, 1991), at 11–12; E. Orts, 'The Complexity and Legitimacy of Corporate Law' (1993) 50 *Washington and Lee Law Review* 1565 at 1578–1579. Easterbrook and Fischel criticise the use of reification (ibid at 11–12), as do M. Gulati et al, 'Connected Contracts' (2000) 47 *University of California at Los Angeles Law Review* 887 at 888–893.

[146]   W. Klein and J. Coffee, *Business Organization and Finance: Legal and Economic Principles*, 10th ed (New York, Foundation Press, 2007) at 117–118.

[147]   Ibid at 118.

[148]   M. Gulati et al, 'Connected Contracts' (2000) 47 *University of California at Los Angeles Law Review* 887 at 890.

[149]   The word is defined in the *Oxford English Dictionary* (Vol 13, 2nd ed, 1989 at 532) as 'the mental conversion of a person or thing or abstract concept into a thing.' (quoted by G. Crespi, 'Rethinking Corporate Fiduciary Duties: The Inefficiency of the Shareholder Primacy Norm' (2002) *Southern Methodist University Law Review* 141 at 155, n42).

[150]   See, S. Bainbridge, *The New Corporate Governance in Theory and Practice* (New York, Oxford University Press, 2008) at 18, 26.

Companies legislation in the UK, and many other jurisdictions inherit-
ing English law, has contained, for many years, a provision that is usually
referred to as providing for a 'statutory contract'. The section in the
Companies Act 2006 which provides for this is section 33. The section
states that members are bound to each other and to the company. For the
first time in the long history of this statutory contract, it is made clear in
section 33 that the company itself is bound by this contract. The section
clearly reifies the company entity.

Furthermore, we reify other bodies such as the government or the Church.
Economists regularly do it when referring to 'society'. All of the aforementioned bodies, like a company, need to have human agents to act for them,
and the company, like the government, does not function apart from the
human agents;[151] it cannot exist apart from human interaction.[152] Stephen
Bainbridge, a law and economics scholar, admits, after acknowledging the
fact that contracts have to be made with the entity if one wishes to contract
with the company, and if the contract is breached it is the entity that sues
or is sued (with any damages in the latter situation coming out of company
funds and any damages in the former situation going to the company's
accounts), that one cannot dismiss all of these facts as mere reification.[153]

Moreover, some writers seem happy to refer to the entity, and say
that the entity created by the act of incorporation has the power to make
contracts, hold property[154] and to take legal action, but then, in another
context, they seek to vilify the concept on the basis of reification. If we can
talk about companies owning property, why cannot we talk about them
maximising wealth?

Obviously, as acknowledged earlier, a company needs human agents to
act for it. So, does that mean the company is not a real entity? As Lord
Reid said in *Tesco Supermarkets Ltd v Nattrass*:[155]

---

[151]   See, J. Strauss, 'The Entrepreneur: The Firm' (1944) 52 *Journal of Political
Economy* 112 at 112.

[152]   J. Dewey, *Experience and Nature* (Chicago, Open Court, 1925) at 163. Also,
see J. Dewey, 'The Historical Background of Corporate Legal Personality' (1926)
35 *Yale Law Journal* 655 at 673.

[153]   'The Board of Directors as Nexus of Contracts' (2002) 88 *Iowa Law Review*
1 at 16.

[154]   Even law and economics scholars, Henry Hansmann and Reiner
Kraakman ('The Essential Role of Organizational Law' (2000) 110 *Yale Law
Journal* 387) accept that the entity holds assets. This is a key point in their argument that the entity permits asset partitioning, namely providing a separate pool
of assets associated with the entity, but separate from those of the shareholders
('owners' according to Hansmann and Kraakman) and managers.

[155]   [1972] AC 153.

A living person has a mind which can have knowledge or intention or be neg-
ligent and he has hands to carry out his intentions. A corporation has none of
these: it must act through living persons, though not always one or the same
person. Then the person who acts is not speaking or acting for the company. He
is acting as the company and his mind which directs his acts is the mind of the
company . . . He is an embodiment of the company or, one could say, he hears
and speaks through the persona of the company, within his appropriate sphere
and his mind is the mind of the company.[156]

Throughout the case law in common law jurisdictions there are many
anthropomorphisms employed by judges. These are often not strictly
correct. But anthropomorphising the company does not deny the existence of an entity, nor does the fact that humans act for the company.
For instance, when a company is in liquidation the liquidator occupies
the position of agent of the company.[157] He or she has the power to bind
the company.[158] But, notwithstanding this, throughout liquidation the
company is treated as an entity.

While advocating the fact that the directors are not to act in the company's affairs without having consideration for the interests of shareholders, the late Jim Gower did acknowledge that directors could act for the
'economic advantage of the corporate entity.'[159]

In sum, while there are many who criticise the company as an entity
there are clear arguments that support the fact that it exists separately
from the people who formed it and own shares in it.

4. EXPLAINING THE MODEL

Earlier in the Chapter I set out the model in very broad terms. Now it is
intended to deal with it in greater detail. There are two major elements
to it, namely maximisation and sustainability. It is intended to deal with
these separately and then in later chapters to consider certain elements of
the model that warrant consideration and greater explanation.

---

[156] Ibid at 170.
[157] *Re Anglo-Moravian Ry Co.* (1875) 1 Ch D 130; *Knowles v Scott* [1891] 1 Ch
717; *Butler v Broadhead* [1975] Ch 97 at 108; *Re Timberland Ltd; Commissioner
for Corporate Affairs v Harvey* (1979) 4 ACLR 259 at 285; *Sydlow Pty Ltd v TG
Kotselas Pty Ltd* (1996) 14 ACLC 846.
[158] See *Re Farrow's Bank Ltd* [1921] 2 Ch 64.
[159] L.C.B. Gower, *Principles of Modern Company Law*, 5th ed (London, Sweet
& Maxwell, 1992) at 554.

4.1   Maximisation

Entity maximisation involves the fostering of entity wealth, which will involve directors endeavouring to increase the overall long-run market value of the company as a whole, taking into account the investment made by various people and groups. In other words, directors should seek to maximise the total wealth-creating potential of the company, so they should do that which value maximises the corporate entity, with the result that the net present value to the company as a whole is enhanced, and so is its strategic importance. The aim is that the company fulfils itself and grows and develops to the best that it can be.[160] All of this means that the directors are to foster the success of the company in terms of meeting its individual goals. In doing all of this directors should have concern for 'the community of interest'.[161] This means that the common interest of all who have invested in the company is to be fostered, but it does mean that at some point one group might benefit at the expense of another.[162] It also means that the common interest of the investors does not, at any time, supersede the interest of the entity as a whole. If the company is a real entity that is separate from its shareholders, as argued for above, then there is no requirement for the directors to reflect the expectations of the shareholders;[163] they can make decisions for the company itself. EMS means that the directors are not under the direct control of the shareholders or any other stakeholder group. This allows the directors to make decisions which are best for the entity and not any investor. In looking at what a company has achieved it is usually impossible either to say which investors' contribution was most valuable or to rank the usefulness of investor input. But, as discussed in Chapter 6 in detail, many investors contribute

---

[160]   C. Handy, 'What is a Company For?' (1993) 1 *Corporate Governance: An International Review* 14 at 16.

[161]   In *Credit Lyonnais Bank Nederland NV v Pathe Communications Corp* 1991 WL 277613; 1991 Del Ch LEXIS 215; LEXIS 215; reprinted in (1992) 17 *Delaware Journal of Corporate Law* 1099 (Delaware Chancery Court), at [34] per Chancellor Allen. This might be said to overlap with the argument posited by some, namely that directors act as stewards who identify with their company and its corporate aspirations: J. Davis, F.D. Schoorman and L. Donaldson, 'Toward a Stewardship Theory of Management' (1997) 22 *The Academy of Management Review* 20.

[162]   This is accepted even by some advocates of stakeholder theory. See W. Evan and R. Freeman, 'A Stakeholder Theory for Modern Corporations: Kantian Capitalism' in T. Beauchamp and N. Bowie (eds), *Ethical Theory and Business* (Englewood Cliffs, Prentice-Hall, 1988), at 103.

[163]   G. Mark, 'The Personification of the Business Corporation in American Law' (1987) 54 *University of Chicago Law Review* 1441 at 1472–1473.

to the success of a company and it is for directors to determine the value of that contribution to the company and to the company's maximisation and survival.

Maximisation *might*, in concrete terms, lead, inter alia, to improved dividends for shareholders, timely repayment of, and reduction of risk for, creditors, improved working conditions, greater job security and bonuses for employees, improved service of customers, treating suppliers consistently and fairly, and a contribution to a stable living environment in which the company operates, and so on. But, rather than the focus being on the investors and their interests, as stakeholder theory requires, the focus is on the entity and what will enhance its position. Any benefits for investors flow from that very object. EMS turns that around. So that rather than concentrating on what will benefit investors, with a possible consequence being the enhancement of the company entity, EMS focuses on entity benefit and its wealth enhancement, and the benefits to investors will be as a consequence of that. While some kinds of benefits to investors can enhance the entity, others can in fact see the entity's wealth decline. For instance, management needs to be aware of the point where employee benefits just become a drain on company wealth with no quid pro quo for the company. Georges Enderle and Lee Tavis give the example of the benefit of supplying breakfast to workers, which while it benefits employees may also produce benefits for the company. But if breakfast is also given to workers' families this might not be productive for the company;[164] there will be a point reached that any benefit bestowed on an investor will be counter-productive for the company. It is often going to be difficult for managers to know how far they take benefits for any investor group. At some point the cost of the benefit will go beyond the overall advantage to the company. Of course, there always may be long-term benefits to the company in making a short-term loss.

Also, importantly, entity maximisation does not focus solely on profit maximisation, namely maximising earnings per share. It certainly does not focus on what some shareholder primacy theorists would advocate, namely share price maximisation. Companies can maximise without being restricted to maximising profits.[165] What EMS is concerned with is the entity's interests are to be maximised for the long term – this might entail making less profit one year compared with a previous one, but still

---

[164]   'A Balanced Concept of the Firm and the Measurement of Its Long-term Planning and Performance' (1998) 17 *Journal of Business Ethics* 1129 at 1141.

[165]   D. Rose, 'Teams, Firms and the Evolution of Profit seeking Behavior' (1999) at 5, and accessible at <http://papers.ssrn.com/sol3/papers.cfm?abstract_id=224438> (last visited, 30 July 2010).

maximising the entity for the future. There are clear benefits to working for the long term, as recognised by many shareholder value theorists. Some of the benefits are contributions 'to the preservation and expansion of human, natural and social capital – assets without which business cannot operate.'[166] Looking to the long term permits time for research and development work and innovative approaches to come to fruition. Also, long-term approaches can engender trust and confidence in the company's customers[167] and other stakeholders. A long-term approach conveys the idea that the company is not involved in 'smash and grab' but seeking to develop ties with investors over a significant period.

Sometimes there are suggestions that the welfare of the company and the welfare of the shareholders coincide, and what is good for the company is good for its shareholders. For example, note the comment of the American Law Institute that a company: 'should have as its objective the conduct of business activities with a view to enhancing corporate profit and shareholder gain.'[168] And frequently management links its view of its company's well-being with shareholder well-being.[169] But financial theorists have argued for some time that the maximisation of total corporate earnings does not necessarily translate into shareholder wealth.[170] Also, there could be a conflict of interest in relation to the risk between the company and the shareholders.[171] It is a critical implication of the popular modern portfolio theory that the welfare of the company is clearly distinguishable from that of shareholders.[172]

The maximisation process involves more than just profit maximisation, although most maximising activities will aim to be profitable for the company in the long run. Maximisation encompasses wealth in broad

---

[166] A. White, 'What is Long-Term Wealth?' September 2007 at 1, and accessible at <http://www.bsr.org/reports/bsr_awhite_long-term-wealth.pdf> (last visited, 16 October 2009).

[167] I. Davis, 'What is the Business of Business?' (2005) *McKinsey Quarterly* 18 (Issue 3) at 19.

[168] *Principles of Corporate Governance: Analysis and Recommendations*, s.2.01(a) at 69 (Proposed Final Draft 11, 31 March 1992)

[169] R. Miller, 'Ethical Challenges in Corporate-Shareholder and Investor Relations: Using the Value Exchange Model to Analyze and Respond' (1988) 7 *Journal of Business Ethics* 117 at 127.

[170] For example, A. Rappaport, *Creating Shareholder Value* (New York, The Free Press, 1986) at 19.

[171] H. Hu, 'New Financial Products, the Modern Process of Financial Innovation and the Puzzle of Shareholder Welfare' (1991) 69 *Texas Law Review* 1273 at 1281.

[172] Ibid at 1307.

terms and embraces such things as augmenting reputation, which can be seen as the most important intangible asset of a company.[173] Firms have economic incentives to have a good reputation in communities where they have offices and factories. Failure to do this might mean that they are subjected to higher taxes or find it hard to recruit workers.[174] The fostering of reputation does not always easily translate into profits. But whilst difficult to measure,[175] an enhancement of it is likely to increase entity wealth in due course, sometimes only in the long term. A company might decline to take on a project that despite being potentially profitable in the short term, might alienate the local or wider community and lead to the entity being derided and see its reputation diminish, something that has happened to large well-known companies in recent years. For instance, Nike in the past established manufacturing facilities in low-wage countries, and the reporting of its alleged exploitation of third-world workers, resulted in significant brand damage.[176] A classic example is that of the James Hardie group in Australia. For many years member companies of the group were involved in using asbestos in producing products. After agreeing to set up a trust fund for employees who suffered from asbestos-related conditions, the group reorganised so that it transferred control of A$1.9 billion of assets of the companies that had used asbestos and could be held liable, to a Dutch company. The fund set up for workers was found to be woefully insufficient to meet claims.[177] The reputation of the group has been affected and its profits affected by what it did in transferring assets off-shore.[178]

---

[173] J. Dean, *Directing Public Companies* (London, Cavendish, 2001) at 107. Also, see S. Letza, X. Sun and J. Kirkbride, 'Shareholding and Stakeholding: a Critical Review of Corporate Governance' (2004) 12 *Corporate Governance: An International Review* 242 at 255; R. Woolley, 'Shareholder Analysis' 31 *Company Secretary's Review* 62, 8 August 2007.

[174] L. Ribstein, 'Accountability and Responsibility in Corporate Governance' (2006) 81 *Notre Dame Law Review* 1431 at 1457–1458.

[175] Australian Parliamentary Joint Committee on Corporations and Financial Services, 'Corporate Responsibility: Managing Risk and Creating Value,' June 2006 at para 4.28 and accessible at <http://www.aph.gov.au/senate/committee/corporations_ctte/completed_inquiries/2004-07/corporate_responsibility/report/index.htm> (last visited, 16 December 2009).

[176] Ibid at para 3.6.

[177] For further details, see the article on the Ethical Corporation website and accessible at <http://www.ethicalcorp.com/content.asp?ContentID=3018> (last visited, 9 January 2010).

[178] S. Long, 'James Hardie profits slump in wake of asbestos cases' Australian Broadcasting Commission website, 14 February 2005, and accessible at <http://www.abc.net.au/worldtoday/content/2005/s1302408.htm> (last visited, 31 August 2010).

There are other actions that can be taken to maximise entity wealth in the long term such as investing in the development of intellectual property, research and development, know-how, brands and ideas. Investing in these sorts of ventures will often only produce profit in the longer term. Also, maximisation can encompass building up the company's tangible assets, such as plant, land and stock for future development as well as its intangible capital. Commitments to customer value, employee satisfaction and creditor protection are able to be seen as enhancing the company's overall position.[179] Overall maximisation could be seen in developing sound corporate strategies (with sustainability in mind), realistic performance aims and constructing a culture that is known for integrity and fairness as well as producing an excellent product for the market. The idea behind EMS is the adding of value.

The vision for the long term and the maximising of entity wealth means eschewing actions such as trimming labour costs, scrimping on health and safety matters that can put the workforce and the community in danger, the delaying of the payment of creditors, the employment of sharp practices with respect to suppliers, and embracing risky ventures so as to increase revenue growth. Invoking EMS means that directors will not be moved to act in order to justify a high share price, or to 'cook the books' (by, for example, manipulating its financial statements), acquire unprofitable assets or firms or undertake investment projects with negative net present value.[180] It permits managers to invest more in research and development (which is a clear investment made so as to generate future cash and profit flows), the training of employees, and to make investments in the local and broader community because it intends to be located there for the long haul. As Jensen has said: 'Value creation does not mean succumbing to the vagaries of the movements in a firm's value from day to day.'[181] Determining what should be done is very much up to the good faith decisions of the directors. Further discussion of their role and what brakes are put on them is found in Chapter 7.

---

[179] S. Thomsen, 'Corporate Values and Corporate Governance' (2004) 4 *Corporate Governance: An International Review* 29 at 37.

[180] See, P. Joerg, C. Loderer, L. Roth and U. Waelchli, 'The Purpose of the Corporation: Shareholder-value Maximization?' European Corporate Governance Institute Finance Working Paper No 95/2005, February 2006 at 13 and available at <http://ssrn.com/abstract=690044> (last visited, 30 June 2009).

[181] M. Jensen, 'Value Maximisation, Stakeholder Theory, and the Corporate Objective Function' (2001) 7 *European Financial Management* 297 at 309.

It might be argued, in the language of hypothetical bargain theory,[182] that as entity maximisation endeavours to increase the value of all investors' interests *ex post* (as the entity maximises its wealth potential), the investors would bargain for it *ex ante* if they could have done so.[183] Hypothetical bargain analysis (asking what parties would have agreed to *ex ante*) is just as applicable to contracts between the company and fixed claimants and others as it is to the contract between the firm and the shareholders. Obviously all investors would approach *ex ante* negotiations with widely differing interests. If asked, before entering into a contract, creditors would be likely to expect there to be an implicit term that directors would not act in a way that would undermine the possibility of repayment.[184] Employees and suppliers would expect the company not to take action that would place their jobs in jeopardy. Local government authorities might be willing to provide certain services, or make certain concessions, but on the implicit basis that the company would retain its factory or offices in the same locality for a reasonable period of time.[185]

---

[182]   Sometimes referred to as the 'hypothetical perfect contract.' See C. Rose, 'Stakeholder Orientation versus Shareholder Value – A Matter of Contractual Failures' (2004) 18 *European Journal of Law and Economics* 77 at 79.

[183]   T. Smith, 'The Efficient Norm for Corporate Law: A Neotraditional Interpretation of Fiduciary Duty' (1999) 98 *Michigan Law Review* 214 at 244; A. Chaver and J. Fried, 'Managers' Fiduciary Duty Upon the Firm's Insolvency: Accounting for Performance Creditors' (2002) 55 *Vanderbilt Law Review* 1813 at 1825.

[184]   Creditors could, of course, include in the credit contract some covenants that seek to reduce the creditors' risk in granting credit and restricting the ways in which directors might act. But the construction of such covenants is never easy, for a number of reasons, chief of which are probably the unwillingness of directors to agree to restrictions, and bounded rationality (that is, the limits of the human mind in comprehending and solving complex problems); see A. Keay and H. Zhang, 'Incomplete Contracts, Contingent Fiduciaries and a Director's Duty to Creditors' (2008) 32 *Melbourne University Law Review* 141.

[185]   This approach is used in relation to companies that are undergoing Chapter 11 bankruptcy in the United States. See *In re Johns-Manville Corp* (1985) 52 Bankr 879 (NY); *Official Committee of Unsecured Creditors v R F Lafferty & Co* (2001) 267 F 3d 340 at 348 (3rd Circuit). Also, see, R. Nimmer and R. Feinberg, 'Chapter 11 Business Governance: Fiduciary Duties, Business Judgment, Trustees and Exclusivity' (1989) 6 *Bankruptcy Developments Journal* 1 at 33; R. Campbell and C. Frost, 'Managers' Fiduciary Duties in Financially Distressed Corporations: Chaos in Delaware (and Elsewhere)' 2006 and available at <http://papers.ssrn.com/sol3/papers.cfm?abstract_id=900904> (last visited, 30 July 2010). See, for example, *In re Central Ice Cream* 836 F 2d 1068 at 1072 (7th Circuit, 1988). Although what is meant by this is not articulated clearly: Nimmer and Feinberg refer to the need for the debtor in possession (the company's management) to balance the competing interests present: 'Chapter 11 Business Governance: Fiduciary Duties, Business

But all investors would agree, it is submitted, that they would like to see the directors obliged to maximise the overall wealth of the company as that would be in their collective interest.[186]

Some, such as Jensen, argue that the corporate objective must be one that has a single value, and in his view this should be the maximisation of shareholder value.[187] He states that you cannot tell a manager to maximise current profits, market share, future growth in profits etc as that leaves the manager with no objective. There is much to commend in having one main objective. In fact EMS has one overall goal (it is argued later that maximisation and sustainability are complementary), but how that is implemented will, obviously, depend on a number of issues including the company's circumstances, the business strategy and the market conditions. So how companies actually achieve the objective of maximisation is a matter for them given their business aims, and the market in which they operate.

The issue that is often discussed when it comes to maximising company wealth is the situation where the company determines to make workers redundant and/or close a plant and transfer company operations to another location. It must not be forgotten that in doing this a company does incur significant costs, such as making redundancy payments to workers and paying for the cost of some workers to transfer. What is often overlooked when there is a plant closure and operations are transferred elsewhere is that there will be jobs created at the site of the new plant. But many might argue that there was an existing obligation to workers at the present site and they should take precedence over prospective workers. Stephen Bainbridge posits[188] the instance of a company considering the closing down of an obsolete plant and opening a new one, whereby the workers at the old plant and the local community will be harmed, but shareholders, creditors and employees at the new plant will benefit. To determine which course of action they are to take as directors, Bainbridge states that it is clear; they have to seek shareholder wealth maximisation and that means the closing down of the old plant

---

Judgment, Trustees and Exclusivity' (1989) 6 *Bankruptcy Developments Journal* 1 at 34.

[186] See G. Crespi, 'Redefining the Fiduciary Duties of Corporate Directors in Accordance With the Team Production Model of Corporate Governance' (2003) 16 *Creighton Law Review* 623 at 636.

[187] M. Jensen, 'Value Maximisation, Stakeholder Theory, and the Corporate Objective Function' (2001) 7 *European Financial Management* 297 at 300.

[188] S. Bainbridge, *The New Corporate Governance in Theory and Practice* (New York, Oxford University Press, 2008) at 66–67.

and opening a new one. Whilst under EMS the same decision might well be made, the determining factor would be: what benefits the company in the long run?

Another example is worth considering. A company improves a product at a significant cost to itself, and it has to decide whether to increase the price it charges for it. It is effectively giving more to its customers, and if it is sold at the same price, customers have a clear benefit. If a price increase is made the customer gets a benefit but pays for it. The board must decide which strategy will ultimately bring long-term wealth to the company. It might be the case that the board decides to charge the same price because not only will customers remain loyal they will publicise how much better the product is, thus increasing sales. Alternatively, the board might reason that it will be more beneficial to increase the price, and to provide some other benefit to customers, such as another product at a lower price if they stay loyal to the improved product and the company makes gains.

One of the concerns that we identified with stakeholder theory was that the balancing of the interests of investors is difficult to implement. Is the entity maximisation approach any different? Directors do not have to engage in active balancing between investors' interests as their aim is to maximise entity wealth. To be sure, the directors will inevitably have to undertake some balancing, as is necessary in applying most principles, including the principle of shareholder primacy. But the balancing, unlike that in stakeholder theory, is not the balancing of interests, but of courses of action, and it has a clear goal, namely the maximisation and sustainability of the entity. The problem with balancing, as it exists in the context of stakeholder theory, is that there is no goal to the balancing; balancing is an end. But with EMS it is only part of the process, in attaining the purpose of the company. EMS does not force directors to weigh up the benefits and harm accruing to different stakeholders as a result of a particular action. Their remit is to act to enhance the wealth of the entity, and any balancing must seek to achieve this. The directors have to be the ones who decide what will maximise entity wealth, based on the circumstances and advice they take. Of course, they are accountable for their decisions, and this issue is discussed later in Chapter 7.

It is submitted that EMS is able to be fair and efficient. The former because those investing in the company have its affairs run so as to enhance the company's wealth and not ultimately for a particular group. If people invest in a company, whilst they can expect their involvement to be respected, they have to accept that the company is to be managed for the benefit of the company itself, and not for them specifically.

EMS is efficient[189] as, inter alia, fewer transaction costs might result because investors are not to be so concerned about the implementation of costly measures to provide them with the same protection that might be implemented if some other corporate objective exists. Also, EMS means that employees and creditors and others want to continue to invest in the company, thus reducing the cost of finding and contracting with new investors. Keeping investors contented will enhance and sustain the company, for, when compared with shareholder primacy, it is more likely to precipitate loyalty from the investors. Arguably without loyalty the future of a company is limited. Loyalty is engendered because the directorial focus is on maximising the entity's wealth and not benefiting the shareholders. Those investors who are creditors might be more willing to grant credit and/or continue lines of credit when they know that the directors are not focusing on shareholder wealth, but entity wealth, for they will know that they are not necessarily going to come second to the shareholders in directorial decision-making. Arguably what is proposed is efficient as there is evidence that the economic interests of shareholders are more and more entwined with those of the leading non-shareholding investors.[190] In Chapter 5 I seek to explain how EMS might be enforced. Permitting all investors to bring proceedings against directors for failing to engage in maximising of company value, something for which I argue in Chapter 5, would be efficient as all investors might have an incentive to enforce EMS.[191]

The benefit of the model also can be seen when a company can be regarded as in financial difficulty. If shareholder primacy applied then the directors would be pursuing those actions which might benefit shareholders, but could be deleterious for the company (and other investors). It is likely when a company is in financial difficulty to be in the shareholders' interests that the directors embrace greater risks,[192] for the

---

[189]   Gregory Crespi's research leads him to the view that it is more efficient if directors owe duties to the company rather than the shareholders: 'Rethinking Corporate Fiduciary Duties: The Inefficiency of the Shareholder Primacy Norm' (2002) *Southern Methodist University Law Review* 141 at 143. This view is also taken by Thomas Smith: 'The Efficient Norm for Corporate Law: A Neotraditional Interpretation of Fiduciary Duty' (1999) 98 *Michigan Law Review* 214.

[190]   V. Ho, '"Enlightened Shareholder Value": Corporate Governance Beyond the Shareholder-Stakeholder Divide' abstract accessible at <http://ssrn.com/abstract=1476116> (last visited, 8 January 2010).

[191]   See, T. Smith, 'The Efficient Norm for Corporate Law: A Neotraditional Interpretation of Fiduciary Duty' (1999) 98 *Michigan Law Review* 214 at 265

[192]   R. Scott, 'A Relational Theory of Default Rules for Commercial Contracts' (1990) 19 *Journal of Legal Studies* 597 at 624; L. LoPucki and W. Whitford,

shareholders have little to lose if a venture is not successful, while if it is successful the shareholders will make a substantial amount. Of course, if the venture is unsuccessful and the company ends up in liquidation the shareholders, because of the concept of limited liability, will not lose any more than they would if the company took no action. But, of course, insolvency would have potentially dire consequences for other investors. Creditors would not get paid in full, employees will lose their jobs (unless the company could be rescued, and even then not all employees might continue in employment), suppliers will lose their customer, the government is not going to recoup all tax owed, and the community will lose an employer.

Of course, the model does not tell managers exactly what to do. What businesses should be pursued, what products should be made or services offered, which people should be hired as employees, how ventures should be funded, from where credit should be sought, where should factories or offices be located etc, are all issues that must be determined by the managers given such things as market conditions, what investors can be obtained and the outlook for its business and commerce in general. What the model does do is to provide the managers with a reference point. All of the issues raised above must be resolved on the basis of maximising the entity's wealth. As indicated earlier, this will involve considering what will benefit the company in the long term, and this is likely to involve weighing up particular strategies. For example, from a practical point of view, it means that if the board resolves that producing X is going to benefit the company in the long term then deviating from that activity must be justified, and that the deviation taken will enhance entity wealth, and is not done simply to benefit some investor interest. The only qualification to the last statement is that the board believes that for some reason the deviation in order to benefit an investor(s) will benefit the entity in the long term.[193] The fact is that the managers have to choose what is the best policy, project or course of action that will maximise the company's position. In making decisions the board must look past whether the project they are considering will make profit (although that is of course a matter

---

'Corporate Governance in the Bankruptcy Reorganization of Large Publicly Held Companies' (1993) 141 *University of Pennsylvania Law Review* 669 at 768; B. Adler, 'A Re-Examination of Near-Bankruptcy Investment Incentives' (1995) 62 *University of Chicago. Law Review* 575 at 590–598; R. de R Barondes, 'Fiduciary Duties of Officers and Directors of Distressed Corporations' (1998) 7 *George Mason Law Review* 45 at 46 and 49.

[193] See, E. Sternberg, *Just Business*, 2nd ed (Oxford, Oxford University Press, 2000) at 43.

that warrants consideration), whether the project 'exceeds a hurdle rate for return on investments'[194] and whether the directors are attracted by it. The board will have to assess the negative and positive factors relating to the project[195] and determine from the data and the opinions of experts, if that is relevant, whether the project will provide entity enhancement over the long term. In doing all of this the views of investors are not irrelevant as the fostering of entity wealth in the direction that the board thinks is appropriate might well be heavily dependent on carrying some or all of the investors with them. The views of investors are not sought and taken into account because the investors are entitled to this (although their reasonable and legitimate expectations should be considered), but because their involvement and support could be a critical feature of the project leading to entity enhancement. So, an investor's view might be ignored if it is likely to derogate from a course of action that is believed will take a company forward in terms of EMS.

A significant advantage of EMS is that the directors, while respecting investors and recognising their importance to the company, are not especially accountable to any specific group. However, pursuing EMS is likely to promote the long-term interests of all investors, although as we will see shortly, it might be that a particular course of action will be deleterious for one or more of the investors. Developing long-term relationships with investors can enable the company (and the investors) to obtain the full value from the investment made.[196] EMS should generally serve investors well, for increasing organisational wealth will, for the most part, pay off for investors.[197]

An important element of this model as with any model is that the managers, while not formally accountable to investors, inform the investors of their major decisions and then explain why they have taken these decisions and how they will maximise the company's interests. If this is done then there is less likelihood of investors becoming disillusioned, and of the company losing them.

How do directors maximise entity wealth? Well this is going to depend on each company, but they obviously need to consider what produces wealth. Margaret Blair, in her excellent book, *Ownership and Control*,[198]

---

[194]   Ibid at 56.
[195]   Ibid.
[196]   M. Blair, *Ownership and Control* (Washington DC, The Brookings Institute, 1995) at 244.
[197]   J. Davis, F. Schoorman and L. Donaldson, 'Towards a Stewardship Theory of Management' (1997) 22 *Academy of Management Review* 25.
[198]   Washington DC, The Brookings Institute, 1995 at 240–241.

asserted[199] that there are three different ways that wealth can be generated. First, providing to the market 'products and services that are worth more to the customer than the customer pays for them.' Second, providing 'opportunities for workers to be more productive at their jobs than they could be in other available employment.' Third, the company is able to 'provide a flow of profits to its investors that is greater than those investors could get by investment in alternative activities.' This approach addresses the questions asked by Allan Kennedy when, in questioning shareholder primacy, he states:

> How many companies would spend their wealth on stock buyback programs if their objective was to create wealth? How many companies would see fit to cut R & D expenditure if their objective was to build wealth? How many companies would cavalierly shed long-term, loyal employees, their heads crammed full of information valuable to the company, if their objective was to create wealth?[200]

The approach taken in this Chapter accords somewhat with what Keynes had to say in the mid-1920s when he said that managers wishing to 'avoid criticism from the public and customers' were going to be concerned with 'the general stability and reputation of the institution than with "maximum profit."'[201] Allied to this is the fact that the managers need to anticipate and, perhaps, respond to the market's view of a company's corporate responsibility, for if they do not then that may well impact on the company's wealth and development, and, even, survival.[202]

What EMS does is to enable the managers to do what they are effectively employed to do, namely to act in the best interests of the company, which is the overarching duty of directors in over 40 jurisdictions around the world.[203]

---

[199] The points were repeated in M. Blair, 'Directors' Duties in a Post-Enron World: Why Language Matters' (2003) 38 *Wake Forest Law Review* 885 at 898–899.

[200] *The End of Shareholder Value: Corporations at the Crossroads* (Cambridge, Massachusetts, Perseus, 2000) at 207.

[201] J. Keynes, *The End of Laissez-Faire* (1926) reprinted in *Essays in Persuasion* (1931) at 314–315 and quoted by P. Ireland, 'Corporate Governance, Stakeholding and the Company: Towards a Less Degenerate Capitalism?' (1996) 23 *Journal of Law and Society* 287 at 291.

[202] See R. Aguilera, D. Rupp, C. Williams and J. Ganapathi, 'Putting the S Back in Corporate Social Responsibility: A Multi-Level Theory of Social Change in Organizations' at 20 (2007) <http://ssrn.com/abstract=567842> (last visited, 12 December 2009); L. Ribstein, 'Accountability and Responsibility in Corporate Governance' (2006) 81 *Notre Dame Law Review* 1431 at 1451.

[203] Special Representative of the Secretary-General on the Issue of Human Rights and Transnational Corporations and other Business Enterprises,

So what does maximisation entail? It is not intended to lay down an objective statement that deals with that issue. It would not be possible. Even shareholder primacy, which is lauded for providing a single objective that allows directors to know what they should be aiming for, fails to do so. Robert Kaplan and David Norton have noted that 'They [senior executives] realize that no single measure can provide a clear performance target or focus attention on the critical areas of the business.'[204] It is not possible simply to look at and compare the share value of the company at the end of the last financial year and the end of the present one, and then decide whether the company has maximised its wealth. EMS is far more subtle than that. It is necessary to consider a number of factors.

What is maximisation depends on a number of factors including the type of company involved, its financial position, market conditions, its position in the relevant market(s), its history, and so on. There are factors that directors clearly need to consider, such as aiming to increase the total aggregate value of the corporate entity. But, as already noted, entity maximisation does not just mean a focus on profit maximisation alone,[205] for it encompasses such things as augmenting reputation, which have a longer term impact on the financial standing of the company, and enhancing overall productivity and morale within the company. Also, it could include the capacity to attract credit on competitive terms and to ensure the pre-emption of litigation. It would be possible for the company to set its own idea of entity maximisation, perhaps in mission statements and at annual general meetings. The argument may be put forward that as objective standards are not set, such as increase in the share value, it is not possible to ascertain whether the directors have, or have not, done a competent job. It is facile to use a standard like share value as the only determining factor, for large public companies are, as discussed in Chapter 1, far too complex to use such an approach, and it smacks of short termism, something that the majority of commentators condemn.[206] The bottom line is that if the directors have not managed the company appropriately then investors will exit or take the kind of action discussed in the next Chapter.[207] The fact of

'Corporate Law Project: Overarching Trends and Observations,' July 2010, (accessible at <http://www.reports-and-materials.org/Ruggie-corporate-law-project-Jul-2010.pdf>) (last visited, 29 July 2010).

[204]   R. Kaplan and D. Norton, 'The Balanced Scorecard – The Measures that Drive Performance' (1992) *Harvard Business Review* (January–February) 71 at 71.

[205]   A. Keay, 'Ascertaining the Corporate Objective: An Entity Maximisation and Sustainability Model' (2008) 71 *Modern Law Review* 663 at 685.

[206]   This is including many shareholder primacists.

[207]   Below at pp. 241–242.

the matter is that even if one prescribed an increase in share value as the goal for the directors, shareholders might not be happy with the increase or because of market conditions an increase could have occurred whether the directors acted or failed to act.

Subsequent Chapters explore the theory in a practical setting and deal with issues such as how is the theory enforced, how are managers held accountable, and how is the company to treat profits? But for the next part of the Chapter consideration is given to issues and scenarios that might be regarded as raising difficulties for the application of the theory.

4.2 Hard Decisions

At the outset it must be acknowledged that no model is able to eliminate difficult choices. There are obviously hard decisions that have to be made with any model that is applied, and it is no different under EMS. The most difficult decisions that are likely to have to be made are those where a course of action will deleteriously affect one or more investors. There are countless fact situations that could present directors with hard decisions, and, of course, much will turn on the actual circumstances, the position of the company and the nature of the market. Here are a couple of instances of hard decisions. First, a company is clearly profitable, but it has ascertained that it might be able to make more profit in another location. Let's say the certain return to be made if the company re-locates is £8 million. This action though would involve closing down its factory in its present location. Relocation will obviously affect both employees, many of whom will be made redundant or relocated, and the community where the existing plant is situated, with likely effects on the company's reputation. If the company does not relocate the certain return to the company is £3 million. The directors might reason that the relocation might not be sensible taking into account the effect, certainly in the short-medium term, on reputation and general disruption. However, on the other hand, if the closing down might be good for the long-term benefit of the company, then the directors might take the view that the entity is best maximised if it were to relocate. It might be argued that the £3 million profit from staying in the original location should be sufficient. But it is not as much as the company could make. While not relocating might be seen as the most compassionate option, certainly in the short term, as it does not affect the existing employees or the community, in the long term there might be a severe reduction in the company's competitiveness which will undermine the company's development and will, ultimately affect most, if not all, investors. It might eventually mean the need to refrain from replacing workers who resign or retire, or for there to be compulsory redundancies. Of course, one has to take into account the impact that the setting up of a new plant would have on the community in which it is sited. It will lead to benefits, inter alia, for that community and to potential employees. The decision would depend, to a large degree, on directors balancing the benefits against the drawbacks, and considering many factors, too complex and variable to enumerate here. But, unlike under stakeholder theory there would not be a balancing of stakeholder interests, but a balancing of factors to ascertain the overall benefit for the entity.

Second, and going back to an example mentioned earlier, what if a company devises a way of producing products for their customers so that the products are as good as they have always been, but the process is less costly. Should the company charge customers the same price and make more profit, or should they pass the benefit on to customers? Perhaps the latter is better for the long term, as it might well enhance goodwill and loyalty, but the directors have to take into account any adverse responses from investors, particularly the shareholders, and the fact that less profit (less than if the company increased the amount charged to customers) would be made, certainly in the short term.

How does EMS deal with the facts of the well known US case of *Shlensky v Wrigley*?[208] In this case the directors of the company that ran the Chicago Cubs baseball team refused to erect lights at the team's stadium to permit night games to be played because they were concerned that it would have a deleterious effect on the lives of people living in the surrounding community. The shareholders brought an action against the directors for failing to construct lights and failing to pursue, therefore, benefits for shareholders. The decision of the directors could very well be justified under EMS on the basis that any ill-will created in the community would not be good for the maximisation of the company in the long term. What short-term profit is made might be off-set by a diminution of its reputation.

A good example of the issues facing directors is the situation encountered by General Motors in 1980.[209] The company was looking at a net loss in income for the first time since 1921. It was determined by the managers that capital expenditure was needed in order for the company to regain its competitive edge and enhance profits. A large five-year capital spending programme was planned, involving things like the latest techniques to produce more efficient cars. It was decided that two ageing plants in Detroit should be replaced, and this would mean the termination

---

[208]   237 NE 2d 776 (Illinois, 1968).
[209]   The following is taken from K.Goodpaster, 'Business Ethics and Stakeholder Analysis' (1991) 1 *Business Ethics Quarterly* 53 at 54–55.

of 500 jobs. The only site that would meet the company's requirements for the construction of a new plant was a densely settled area of Detroit. An alternative site, a 'green field site,' was available in another state in the US. Building on the new Detroit site was more costly ($200 million as against $80 million on the site in the other state). Detroit had significant unemployment and the building of the new plant in Detroit was supported by local government and the relevant car workers' union. The residents of the area in Detroit where GM was considering building were unhappy. The directors had to decide whether it was better to relocate or not.

A mechanism used by BT to address problems raised by the most recent recession, including £1.3 billion loss for the first quarter of 2009, was to ask staff to take a pay cut in return for long-term holidays,[210] rather than making workers redundant. The strategy devised by BT would take into account two factors. First, the company was cognisant of the bad publicity that is so often a concomitant of laying-off staff, and it wished to avoid that effect. Second, it did not wish to lose many of its skilled workers that it had trained, for when the economy strengthened they would need these workers again.[211]

A good example of a hard decision is represented by the situation facing the American company, Johnson and Johnson in 1982. The company produced a mild painkiller, Tylenol, that could be obtained by members of the public without prescription. It was very popular. Seven people died after taking Tylenol because the packets had been subject to contamination. The company reacted by recalling all capsules and introduced 'tamper-resistant' packaging. Although the company's sales fell initially on the publicising of the deaths, the company eventually regained market share. The action of recalling all capsules cost the company a lot of money. In this situation, which could be categorised as extreme, the company placed emphasis on one investor, the customer. It could be argued that the company's wealth was maximised eventually, even though in the short term it cost it significantly.

Returning to a fictional illustration, let us say that there are two projects, both costing £1 million, that is the company will make an outlay of £1 million. Project A offers a safe return of £1.1 million (the initial outlay together with a clear profit, albeit modest). Project B offers a 50:50 chance of success, whereby if it does not succeed the company will only

---

[210] R. Henry, 'BT in bid to cut staff pay in return for holidays' *The Times*, 4 July 2009.
[211] This second issue is illustrative of the change of circumstances in companies in recent times. Many companies are reliant on a skilled workforce that is not easy to replace. See L. Zingales, 'In Search of New Foundations' (2000) 55 *Journal of Finance* 1623.

have returned to it the sum of £500 000 from its investment, but if it succeeds the company will get £1.5 million. The shareholders will generally prefer B to A and other stakeholders will prefer A to B. B will involve a virtual transfer of wealth from the non-shareholders to the shareholders. Ordinarily, applying a shareholder primacy approach, if B succeeds then the shareholders will gain most from it, for other investors might not receive any benefits. If, however, B fails, the other investors might have to absorb most of the loss, for example creditors might not get paid or at least on time, and some employees might be made redundant. Under EMS the directors would have to consider which project best increases entity wealth. Obviously, B does if it is successful, but A does give a guaranteed return. It is impossible to make a decision as to which project should be favoured, without knowing the state of the market, the company's exact financial affairs and business position, and the full details of the relevant projects. If the company is very healthy from a financial point of view, it might be thought that B could be pursued, for if the company were to make a loss it would not affect the payment of creditors and the retention of staff. It becomes more difficult the less healthy a company's affairs are, and it also becomes more difficult the larger the sums involved. For instance, what if the figures were changed so that the outlay was £10 million with A producing a guaranteed return of £11 million while with B (again there is a 50:50 chance of success), if it does not succeed the company will only have returned to it the sum of £5 million (therefore, making a loss of £5 million), but if it succeeds the company will get £15 million (making a profit of £5 million). In considering what to do the issue of sustainability (to be discussed shortly) comes into play. Embracing B might not only mean that the investors take a hit, but the very solvency of the company might be under threat.

A matter that is likely to cause some concern in any situation is if the company is the subject of a takeover offer. How do the directors proceed under EMS? The prima facie problem is that a takeover can be beneficial for some investors, usually the shareholders,[212] and not for others.[213] Generally, in Anglo-American jurisdictions the shareholders' interests

---

[212] B. McDonnell, 'Corporate Constituency Statutes and Employee Governance' (2004) 30 *William Mitchell Law Review* 1227 at 1236.

[213] The Unite union which represents workers at Cadbury factories in the UK were concerned that the planned takeover of Cadbury by Kraft would lead to massive job losses in the former company: R. Lindsay, 'Cadbury union warns Kraft my axe jobs' *The Times*, 30 November 2009. Eventually 400 jobs were lost after Kraft closed a plant post-takeover: C. Boyle, 'Kraft censured for breaching the Takeover Code on Cadbury' *The Times*, 27 May 2010.

have been a priority and it has been thought that this was a form of stakeholder exploitation,[214] as the shareholders could transfer employee, creditor and community wealth to themselves during takeovers.[215] Andrei Schleifer and Larry Summers have said that apparent gains from takeovers can often involve losses of wealth from non-shareholding stakeholders to shareholders, such as a decline in the value of workers' human capital or sub-contractors' firm-specific capital.[216] Certainly there is empirical research that has been conducted suggesting that shareholders in target companies, where a takeover is successful, achieve large, abnormal gains.[217] It is in the context of takeovers that most US constituency statutes require[218] or permit[219] directors to consider the interests of investors, other than the shareholders. The shareholder primacy theory requires directors to determine what would be best for the shareholders, and in Delaware, which might be regarded as the bastion of shareholder primacy (although some might disagree), courts have required directors to prove the reasonableness and good faith of their actions if they fight a hostile takeover.[220] In fact in one UK case, *Dawson International Plc v Coats Paton Plc (No.1)*,[221] it was said that where a takeover is involved directors

---

[214] W. Allen, 'Our Schizophrenic Conception of the Business Corporation' (1992) 14 *Cardozo Law Review* 261 at 274.

[215] M. van der Weide, 'Against Fiduciary Duties to Corporate Stakeholders' (1996) 21 *Delaware Journal of Corporate Law* 27 at 78. It is to be noted that the Scottish court in *Dawson International Plc v Coats Paton Plc (No 1)* 1988 SLT 854 at 860; [1989] BCLC 233 at 241 was of the view that the directors had to consider what was in the best interests of the company.

[216] A. Schleifer and L. Summers, 'Hostile Takeovers as Breaches of Trust,' Discussion Paper No 0008, London School of Economics Financial Market Group and referred to in J. Plender, 'Giving People a Stake in the Future' (1998) 31 *Long Range Planning* 211 at 215. But compare, J. MacIntosh, 'Designing an Efficient Fiduciary Law' (1993) 43 *University of Toronto Law Journal* 425 at 462.

[217] S. Ross et al, *Corporate Finance* (London, McGraw-Hill, 1993) at 854 and referred to by M. van der Weide, 'Against Fiduciary Duties to Corporate Stakeholders' (1996) 21 *Delaware Journal of Corporate Law* 27 at 79.

[218] For example, see Connecticut: Connecticut General Statute s.33-313 (2003); Arizona: Arizona Revised Statute, s.10-1202 (2002); Idaho: Idaho Code, s.30-1602 (2002).

[219] For example, see Indiana, Indiana Code, s.23-1-35-1(d); Ohio, Ohio Revised Code, s.1701.59(E) (Supp 1989).

[220] W. Allen, J. Jacobs and L. Strine, 'The Great Takeover Debate: A Meditation on Bridging the Conceptual Divide' (2002) 69 *University of Chicago Law Review* 1067 at 1079. There are cases where courts have upheld what directors have done. For example, see *Moran v Household International Inc* 500 A 2d 1346 (Del, 1985); *Unocal v Mesa Petroleum Co* 493 A2d 946 (Del, 1985)

[221] 1988 SLT 854; [1989] BCLC 233.

might have a duty to shareholders if they make recommendations to the shareholders in light of a takeover offer.[222] But in this case Lord Cullen said:

> At the outset I do not accept as a general proposition that a company can have no interest in the change of identity of its shareholders on a take-over. It appears to me that there will be cases in which its agents, the directors, will see the take-over of its shares by a particular bidder as beneficial to the company. For example, it may provide the opportunity for integrating operations or obtaining additional resources. In other cases the directors will see a particular bid as not in the best interests of the company.[223]

This opinion is consistent with the idea that a company can have an interest in the takeover. The reason why it should be able to have an interest is that the identity of its investors is changing constantly, and accepting a takeover could be deleterious for the company in the long term.[224] This could occur, for instance, where the corporate raider is an asset stripper whose actions could weaken the company for the future, or the raider decided to make wholesale redundancies or factory closures, which could prejudice the company's reputation. Even where the raider does not have asset-stripping intentions a takeover can lead to the company not generating the wealth that it could have if left alone.[225] Where there is a takeover offer the directors should be able to make a decision based on the integrity, personality and life of the company.[226] It is submitted that all of the above is consistent with the fact that independent directors who are to advise shareholders under rules 3 and 25 of the UK's Takeover Code might take the view that they had a duty to not only consider the value of the bid for the present shareholders, but to ascertain what risk there might be to the company as an entity if the takeover proceeded.[227]

---

[222]   *Dawson International Plc* v *Coats Paton Plc (No1)* 1988 SLT 854; [1989] BCLC 233.

[223]   [1989] BCLC 233 at 242–243.

[224]   This is envisaged by R. Mitchell, A. O'Donnell and I. Ramsay, 'Shareholder Value and Employee Interests: Intersections Between Corporate Governance, Corporate Law and Labor Law' (2005) 23 *Wisconsin International Law Journal* 417 at 438.

[225]   W. Allen, J. Jacobs and L. Strine, 'The Great Takeover Debate: A Meditation on Bridging the Conceptual Divide' (2002) 69 *University of Chicago Law Review* 1067 at 1077.

[226]   M. Phillips, 'Reappraising the Real Entity Theory of the Corporation' (1994) 21 *Florida State University Law Review* 1061 at 1097.

[227]   A. Alcock, 'An Accidental Change to Directors' Duties' (2009) 30 *The Company Lawyer* 362 at 366.

While the focus is not on the benefits for shareholders, shareholders would benefit from the directors considering what would maximise the corporate entity's position. Investors would need to monitor the actions of directors carefully as there would always be the temptation for managers to act to resist the takeover for purely personal reasons, namely they stay in their positions whereas a new controlling shareholder might well oust them. The fact is that managers are often replaced when a takeover occurs.[228] Managers might be said to be aligned with employees and the community, so it is probable that shareholders would need to satisfy themselves that in rejecting a takeover offer the managers were not merely seeking to retain their posts.

The problem that the late John Parkinson would likely have had with this approach is that:

> [E]xpressing such a duty as a duty to further the interests of the enterprise would be unhelpful, since the formulation has very limited information content: it fails to identify the relevant constituencies and gives no indication of what priority should be given to them inter se.[229]

But, as has been stated earlier, EMS is not concerned with identifying constituencies for the purpose of considering their interests directly. EMS focuses on the benefit of the entity, and the views of constituencies, or investors as they are referred to in this Chapter and subsequently, are only taken into account in order to determine what is going to enhance entity wealth.

One of the real issues of difficulty comes with respect to the distribution of profits made by the company. This is discussed in detail later in Chapter 8.

4.3 Sustainability

A word about the term 'sustainability' is appropriate, before discussing this aspect of EMS. The term has in many ways become 'a mantra for the 21st century.'[230] Yet it does not have a consistent meaning. It is a

---

[228] For instance, the key executives of Cadbury left the company very soon after the completion of the takeover by Kraft in January 2010: C. Boyle, 'Cadbury executives exit hours after deal closes' *The Times*, 3 February 2010.

[229] J. Parkinson, *Corporate Power and Responsibility* (Oxford, Oxford University Press, 1993) at 79.

[230] T. Dyllick and K. Hockerts, 'Beyond the Business Case for Corporate Sustainability' (2002) 11 *Business Strategy and the Environment* 130 at 130.

'contested concept'[231] and deciding on a meaning is a vexed problem.[232] It has been defined as 'the activities, demonstrating the inclusion of social and environmental aspects in the normal business operations of a company and its interaction with its stakeholders.'[233] Some might say that it is inextricably linked to stakeholder theory as it might be defined as meeting the needs of a firm's stakeholders without compromising the ability of the company to meet the needs of future stakeholders as well.[234] The concept is seen by some as having three dimensions – the economic, the social and the environmental, and often known as the triple bottom line of corporate sustainability.[235] It involves growing the economic, social and environmental capital base, with rejection of simply focusing on economic sustainability.[236] However, entity sustainability in this article simply means, for the most part, the survival of the company, namely the company does not fall into an insolvent position from which it cannot escape. But, sustaining a company could well involve, as a matter of necessity, having concern for social and environmental sustainability, as well as the economic, and the extent of concern will depend on the nature of the company's business and the position in which it finds itself at a particular juncture. Keeping a workforce satisfied, and refraining from abusing the environment could set the scene for wealth maximisation, as there is evidence that there is congruence of social and financial performance.[237]

---

[231] D. Dunphy, 'Corporate Sustainability: Challenge to Managerial Orthodoxies' (2003) 9 *Journal of the Australian and New Zealand Academy of Management* 2 at 3.

[232] Jeremy Cooper, Deputy Chairman of ASIC in a submission to the Australian Parliament's Joint Committee on Corporations and Financial Services and referred to in its report, 'Corporate Responsibility: Managing Risk and Creating Value' June 2006 at para 2.3. and accessible at <http://www.aph.gov.au/senate/committee/corporations_ctte/completed_inquiries/2004-07/corporate_responsibility/report/index.htm> (last visited, 16 December 2009).

[233] A. Caldelli and M. Parmigiani, 'Management Information System – A Tool for Corporate Sustainability' (2004) 55 *Journal of Business Ethics* 159 at 159.

[234] T. Dyllick and K. Hockerts, 'Beyond the Business Case for Corporate Sustainability' (2002) 11 *Business Strategy and the Environment* 130 at 131.

[235] Ibid at 132. The triple considerations are sometimes known as 'People, planet and profit.' See, T. Hardjono and P. de Klein, 'Introduction on the European Sustainability Framework (ECSF)' (2004) 55 *Journal of Business Ethics* 99 at 99.

[236] T. Dyllick and K. Hockerts, 'Beyond the Business Case for Corporate Sustainability' (2002) 11 *Business Strategy and the Environment* 130 at 132.

[237] R. Aguilera et al, 'Putting the S Back in Corporate Social Responsibility: A Multi-Level Theory of Social Change in Organizations' (2007) 32 *Academy of Management Review* 836.

Clearly it is generally necessary to keep a company's primary investors involved in the company, and involvement presupposes contentment.[238] Sustainability from an economic perspective will involve taking into account the arrival of new competitors and changes in social habits and changes in preferences of customers and commercial outlets for goods and services. Economic sustainability has to involve thinking in the long term so that cyclical downturns and changes in commercial life can be addressed.

Maximisation of entity value is designed to lead to growth, but it is only half of the story. It is also necessary for the company, under Post-Keynesian theory, to aim for long-term survival. 'Growth and survival are two sides of the same coin,'[239] and the focus on only one of these aims does not necessarily mean either or both can be achieved. A stakeholder theorist, Frederick Post, recognises the importance of the long-term survival of a company. He posits that if it is not possible for management to decide between various interests, 'there is always a tiebreaker that determines the interest to be weighed the most heavily, the long-term survival of the corporation.'[240]

Profit is an essential element of sustainability,[241] for many argue that if a company fails to maximise profits then it will lose out to its competitors and not survive.[242] An emphasis on long-term survival will mean embracing a less risky strategy compared with the company that is concerned with short-term gain.

The aspect of the model that is discussed in this section is designed to foster the existence of the entity as a going concern. It is critical that the company does not become insolvent, or if it does, it is only a very temporary phenomenon. The merit of seeking to ensure survival should

---

[238] See, J. Post, L. Preston and S. Sachs, 'Managing the Extended Enterprise' (2002) 45 *California Management Review* 6 at 7.

[239] M.J. Gordon, *Finance, Investment and Macroeconomics: The Neoclassical and a Post-Keynesian Solution* (Aldershot, Edward Elgar, 1994) at 94.

[240] F. Post, 'A Response to "The Social Responsibility of Corporate Management: A Classical Critique' (2003) 18 *Mid-American Journal of Business* 25 at 32.

[241] L. Mitchell, *Corporate Irresponsibility* (New Haven, Yale University Press, 2001) at 11.

[242] D. Schrader, 'The Corporation and Profits' (1987) 6 *Journal of Business Ethics* 589 at 590. Schrader does argue that non-maximising firms do survive. But he recognises that there have to be positive profits as a necessary condition of survival (ibid at 591, 597).

be self-evident,[243] for if a company does not sustain itself, it cannot make wealth for itself or anyone. When investors sign up to be involved with a company they envisage that the focus will not only be on maximisation, but also on survival (so that the capital of shareholders is safe, the loans of financiers are paid, the wages of employees are able to be satisfied etc).

It has been asserted that all approaches to business enterprise begin with asking what are the survival needs of a business? That is, 'what . . . does it have to be, to do, to achieve – to exist at all?'[244] Companies have to ask: on what does our survival depend? The fact of the matter is that to seek profit maximisation without consideration of survival misses the point for the company might well fail to survive.[245]

It might be argued that if one focuses on maximisation, then survival is taken care of and the issue of survival does not need to be broached. Yet, survival is something that is to be aimed for and not something that is expected.[246] In seeking to maximise, the company must maintain economic (efficient rendering of services) and financial (maintaining an atmosphere conducive to attracting further business capital) competence.[247] It cannot expect to survive or else complacency sets in. Companies, even the most solvent ones, might well be only one decision away from insolvency.[248] All it takes is one risk that goes wrong for a company to find itself in an insolvent state. A prime example is Barings Bank, which was once highly respected and solvent, but which became insolvent as a consequence of huge losses on derivatives.[249] A trader, Nick Leeson, was left in control of both the dealing and settlement functions (a very powerful position) at the bank's Singapore office. Leeson traded in derivatives. If the actions of Leeson, which can be referred to as 'bets,' succeeded, the shareholders of

---

[243]   M.J. Gordon, *Finance, Investment and Macroeconomics: The Neoclassical and a Post-Keynesian Solution* (Aldershot, Edward Elgar, 1994) at 93.

[244]   P. Drucker, 'Business Objectives and Survival Needs: Notes on a Discipline of Business Enterprise' (1958) 31 *The Journal of Business* 81 at 84.

[245]   A recent example is Enron Inc.

[246]   D. Li, 'The Nature of Corporate Residual Equity Under the Equity Concept' (1960) 35 *The Accounting Review* 258 at 259.

[247]   Ibid at 259, 262.

[248]   T. Smith, 'The Efficient Norm for Corporate Law: A Neotraditional Interpretation of Fiduciary Duty' (1999) 98 *Michigan Law Review* 214 at 223 and referring to C. Loomis, 'A House Built on Sand: John Meriwether's Once Mighty Long-Term Capital Has All But Crumbled' *Fortune*, 26 October 1998 at 110.

[249]   N. Denton, 'The Barings Crisis: Disaster, Just When Most Things Were Going Right' *The Financial Times*, 27 February 1995 at 3.

Barings would have benefited substantially.[250] The risks did not work out, and they precipitated the collapse of the bank. Even a company that is delivering high shareholder value might well be on the brink of financial collapse in the near future.[251] Focusing on survival will affect how managers will run a company, and it might moderate maximisation plans.

While the directors are seeking to maximise, the company must sustain itself – it is no good if the strategies will bring benefits down the track if the company is not able to meet financial demands in the short-medium term. Managers must develop a strategy that combines the maximisation of long-term value and survival, particularly in the short term. Creditors are not necessarily going to wait for any master plan to unfold – they will have to be convinced that the company will be able to sustain itself. The need to ensure survival will prevent short termism, for the company must ensure that its value will continue to develop and that wringing out profits today does not mean insolvency tomorrow. There is a need to achieve a balance so as to ensure there is both survival and growth.[252]

Survival is the necessary precursor of all of a company's specific goals.[253] Without survival a company, naturally, cannot achieve anything. This is why it is argued that it must be factored into any formulation of the corporate objective. But, it cannot be regarded as the only objective as it does not provide sufficient direction and aspiration needed for a corporate objective. Survival entails ascertaining the minimum profit that is required to meet the risks that are assumed,[254] but it is only a minimum point. Seeking merely to survive means there is a lack of ambition. More importantly, firms cannot in fact survive without making profits.[255] A company has to seek to grow as it cannot just stand still. Where, for instance, a company is in a market where there are a large number of competitors,

---

[250] T. Smith, 'The Efficient Norm for Corporate Law: A Neotraditional Interpretation of Fiduciary Duty' (1999) 98 *Michigan Law Review* 214 at 225.

[251] A. Campbell, 'Stakeholders: The Case in Favour' (1997) 30 *Long Range Planning* 446 at 449.

[252] P. Drucker, 'Business Objectives and Survival Needs: Notes on a Discipline of Business Enterprise' (1958) 31 *The Journal of Business* 81 at 87. Of course, these objectives may pull in different directions.

[253] D. Li, 'The Objectives of the Corporation under the Entity Concept' (1961) 39 *The Accounting Review* 946 at 948.

[254] P. Drucker, 'Business Objectives and Survival Needs: Notes on a Discipline of Business Enterprise' (1958) 31 *The Journal of Business* 81 at 86.

[255] R. Eels and C. Watson, *Conceptual Foundations of Business* (Homewood, Richard D Irwin, 1969) at 535. See D. Rose, 'Teams, Firms and the Evolution of Profit seeking Behavior' (1999) and accessible at <http://papers.ssrn.com/sol3/papers.cfm?abstract_id=224438> (last visited, 8 January 2010).

over a period of time the only strategy that will ensure survival is the one that maximises company wealth.[256] Companies should be making as much as they can, whilst taking into account the need to retain economic and financial stability that will ensure survival. Maximising wealth is to be aspired to while keeping a watchful eye on the survival of the company.

Sustainability will mean managing carefully the company's various types of capital/assets, namely financial capital (equity and debt) tangible capital such as plant, land, stock and intangible capital, such as reputation, intellectual property, and know-how. If a company is sustained economically then it will guarantee a cash flow sufficient to ensure liquidity. To survive a company must do certain things.[257] First, it has to have a human resource structure that is effective in that people work for a common cause and are organised for joint performance. This human resource must be able to perpetuate itself. Second, the company must be able to adapt to the society and economy in which it operates. Third, there is the need to attain a minimum profitability that is adequate taking into account the risks which are assumed.

It is likely that sustainability will fit well with long-term maximisation as companies looking to the long term are more likely to refrain from making risky choices that could place them in danger of insolvency. Building a company for long-term gain often will involve steady development and not looking for the 'quick fix' which can endanger a company's financial well-being.

To be sustainable a company must be able to pay its business expenses. They are often referred to as 'overheads,' and feature the costs associated with borrowing money, payment of employees, purchasing materials needed for the business, paying for licences etc.

It has been argued that to survive it is necessary to ensure that all critical investors remain with the company.[258] While this has merit, it is probably rather a general statement. For some companies, requiring specialist investors, it is often going to be correct. Other companies, though, would be able to use other investors if some chose to exit.

Arguably, directors have an interest in sustainability as it enables them to keep their jobs, and it enhances their reputation as far as the labour

---

[256] S. Enke, 'On Maximizing Profits: a Distinction between Chamberlain and Robinson' (1951) 41 *American Economic Review* 566.

[257] The following points are adapted from P. Drucker, 'Business Objectives and Survival Needs: Notes on a Discipline of Business Enterprise' (1958) 31 *The Journal of Business* 81 at 85–87.

[258] M. Clarkson, 'A Stakeholder Framework for Analyzing and Evaluating Corporate Social Performance' (1995) 20 *Academy Management Review* 92 at 107.

market for directors is concerned; the reputation of executive directors is likely to plummet if they oversee a company's slide into insolvency. Also, investors have an interest in sustainability as they all hope that the company will continue to operate or else shareholders lose their capital, employees lose their jobs, creditors do not get paid, or at least in full, suppliers lose their customers, customers lose the product that they like and the community in which the company operates will be severely hurt and could in fact be devastated. [259]

Aiming to sustain can have a beneficial effect generally, because if a company suffers financial distress and its survival is in the balance, even if it is quite temporary, it might well have very long-term consequences on the value of the firm.[260] There is evidence to suggest that financial distress of a company can lead to underinvestment in valuable projects.[261] So, a company that focuses on sustaining itself might well reduce the chances of it experiencing distress and, therefore, detrimental effects in terms of value. Experiencing financial distress can affect companies attracting finance and can severely damage reputation.

The sustainability over time of sound economic and financial conditions is the necessary requirement for the company to remain a 'going concern.'[262] Development of the business activity under sound economic and financial conditions when resulting in the survival and development of the business satisfies all investor interests.[263]

4.4 Fitting it into the Law

It is not possible to consider how EMS could be accommodated in all legal systems, but we can look at a couple of the leading developed countries. First, the UK. At the moment UK law arguably provides for a variation of shareholder primacy.[264] This is found in s.172 of the Companies Act

---

[259] An example is the British car-maker, Rover, when it closed its major operations at Longbridge in the West Midlands of England in 2005.

[260] L. Zingales, 'In Search of New Foundations' (2000) 55 *Journal of Finance* 1623 at 1633.

[261] Ibid at 1636.

[262] L. Cerioni and A. Keay, 'Corporate Governance and the Corporate Objective in the European Community: Proposing a Redefinition in Light of EC Law' (2008) 19 *European Business Law Review* 405.

[263] Ibid.

[264] The same might be said for those US states that have enacted so-called 'constituency statutes'. Although it might be argued that apart from in Connecticut (see Connecticut General Statute s.33-313(e) (2003), where directors have to take into account non-shareholder rights, directors clearly have a discretion as to whether

2006. The variation is known as 'enlightened shareholder value' (ESV).[265] Virginia Ho puts it adroitly when she states that: 'To no small degree, then, "enlightened shareholder value" looks like the standard Anglo-American corporate governance model. As the name suggests it is grounded squarely within a shareholder-primacy paradigm . . .'[266]

To implement EMS little needs to be done from a legislative perspective. Under s.170(1) of the Companies Act 2006, the duties of directors (fiduciary duties and duties of care and skill) are owed to the company. In this context the words 'the company' have been variously interpreted in cases as meaning the entity[267] or the company's present and future shareholders,[268] or even both.[269] So, the provision could certainly be interpreted as meaning the company as a whole, namely the entire corporate enterprise, as argued for earlier in this Chapter. The problem for any change at the moment comes in the form of s.172(1) as it provides:

---

they have regard for stakeholder interests or not. For a list of most of the statutes that have been enacted, see K. Hale, 'Corporate Law and Stakeholders: Moving Beyond Stakeholder Statutes' (2003) 45 *Arizona Law Review* 823 at 833, n78.

[265] See A. Keay, 'Enlightened Shareholder Value, the Reform of the Duties of Company Directors and the Corporate Objective' [2006] *Lloyds Maritime and Commercial Law Quarterly* 335; A. Keay, 'Tackling the Issue of the Corporate Objective: An Analysis of the United Kingdom's "Enlightened Shareholder Value Approach" (2007) 29 *Sydney Law Review* 577. Section 417 of the Companies Act 2006 is also of potential importance as it provides for part of the idea of ESV. This provision requires companies, other than small ones, to include a fair review of the company's business and a description of the principal risks and uncertainties faced by the company (s.417(3)), and quoted companies have to include, to the extent necessary to understand the development, performance and position of the company's business, information about environmental matters, the employees, social and community issues and the people with whom the company has contractual arrangements (s.417(5)). See, A. Johnson, 'After the OFR: Can UK Shareholder Value Still Be Enlightened?' (2006) 7 *European Business Organizations Review* 817.

[266] V. Ho, '"Enlightened Shareholder Value": Corporate Governance Beyond the Shareholder-Stakeholder Divide' abstract accessible at <http://ssrn.com/abstract=1476116> (last visited, 8 January 2010)

[267] For example, see *Lonrho Ltd v Shell Petroleum Co Ltd* [1980] 1 WLR 627; *Fulham Football Club Ltd v Cabra Estates plc* [1994] 1 BCLC 363; *Nicholson v Permakraft (NZ) Ltd* (1985) 3 ACLC 453; *Brunninghausen v Glavanics* [1999] NSWCA 199; (1999) 17 ACLC 1247; *Peoples' Department Stores v Wise* [2004] SCC 68; (2004) 244 DLR (4th) 564.

[268] For example, see *Parke v Daily News Ltd* [1962] Ch 927; *Brady v Brady* (1987) 3 BCC 535. Also, see *Greenhalgh v Arderne Cinemas* [1951] Ch 286 in a different context.

[269] *Darvall v North Sydney Brick and Tile Co Ltd* (1987) 12 ACLR 537 at 554; (1988) 6 ACLC 154 at 176.

A director of a company must act in a way that he considers, in good faith, would be most likely to promote the success of the company for the benefit of its members as a whole, and in doing so have regard (amongst other matters) to –

(a) The likely consequences of any decision in the long term;
(b) the interests of the company's employees;
(c) the need to foster the company's business relationships with suppliers, customers and others;
(d) the impact of the company's operations on the community and the environment;
(e) the desirability of the company maintaining a reputation for high standards of business conduct; and
(f) the need to act fairly between the members of the company.

While this subsection appears to provide for a stakeholder-oriented approach to corporate governance,[270] it clearly does not. It is based on shareholder value and involves directors having to act in the collective best interests of shareholders;[271] but what it does do is eschews 'exclusive focus on the short-term financial bottom line' and seeks a more inclusive approach that values the building of long-term relationships.[272] As we saw in Chapter 2, many shareholder primacists[273] do favour companies looking to the long term even when practising shareholder value theory on the basis that this will enhance shareholder wealth in due course. This is well illustrated by reference to the well-known and provocative article, 'The End of History for Corporate Law,'[274] where Henry Hansmann and Reiner Kraakman, adherents of shareholder primacy, said that there was 'no longer any serious competitor to the view that corporate law should principally strive to increase *long-term* shareholder value.' (my emphasis) What ESV does, as it is encapsulated in UK legislation, is to recognise

---

[270] See, A. Keay, 'Moving Towards Stakeholderism? Constituency Statutes, Enlightened Shareholder Value and All That: Much Ado About Little?' (2011) 22 *European Business Law Review* 1.

[271] Company Law Review, *Modern Company Law for a Competitive Economy: Developing the Framework* (DTI, London, 2000), para 2.22.

[272] Ibid. See, A. Keay, 'Moving Towards Stakeholderism? Constituency Statutes, Enlightened Shareholder Value and All That: Much Ado About Little?' (2011) 22 *European Business Law Review* 1.

[273] For example, M. Jensen, 'Value Maximisation, Stakeholder Theory, and the Corporate Objective Function' (2001) 7 *European Financial Management* 297; 'Value Maximisation, Stakeholder Theory and the Corporate Objective Function' (2001) 14 *Journal of Applied Corporate Finance* 8.

[274] (2001) 89 *Georgetown Law Journal* 439.

the instrumental importance of stakeholders in maximising shareholder wealth, but it still emphasises shareholder primacy.[275]

To implement EMS s.172(1) could be amended to remove all of the words following 'the success of the company.' Importantly this would see the omission of the words, 'for the benefit of the members as a whole,' and the list of stakeholders who are set out in the subsection. This action would provide for a focus on the company as an entity.[276] At the moment the meaning of 'success of the company' is uncertain.[277] An indication could be given in the section that it means maximising the wealth of the entity.

The directors will owe a fiduciary duty to the company as an entity, and, therefore, their duty is to act to promote its best interests. Undoubtedly, there is room for directors to act opportunistically or to shirk, but this is also the case with companies operating under shareholder primacy (and stakeholder theory). Shareholder primacy prides itself as providing the best answers to the agency problem, namely how do you control and monitor the directors who are regarded as the agents of the shareholders and who manage the company's affairs? Nevertheless, there are spectacular examples, such as Enron and WorldCom in the United States, Maxwell Communications in the UK and HIH Insurance and One.Tel in Australia, of the failure to monitor and rein in directors in the context of the practice of shareholder primacy. Clearly, managers have, under shareholder primacy, plenty of scope for self-serving activity.[278]

Second, we will consider, briefly, the US. Over 40 US states have provisions that are similar to s.172 in what the Americans call 'constituency statutes.' [279]

---

[275]   A. Alcock, 'An Accidental Change of Directors' Duties?' (2009) 30 *The Company Lawyer* 362 at 368.

[276]   Gregory Crespi advocates such an approach for the US: 'Redefining the Fiduciary Duties of Corporate Directors in Accordance with the Team Production Model of Corporate Governance' (2003) 16 *Creighton Law Review* 623 at 633.

[277]   A. Keay, *Directors' Duties* (Bristol, Jordan Publishing, 2009) at 129–130.

[278]   T. Donaldson and L. Preston, 'The Stakeholder Theory for the Corporation: Concepts, Evidence, Implications' (1995) 20 *Academy Management Review* 65 at 87.

[279]   K. Hale, 'Corporate Law and Stakeholders: Moving Beyond Stakeholder Statutes' (2003) 45 *Arizona Law Review* 823 at 833. For a list of the states and the statutes, see Hale at n78. The literature on these statutes is too voluminous to cite in full. Some examples are, Committee on Corporate Laws, 'Other Constituencies Statutes: Potential for Confusion' (1990) *Business Lawyer* 2253; J. Hanks Jr, 'Playing With Fire: Nonshareholder Constituency Statues in the 1990s' (1991) 21 *Stetson Law Review* 97; L. Mitchell, 'A Theoretical and Practical Framework for Enforcing Corporate Constituency Statutes' (1992) 70 *Texas Law Review* 579; S. Bainbridge, 'Interpreting Nonshareholder Constituency Statutes' (1992)

Most of the statutes were passed in the 1980s, but several were enacted in the 1990s and one, in Washington State, as recently as 2007.[280] The first constituency statute was enacted in Pennsylvania in 1983. By way of example, and fairly representative of a number of provisions in constituency statutes, s.1715 of the Pennsylvanian statute provided, when it was first enacted that:[281]

(a) In discharging the duties of their respective positions, the board of directors . . . may, in considering the best interests of the corporation, consider to the extent they deem appropriate:
(1) the effects of any action upon any or all groups affected by such action, including shareholders, employees, suppliers, customers and creditors of the corporation, and upon communities in which offices or other establishments of the corporation are located.

Constituency statutes in general terms 'purport to allow directors of public corporations to consider an expanded group of "interests" when making decisions on behalf of the corporations or, more precisely, decisions concerning the course of the corporation's business.'[282] So, these statutes permit the welfare of constituencies other than shareholders to be considered by the directors. Unlike s.172, these statutes, save for the one applying in Connecticut,[283] do not require directors to consider the interests of stakeholders. The statutes merely permit directors, in their

---

19 *Pepperdine Law Review* 971; E. Orts, 'Beyond Shareholders: Interpreting Corporate Constituency Statutes' (1993) 61 *George Washington Law Review* 14; T. Fort, 'The Corporation as Mediating Institution: An Efficacious Synthesis of Stakeholder Theory and Corporate Constituency Statutes' (1998) 73 *Notre Dame Law Review* 173; J. Springer, 'Corporate Constituency Statutes: Hollow Hopes and False Fears' (1999) *Annual Survey of American Law* 85; E. Adams and J. Matheson, 'A Statutory Model for Corporate Constituency Concerns' (2000) 49 *Emory Law Journal* 1085; B. McDonnell, 'Corporate Constituency Statutes and Employee Governance' (2004) 30 *William Mitchell Law Review* 1227; A. Bisconti, 'The Double Bottom Line: Can Constituency Statutes Protect Socially Responsible Corporations Stuck in Revlon Land?' (2009) 42 *Loyola of Los Angeles Law Review* 765.

[280] HB 111, 60th Leg, Regular Session (2007).

[281] Pennsylvania (PA, 15 Consolidated Statutes) (1990). The provision is now s.516 and it has been changed in minor ways.

[282] J. Macey, 'Fiduciary Duties as Residual Claims: Obligations to Nonshareholder Constituencies From a Theory of the Firm Perspective' (1999) 84 *Cornell Law Review* 1266. This is except for Arizona and Idaho where directors are required simply to consider long-term as well as short-term interests of the company: Arizona: Revised Statute, s.10-1202 (2002); Idaho Code, s.30-1602 (2002).

[283] Connecticut: General Statute, s.33-756 (2005).

discretion, to consider these interests. Besides referring to stakeholders and their interests, the legislation, in a number of states, provides that the directors could consider the long-term, as well as the short-term, interests of the corporation.[284]

Importantly, the statutes allow the directors to take account of constituencies in the course of considering the 'best interests of the corporation.' So, the provisions cannot be seen as stakeholder provisions per se, as the end of the directors' deliberations is to be the benefit of the company. The phrase, 'best interests of the corporation,' has caused no little debate in the US as well as in other jurisdictions. It has been argued that the phrase can only be defined by reference to the interests of the shareholders.[285] But in some cases courts have clearly distinguished between the corporation and the shareholders.

EMS could be introduced into US law by amending the existing constituency statutes and enacting new statutes in the few states not having a constituency statute, so that there is a requirement that directors are to act in the best interests of the corporation and it is made clear that the reference to 'the corporation' means the corporate entity and not the shareholders. Also, it might be necessary to provide in legislation something akin to s.170 of the UK legislation, namely that the directors' duties are owed to the corporation as an entity.

5. DISTINGUISHING THE MODEL

It is important to identify how EMS is different from others. First, it is clearly different from shareholder primacy because with the latter there is the temptation to subtract from other investors (sometimes known as 'hold up') in order to boost shareholder benefits, namely a company might find that it is appropriate to transfer value away from one or more investors to ensure that shareholders benefit. For example, the management lays off workers, or embraces a high risk strategy that might jeopardise the payment of creditors, so that there are funds available to pay shareholders a larger dividend. EMS seeks to take the course of action that will enhance entity wealth, and not only the wealth of shareholders. With EMS

---

[284]   For example, see Minnesota (s.302A.251(5) (West 1985 & 2001).

[285]   S. Wallman, 'The Proper Interpretation of Corporate Constituency Statutes and Formulation of Director Duties' (1991) 21 *Stetson Law Review* 163 at 170. This has also been the case in the UK. See, A. Keay, 'Enlightened Shareholder Value, the Reform of the Duties of Corporation Directors and the Corporate Objective' [2006] *Lloyds Maritime and Commercial Law Quarterly* 335 at 341–343.

shareholder wealth comes as a consequence of maximising the wealth of the company, namely as a by-product of corporate welfare, whereas under shareholder primacy the maximisation of the wealth of the shareholders is sought directly.

Unlike with stakeholder theory, in EMS the directors are not required to balance all investors' interests or resolve conflicts per se, but merely to ascertain what action will maximise the wealth of the entity. Directors might have to take action which damages one investor because that is best for the entity as a whole, e.g., the closing of a plant which makes employees redundant. The managers are seen as representatives and guardians of all stakeholder interests in stakeholder theory,[286] whilst under EMS the emphasis is on the directors acting as agents for the corporate entity and owing the entity fiduciary duties and duties of care and skill. Directors are not referees;[287] they will take the action that serves the continuing prosperity and development of the company as an entity.

An interesting and important theory, to which the book has made reference on several occasions, known as 'team production,' (TP) was formulated in 1999 by Blair and Stout[288] and warrants some consideration, and particularly as to whether it affects the theory discussed in this Chapter, and to explain how it differs from EMS. In a nutshell the main thrust of TP is to say that the company is a team to which different persons contribute, and from which they can expect returns. The theory sees an independent board of directors as mediating hierarchs in monitoring inputs and outputs, with shareholders not having control rights. The directors have ultimate power in both determining how company assets are to be used and in reconciling conflicts between the various interests of team members. The problem with this approach, as with the stakeholder approach, appears to be that it does not indicate how directors are to reconcile conflicting interests. EMS differs from TP in that it sets an objective for a company that is not directly related to the investors (the team under TP), while the team approach requires directors, without any guidance,

---

[286]   K. Hall, *The Magic Mirror: Law in American History* (New York, Oxford University Press, 1989) and referred to in S. Letza, X. Sun and J. Kirkbride, 'Shareholding and Stakeholding: a Critical Review of Corporate Governance' (2004) 12 *Corporate Governance: An International Review* 242 at 250.
[287]   See W. Leung, 'The Inadequacy of Shareholder Primacy: A Proposed Corporate Regime that Recognizes Non-Shareholder Interests' (1997) 30 *Columbia Journal of Law and Social Problems* 589 at 590.
[288]   'A Team Production Theory of Corporate Law' (1999) 85 *Virginia Law Review* 247. The theory built on the work of others, such as A. Alchian and H. Demsetz, 'Production, Information Costs and Economic Organization' (1972) 62 *American Economic Review* 777.

to look after the team members' interests. Also, and importantly, TP does not formulate a corporate objective; rather it is a theory of the firm (the authors seek to depose the agency theory in this respect) and seeks to describe what actually happens in the company (and answers the question: why are directors given so much discretion in public companies?). In contrast, EMS seeks to provide a normative objective of the company, and not to provide a theory of the firm. Finally, TP provides that the stakeholders make up the firm,[289] whereas EMS does not propound that viewpoint.

6. CONCLUSION

Rather than relying on either of the dominant theories, discussed in Chapters 2 and 3, this Chapter has advocated another approach for the corporate objective, namely the entity maximisation and sustainability theory. This focuses on the company as a separate legal entity and maintains that the objective of the company is to maximise the wealth of the entity as an entity and, at the same time, to ensure that the company is sustained. The theory involves directors endeavouring to increase the overall long-run market value of the company as a whole, taking into account the investment made by various people and groups. But it maintains that maximisation must be combined with aiming to ensure entity survival. The theory values the broad range of people and groups who invest in the company and maintains that they should benefit from their investment. How they benefit will depend on what is best for maximisation of the entity.

While there is no clear empirical evidence that suggests that directors are in fact employing an EMS approach, and, in any event this book focuses on the normative, anecdotal evidence is such that many directors appear to be implementing a real entity approach. In addition there are indications from a study of the mission statements and other public documents of FTSE 100 companies that an EMS approach might well be invoked in practice.

Having explained EMS and considered its foundations, it is now necessary to discuss elements of the theory and to deal with important issues such as how the theory can be enforced. This latter issue is the subject of the next Chapter.

---

[289] 'A Team Production Theory of Corporate Law' (1999) 85 *Virginia Law Review* 247 at 305.

5. The enforcement of the entity maximisation and sustainability model

1. INTRODUCTION

In the last Chapter a new normative model, the entity maximisation and sustainability model (EMS) was proposed. It was explained in that Chapter that the model has two elements to it, namely the maximising of entity wealth and contemporaneously ensuring the entity's financial sustainability. This Chapter deals with the first issue that is raised concerning the model, namely how is compliance with the model to be enforced? What if the directors fail to manage the company in line with the tenets of the model which lay down what a company's objective should be? How can their action be contested? As Morey McDaniel has said, 'a right without a remedy is worthless,'[1] so there must be some enforcement mechanism for the model to be of any practical use.[2] There must be enforceable standards that ensure that the directors discharge their stewardship of the company's affairs and assets properly and in accord with the objective of a company. This is merely consistent with the fact that any system must have safeguards built into it.[3] Providing for some process which permits the contesting of what the directors have done operates as a legitimating mechanism.[4]

It is critical that those who have invested in the company, and this includes shareholders, creditors, employees and others, have an avenue

---

[1] M. McDaniel, 'Bondholders and Stockholders' (1988) 13 *Journal of Corporation Law* 205 at 309.

[2] See the comments in J. Parkinson, *Corporate Power and Responsibility* (Oxford, Oxford University Press, 1993) at 237. The OECD *Principles of Corporate Governance* state that legal requirements that affect corporate governance should be enforceable (Clause IB), 2004. Accessible at <http://www.oecd.org/dataoecd/32/18/31557724.pdf> (last visited, 1 February 2010).

[3] Company Law Review, *Modern Company Law for a Competitive Economy*: 'The Strategic Framework' 1999, London, DTI, at para 5.1.30.

[4] S. Bottomley, *The Constitutional Corporation* (Aldershot, Ashgate, 2007) at 144.

available to them to take some form of action if they have legitimate concerns in relation to how the company is being managed, namely that it is not being run in such a way as to maximise entity wealth and to ensure the entity's sustainability. They should be entitled to do so because of the contribution that they have made to the company. The mechanism that is employed to permit contesting of what the directors have done or have not done should be such that it will encourage a board of directors to be diligent and mindful of the way that they exercise their powers and duties. The mechanism utilised must be effective and something which can be embraced without inordinate costs in terms of finance and time.[5] Moreover, any mechanism should not be easily or frequently employed as it could be costly and precipitate loss of business opportunities, and eventually prejudice the company's reputation.[6] If it was necessary to use the mechanism frequently then one would fear for the sustainability of the company.

An important aspect of having an enforcement mechanism is that it can have positive effects, for it can act as both an incentive to adhere to the objective and ensure better directorial behaviour, and a deterrent not to engage in non-compliant action.[7] Directors will know that their decision-making is being monitored and can be called into question in a formal way, and knowing this might encourage relevant parties to resolve any disagreement without the need for any formal action.

The issue of enforcement has been something that has been a problem for many aspects of company law for a significant number of years (and continues to be so) and it has plagued the stakeholder theory ever since its popularisation in the early 1980s. If the directors fail to take into account a particular stakeholder's interests, what can that stakeholder do? Absent the shareholders, who are entitled to seek permission to continue a derivative claim,[8] the answer, as far as the law goes, appears to be: very little.

The Chapter explores the measures which might be employed in order to enforce EMS, and then argues for one particular mechanism. The Chapter seeks to do this primarily in the context of UK law, but much of the discussion is relevant to many jurisdictions, particularly those that are able to be classified as Anglo-American jurisdictions.

---

[5]   Ibid at 148.

[6]   Ibid at 146.

[7]   The function of enforcement is deterrence: C. Hill and T. Jones, 'Stakeholder-Agency Theory' (1992) 29 *Journal of Management Studies* 131 at 141.

[8]   Even the shareholders may have problems in taking action. See, A. Keay, 'Company Directors Behaving Poorly: Disciplinary Options for Shareholders' [2007] *Journal of Business Law* 656.

It is emphasised that the Chapter is dealing with non-contractual enforcement options. Obviously, some investors who have contracts with the company will often be able to take action for breach of the contract or have specific mechanisms in their contracts which permit them to take some form of self-help action; but this action is based on a breach of the specific contract entered into, and might have little to do with the objective of a company. Also, it does not take into account that arguably some investors do not have any contractual rights.

The Chapter develops in the following manner. Part II considers what has been said in relation to the enforcement of the shareholder primacy and stakeholder theories. Part III, the principal part of the Chapter, identifies and examines various alternative ways of enforcing the model and then argues for the use of one. This is followed by some concluding remarks.

2. ENFORCEMENT UNDER OTHER THEORIES

Under the shareholder primacy approach the directors have a duty to act in the best interests of the company and this is taken, effectively, to mean the shareholders.[9] This duty involves focusing on maximising shareholder interests. If directors fail to do so, they are in breach. Shareholders have been given the right, for many years at common law, to bring derivative actions against directors where they have breached their duties to the company. Some have even said that this right is provided because the shareholders are perceived as the owners of the company.[10] The most frequently argued reason for granting shareholders the right to take action is that they are the residual claimants to the income generated by the company.[11] Arguably, one of the strengths of

---

[9]   The literature discussing the theory is extensive. For some of the leading works on the principle, see J. Macey, 'An Economic Analysis of the Various Rationales for Making Shareholders the Exclusive Beneficiaries of Corporate Fiduciary Duties' (1991) 21 *Stetson Law Review* 23; S. Bainbridge, 'In Defense of the Shareholder Maximization Norm: A Reply to Professor Green' (1993) 50 *Washington and Lee Law Review* 1423; B. Black and R. Kraakman, 'A Self-Enforcing Model of Corporate Law' (1996) 109 *Harvard Law Review* 1911; D. G. Smith, 'The Shareholder Primacy Norm' (1998) 23 *Journal of Corporation Law* 277.

[10]   L. Mitchell, 'The Fairness Rights of Bondholders' (1990) 65 *New York University Law Review* 1165 at 1192–1193; M. Stokes, 'Company Law and Legal Theory' in S. Wheeler (ed), *The Law of the Business Enterprise* (Oxford, Oxford University Press, 1994) at 94.

[11]   S. Deakin and G. Slinger, 'Hostile Takeovers, Corporate Law, and the Theory of the Firm' (1997) 24 *Journal of Law and Society* 124 at 126; A. Licht, 'The

this approach is that the shareholders have rights which might allow them to remedy in some way the wrongs perpetrated by the directors in not adhering to the objective of the company. Derivative actions are provided for under company law in many common law jurisdictions. Most common law jurisdictions that allow for derivative actions have now codified the right to bring such actions, the UK doing so quite recently in its Companies Act 2006.[12] The aim behind the UK's decision is the simplification and modernisation of the law in order to improve its accessibility.[13] Whether or not there will be an increase in derivative claims under this legislation is moot. The legislation was only put in force from 1 October 2007 and there are relatively few cases that have been reported.[14] Australia, which has similar legislation, introduced in 2000, has not seen an upsurge in litigation,[15] and it has been suggested that the same situation is likely to occur in the UK.[16] While arguably shareholders might be able to mount derivative claims more easily, they still have to get over a significant hurdle, namely persuading a court to give them permission (in England, Wales and Northern Ireland ('leave' in Scotland)) to continue a derivative claim.[17]

Maximands of Corporate Governance: A Theory of Values and Cognitive Style' (2004) 29 *Delaware Journal of Corporate Law* 649 at 652. This seems to be what was being said in the English case of *Brady v Brady* (1988) 3 BCC 535.

[12]   See Part 11.

[13]   Law Commission, *Shareholder Remedies: Report on a Reference under section 3(1)(e) of the Law Commissions Act 1965* (Law Com No 246, Cm 3769) (London, Stationery Office, 1997) at p7. There have been some adjustments to the original recommendations – in England and Wales, for example, the Law Commission's recommendation that a member be required to give notice of 28 days to the company before initiating proceedings was not adopted: ibid at 91.

[14]   For example, see: *Franbar Holdings Ltd v Patel* [2008] EWHC 1534 (Ch); *Wishart* [2009] CSIH 65; 2009 SLT 812; *Stimpson v Southern Landlords Association (2009)* [2009] EWHC 2072 (Ch); *Iesini v Westrip Holdings Ltd* [2009] EWHC 2526 (Ch); *Kiani v Cooper* [2010] EWHC 577 (Ch); *Stainer v Lee* [2010] EWHC 1539 (Ch). For a discussion of them and other case law, see A. Keay and J. Loughrey, 'Derivative Proceedings in a Brave New World for Company Management and Shareholders' [2010] *Journal of Business Law* 151.

[15]   See, I. M. Ramsay and B. Saunders, 'Litigation by Shareholders and Directors: An Empirical Study of the Statutory Derivative Action' (2006) 6 *Journal of Corporate Law Studies* 397 at 417.

[16]   A. Keay and J. Loughrey, 'Something Old, Something New, Something Borrowed: An Analysis of the New Derivative Action Under the Companies Act 2006' (2008) 124 *Law Quarterly Review* 469 at 499–500.

[17]   For a discussion of the process and issues relating to it, see ibid; A. Reisberg, *Derivative Actions and Corporate Governance* (Oxford, Oxford University Press, 2007); R. Hollington, *Shareholders' Rights*, 5th ed (London, Sweet and Maxwell,

Theoretically, where there is a failure to maximise shareholder interests, shareholders might be able to mount an action under provisions similar to s.994 of the UK's Companies Act 2006, on the basis that the affairs of the company have been conducted in a way that is oppressive or unfairly prejudicial to them. Such actions have been rare where public companies are concerned. While there is nothing in the legislation which prevents a member in a public company bringing proceedings under s.994, and they are possible, given the decision of the English Court of Appeal decision in *Clark v Cutland*,[18] clearly it has been used overwhelmingly in relation to private companies where a member can establish that he or she had, when joining the company, certain legitimate expectations that have not been fulfilled. The reason why disenchanted shareholders of public companies have not invoked s.994 and its legislative forebears is probably primarily due to the fact that they favour selling their shares rather than resorting to what is potentially costly litigation. In any event, with public companies, where people tend to become involved without being given any expectations by directors or managers, a claim under the precursor of s.994 has not generally been successful.[19]

Besides the aforementioned legal actions, shareholders are able in a number of jurisdictions, provided that they can secure sufficient support, to have directors removed from office,[20] or they are entitled to refrain from supporting them at re-election time.[21] However, there are significant practical hurdles that shareholders have to face in order to see these options to a successful end.[22]

Another process that is often said to protect shareholders where shareholder primacy applies, is the market for corporate control. This is said to deter managers from failing to maximise shareholder wealth because if a company is run down, and operating below its potential, its share price will be depressed, and corporate raiders might see an opportunity to acquire the company at a good price and then run it efficiently to produce a profit. In such circumstances the shareholders will usually

---

2007) Chapter 6; V. Joffe et al, *Minority Shareholders: Law, Practice and Procedure* (Oxford, Oxford University Press, 2008), Chapter 1.

[18]   [2003] EWCA Civ 810; [2004] 1 WLR 783.

[19]   See *Re Astec (BSR) plc* [1998] 2 BCLC 556 at 589. For a case where a petition in relation to a public company failed, see *Re Blue Arrow plc* [1987] BCLC 585.

[20]   For example, see s.168 of the UK Companies Act 2006. For a discussion of this provision and removal in general, see, A. Keay, 'Company Directors Behaving Poorly: Disciplinary Options for Shareholders' [2007] *Journal of Business Law* 656.

[21]   For a discussion of the avenues shareholders might take, see ibid.

[22]   See ibid.

benefit because either they will sell their shares to the raider at a much better price compared with the listed price or the price that is generally available, or they remain in the company after the takeover while the company's performance improves. The managers though will usually lose their jobs as the raider will replace them with its own nominees. But there has been theoretical argument[23] and some empirical research[24] that denies the efficacious nature of the takeover in this regard. The use of the market for corporate control has also been questioned as an adequate device for disciplining directors.[25]

In shareholder primacy the ones who enforce the duties of the directors, if the board does not take action against the miscreant directors, are the shareholders. There have been a number of commentators who have argued for greater powers for shareholders in the US, but even in the UK where shareholders are regarded as having more powers to control directors,[26] they are not, practically, well endowed with powerful weapons.[27]

Whilst it might be said that one of the strengths of shareholder primacy is the fact that it is a theory that can be enforced by the shareholders, even though there are problems in doing so, undoubtedly one of the main drawbacks with stakeholder theory is that there are significant problems in enforcing it. Stakeholder theory demands that directors manage the company's business for the betterment of the interests of all those who can be counted as stakeholders in the company.[28] Enforcing adherence to this

---

23   M. Lipton and S. Rosenblum, 'A New System of Corporate Governance: The Quinquenial Election of Directors' (1991) 58 *University of Chicago Law Review* 187 at 188; R. Booth, 'Stockholders, Stakeholders and Bagholders (or How Investor Diversification Affects Fiduciary Duty)' (1998) 53 *The Business Lawyer* 429 at 440. For a more recent view, see L. Bebchuk, 'The Myth of the Shareholder Franchise' (2007) 93 *Virginia Law Review* 675.
24   J. Franks and C. Mayer, 'Hostile Takeovers in the UK and the Correction of Managerial Failure' (1996) 40 *Journal of Financial Economics* 163.
25   See I. Anabtawi, 'Some Skepticism About Increasing Shareholder Power' (2006) 53 *University of California at Los Angeles Law Review* 561 at 568.
26   Certainly this is the perception of some esteemed American commentators. For example, see L. Bebchuk, 'The Case for Increasing Shareholder Power' (2005) 118 *Harvard Law Review* 833.
27   See A. Keay, 'Company Directors Behaving Poorly: Disciplinary Options for Shareholders' [2007] *Journal of Business Law* 656
28   The literature discussing the theory is extensive. For some leading works, see R. Edward Freeman, *Strategic Management: a Stakeholder Approach* (Boston, Pitman/Ballinger, 1984); R. Karmel, 'Implications of the Stakeholder Model' (1993) 61 *George Washington Law Review* 1156; T. Donaldson and L. Preston, 'The Stakeholder Theory for the Corporation: Concepts, Evidence, Implications'

theory has been identified as a problem ever since the time of the debates entered into between Berle and Dodd in the early 1930s. Berle indicated[29] that he, like Dodd, favoured an approach closer to what we know as stakeholder theory today, but he confessed that he could not see it being workable. His inevitable conclusion from his thinking was that you cannot abandon an emphasis on:

> the view that business corporations exist for the sole purpose of making profits for their shareholders until such time as [you] are prepared to offer a clear and reasonably enforceable scheme of responsibilities to someone else.[30]

Berle saw shareholder primacy as a second-best solution so as to mitigate the amount of opportunism which managers engaged in, but it was more practicable than stakeholder theory. Dodd conceded that it was necessary to introduce strong legal measures in order to provide for the regulating of the actions of management.[31] The disagreement between the two scholars was in relation to how the duty could be enforced.[32] Much later Oliver Hart asserted that there could be no enforcement of the stakeholder theory because the idea of requiring a director to take into account the interests of all constituencies is 'essentially vacuous'[33] as directors would be able to justify any decision on the basis that it benefited some person or some group.[34] Of concern was that the directors might be able to act opportunistically and then hide behind an assertion that they acted in order to benefit a particular stakeholder group. Far more recently the Company Law Review Steering Group in its review of UK company law

---

(1995) 20 *Academy Management Review* 65; R. Mitchell, 'Toward a Theory of Stakeholder Identification and Salience: Defining the Principle of Who and What Really Counts' (1997) 22 *Academy Management Review* 853; A. Campbell, 'Stakeholders: The Case in Favour' (1997) 30 *Long Range Planning* 446; J. Dean, *Directing Public Companies* (London, Cavendish, 2001).

[29]   A. A. Berle Jr, 'For Whom Corporate Managers are Trustees: A Note' (1932) 45 *Harvard Law Review* 1365.

[30]   Ibid at 1367.

[31]   'The Modern Corporation and Private Property' (1933) 81 *University of Pennsylvania Law Review* 182 at 785.

[32]   A. Licht, 'The Maximands of Corporate Governance: A Theory of Values and Cognitive Style' (2004) 29 *Delaware Journal of Corporate Law* 649 at 652.

[33]   'An Economist's View of Fiduciary Duty' (1993) 43 *University of Toronto Law Journal* 299 at 303.

[34]   Ibid

said that there is little sense in requiring a duty to be owed to a group that is unable to enforce it.[35]

It might be said that as stakeholder theory tends to espouse the trustworthiness and professionalism of directors, there is no need for any enforcement mechanism. Under the stewardship theory, embraced by many favouring stakeholder theory or something akin to it, there is a focus on directors' need for achievement, responsibility, recognition, altruism and respect for authority, and as a result they can be seen not as opportunistic, but as good stewards who will act in the best interests of the stakeholders.

Janice Dean has said that if stakeholding is to be implemented in practice then there has to be a power to protect stakeholder expectations and to compensate stakeholders whose interests have been disregarded.[36] First of all, it is never going to be easy to assess if the interests of some stakeholders have been prejudiced, and then secondly, it may well be difficult to quantify the extent of the loss. Gregory Crespi has attempted to explain how a court might go about determining whether a stakeholder had been injured by the decision-making of the directors, and, if so, to what extent.[37] But, with respect, the process with which a court would be faced, if Crespi's explanation were applied, is extremely complex. Crespi seemed to acknowledge this problem as he states that any obligation on a director in relation to stakeholder interests would have to be an aspirational norm rather than a legal directive.[38] This obviously does not provide what Dean asserts is needed for stakeholder theory to become operative. The problem with this issue is manifested by the fact that the UK's Company Law Review Steering Group recorded that few who responded to their request for replies on various topics, and who argued for a stakeholder approach, sought to give stakeholders the right to be heard by a court if they felt that their interests were not being taken into account by the directors.[39]

Wai Leung,[40] adopting the arguments of Larry Mitchell in addressing

---

[35]   Company Law Review, *Modern Company Law for a Competitive Economy*: 'The Strategic Framework' 1999, London, DTI, note 31, p40.

[36]   *Directing Public Companies* (London, Cavendish Publishing, 2001) at 169, 176

[37]   'Redefining the Fiduciary Duties of Corporate Directors in Accordance with the Team Production Model of Corporate Governance' (2002-03) 16 *Creighton Law Review* 623 at 637–639.

[38]   Ibid at 641.

[39]   Company Law Review, *Modern Company Law for a Competitive Economy*: 'Developing the Framework,' 2000, London, DTI, at para 2.12.

[40]   W. Leung, 'The Inadequacy of Shareholder Primacy: A Proposed Corporate Regime that Recognizes Non-Shareholder Interests' (1997) 30 *Columbia Journal of Law and Social Problems* 589 at 627–628.

the enforcement of US constituency statues,[41] has advocated permitting stakeholders who have been injured because of the way the directors have run the company, to bring proceedings against the directors. On this argument, the stakeholder would need to establish that he or she was injured and that the injury sustained was to a legitimate expectation which he or she had as a stakeholder in the company. This is similar to the requirement for relief that exists under s.994 of the UK's Companies Act 2006.[42] The concept of legitimate expectations[43] in essence is a contract-based idea, the object of which is to fill in the gaps in a contractual relationship. It involves asking what reasonable parties would have wanted to have included in their contract had they thought about the issue.[44] The argument might be put that as stakeholders make firm specific investments in the company then they have certain high expectations of how the company will be managed. Nevertheless, this does not help with the enforcement issue.

It has been suggested, adroitly, it is respectfully submitted, that to provide non-shareholder stakeholders with a legally enforceable right in the governance of companies will require a fundamental change in the organisation of corporate affairs,[45] and that is unlikely to happen in Anglo-American jurisdictions, certainly in the short-medium term.

Finally, reference should be made to the now repealed s.309 of the UK's Companies Act 1985.[46] This provision stated that in performing their functions directors were to have regard to the interests of the employees. While this might, prima facie, look attractive for employees, the provision was effectively 'a lame duck' because of the fact that neither the employees nor anyone acting on behalf of the employees could enforce the section.[47]

There are several ways that may be used to prevent or limit directors

---

[41]   See above at pp. 227–228.

[42]   See *O'Neill v Phillips* [1999] 2 BCLC 1; [1999] BCC 600 (HL).

[43]   It is a concept that was regularly considered in cases brought under s.459 of the Companies Act 1985 (now replaced by s.994 of the Companies Act 2006) and claiming that a company's affairs have been conducted in an unfairly prejudicial way. For example, see *O'Neill v Phillips* [1999] 2 BCLC 1; [1999] BCC 600 (HL).

[44]   L. Mitchell, 'The Fairness Rights of Bondholders' (1990) 65 *New York University Law Review* 1165 at 1225.

[45]   A. Schall, L. Miles and S. Goulding, 'Promoting an Inclusive Approach on the Part of Directors: The UK and German Positions' (2006) 6 *Journal of Corporate Law Studies* 299 at 300.

[46]   In fact much of the Act has now been repealed and replaced by Companies Act 2006.

[47]   See, J. Parkinson, *Corporate Power and Responsibility* (Oxford, Oxford University Press, 1993) at 82–83.

from shirking or acting opportunistically. There is a mixture of contractual, regulatory, market and fiduciary constraints on the actions which directors can take. For instance, managers remain subject to the financial markets, the market for control and the product markets[48] and these provide, according to some, highly objective and demanding guidelines.[49] But these constraints do not give any investors in the company a straightforward route which they can pursue either to rein in directors' conduct or make them accountable for what they have done. For example, as noted earlier, no one but a shareholder is generally able to commence proceedings if the directors breach their duties and the company decides not to take action against them.

3.   ENFORCEMENT OPTIONS UNDER EMS

This part of the Chapter considers the options which are available, or potentially available, to ensure that the EMS model is enforced. What we are considering is whether any action, and in particular, although not exclusively, any kind of legal action can be introduced to ensure that directors show appropriate regard for the maximisation of entity wealth together with making sure that the entity is sustained financially. Under UK law (and many common law jurisdictions), as we have seen, the only investors who have any significant structural protection within the company are the shareholders, and it is arguable whether that is particularly effective.[50]

Importantly, any enforcement mechanism that is implemented must be credible if it is to be successful.[51] If a mechanism is not credible then the directors are likely to ignore it,[52] and investors are not going to attempt to utilise it.

---

[48]   See, for example, E. Fama, 'Agency Problems and the Theory of the Firm' (1980) 88 *Journal of Political Economy* 288; E. Fama and M. Jensen, 'Separation of Ownership and Control' (1983) 26 *Journal of Law and Economics* 301; M. Jensen and W. Meckling, 'Theory of the Firm: Managerial Behavior, Agency Costs and Ownership Structure' (1976) 3 *Journal of Financial Economics* 305.

[49]   A. Campbell, 'Stakeholders: The Case in Favour' (1997) 30 *Long Range Planning* 446 at 448.

[50]   See A. Keay, 'Company Directors Behaving Poorly: Disciplinary Options for Shareholders' [2007] *Journal of Business Law* 656.

[51]   T. Schelling, *The Strategy of Conflict* (Cambridge, Massachusetts, Harvard University Press, 1960) and referred to in C. Hill and T. Jones, 'Stakeholder-Agency Theory' (1992) 29 *Journal of Management Studies* 131 at 141.

[52]   C. Hill and T. Jones, 'Stakeholder-Agency Theory' (1992) 29 *Journal of Management Studies* 131 at 141.

The following discussion does not encompass any contractual options available to investors. Such options are usually considered in relation to creditors and, on some occasions, employees. It might be argued that there should not be any dedicated enforcement mechanism as investors can rely on contract and, in addition, the market to ensure that they are protected. But with EMS we are not looking at investors taking action to protect their own positions directly, as with any options envisaged by stakeholder theory, but to enforce any failure of the directors to comply with the objective of the company, namely to maximise entity wealth.

One other matter should be noted. It is often argued that the markets themselves, such as the market for corporate control, will act as constraints on the actions of directors.[53] As with the issue of contractual protection, it is arguable that many investors are not protected by market forces, and in any event market forces do not constrain directors adequately.[54] Before dealing with pure legal mechanisms it is appropriate to consider other methods that might be invoked.

3.1 Exit

If dissatisfied with the way that the directors are acting, most investors can decide to exit from their relationship with the company. For instance, shareholders can sell their shares, employees can resign and suppliers can decline to supply the company any longer. This option might, however, be of little, or no, use. In fact it might be totally impracticable for an investor to leave. Shareholders might not be able to get the price for their shares that they believe they are worth, and they believe that they cannot afford to sustain the loss.[55] Institutional investors or other large shareholders are often not going to be in a position where they can liquidate their shareholding easily. It is often inconvenient and even disruptive for company employees (and their families) if they decide to leave their posts, especially if they have either to leave the area in which they live or commute

---

[53] For example, in relation to the market for corporate control, see H. Butler and L. Ribstein, 'Opting Out of Fiduciary Duties: A Response to the Anti-Contractarians' (1990) 65 *Washington Law Review* 1 at 21–28.

[54] For example, there is empirical research (J. Franks and C. Mayer, 'Hostile Takeovers in the UK and the Correction of Managerial Failure' (1996) 40 *Journal of Financial Economics* 163) and theoretical research (I. Anabtawi, 'Some Skepticism About Increasing Shareholder Power' (2006) 53 *University of California at Los Angeles Law Review* 561 at 568) that casts doubt on the efficacy of the market for corporate control.

[55] There is also the expense of transaction costs, such as a brokerage fee.

long distances to take up new employment. Some suppliers either might have built their businesses around the company or cannot replace the company's custom readily. Other investors, such as lenders, are not able, absent breaches of restrictive covenants or other covenants in the loan agreement (such as a failure to repay instalments under loans), to exit the relationship in the short term as they are contractually bound. Clearly, the local community is not able to exit the relationship, although it might withdraw support in some way.

In any event exit of investors is not, of itself, going to permit enforcement of the directors' obligations under EMS. It is merely going to permit an investor to escape. At best the exit of an investor might limit its losses and lead to directors modifying their actions, but this is far from guaranteed.

3.2 Voice

Exit might be regarded as an extreme measure, so what else is available that is less extreme? One would expect that any investor or group of investors who were disgruntled with the manner in which the directors were acting, could approach the board with their concerns in the hope that the board would modify its proposed action(s) or at least enter some form of dialogue and negotiation. There are numerous examples of shareholders doing this in recent years,[56] particularly as shareholder activism has developed and become far more common. Influential creditors, such as banks which have lent large sums, may well be able to go to the board and register concern, but most investors will either not have enough information to do anything, because of information asymmetry, or will not be able to get the attention of the directors. Directorial response to voice is likely to be commensurate with the power that the investor can bring to bear.

3.3 Pressure

It is very possible that the overtures of most investors to directors, if made, will go unheeded. If that is the case, what else might investors seek to do? One possible extra-legal action that an investor might take is to exert some form of pressure on the board. This could take a variety of forms. Pressure is something that has long been recognised as something emanating from

---

[56] See A. Keay, 'Company Directors Behaving Poorly: Disciplinary Options for Shareholders' [2007] *Journal of Business Law* 656.

investor groups[57] and one or more investor groups could exert pressure with one of two aims in view. First, an investor might act in order to convince the directors that they should be doing something differently in order to enhance the company's wealth. But, alternatively, an investor could seek to persuade the board to act in such a way as to benefit him or her. This latter approach could lead to more investors engaging in rent-seeking activities as they compete with one another in order to gain greater advantages.[58] Pressure by investors on the board to benefit them must be resisted by a board or else it is likely to be highly deleterious for the company, and certainly it would not enhance entity wealth. It might lead, conceivably, to other investors deciding to exit. Leaving aside this issue, what avenues are there available to investors who seek to exert pressure so as to benefit the company?

Under any model of the corporate objective there is the possibility of an economic enforcement mechanism that is able to be undertaken by several investors and others, if directors do not adhere to the company's objective.[59] First, investors might threaten to exit,[60] engendering concern in the board that this threat, if put into action, might lead to a reduction in the company's share price. Of course, such a threat might be, or seen by the directors and others to be, a bluff. All of this could lead to brinkmanship, which is unlikely to be good for the company. Second, there might well be available to some investors various forms of political pressure that can be brought to bear on directors. There are a range of political pressure mechanisms that can be used, such as the formation of coalitions, public relations campaigns, referring matters to regulatory agencies etc. Some investors may be willing to take action which will see their concerns about the company become public and, therefore, possibly be detrimental to the company's reputation. This might be prejudicial to the investor, but it might be reasoned that the damage to the company will only be short term, and the action might bear fruit in the long term. Robert Monks,

---

[57]   D. Greening and B. Gray, 'Testing a Model of Organizational Response to Social and Political Pressure' (1994) 37 *Academy of Management Journal* 467 at 476.

[58]   D. Millon, 'New Game Plan or Business as Usual? A Critique of the Team Production Model of Corporate Law' (2000) 86 *Virginia Law Review* 1001 at 1004.

[59]   See, N. Gunningham, R. Kagan and D. Thornton, 'Social License and Environmental Protection: Why Businesses Go Beyond Compliance' (2004) 29 *Law and Social Inquiry* 307.

[60]   C. Kirchner, 'Shareholder Value: A New Standard for Company Conduct' in K. Hopt and E. Wymeersch (eds), *Capital Markets and Company Law* (Oxford, Oxford University Press, 2003) at 344.

the corporate governance commentator, embraced the publicity option successfully in relation to the American retailer, Sears (see below).

Shareholders have what might be regarded as the ultimate pressure tactic, and which was dealt with earlier, that is, threatening to use their power to remove one or more directors.[61] They may also threaten to exercise their voting rights to not re-elect a director. Whether these measures will have any effect will depend on a number of factors, including the level of shareholding held by the shareholder and his or her allies, and the shareholder's power to influence and co-ordinate more like-minded shareholders.

The ultimate pressure tactic for employees is to withdraw their labour. The number of strikes has reduced in the UK over the past decade compared with previous years and this might be due to diminished unionisation.[62] It has been asserted that the influence of union on management and governance of companies has been severely affected in recent times.[63] Unless large portions of a company's workforce are members of a union it is unlikely that this option is of great benefit as there could be different views leading to only some of the workforce deciding to strike. This is likely to produce relatively little benefit. Alternatively, employees could threaten to resign. Whether this is potentially effective will depend on the worth, or perceived worth, of the employees to the company.

There might be other means (besides court action), such as pressure on the board so as to encourage the board to take a different course of action or approach. One method is to place pressure on directors as Robert Monks did in relation to the American retailer, Sears. He did this by influencing public opinion. Monks inserted full-page advertisements in the *Wall Street Journal* exposing the identities of the directors of the company and describing them as 'non-performing assets.' The subsequent embarrassment for the directors led to the changes Monks sought.[64] The

---

[61] See s.168 of the Companies Act 2006.

[62] D. Bradley, 'Be prepared to act fast when industrial action strikes' Personnel Today and accessible at <http://www.personneltoday.com/art icles/2007/09/10/42221/be-ready-to-act-fast-when-industrial-action-strikes.html> (last visited, 22 May 2009). See the Department of Business Enterprise and Regulatory Reform statistics <http://stats.berr.gov.uk/UKSA/tu/tum2008.pdf> (last visited, 22 May 2009).

[63] G. Proctor and L. Miles, *Corporate Governance* (London, Cavendish Publishing, 2002) at 58.

[64] R. Monks and N. Minnow, *Watching the Watchers: Corporate Governance for the Twenty-first Century*, (Malden, Mass, Blackwell Publishing, 1995) and referred to in L. Zingales, 'In Search of New Foundations' (2000) 55 *Journal of Finance* 1623 at 1627–1628.

drawback with this type of approach is that it might attract very bad publicity from which it might take the company a long period to recover, even if the sought-after reforms are introduced. Pressure was successful in 2005 in relation to Asset Management Investment Company plc, a specialist investor in the asset management industry. Its board was accused of overseeing disastrous performance and under substantial pressure the directors resigned.[65] Besides possible effects on the company's reputation, the danger of instituting a publicity campaign against a board is that it could deter future investment and/or affect the company's place in the marketplace, both of which would prejudice the entity and, indirectly, all investors, so any action has to be measured.

Consumers can seek to engineer a boycott of the company's products, action which might place pressure on other investors to take action to persuade or force the board to change its actions, as a boycott could affect them ultimately. Of course, a boycott might not be an option where the company is either the only producer of a line of goods, or is the cheapest producer of those goods. Nor will it be an option where the company does not have a ready consumer market or does not need, or is not prepared, to protect a brand.[66]

Communities that are affected by companies might take political action in order to try and enforce adherence to EMS as this action is something which Jonathon Macey has argued is capable of being effective.[67] The action that might be taken could include demonstrations, particularly at the gates of factories or retail outlets of the company, as these tend to cause the most publicity. Less direct action is to lobby local councillors, members of the legislature and even government ministers to have such officials influence boards of directors or exert pressure through the political process.

Suppliers could exert pressure by way of a threat to refuse to continue to supply necessary supplies to a company, although of course this might lead to the company going elsewhere for those supplies (if it could), and many suppliers would rather not take the risk of alienating the company's directors, especially if the company is a major customer.

Lenders could threaten to decline to continue existing credit

---

[65] P. Hosking, 'Amic board makes quiet exit' *The Times*, 9 June 2005.

[66] N. Gunningham, R. Kagan and D. Thornton, 'Social License and Environmental Protection: Why Businesses Go Beyond Compliance' [2004] *Law and Social Inquiry* 307 at 334.

[67] 'An Economic Analysis of the Various Rationales for Making Shareholder the Exclusive Beneficiaries of Corporate Fiduciary Duties' (1991) 21 *Stetson Law Review* 23 at 42–43.

arrangements, save where they are constrained by contractual terms, or indicate that any request for new credit facilities will be refused unless directors change direction. Lenders could seek to influence other lenders accordingly, thus making it more difficult for the company to obtain further loan funds. But the latter option is not likely to succeed in relation to all possible financiers and in fact some might be encouraged to lend by the fact that a finance competitor has withdrawn funding; an opportunity might be seen to steal a march on a competitor.

Many of the aforementioned options cannot work across all companies and not even across all investors in a particular company. It is limited in efficacy to those situations where the investor is offering something unique to the company, or all, or a significant number, of the investors are disgruntled and they agree to engage in economic action. For, unless these circumstances exist, it is probable that the company can go elsewhere to obtain its investment.

As adverted to above, the problem with extra-legal pressure is that an investor can endeavour, by taking such action, to obtain a benefit for himself or herself, whereas EMS is seeking to enhance company wealth. With pressure there is the danger that it might in fact lead to directors being forced to take action which fails to achieve EMS, but surrenders to the pressure being exerted by a particular investor, and benefits that investor.

3.4 Board Representation

One mechanism that has been suggested for enforcement, in the context of stakeholder theory,[68] is to install representatives on the board from various investor groups, so it is not only shareholders who get to vote for the directors. Indeed this does happen in some companies. In many companies in continental Europe and East Asia there is representation on boards. This will usually consist of representation on supervisory boards where there is a two-tier board system. Although, companies in Denmark, Sweden and Luxembourg all have employee representatives on one-tier boards of directors.[69]

---

[68]   For example, see, K. Greenfield, 'Reclaiming Corporate Law in a New Gilded Age' (2008) 2 *Harvard Law and Policy Review* 1 at 24; K. Greenfield, 'Saving the World With Corporate Law' (2008) 57 *Emory Law Journal* 947 at 978; F. Post, 'A Response to "The Social Responsibility of Corporate Management: A Classical Critique"' (2003) 18 *Mid-American Journal of Business* 25 at 32.

[69]   F. Allen, E. Carletti, and R. Marquez, 'Stakeholder Capitalism, Corporate Governance and Firm Value,' 4 August 2007, Working Paper, University of

The attractiveness of doing this is that firms will be seen as recognising formally the importance of the role of stakeholders who are represented on the board.[70] Kent Greenfield asserts that the best way for a board to engage in decision-making is to have all important stakeholders represented on it. He acknowledges that this mechanism presents difficulties but argues that employees, the communities in which the company employs a significant portion of its workers, long-term business partners and creditors could all be represented.[71] In fact representation on the supervisory board of German companies is necessary under that country's co-determination law. Could this approach be used for enforcing adherence to EMS? There are at least four obvious drawbacks with this action. Before discussing these, it should be noted that Hillman, Keil and Luce found in an empirical study that the existence of stakeholder directors in the companies they considered had no effect on stakeholder relations and they concluded that a board does not need stakeholder representation to address the needs of stakeholders.[72]

Now returning to the drawbacks of having representative boards. First, each investor is, naturally, going to be concerned to act to its benefit, and often options that are available to a board will not favour all investors. It has been asserted that no stakeholder would hurt the company just so that a larger piece of the pie could be secured.[73] But, with respect, that does not necessarily ring true, and it is rather naive. Some stakeholders might see the opportunity of taking benefits in the short term, just as shareholders are often alleged to want to do. Second, a company could have many trading partners and it would be unwieldy to have them all represented, and yet it would be impossible to have them represented as a group as they are likely to have many conflicting interests,[74] and it could produce severe internecine disputes. Also, if one had trading partners

---

Pennsylvania, at 6, and accessible at: <http://knowledge.wharton.upenn.edu/papers/1344.pdf> (last visited, 3 August 2009).

[70]   R. Mitchell, B. Agle and D. Wood, 'Toward a Theory of Stakeholder Identification and Salience: Defining the Principle of Who and What Really Counts' (1997) 22 *Academy Management Review* 853 at 876.

[71]   'Reclaiming Corporate Law in a New Gilded Age' (2008) 2 *Harvard Law and Policy Review* 1 at 24.

[72]   A. Hillman, G. Keim and R. Luce, 'Board Composition and Stakeholder Performance: Do Stakeholder Directors Make a Difference?' (2001) 40 *Business and Society* 295 at 308 and 309.

[73]   K. Greenfield, 'Reclaiming Corporate Law in a New Gilded Age' (2008) 2 *Harvard Law and Policy Review* 1 at 28.

[74]   See, J. Parkinson, *Corporate Power and Responsibility* (Oxford, Oxford University Press, 1993) at 391.

represented individually, it would not be possible to have all of them represented, and those who were omitted from this process might be severely miffed. Third, it is possible that it might encourage factions to develop in the board that could lead to difficulty in decision-making at board level. Fourth, any restructuring of corporate governance to permit stakeholders to have some control is unlikely to be attractive to many, and particularly to shareholders. The UK's Company Law Review Steering Group, when considering the review of UK company law at end of the last century and the beginning of the present, stated in one of its reports that: 'Proposals to alter board composition to require wider representation as a mandatory requirement would represent a very radical change to British corporate culture [and that of many Anglo-American jurisdictions] and would be unlikely to command wide support.'[75] It has been suggested that placing stakeholders on boards would be frowned on by present and potential shareholders.[76] It is quite probable that potential shareholders would be reluctant to invest in a company where the board had wide representation as they would be concerned about decisions being made against their interests. Even if one had board representation that does not mean that there would, necessarily, be adherence to the objective provided for in the model, and so one still needs an enforcement mechanism in case the board fails to act appropriately. Therefore, one is back to the beginning to find a method to permit the contesting of the action.

3.5 Administration/Liquidation

A mechanism that is available to creditors in the UK, and other jurisdictions like Australia and New Zealand, in order to enforce adherence to EMS is to threaten, or apply, to put the company into liquidation or administration.[77] This would concern the directors as the commencement of such regimes would see the directors losing their positions, for an independent insolvency practitioner (acting as an administrator or

---

[75] Company Law Review, *Modern Company Law for a Competitive Economy*: 'The Strategic Framework' 1999, London, DTI, at para 5.1.32. The same could be applied to the culture that exists in companies in places such as the US, Australia, and Canada, as well as in companies in many countries.

[76] L. Ribstein, 'Accountability and Responsibility in Corporate Governance' (2006) 81 *Notre Dame Law Review* 1431 at 1440.

[77] Administration is a shelter regime for insolvent companies, and it has some similar features to Chapter 11 bankruptcy in the US, voluntary administration in Australia and sauvegarde in France. See A. Keay and P. Walton, *Insolvency Law: Corporate and Personal*, 2nd ed (Bristol, Jordan Publishing, 2008) at 89–140.

liquidator) would take control of the company's affairs,[78] and actions might be brought against the directors by the liquidator or administrator for breach of duty. While this might seem attractive, the board will know that although an application to have the company liquidated or placed in administration would be annoying, if their company is clearly solvent then an application would not succeed as a creditor seeking liquidation or administration will usually have to demonstrate that the company is unable to pay its debts, and that would obviously not be the case.[79] Also, an application for administration or liquidation could be potentially damaging as far as the reputation of the company is concerned,[80] and this might not be the best outcome for a creditor ultimately.

A problem with administration is that it cannot be sought by any investor other than a creditor, and in Australia administration can only be commenced by a secured creditor.[81] Furthermore, apart from shareholders who are able to be categorised as contributories,[82] other investors cannot present a liquidation petition.

In the UK the Secretary of State for Business, Innovation and Skills is empowered to present against a company a petition for winding up, pursuant to s.124A of the Insolvency Act 1986, where it is in the public interest to do so.[83] Could such a power be invoked by the Secretary of State where a company's board has acted in a way that is not consistent with the objective of a company? It might be argued that the public interest here means a very wide-ranging interest. It is suggested that in the context of s.124A 'in the public interest' means something that is in the interest of society as a whole, as opposed to specific sectors of the community or certain people, such as investors, who are interested in the company which is the subject of the petition. This seems to be in line with two judicial comments in England. First, in *In re Rubin, Rosen and*

---

[78] Compare debtor-in-possession regimes, like Chapter 11 bankruptcy in the US.

[79] See s.122(1)(f) and Schedule B1, para 11(a) of the Insolvency Act 1986.

[80] The reason why companies are able to apply for an injunction to prevent a petition to wind up being advertised (as is required by the Insolvency Rules 1986) is that the advertising could damage the company's reputation: *Re a Company (No. 007923 of 1994)* [1995] BCC 634 at 639.

[81] In Australia administration can only be commenced out of court.

[82] s.124 of the Insolvency Act 1986 prescribes who may petition for winding up. Subsection (1) permits contributories to do so, but no other investor.

[83] See A. Keay, 'Public Interest Petitions' (1999) 20 *The Company Lawyer* 296; V. Finch, 'Public Interest Liquidation: PIL or Placebo?' [2002] *The Insolvency Lawyer* 157.

Associated Ltd,[84] Megarry J referred, in the context of the public interest, to the Secretary of State acting in the interests of the public at large, and the public at large is a similar idea to society as a whole. Second, Nicholls LJ in the Court of Appeal, in the case of *Re Walter L Jacob Ltd*,[85] said that the public interest requires that individuals and companies who are involved in dealing in securities with the public, should be ready to assume minimum standards of commercial behaviour and those who do not do so should be stopped from engaging in such activities.[86] In referring to the public interest his Lordship was obviously adverting to society as a whole, for it is the concern of society that business affairs are conducted in a commercially moral way. In addition to the above, most s.124A petitions have been presented where the Secretary of State is concerned about the public being misled and/or companies that have acted unscrupulously. It is highly unlikely that the Secretary of State would want to get involved in taking action against a solvent company that has not committed any wrongdoing where there were broad consequences.

3.6   Government Intervention

The Company Law Review Steering Group indicated in its review of UK company law that supporters of the pluralist view of the company wanted either a power for the Secretary of State to intervene in a company, or some form of consultative system.[87] The problem with the Secretary of State having the former power is that intervention could be very arbitrary, and its use could always be heavily influenced by political reasons rather than reasons of justice and fairness. Allied to this is the fact that the government might well have insufficient resources to act in relation to a number of companies. Furthermore, what does the Secretary of State do when he or she intervenes? We have seen that, certainly in more recent times, UK governments prefer generally not to intervene in business affairs.[88] Any government intervention would be unpalatable to many who would see such a mechanism as favouring the idea that companies carry out a public function, whereas they would say that companies are involved in private

---

[84]   [1975] 1 WLR 122 at 129.

[85]   (1989) 5 BCC 244.

[86]   Ibid at 256.

[87]   Company Law Review, *Modern Company Law for a Competitive Economy*: 'Developing the Framework,' 2000, London, DTI at para 2.12.

[88]   There has been partial nationalisation of the banks recently, but that was regarded by many as judicious use of government power, and designed to deal with a very unusual situation.

functions only. This is, of course, an issue that is very wide and has been ongoing since the time of Berle and Dodd in the 1930s.

The Secretary of State for Business, Innovation and Skills is empowered, pursuant to s.438 of the Companies Act 1985, to bring proceedings in the name of a company, if it is in the public interest. But this can only occur following a report or information obtained through an investigation by an inspector appointed under s.431.[89] The problem is that for an inspector to be appointed there must be an application by the company itself, a large number of members, or a small group of members with a large shareholding in the company. It is likely that in most cases no application could be made.

3.7 Oppression/Unfair Prejudice Provision

Several common law jurisdictions have had an 'oppression remedy'[90] for some time, in order to protect minority shareholders. The UK has had an oppression/unfair prejudice section since the enactment of s.210 of the Companies Act 1948. Most US states have provisions allowing for action to be taken for oppression, although the remedies available are limited, and in some states are limited to dissolution of the company. Many Commonwealth jurisdictions, such as Australia, still have an oppression remedy that was based on the aforementioned UK provision.[91] The Australian provision effectively provides that if the company's affairs are being conducted in a manner that is oppressive to, unfairly prejudicial to, or unfairly discriminatory against, a member or members whether in that capacity or in any other capacity relief might be given by a court. The former and present UK provisions, like the present Australian provision, were limited to granting a right to members to bring action. Usually, as with the unfair prejudice ground that is now found in s.994 of the Companies Act 2006,[92] the provision tended to be used to take action against the directors and/or controlling shareholder in quasi-partnerships in a variety of situations, but often where the complainant had been removed from a management role in the company.

---

[89] In such a situation the Secretary of State could also bring proceedings under s.995 if there is unfair prejudice.

[90] 'Oppression' in this context has been said to involve 'burdensome, harsh and wrongful' conduct: *Scottish Co-operative Wholesale Society Ltd v Meyer* [1959] AC 324 at 342 (HL).

[91] s.232 of Corporations Act 2001.

[92] The Australian provision also provides that if conduct that is unfairly prejudicial is established the courts are permitted to grant relief.

Canada has developed perhaps the most broad oppression provision as far as the persons who qualify as applicants for relief are concerned. The provision is s.241 of the Canada Business Corporations Act 1985. Section 241(2) provides that an applicant may succeed if he or she establishes conduct that amounts to oppression or unfair prejudice. Section 241(2) (c) (and provincial statutes based on this Federal provision) states that the court is able to give a remedy if the directors' powers have been exercised 'in a manner that is oppressive or unfairly prejudicial to or unfairly disregards the interests of any security holder,[93] creditor, director or officer.'[94] The Part in the Canada Business Corporations Act that houses s.241 does allow a potentially broad range of people who can bring proceedings. Section 238 provides that applications may be made by people including members, secured creditors[95] and directors. Importantly, in subsection (d) it also includes 'any other person who, in the discretion of a court, is a proper person.' Who is a proper person is squarely within the discretion of the court.[96] In Canada creditors have sought to initiate most actions under this provision. The courts have been aware of the potential width of the provision and have restricted who can take action. For example, it has been said that for a creditor to be able to proceed, it must be demonstrated that the creditor has a legitimate interest in the manner in which the company is being run or has a direct financial interest in how directors are managing the company's affairs.[97] One example of the use of the provision is *Prime Computer of Canada Ltd v Jeffrey*[98] where a director had increased his salary substantially at a time when he was aware that his company was in financial straits. On the application of a creditor the court ordered the director to repay the increase in salary on the basis that the

---

[93]   According to s.2 of the Canada Business Corporations Act 1985 this means a person who holds a share of any class or series of shares or a debt obligation of a corporation and includes a certificate evidencing such a share or debt obligation.

[94]   See D. Thomson, 'Directors, Creditors and Insolvency: A Fiduciary Duty or a Duty Not to Oppress' (2000) 58 *University of Toronto Faculty of Law Review* 31.

[95]   Interpreted very broadly by the Ontario Superior Court of Justice in *Fedel v Tan* 2008 CanLII 46697.

[96]   s.241(3) gives courts an unfettered discretion as to what order they think appropriate, although some examples of orders are set out, in a similar manner to s.996 of the UK's Companies Act 2006.

[97]   *Hordo*; *Jacobs Farms Ltd v Jacobs* [1992] OJ No 813 at 12–14, and referred to by J. Sarra, 'Taking the Corporation Past the "Plimsoll Line" – Director and Officer Liability When the Corporations Founders'' (2001) 10 *International Insolvency Review* 229 at 240.

[98]   (1991) 6 OR (3d) 733.

director's action was unfairly prejudicial to the creditor, as the funds used to increase the director's salary were largely, in effect, those of the creditor.

Could a provision like the Canadian one be used to enforce EMS? A possible objection to this approach might be that it will precipitate a proliferation of litigation, as well as the abuse of proceedings in order to disrupt the management of a company. Yet, this is not the Canadian experience. Its legislation has not, interestingly, precipitated a large number of claims.[99]

Dean appears to think that the UK's counterpart to the Canadian provision, namely s.994 of the Companies Act 2006, is the most promising for the enforcing of stakeholder theory.[100] She argues that a personal action provided for by the unfair prejudice remedy is best as it provides benefits for those who have been deprived of some advantage by the company.[101] At first blush the oppression remedy is attractive for enforcement of EMS. However, it is submitted that it is not ultimately appropriate. The main reason is that s.994, at present is limited to actions by members, and requires the applicant to establish that the company's affairs have been conducted in a manner that is unfairly prejudicial to the interests of members (including the applicant for relief). But even if 'investors' were substituted for members it would still not be appropriate, as EMS is all about preventing action that fails either to maximise entity wealth or to sustain the entity. The oppression/unfair prejudice remedy tends to personalise the effects of the board's wrongful action, and it is focused on personal rights. That is, the applicant for relief is complaining that he or she has been oppressed or unfairly prejudiced by the action of which he or she complains, and while an action can lead to any relief deemed fit and proper by the courts, it is generally regarded as providing for a personal remedy, with the most frequent relief being an order that the petitioner's shares be purchased.[102] There is certainly room for such proceedings for shareholders, particularly

---

[99] J. Ziegel, 'Creditors as Corporate Stakeholders: The Quiet Revolution – An Anglo-Canadian Perspective' (1993) 43 *University of Toronto Law Journal* 511 at 527; D. Thomson, 'Directors, Creditors and Insolvency: A Fiduciary Duty or a Duty Not to Oppress' (2000) 58 *University of Toronto Faculty of Law Review* 31 at 47.

[100] *Directing Public Companies* (London, Cavendish Publishing, 2001) at 177. The defence that would be available is that the directors had properly examined all the relevant options with appropriate reference to stakeholder interests.

[101] Ibid at 167.

[102] In light of the Privy Council decision in *Gamlestaden Fastigheter AB v Baltic Partners Ltd* [2007] UKPC 26; [2008] 1 BCLC 468 (Jersey) the unfair prejudice ground may not be as restricted as once thought. See B. Hannigan, 'Drawing Boundaries between Derivative Claims and Unfairly Prejudicial Petitions' [2009] *Journal of Business Law* 606.

in closely-held companies as they are often unfairly locked in to a company and cannot exit if they so desire, or certainly not as easily as shareholders of large companies, but what we are seeking to construct is a mechanism that facilitates an investor to enforce the obligation of directors to adhere to EMS, and not to obtain some personal benefit.

3.8   Derivative Claims

3.8.1   Introduction[103]

In many common law jurisdictions provision is made in company law for the bringing of derivative actions. Such actions permit shareholders to commence or continue proceedings on behalf of their company against persons who have wronged the company in some way, and in circumstances where the company fails, or refuses, to initiate proceedings itself. This is because the board, which is usually granted by the articles of association or charter the power to manage the business of the company,[104] including bringing and defending litigation, has decided not to take action against someone who has harmed the company. Most often this is because the claim involves misconduct on the part of one or more directors, or even the whole board. Over the years many actions have been brought in the US, whilst actions in other common law jurisdictions have been less frequent.

While provision for the bringing of such actions was at one stage permitted only by case law,[105] the legislatures in many countries have enacted statutory derivative action schemes either to replace the common law or to sit alongside the common law scheme.[106] The UK was one of the latest to do so, and quite recently.[107]

---

[103]   For a recent substantive study of derivative actions in the UK, see, A. Reisberg, *Derivative Actions and Corporate Governance* (Oxford, Oxford University Press, 2007).

[104]   For example, see the UK's art. 70 of Table A (Companies (Tables A–F) Regulations 1985 (SI 1985/805).

[105]   In the US, see *Kusner v First Pa Corp*, 395 F. Supp. 276 at 280–83 (ED Pa 1975); *Dorfman v Chem Bank,* 56 FRD 363 at 364 (SDNY 1972) .

[106]   Hong Kong is an example of a jurisdiction where the common law right to bring a derivative action remains notwithstanding the fact that a statutory derivative scheme has been introduced (see, *Waddington Ltd v Chan Chu Hoo Thomas* [2008] HKCA 196). This is to be compared with the UK where the common law action has been terminated by statute.

[107]   Also, see Canada (s.239 of the Canada Business Corporations Act 1985), Part 2F1A of the Australia (Corporations Act 2001), Singapore (s.216A of the Companies Act), New Zealand (s.165 of the Companies Act 1993), Hong Kong (s.168BC of the Companies Ordinance).

The need for a derivative action, in the law of the UK and those jurisdictions which have taken their law from the UK, follows from the decision in *Foss v Harbottle*[108] where it was held that if a company is wronged, it, and it alone, must bring proceedings to seek relief.[109] At common law the courts developed several exceptions to the rule in this case because they felt that the rule could produce unfairness. The reason for enacting a statutory scheme for derivative actions[110] is the simplification and modernisation of the law in order to improve its accessibility.[111] Also, the existence of any statutory scheme is to ensure that the company receives an appropriate remedy for actions that have prejudiced its interests, and to deter the directors from acting improperly.[112]

As indicated above, while an oppression/unfair prejudice action is an action focused on personal rights, namely, the applicant for relief is complaining that he or she has been oppressed or unfairly prejudiced by the action of the company, the derivative action is a mechanism for 'corporate-regarding behaviour,'[113] that is the emphasis is on corporate concerns, and is, therefore, far more appropriate for EMS. It is 'oriented towards collective outcomes,'[114] rather than purely personal benefits.

The problem with utilising this process in the UK and some other jurisdictions is that only members are permitted to initiate derivative proceedings. Yet it has been said that the scheme is an imperfect device because there is a 'dissonance between the corporation's gains and losses and those of the shareholders,'[115] and so it is not, as presently drafted, appropriate when one is trying to ensure compliance with EMS. But there is a problem

---

[108]   (1843) 2 Hare 461; 67 ER 189.

[109]   Whilst not following UK law, the US law came to the same point as UK law did with *Foss v Harbottle*.

[110]   For a discussion of which, see A. Keay and J. Loughrey, 'Something Old, Something New, Something Borrowed: An Analysis of the New Derivative Action Under the Companies Act 2006' (2008) *Law Quarterly Review* 469.

[111]   Law Commission, *Shareholder Remedies: Report on a Reference under section 3(1)(e) of the Law Commissions Act 1965* (Law Com No 246, Cm 3769) (London, Stationery Office, 1997) at p7. There have been some adjustments to the original recommendations – in England and Wales, for example, the Law Commission's recommendation that a member be required to give 28 days notice to the company before initiating proceedings was not adopted: ibid at 91.

[112]   See, J. Coffee and D. Schwartz, 'The Survival of the Derivative Suit: An Explanation and a Proposal for Legislative Reform' (1981) 81 *Columbia Law Review* 261 at 302–309.

[113]   S. Bottomley, *The Constitutional Corporation* (Aldershot, Ashgate, 2007) at 166.

[114]   Ibid at 167.

[115]   Ibid at 158.

with leaving the derivative action only to the shareholders. In articulating their team production approach to corporate law, Blair and Stout argue that the shareholders in bringing derivative actions act as proxies for all those with claims on the company.[116] But, while such an action is designed to recover for the company, it might be argued that shareholders do not take proceedings save where they are convinced that either they will benefit from the action, at least indirectly, or that the action was likely to harm them in the short term or even in the long term. It is probable that whether or not shareholders would be prepared to institute derivative proceedings will very much depend on what the directors have done. Some actions that the directors take, in contravention of EMS, might well lead shareholders to reasoning that the action taken would end up indirectly affecting the shareholders, so they will consider proceeding. But other actions will not adversely affect shareholders, or they might even benefit them, and in either case no shareholder is going to take proceedings. The upshot is that while it may make sense to limit derivative actions to shareholders if a shareholder value approach is implemented, if an EMS approach is taken it makes sense to give the right to a wider category of investors to bring proceedings.[117]

As Dean has asserted in relation to derivative claims: 'there seems to be no a priori reason why others [besides shareholders] should not enjoy similar access to the courts to protect the company from harm, under a regime of judicial supervision similar to that envisaged to "manage" shareholder actions.'[118] Implicit in the EMS model is a recognition that all investors should be entitled to take action to safeguard the wealth of the company entity, in which they have a potential distinct interest, albeit one that is not vested or able to be calculated. As a consequence there needs to be an enforcement mechanism that is more encompassing. Also, it is often recognised that shareholders frequently do not know what is going on in a company; they are poor monitors. Broadening the range of those who can bring proceedings increases the chances of a company's interests being protected, because another investor might well be aware

---

[116] M. Blair and L. Stout, 'A Team Production Theory of Corporate Law' (1999) 85 Va L R 247 at 293. David Millon doubts this ('New Game Plan or Business as Usual? A Critique of the Team Production Model of Corporate Law' (2000) 86 *Virginia Law Review* 1001 at 1013).

[117] One commentator accepts the need for it in relation to creditors: R. B. Campbell Jr, 'Corporate Fiduciary Principles for the Post-Contractarian Era' (1996) 23 *Florida State University Law Review* 561 at 606.

[118] *Directing Public Companies* (London, Cavendish Publishing, 2001) at 155.

of something that the shareholders and others are not. For example, employees may be more conversant with the activities of directors, and may, therefore, be far better monitors. This is perhaps demonstrated to some degree by the fact that we see, not infrequently, employees acting as 'whistleblowers,' namely disclosing some improper or inappropriate practice of managers.

3.8.2 What is needed?

While the UK restricts those who can initiate derivative actions to shareholders, [119] many other jurisdictions permit a greater range of possible applicants. For instance, s.236 of the Australian Corporations Act 2001 allows, besides members, former members and officers of the company to bring derivative proceedings.[120] Interestingly, the Company and Securities Law Review Committee, a body that reviewed company law and considered changes to corporate legislation in Australia, favoured giving a derivative action to creditors as well as shareholders,[121] but this view did not gain the imprimatur of Parliament and, hence, did not find its way into legislation. Importantly though, in the general scheme of things, Australian creditors arguably could secure relief under s.1324 of the Corporations Act 2001, which enables anyone affected, or who could be affected, by a contravention, or proposed contravention, of the Act to seek injunctive relief. Such relief is not available under the companies legislation in the UK.

It would be necessary to provide a broad category of persons who could apply, because the range of people who can be regarded as investors for the purpose of EMS is wide. But, it is probably impossible to include all persons who may be within the purview of the concept of investor. If standing to bring proceedings were limited, then there would be no one who would apply where a decision of the board damaged the company entity but fostered the interests of the subset of investors who did have the right to bring an application to challenge directorial action through the derivative claim process.[122] Therefore, it is suggested that the legislation

---

[119] Hong Kong in s.168BC of the Companies Ordinance also limits actions to shareholders.

[120] New Zealand also permits directors to apply: s.165 of the Companies Act 1993.

[121] *Enforcement of the Duties of Directors and Officers of a Company by Means of a Statutory Derivative Action*, Report No 12, 1990.

[122] G. Crespi, 'Redefining the Fiduciary Duties of Corporate Directors in Accordance with the Team Production Model of Corporate Governance' (2002–03) 16 *Creighton Law Review* 623 at 634.

should provide that an application could be made by 'anyone who appears to the court to be interested in the company.' Courts could be granted, by a revised statutory derivative scheme, a discretion as to whether any applicant legitimately fell within the category suggested. The permission procedure which is provided for in the Companies Act 2006 before derivative proceedings can be continued, and the accompanying criteria for determining whether the proceedings can go ahead, could and should remain. This would ensure that the floodgates would not be opened as far as applications are concerned. Added to the court's deliberations about whether permission should be given could be consideration of whether the applicant for permission did fall within the range of investors entitled to apply.

It is submitted that in deciding whether 'anyone who appears to the court to be interested in the company' is able to bring a derivative action a court should be convinced that they have either a direct financial interest in the affairs of the company or a particular legitimate interest in the way that the company is being managed.

The suggestion made here is not unprecedented for there are at least two common law jurisdictions where derivative proceedings are able to be instigated by, potentially, a very broad range of persons. First, s.238(d) of the Canada Business Corporations Act 1985 includes amongst those who may make applications to bring derivative proceedings, 'any other person who, in the discretion of a court, is a proper person to make an application.' In a similar vein, s.216A(1)(c) of the Singaporean Companies Act provides that the range of persons who can apply for a derivative action includes 'any other person who, in the discretion of the Court, is a proper person.'

It is envisaged that if the proposal to widen the range of people who could take derivative action were implemented, the courts would be granted broad discretion when it came to giving permission to the pursuit of such actions (as is granted under the present regime in the Companies Act 2006) and then making final orders in the derivative action if permission were granted to continue it. Where a case initiated by an investor establishes that action had been taken by the board that did not maximise and sustain the entity, then the courts might make an order that would remedy what the directors had done. For instance, the court might make an order that goes so far as preventing the redundancy of employees, or an order voiding a decision to declare a dividend.[123] It is likely that under the

---

[123] This latter instance would only be fair and effective if an injunction stopping payment could be secured before the shareholders were actually paid out.

scheme proposed courts would make more orders that are declaratory or requiring action to be taken, rather than orders that involve damages or the taking of accounts which is more often the kind of orders made when directors have breached their duties to the company.

For the most part it is likely in practice that the party who decides to make a derivative claim and institutes proceedings, because he or she would be motivated sufficiently, would be one who has felt that the directors' actions have prejudiced, or are likely to prejudice his or her position, but it would not be limited to such persons. Some investors might feel very strongly about action that the directors intend to take, or have taken, even though it might not affect their interests directly. The fact of the matter is that if an action is not in accordance with EMS it is likely to affect some or even many investors. Of course, the prospective applicant would have to make out a case that the directorial action offends the notion of entity maximisation and sustainability, and not that his or her position is damaged, even though it might be clear that the directors' actions have prejudiced or will prejudice the applicant's position in some way. This latter requirement would have the advantage of ensuring that applicants would not only be focused on their own interests, but also the interests of the company, and they would have to be able to demonstrate, as with the present derivative scheme, that the company's interests have been harmed. This does produce a possible proof problem. How might an investor obtain the necessary evidence that is needed to establish the fact that the company's interests are prejudiced? But this is the same problem that faces shareholders under the present system and no one has suggested that this makes the derivative claim otiose. A further advantage of introducing this process for a broader class of investor is that there would be more potential applicants for permission to take derivative action if directors breach their duties to the company. It is possible that some investors, such as creditors, suppliers and some employees will have either, or both, more resources and more information than most shareholders. Investors might form a loose coalition to bring proceedings.

Under the present UK law a court must refuse permission to continue a derivative action if directors have had their actions ratified by a general meeting of members. Under what is proposed here, this provision would need to be removed as the shareholders could stymie an application by another investor for permission. As it is at the moment where only members can bring derivative claims one can see why ratification by the members might qualify as an event that should block derivative proceedings. But under the proposal made here, failure to remove the provision concerning ratification could effectively mean directors would be able to run the company for shareholders and the latter could ratify the breach of duty as they might well be quite content with what the directors have done. So, the present UK provisions would have to be amended, not only to broaden the right of those who are eligible to bring proceedings, but also to omit any reference to ratification[124] so as not to favour shareholders when compared with other investors. This should not be a problem. It is notable that the derivative action provisions of both Australia[125] and Canada[126] do not include the possibility of ratification as an element that should be considered by courts in determining whether to give permission for someone to be able to continue a derivative action.

The advantage of the proposal advocated here is that it does not revolutionise the law that has been introduced in many jurisdictions, for derivative actions are only permitted now when the company has been subject to harm. All that the proposed action does is to extend the range of possible applicants for permission to take forward a derivative action and to permit derivative actions where the directors have not only done something that has harmed the company, but what they have done or intend to do would fail to ensure the company's maximisation and sustainability. It could be argued that the use of the derivative action in the circumstances envisaged here seems to be consistent with the rationale for such an action, namely to nurture 'as a corrective for managerial abuse in economic units which by their nature deprived some participants of an effective voice in their administration.'[127]

Finally, the employment of a judicial process might well encourage investors to invoke, or at least seek to invoke, other options which will be less costly and less time-consuming.[128]

When hearing a derivative action along the lines set out here, a court must hear the evidence and make a decision as to whether the directors' actions/decisions etc could be said reasonably to involve conduct that would maximise entity wealth and sustain it. The court's decision will be heavily dependent on the facts of each case and each company. It would be incumbent on the applicants to demonstrate that the directors' actions/decisions failed to maximise or sustain the company. The evidence produced by the directors would, provided that the applicant's evidence was sufficiently compelling to indicate a case to answer, have to manifest that

---

[124]   In s.263(2)(c) for England and Wales, and Northern Ireland.
[125]   s.237 of the Corporations Act 2001.
[126]   s.239 of the Canada Business Corporations Act 1985.
[127]   B. Prunty, 'The Shareholders' Derivative Suit: Notes on its Derivation' (1957) 32 *New York University Law Review* 980 at 982.
[128]   S. Bottomley, *The Constitutional Corporation* (Aldershot, Ashgate, 2007) at 149.

their decision/action was intended to maximise company wealth. In assessing the directors' evidence and particularly their reasons for acting in the way that is impugned the courts must be careful, as discussed later, not to depend on hindsight.

3.8.3 Criticisms and retorts

What are the arguments against the use of the process advocated? First, those who do not take action might be regarded as free-riding on those who can and do take action. But free-riding takes place all of the time. For instance, creditors free-ride on the monitoring that is conducted by bigger and more powerful creditors,[129] such as banks, and individual and corporate shareholders will often leave the monitoring of directors' actions to institutional investors.

Second, one of the reasons given for the rule in *Foss v Harbottle* was to limit the number of actions that could be commenced. Is there a danger that allowing a potentially wide group of investors to bring proceedings could lead to an avalanche of litigation? This was even a concern when the introduction of the present statutory scheme in the UK was proposed.[130] But, this is unlikely; the concern over a deluge of claims is often over-emphasised. Certainly the floodgates do not appear to have opened as far as litigation is concerned in either Canada or Singapore, even though they allow a potentially broad range of applicants. It would appear that the leave hurdle has been used in Canada[131] successfully, so as to prevent the litigation floodgates from opening.[132] The Australian experience is that there has not been a marked increase in litigation since the advent of the statutory derivative action. In fact Stephen Bottomley is of the view that such actions are under-used in Australia.[133] Concern over

---

[129] 'Free-riding' occurs where economic actors 'are able to enjoy their share of the benefits from some costly activity . . . without shouldering their share (or any) of the costs of the activity': J. Macey, *Corporate Governance* (Princeton, Princeton University Press, 2008) at 131. See, S. Levmore 'Monitors and Freeriders in Commercial and Corporate Settings' (1982) 92 *Yale Law Journal* 49.

[130] J. Loughrey, A. Keay and L. Cerioni 'Legal Practitioners, Enlightened Shareholder Value and the Shaping of Corporate Governance' (2008) 8 *Journal of Corporate Law Studies* 79 at 87.

[131] s.239(1) of the Canada Business Corporations Act 1985.

[132] See, I. M. Ramsay and B. Saunders, 'Litigation by Shareholders and Directors: An Empirical Study of the Statutory Derivative Action' (2006) 6 *Journal of Corporate Law Studies* 397.

[133] S. Bottomley, *The Constitutional Corporation* (Aldershot, Ashgate, 2007) at 161.

mass litigation was one reason why the Law Commission for England and Wales recommended that court permission had to be obtained in relation to a proposed derivative action,[134] and the Companies Act 2006 implemented the recommendation. In the past three or so years that the new scheme has been in operation in the UK, there has not been a huge number of cases.[135]

In Canada, it is actually the oppression provision which has spawned a significant amount of litigation, with few applications made for relief under derivative proceedings except where shareholders are the applicants. Also, as indicated above, the permission/leave process that is in existence in the UK and other jurisdictions would be retained. This process should enable the filtering out of unmeritorious or vexatious claims.[136] For countries without legislation covering derivative actions there would need to be provisions introduced into companies legislation to enable a wider range of applicants, taking into account the fact that in common law jurisdictions the common law only permits shareholders generally to bring proceedings.[137]

Whilst there may well be some increase in litigation it is unlikely that it would involve a significant increase. As far as non-shareholders are concerned, in Canada, as with the oppression remedy, it is creditors who have sought to utilise the broad derivative process. The courts have not encouraged proceedings and they have required creditors to establish that they have either a direct financial interest in the affairs of the company or a particular legitimate interest in the way that the company is being managed.[138] Also, the courts have required creditors to demonstrate that

---

[134] *Shareholders Remedies*, Report No 246, 1997, at para 6.69.

[135] See, A. Keay and J. Loughrey, 'Derivative Proceedings in a Brave New World for Company Management and Shareholders' [2010] *Journal of Business Law* 151.

[136] It has been suggested that in the context of implementing stakeholder theory relief might be limited to injunctions (W. Leung, 'The Inadequacy of Shareholder Primacy: A Proposed Corporate Regime that Recognizes Non-Shareholder Interests' (1997) 30 *Columbia Journal of Law and Social Problems* 589 at 625), but this would not be necessary with a permission process in effect.

[137] If a company is insolvent in the US creditors are permitted to bring derivative actions: *North American Catholic Educational Programming Foundation, Inc v Gheewalla*, 18 May 2007, <http://courts.delaware.gov/opinions/(nbvy0wjdzka5xj55yeyw1n55)/download.aspx?ID=92000> (last visited, 6 January 2010).

[138] *Re Daon Development Corp* (1984) 54 BCLR 235 at 243; *Jacobs Farms Ltd v Jacobs* [1992] OJ No 813 at 6–7 and referred to by J. Sarra, 'Taking the Corporation Past the "Plimsoll Line" – Director and Officer Liability When the Corporations Founders' (2001) 10 *International Insolvency Review* 229 at 244.

they are in a position that is analogous to minority shareholders who have no legal right to influence the things that they regard as abuses of management.[139] The Canadian cases seem to indicate that if an applicant can establish that he or she is bringing action to address conduct that harms the corporation's interests then the courts will grant leave to take the derivative proceedings.[140] This case law is consistent with the views provided in the recent Canadian Supreme Court case of *BCE Inc v 1976 Debentureholders*.[141]

One other possible concern in this regard is that the board could be held to ransom by an investor, who might threaten litigation unless the directors agree to take some form of action, and this action might not be conducive to fostering EMS for what is sought is action that will benefit the investor who is making the threat. But with respect to this, and generally when it comes to considering whether derivative claims will be pursued, we must take into account the fact that there are sufficient hurdles for an investor to get over, such as having the onus of instructing lawyers and obtaining evidence, as well as the leave/permission process, to dissuade all but the most committed investor. And there is the fact that litigation will precipitate some costs.[142] There is always the possibility of a costs order being made against an investor if an application is unsuccessful at either the permission stage or when the matter is finally decided as a derivative proceeding, if permission were obtained. Furthermore, as with the present system it will be necessary in the UK to persuade a judge that the claim by the investor/applicant is warranted and the criteria set out in s.263 of the UK legislation (s.268 for Scotland), and to be considered by a court in determining whether to grant permission to an investor to continue derivative proceedings, are to be resolved in the applicant's favour. Inter alia this includes the fact that the applicant is acting in good faith. The legislation in other jurisdictions such as Canada and Australia set out several criteria that an application for leave to take or continue derivative proceedings must fulfil.

One possible way of ensuring that derivative proceedings do not get out of hand, or investors are minded to use the proceedings to 'feather their own nest,' would be to enable other investors to appear at the leave/permission hearing. Investors who are concerned that the applicant under the derivative process is seeking to benefit his or her own interests or that

---

[139] *Re Daon Development Corp* (1984) 54 BCLR 235 at 243.
[140] *Re Daon Development Corp* (1984) 54 BCLR 235.
[141] [2008] SCC 69.
[142] See, A. Reisberg, *Derivative Actions and Corporate Governance* (Oxford, Oxford University Press, 2007) at 20.

there is really no harm done to the company, might seek to argue that leave/permission not be given to enable the proceedings to proceed. This process is permitted with petitions presented by creditors in England (and many other countries) to liquidate companies, and courts are entitled to take into account the views of other creditors who appear to oppose the making of a winding-up order. The reason is that liquidation is regarded as a collective regime, and the petitioner is not only acting for himself or herself but for all creditors.[143] Likewise, an investor who seeks leave to continue a derivative action would be seen as acting collectively on behalf of all investors in ensuring the enforcement of EMS. One thing that an investor might be concerned about, and which might motivate his or her opposition to an application for leave/permission by another investor is that the company might well end up being responsible for most, if not all, of the legal costs of any action, and that will not only affect the company, but also investors indirectly.

A fourth objection might be that the process proposed is too uncertain, on the basis that what is proposed is leaving open and undefined the class of investors who could apply for leave/permission to continue derivative proceedings. But, gradually a jurisprudence would develop to provide more certainty. Also, the main players (employees, creditors, suppliers, the community etc) would be likely to be covered by the formula proposed. It would be impossible to provide an exhaustive list of those who could or should be entitled to bring proceedings, but this fact does not appear to have caused insurmountable, or any, problems in Canada and Singapore.

Fifth, it might be argued that investors would not bother taking action if they are not going to get any direct benefit. Frank Easterbrook and Daniel Fischel have observed that: 'A dominating characteristic of the derivative action is the lack of any link between stake and reward – not only on the judge's part but on the plaintiff's.'[144] But shareholders do institute derivative proceedings now when they do not receive any direct benefit. Also, it is likely that the investors who will take action are those who are likely to be prejudiced in some way as a result of what the directors have done or propose to do. The difficulty might be that investors cannot always see how an action will affect the entity and are less likely to see how it will affect them. In addition, there is always the possibility that they might be rather reluctant to take action as they might feel that other investors are free-riding on what they are doing.

---

[143] See *Re Esal (Commodities) Ltd* [1985] BCLC 450.
[144] *The Economic Structure of Corporate Law* (Cambridge, Massachusetts, Harvard University Press, 1991) at 101.

Sixth, any investor who wishes to bring proceedings has to deal with certain practical issues, some of which have been adverted to earlier, namely access to information to formulate a claim, the time involved in being embroiled in litigation and the possibility of being responsible for costs. The short answer to this is that these are the issues which face shareholders under the present scheme,[145] and while there is not an avalanche of proceedings in the UK there is no suggestion as yet that members will be dissuaded by these issues. In fact, there is a case for saying that the present UK statutory scheme together with other provisions in the new companies legislation assist investors compared with the position that existed at common law. For instance, directors of all companies not subject to the small companies' regime must now include in the directors' report a business review.[146] This requires directors to provide a fair review of the company's business and a description of the principal risks and uncertainties facing the company.[147] The review must also provide a balanced and comprehensive analysis of the development and performance of the company business during the financial year[148] and it must contain analysis using financial key performance indicators.[149] To facilitate the acquisition of information, investors might be permitted to seek pre-action discovery of documents from the directors under rule 31.16 of the Civil Procedure Rules.[150]

3.8.4 The use of a company litigation committee

Before applying to the courts for review of what the directors have done, is it feasible and/or appropriate to require the complaint of the investor to go before a litigation committee[151] that is comprised of independent members of the board? This is an option used in the US in relation to shareholders'

---

[145] See the discussion in A. Reisberg, *Derivative Actions and Corporate Governance* (Oxford, Oxford University Press, 2007) at 85–86 in relation to access to information and Chapter 6 in relation to costs.

[146] s.417 of the Companies Act 2006.

[147] Companies Act 2006, s.417(3).

[148] Companies Act 2006, s.417(4)(a).

[149] Companies Act 2006, s.417(6)(a).

[150] It is acknowledged that this procedure is susceptible to abuse, and the English courts have been concerned that applications for discovery might constitute 'fishing expeditions.' See *Anglo Irish Bank Corp plc v West LB AG* [2009] EWHC 207 (Comm).

[151] The concept of such committees is based on litigation committees in the US. See G. Dent, 'The Power of Directors to Terminate Shareholder Litigation: The Death of the Derivative Suit' (1980) 75 *Northwestern University Law Review* 96.

derivative claims. The obvious benefits of this process are to keep down costs and to 'nip in the bud' a dispute before it becomes too serious and which could, conceivably, prejudice the company's public reputation.[152] Also, the directors would usually be able to access more information than an investor and would be in a better position to assess the effects of what directors have done, and whether it would affect entity maximisation.[153] But there are undoubted problems with this approach. The directors who are members of the committee would have to be independent in that they could not have been involved in taking the action against which the investor complains, or else, obviously, one would have to question how open-minded they would be at a hearing. It might be very difficult in many companies to have truly independent directors. Those selected to act have an inherent conflict of interest in having to pass judgment on one or more of their colleagues.[154] The directors would have to be non-executives as it is likely that if executives were to have to determine allegations against other executives they would tend to side with the executives as a matter of course, and especially if their promotion or benefits depended on those about whose actions the investor is complaining.[155] One would expect many investor complaints in the context of EMS to be brought against the board for its collective decisions. In today's commercial climate all directors are expected to be actively involved in overseeing all facets of the company's business and they cannot avoid liability by relying on being passive.[156] So, it is likely that all, or nearly all, of the directors would be involved in the decision that is subject to complaint.

Where the action of the investor is aimed at one, two or a small number of directors it will be easier to convene a meeting of independent directors, but in such a situation the independent directors will realise that they would have to work in the future with the directors who took the action that is under attack, unless these latter directors were removed, and then they might feel uncomfortable about acceding to the investor's request. It is not unusual for non-executive directors to be familiar with

---

[152] As Hale has said: 'there will often be sound reasons for avoiding the washing of corporate linen in the courtroom.': 'What's Right With the Rule in Foss v Harbottle?' [1997] *Company, Financial and Insolvency Law Review* 219 at 225.

[153] A. Reisberg, *Derivative Actions and Corporate Governance* (Oxford, Oxford University Press, 2007) at 104.

[154] Ibid at 114.

[155] Ibid at 111

[156] For instance, see *Re Park House Properties Ltd* [1999] 2 BCLC 530; *Re Kaytech International plc* [1999] BCC 390; *Cohen v Selby* [2000] BCC 275; *Lexi Holdings plc (In Administration) v Luqman* [2007] EWHC 2265 (Ch).

those directors who are subject to the complaint, having, in the course of working together, forged a friendship with them. In any event it is quite possible that those who select the directors to be members of the litigation committee will seek to select persons who are more likely not to 'cause waves'. If the ones whose action is impugned are more junior executives the independent directors might feel that if they were to find against the former the junior executives might take the view that there is no loyalty within the board and they might well be less loyal or effective in the future.[157]

Finally, the fact is that US experience indicates that rarely will it be recommended that a derivative action be continued.[158] All of this is likely to cause the independence of the committee to be called into question.[159] Consequently, any submission that a litigation committee should deal with the claim of an investor is not strong, and should be dismissed.

3.8.5   Court review

Perhaps one of the primary arguments against the proposal propounded here is that courts should not be employed to review actions of directors. The argument effectively casts aspersions on either the competence or appropriateness of a court making the kind of decisions that are envisaged by derivative litigation initiated by a wide range of investors. It might be said that it involves courts getting involved in the management of companies, and this is something that courts have steadfastly refused to do for many years.[160] One American bankruptcy court has said that short of cases of obvious abuse in cases involving Chapter 11 of the Bankruptcy Reform Act 1978, business judgments should be made in the boardroom and not in the courts.[161]

If a derivative action in the form suggested above were available, and permitted to proceed, then the courts would have to determine whether or not the directors had failed to adhere to EMS. The bottom line is that the

---

[157]   G. Dent, 'The Power of Directors to Terminate Shareholder Litigation: The Death of the Derivative Suit' (1980) 75 *Northwestern University Law Review* 96 at 111.

[158]   D. DeMott, 'Shareholder Litigation in Australia and the United States: Common Problems, Uncommon Solutions' (1987) 11 *Sydney Law Review* 259 at 275–279; J. Coffee, 'New Myths and Old Realities: The American Law Institute Faces the Derivative Action' (1993) 48 *Business Lawyer* 1407 at 1422–1424.

[159]   A. Reisberg, *Derivative Actions and Corporate Governance* (Oxford, Oxford University Press, 2007) at 105.

[160]   See the concerns of John Parkinson in *Corporate Power and Responsibility* (Oxford, Oxford University Press, 1993) at 94.

[161]   *In re Simasko Production Co* 47 Bankr 444 at 449 (Col) (1985)

courts would have to assess the actions of the directors and possibly the effect of those decisions. Many have had severe misgivings about judges sitting in judgment on what directors have done in making business decisions. David Wishart has asserted that: 'Judges simply do not have or would not be seen to have the expertise to determine the limits of acceptable business decisions.'[162] Blair and Stout have said that:

> once we leave behind the narrow objective of maximising 'share value,' it is impossible for an outsider like a court to design an algorithm to measure whether a board is maximizing returns to the corporate team, and dangerous to invite courts to try.[163]

But if that is the case how do you enforce any breaches? The theory of the firm which Blair and Stout advocate, namely the team production approach, places great responsibility on, and trust in, the directors (known as 'mediating hierarchs'[164]) but surely the commentators do not envisage the absence of some form of review process. As the UK Company Law Review Steering Group said in 1999, any system must have safeguards built into it[165] and court review is the ultimate safeguard.

Doug Baird and Todd Henderson refer to an additional reason for not permitting judges to adjudicate on directors' decisions.[166] They assert that besides judges lacking expertise, they lack information to police directorial actions.[167] I will deal with that issue in a moment.

Admittedly, the judges themselves have, from time to time, expressed

---

[162] 'Models and Theories of Directors' Duties to Creditors' (1991) 14 *New Zealand Universities Law Review* 323 at 340. In a similar vein, see M. Whincop, 'Overcoming Corporate Law: Instrumentalism, Pragmatism and the Separate Legal Entity Concept' (1997) 15 *Company and Securities Law Journal* 411 at 426; D. Oesterle, 'Corporate Directors' Personal Liability for "Insolvent Trading" in Australia, "Reckless Trading" in New Zealand and "Wrongful Trading" in England: A Recipe for Timid Directors, Hamstrung Controlling Shareholders and Skittish Lenders' in I.M. Ramsay (ed), *Company Directors' Liability for Insolvent Trading* (Melbourne, Centre for Corporate Law and Securities Regulation and CCH Australia, 2000).

[163] 'Specific Investment: Explaining Anomalies in Corporate Law' (2006) 31 *Journal of Corporation Law* 719 at 741.

[164] M. Blair and L. Stout, 'A Team Production Theory of Corporate Law' (1999) 85 *Virginia Law Review* 247 at, for example, 281.

[165] Company Law Review, *Modern Company Law for a Competitive Economy*: 'The Strategic Framework' 1999, London, DTI, at para 5.1.30.

[166] Of course, in the US it is normally the case that the business judgment rule will come into play. It is possible that this is going to be the case in many situations in Australia where a business judgment rule is also provided for in statute.

[167] 'Other People's Money' (2008) 60 *Stanford Law Review* 1309 at 1313.

misgivings, or even fear, in making decisions about how directors have acted in any given business situation.[168] Undoubtedly one can point to many old cases where courts have taken such a view. Even in the mid-1980s in *Kinsela v Russell Kinsela Pty Ltd*[169] when dealing with the issue of directors' duties to take into account the interests of creditors, Street CJ of the New South Wales Court of Appeal accepted that courts have traditionally and properly been cautious about entering boardrooms when deciding the commercial justification of executive actions.[170] But his Honour approved[171] of the opinion of Cooke J of the New Zealand Court of Appeal in *Nicholson v Permakraft (NZ) Ltd*[172] who said that, inter alia, creditors' interests were to be considered 'if a contemplated payment or other course of action would jeopardise its solvency,'[173] and this requires, as a matter of necessity, an examination of the decision of a board, by a court.

It is arguable that in more recent times there are indications that many judges no longer see the boardroom as sacrosanct and have not resiled from assessing decisions of management. There are many examples of UK courts in the past 20 years demonstrating a readiness to review the way in which companies operate and the merits of decisions which have been made at a managerial level.[174] This is most patent in cases involving claims

---

[168] See L.S. Sealy, *Company Law and Commercial Reality* (London, Sweet and Maxwell, 1984) at 53–54. Gregory Crespi ('Redefining the Fiduciary Duties of Corporate Directors in Accordance with the Team Production Model of Corporate Governance' (2003) 16 *Creighton Law Review* 623 at 640) expresses the view that the courts would show the same degree of deference to board decisions as they do now if duties were owed to the company, but the learned commentator was referring to the duty of care and in the US there is always difficulty in challenging directors' decisions as breach of the duty of care because of the existence of the business judgment rule.

[169] (1986) 4 ACLC 215.

[170] Ibid at 223.

[171] Ibid.

[172] (1985) 3 ACLC 453.

[173] Ibid at 457.

[174] For example, *Re D'Jan of London* [1993] BCC 646; *AWA Ltd v Daniels* (1992) 10 ACLC 933 and on appeal *Daniels v Anderson* (1995) 13 ACLC 614; *Re Barings plc* [1998] BCC 583; *Re Westmid Services Ltd* [1998] 2 BCLC 646; [1998] BCC 836; *Re Barings plc (No5)* [1999] 1 BCLC 433; *Re HIH Insurance Ltd (in prov liq); ASIC v Adler* [2002] NSWSC 171; (2002) 41 ACSR 72; (2002) 20 ACLC 576; *Re One.Tel Ltd (in liq); ASIC v Rich* [2003] NSWSC 85; (2003) 44 ACSR 682; *ASIC v Vines* (2003) 48 ACSR 322; *Re AG (Manchester) Ltd* [2008] EWHC 64 (Ch); [2008] 1 BCLC 321; *Lexi Holdings Ltd (in administration) v Luqman* [2008] EWHC 1639 (Ch).

for directors' breach of duty of care,[175] breach of duty to take into account the interests of creditors against directors[176] and in the UK in relation to applications to disqualify directors under the Company Directors' Disqualification Act 1986.[177] The courts have clearly conceded that there is a potential danger that they might see everything that was done many years before a matter comes to trial with hindsight, but the fact that they have adverted to this danger, and warned that it must be avoided, is at least a positive step, and is likely to mean that courts will not unfairly rely on second-guessing what directors did and allow hindsight to influence them in the final outcome of a case.[178] In fact it seems that courts take great care to ensure that their assessment of the conduct of the directors is not coloured by hindsight. This is demonstrated clearly by the comments in *Re Sherborne Associates Ltd,*[179] a wrongful trading case (brought under s.214 of the UK's Insolvency Act 1986),[180] where the judge warned that it is dangerous to assume that 'what has in fact happened was always bound to happen and was apparent.'[181] Likewise in *Facia Footwear Ltd,* Sir Richard Scott V-C said that 'the benefit of hindsight was not available to the directors at the time,' implying that he was not going to rely on it. The same approach is evident in the director disqualification case, *Secretary of State for Trade and Industry v Gill,*[182] where the past activities of a director were examined. Blackburn J made it clear that hindsight should not be employed when dealing with a consideration of the finely balanced judgments of directors.

---

[175]   For instance, see most of the cases in preceding note.

[176]   For instance, see *Nicholson v Permakraft (NZ) Ltd* (1985) 3 ACLC 453; *Kinsela v Russell Kinsela Pty Ltd* (1986) 4 ACLC 215; 10 ACLR 395; *Liquidator of West Mercia Safetywear v Dodd* (1988) 4 BCC 30; *Facia Footwear Ltd (in administration) v Hinchliffe* [1998] 1 BCLC 218; *Re Pantone 485 Ltd* [2002] 1 BCLC 266; *Gwyer v London Wharf (Limehouse) Ltd* ([2003] 2 BCLC 153; [2002] EWHC 2748; *Peoples' Department Stores v Wise* [2004] SCC 68; (2004) 244 DLR (4th) 564; *Re MDA Investment Management Ltd* [2004] BPIR 75; [2003] EWHC 227 (Ch); *Re Cityspan Ltd* [2007] EWHC 751 (Ch); [2007] 2 BCLC 522.

[177]   For instance, see *Re Barings plc* [1998] BCC 583; *Re Westmid Services Ltd* [1998] 2 BCLC 646; [1998] BCC 836; *Re Barings plc (No 5)* [1999] 1 BCLC 433; *Secretary of State for Trade and Industry v Swan* [2005] EWHC 603 (Ch); *Secretary of State v Thornbury* [2007] EWHC 3202 (Ch); [2008] 1 BCLC 139.

[178]   *Linton v Telnet Pty Ltd* (1999) 30 ACSR 465 at 475.

[179]   [1995] BCC 40.

[180]   Wrongful trading is similar in scope to what is known as, for example, 'insolvent trading' in Australia, and 'reckless trading' in Ireland, New Zealand and South Africa.

[181]   [1995] BCC 40 at 54.

[182]   [2004] EWHC 933.

In the famous, but rather old, US case of *Dodge v Ford Motor Co*,[183] the court opined that 'judges are not business experts.'[184] But do they have to be? In several jurisdictions specialised courts and/or judges hear corporate law matters. For example, in England and Wales the Companies Court (part of the Chancery Division) deals with all company law proceedings (as well as other proceedings, such as insolvency actions) and all judges will have had some significant commercial experience,[185] and, most importantly (perhaps addressing the Baird and Henderson concern referred to earlier), the parties can present expert evidence to the court to assist the judge who hears the case. In any event all judges can assess the evidence, both oral and documentary, and decide what is in the interests of the company even if they cannot readily quantify those interests.[186] Importantly, it must not be forgotten that judges in the Companies Court have regularly assessed the conduct of directors in relation to actions, by way of example, for wrongful trading[187] and breaches of directors' duties,[188] some of which have been difficult to resolve and/or involving complicated facts and issues. The UK Parliament has, arguably, in the Companies Act 2006 demonstrated recognition that courts can engage ably in assessing the actions of directors. The courts will have to assess, for instance, whether directors have acted in such a way as to promote the success of their company under s.172(1). The UK Parliament seems to be content to bestow on the courts the responsibility of assessing decisions made by administrators in relation to actions taken in administrations under Schedule B1 of the Insolvency Act 1986. This responsibility includes evaluating business decisions that administrators have to make.

---

[183]   204 Mich 459; 170 NW 668.

[184]   170 NW 668 at 684.

[185]   Another example is the Chancery Court of the State of Delaware in the US.

[186]   S. Wallman, 'The Proper Interpretation of Corporate Constituency Statutes and Formulation of Directors' Duties' (1991) 21 *Stetson Law Review* at 163 at 191.

[187]   For example, see *Re Brian D. Pierson (Contractors) Ltd* [1999] BCC 26; [2001] BCLC 275; *Re Continental Assurance Ltd* [2001] BPIR 733; *The Liquidator of Marini Ltd v Dickensen* [2003] EWHC 334 (Ch); [2004] BCC 172.

[188]   For example, *AWA Ltd v Daniels* (1992) 10 ACLC 933; *CAS (Nominees) Ltd v Nottingham Forest plc* [2002] BCC 145; *Criterion Properties plc v Stratford UK Properties LLC* [2002] EWHC 496 (Ch); [2002] 2 BCLC 151; *In Plus Group Ltd v Pyke* [2002] EWCA Civ 370; [2002] 2 BCLC 201; *Re HIH Insurance Ltd (in prov liq)*; *ASIC v Adler* [2002] NSWSC 171; (2002) 41 ACSR 72; (2002) 20 ACLC 576; *Extrasure Travel Insurances Ltd v Scattergood* [2003] 1 BCLC 598; *British Midland Tool Ltd v Midland International Tooling Ltd* [2003] EWHC 466 (Ch); [2003] 2 BCLC 523; *Shepherds Investments Ltd v Walters* [2006] EWHC 836; *Wrexham Association Football Club Ltd v Crucialmove Ltd* [2006] EWCA Civ 237; [2008] 1 BCLC 508.

In Australia the federal Parliament has granted the courts, in s.447A of the Corporations Act 2001, very broad powers to determine how the voluntary administration scheme is to work and that involves considering the actions of directors and administrators. Also, the Australian legislation endows, in s.447E, the court with the power to determine whether it is satisfied that the administrator of a company under voluntary administration has managed, or is managing, the affairs of the company in a manner which is prejudicial to the interests of some or all of the company's creditors or members or has acted, is intending to act, or has failed to act and prejudiced interests of creditors or members. The UK Parliament has provided something very similar in relation to administration in paragraph 71 of Schedule B1 of the Insolvency Act 1986.

It is submitted that, hitherto, courts, when reviewing what has occurred to companies, often some years before the hearing of an action, have demonstrated a good deal of understanding of the positions in which directors found themselves at the relevant time. It has already been noted that judges have warned about second guessing the judgments of directors.[189] Decisions like *Nicholson v Permakraft (NZ) Ltd,*[190] *Re Welfab Engineers Ltd,*[191] *Linton v Telnet Pty Ltd*[192] and *Brady v Brady*[193] manifest the fact that courts are capable of weighing up business decisions. In *Facia Footwear Ltd (in administration) v Hinchliffe,*[194] Sir Richard Scott V-C acknowledged that in continuing trading the directors were taking a risk, but his Lordship went on to say, with, it is respectfully suggested, an understanding of business practice, that 'the boundary between an acceptable risk that an entrepreneur may properly take and an unacceptable risk . . . is not always, perhaps not usually, clear cut.'[195]

Furthermore, the courts have been judging the actions of different kinds of fiduciaries for many years and, it is submitted, they are now more adept at doing so than ever before. It is contended that the reported cases demonstrate the fact that UK courts as well as courts in other jurisdictions such as Canada, Ireland, Australia and New Zealand have increasingly become more competent at assessing the actions of directors.

---

[189]   Law Commission, *Company Directors: Regulating Conflicts of Interests and Formulating a Statement of Duties* (Law Commission Consultation Paper No 153, London, 1998), at para 15.30.
[190]   (1985) 3 ACLC 453.
[191]   [1990] BCC 600.
[192]   (1999) 30 ACSR 465.
[193]   (1988) 3 BCC 535.
[194]   [1998] 1 BCLC 218.
[195]   Ibid at 228.

Where a claim is that the directors have been involved in some form of self-dealing or have allegedly breached their duty of care, the courts could approach the matter as they presently do. Where the allegation is that the directors have failed to maximise entity wealth, then the courts will have to consider whether this is indeed the case. Undoubtedly there are likely to be some significant measurement issues that have to be considered in determining whether the directors did maximise entity wealth in the circumstances in which they found themselves.[196] If EMS was only focused on financial wealth at a given time then it would be preferable if the judges could engage in a comparison of the total aggregate value of the corporate entity before the directors took the action that is impugned and the total aggregate value after they had taken the action, to ascertain the effect of what they had done. But entity maximisation does not just mean a focus on profit maximisation,[197] for it encompasses such things as augmenting reputation, which have a longer-term impact on the financial standing of the company. Any assessment cannot be purely objective. A court cannot simply look, for instance, at the share value of the company before and after the impugned action. EMS is far more subtle than that. A court would have to consider how the action has impacted on the company overall, and this might involve examining a number of factors. What the court does consider will, to a large extent, depend on what is presented to it by the party claiming under the derivative claim. It is obviously the responsibility of the claimant to introduce cogent and convincing evidence that demonstrates that the directors have fallen short of the necessary standard, and the claimant obviously will bear the burden of proof. The judicial review of the directors' actions is to prevent a serious abuse of power.[198] The courts will be required to determine whether the claimant's or the directors' view of what is best for the company will prevail,[199] and it is submitted that the courts are able to ascertain whether any exercise of powers is designed to enhance entity interests or derogate from them.[200]

---

[196] See, G. Crespi, 'Redefining the Fiduciary Duties of Corporate Directors in Accordance with the Team Production Model of Corporate Governance' (2003) 16 *Creighton Law Review* 623 at 636. The learned commentator does not seek to ascertain whether the company entity has been maximised, but is more concerned with the value of any action to each stakeholder.

[197] A. Keay, 'Ascertaining the Corporate Objective: An Entity Maximisation and Sustainability Model' (2008) 71 *Modern Law Review* 663 at 685.

[198] G. Frug, 'The Ideology of Bureaucracy in American Law' (1983–84) 97 *Harvard Law Review* 1276 at 1334.

[199] Ibid.

[200] S. Worthington, 'Shares and Shareholders: Property, Power and Entitlement (Part 2)' (2001) 22 *The Company Lawyer* 307 at 313.

There has to be an avenue for review of what directors have done; they cannot be immune from scrutiny of their actions. Just as there is provision for the review of decisions of office-holders from the private sector who are administering the affairs of insolvents, such as administrators, liquidators, trustees and others, so there must be provision for the review of what directors do. The approach being suggested here is a parallel to judicial review in administrative law. In administrative law courts take it upon themselves to engage in the review of the decisions of public servants and other public office-holders, where they have been granted broad discretionary powers, so as to ensure that unreasonable decisions are not made, and decisions are not based on improper motives.[201]

Finally, it can be argued that judges are able to be flexible and adjust their analysis to case-specific issues and to address innovations in commercial practice.[202]

In sum, while judges will, it is acknowledged, often have to wrestle with difficult questions flowing from differing views of what constitutes right action in the circumstances in which companies operated,[203] they are able to make a fair assessment of the actions of directors on the evidence that is presented to them, and are now more than ever probably better able and better equipped to take practical and commercial decisions.[204] As Sheldon Leader has said: 'management need not always have the last word on the matter either. It must be open to the outside influence of a court of law.'[205]

---

[201] M. Stokes, 'Company Law and Legal Theory' in S. Wheeler (ed), *The Law of the Business Enterprise: Selected Essays* (Oxford, Oxford University Press, 1994) at 99.

[202] J. Fisch, 'Measuring Efficiency in Corporate Law: The Rule of Shareholder Primacy' December 2005, Fordham Law Legal Studies, Working Paper No 105 at p40 and available at <http://ssrn.com/abstract=878391> (last visited, 27 July 2009).

[203] W. Allen, 'Ambiguity in Corporation Law' (1997) 22 *Delaware Journal of Corporate Law* 894 at 899.

[204] A point accepted as far back as 1982 by the Insolvency Law Review Committee, *Insolvency Law and Practice* (generally referred to as 'the Cork Report') Cmnd 858, HMSO, 1982 at para 1800.

[205] 'Private Property and Corporate Governance. Part I: Defining the Interests' in F. MacMillan Patfield (ed), *Perspectives on Company Law: 1* (London, Kluwer, 1995) at 113.

4. CONCLUSION

This Chapter has sought to ascertain what enforcement measure could be utilised in relation to the entity maximisation and sustainability model. It has been noted that providing an enforcement mechanism has been problematic for the stakeholder theory, and devising an enforcement process is far from easy. However, it is, arguably, significantly easier as far as EMS is concerned, when compared with the stakeholder theory, because with the former there is no need to determine whether a stakeholder/investor has suffered prejudice. It will only be necessary to establish that the affairs of the company have not been carried out in such a way as to maximise and sustain it.

The Chapter has considered various options to accommodate enforcement of the model, including the use of oppression/unfair prejudice proceedings, but it has been argued that the derivative action is the most appropriate enforcement process. To ensure that all appropriate investors might have standing, the process must be open to more than just shareholders. The availability of a derivative action requires investors to consider the wider interests of the corporate entity, and these interests can be considered by a court in a derivative action. It has been argued that the derivative scheme should allow any investor 'who appears to the court to be interested in the company,' to bring derivative proceedings. Such an application should be subject to a permission/leave process that already exists in most jurisdictions that have provided for a statutory derivative action scheme. Inter alia, it would be necessary for a court to be convinced that the application is brought by someone who has either a direct financial interest in the affairs of the company or a particular legitimate interest in the way that the company is being managed. It has been submitted that in due course a jurisprudence would develop to provide a degree of certainty for those contemplating bringing proceedings and those advising such persons.

6. Investors

1. INTRODUCTION

It is well-recognised that a company cannot be successful without the involvement in, and contribution by, various stakeholders,[1] known in this work as investors,[2] in company life.[3] EMS certainly acknowledges that entity wealth maximisation is something that can only be achieved with a contribution from an array of investors, but, as was said in Chapter 4, the company is not a sum of all the interests of the investors. It could only be so if one were to allocate the investors a fixed priority in relation to one another[4] and that cannot be done, for it is not possible to affix any specific proportion of the result of the company's trading to any particular investor's contribution.[5] Management must remember that a large portion of its role is to coordinate the resources that are invested in their company by investors in order to produce goods or services and ultimately to make a profit. It is contended that ordinary decency requires companies to be obliged not to permit investors to harbour unreasonable expectations from their dealing with the company.[6] But

---

[1]   OECD, *Annotations of the Principles of Corporate Governance* (Clause IV), 2004. Accessible at <http://www.oecd.org/dataoecd/32/18/31557724.pdf> (last visited, 1 February 2010).

[2]   Douglas Baird and Todd Henderson in 'Other People's Money' (2008) 60 *Stanford Law Review* 1309 at 1311 acknowledge the groups discussed in this Chapter as 'investors.' To do otherwise is, according to these commentators, misleading.

[3]   This is acknowledged by General Motors. See <http://www.gm.com/corporate/responsibility/reports/06/300_company/3_thirty/330.html> (last visited, 15 February 2009).

[4]   S. Leader, 'Private Property and Corporate Governance' in F. Patfield (ed), *Perspectives on Company Law: Vol 1* (London, Kluwer, 1995) at 90.

[5]   M. Blair and L. Stout, 'Director Accountability and the Mediating Role of the Corporate Board' (2001) 79 Washington University Law Quarterly 403 at 419.

[6]   E. Sternberg, *Just Business*, 2nd ed (Oxford, Oxford University Press, 2000) at 173.

the company has to be transparent in its dealings with investors, also to evidence decency.

As the investors are crucial to the life of a company, they should be able to share in the value created by their investment.[7] Given the fact that investors are a critical element in any theory of the corporate objective this Chapter is devoted to considering their role, who they are and where they fit in the EMS model. Some discussion of investors was provided in Chapter 3, and it is not intended to go over ground covered in that Chapter.

2. A BROAD RANGE OF INVESTORS

The EMS approach recognises that corporate wealth is not generated solely by the shareholders' input, for it is also fostered by other investors who make 'firm-specific' investments. These investments, perhaps able to be called 'value exchanges,'[8] could be of share capital, human endeavour and finance or something else that is of value. This all follows from the fact that the entity needs: investment capital supplied by shareholders; to borrow money and obtain products and services on credit; employees to contribute their skill and labour; services supplied by local government and utility suppliers; customers to purchase their goods and/services; and so on. The people and groups providing these benefits can be said to have made an investment in the company. They have invested something valuable, whether it be money, labour etc, with the expectation of receiving a return on the investment.

It has been asserted that no business can run without opportunity capital, namely making use of 'a pre-existing knowledge base, (subsidized) education system, police function, and infrastructure (roads, water mains, sewage systems etc).'[9] The point is that companies do draw on the work of many people over a long period of time to provide certain facilities and circumstances, and this is as important to companies as the shareholder funding. There is, to a degree, an interdependence of investors, and EMS recognises that fact. The rights of all investors are not to take precedence

---

[7] T. Kochan, 'Toward a Stakeholder Theory of the Firm: The Saturn Partnership' (2000) 11 *Organization Science* 367 at 370.

[8] See R. Miller, 'Ethical Challenges in Corporate-Shareholder and Investor Relations: Using the Value Exchange Model to Analyse and Respond' (1988) 7 *Journal of Business Ethics* 117 at 121.

[9] E. Schlossberger, 'A New Model of Business: Dual-Investor Theory' (1994) 4 *Business Ethics Quarterly* 459 at 461.

over those of the entity (the community of interest), but those who invest in the company have a legitimate expectation to a return on that investment. Such investors' incentive in investing is going to be greatly reduced[10] if they believe that any benefits received will always depend on what the shareholders want in any given situation. Moreover, it has been suggested that any perceived distinction between the shareholders and outsiders are, for the most part, artificial.[11] While shareholders undoubtedly assume significant economic risk, so do other investors, for example, the employee who leaves a job, sells his or her home and moves half-way across the country to take up a position with a company. Unlike the shareholder, the employee who makes such a move also takes social and emotional risks as well financial ones. However, it might be argued that in the long term the interests of employees and other investors are aligned with those of shareholders.[12]

R. Edward Freeman and his co-authors have said that:

> Business is about putting together a deal so that suppliers, customers, employees, communities, managers and shareholders all win continuously over time. In short, at some level, stakeholder interests have to be joint – they must be traveling in the same direction – or else there will be exit, and a new collaboration formed.[13]

There is much to commend in what Freeman et al have said. Primarily they are correct when they imply the need for co-operation or else investors will exit and go elsewhere.[14] Company entities depend on exchange between, and co-operation from, investors.

Some investors put so much and such a specific investment into a company that they are as entitled to be referred to as residual claimants as

---

[10] W. Allen, J. Jacobs and L. Strine, 'The Great Takeover Debate: A Mediation on Bridging the Conceptual Divide' (2002) 69 *University of Chicago Law Review* 1067 at 1077.

[11] L. Ribstein, 'Accountability and Responsibility in Corporate Governance' (2006) 81 *Notre Dame Law Review* 1431 at 1442.

[12] W. Allen, J. Jacobs and L. Strine, 'The Great Takeover Debate: A Mediation on Bridging the Conceptual Divide' (2002) 69 *University of Chicago Law Review* at 1090.

[13] S. Venkataraman, 'Stakeholder Value Equilibration and the Entrepreneurial Process' in R. E. Freeman and S. Venkataraman (eds), *The Ruffin Series No 3: Ethics and Entrepreneurship* (Charlottesville, Philosophy Documentation Center, 2002) at 45.

[14] This is something that is an important point in the team production approach: M. Blair and L. Stout, 'A Team Production Theory of Corporate Law' (1999) 85 *Virginia Law Review* 247

much as shareholders.[15] One reason is that many investors cannot easily withdraw their investment, and this is highlighted below.

We now consider the leading classes of investors. Of course, it is quite possible these days for a person or organisation to be a member of more than one class.

3. THE INVESTORS

Thus far the focus has been on what investors mean to the company. But the investors do not contribute to the company out of altruism. They do so under the belief that through the company, which will coordinate all contributions and produce outputs, they will benefit.[16] There are many investors that contribute to companies. The main concern for investors is protecting their firm-specific investments in companies. This is a difficult task for many.[17] One reason is that some investors having little bargaining power that they can use in order to protect themselves. Another reason is the insolvency of the company. In many situations investors cannot protect themselves against the company becoming insolvent.

While shareholder primacy holds that it is the shareholders who have the greatest interest in the company's fate, this is not correct for many other investors have such a substantial firm-specific investment in the company that they have an equal or greater interest in: how the company's assets are allocated; the company's future; and the company's ultimate fate. The importance of most of the investors mentioned here is manifested by the fact that the UK Parliament felt it appropriate that they be mentioned specifically in s.172(1) of the Companies Act 2006 as holding interests to which directors have to have regard in making decisions.

---

[15] M. Blair, *Ownership and Control* (Washington DC, Brookings Institute, 1995) at 239; M. Blair and L. Stout, 'Specific Investment: Explaining Anomalies in *Corporate Law*' (2006) 31 *Journal of Corporation Law* 719 at 739. This is even accepted by shareholder primacists: F. Easterbrook and D. Fischel, *The Economic Structure of Company Law* (Cambridge, Massachusetts, Harvard University Press, 1991), at 35–39.

[16] K. Greenfield, 'Defending Stakeholder Governance' (2008) 58 *Case Western Reserve Law Review* 1044 at 1044.

[17] J. Boatright, 'Contractors as Stakeholders: Reconciling Stakeholder Theory with the Nexus-of-Contracts Firm' (2002) 26 *Journal of Banking and Finance* 1837 at 1840.

3.1 The Shareholders

While shareholder primacy acknowledges the fact that constituencies other than the shareholders play an important role in the life of a company, its aim is to ensure maximisation of shareholder wealth. As discussed earlier, non-shareholding constituencies are merely instrumental in achieving shareholder wealth under this scheme. Some even hold that the shareholders are the owners of the company. EMS rejects any notion of ownership. It sees shareholders as one of the investors in a company, without being entitled to any primacy. Of course, the shareholders are important investors whose decision to buy or sell company shares may have a crucial impact on the company's development and overall value. If the interests of shareholders are not provided for then there is the possibility that less capital will flow into the markets, and to companies, which, of course, will lessen economic growth.[18]

Shareholders often hold diversified portfolios, investing as lenders in companies as well as in equities.[19] Also, they are often consumers and employees of companies as well as having other interests in companies. So, shareholders are more likely to benefit overall if EMS is the objective of companies for it is the best way of satisfying their interests; it would mean that the entity would develop and survive and would ensure that they benefit in all their various roles. It is important to emphasise that shareholders are investors and not owners, as sometimes they are so described. This issue was discussed in depth in Chapter 2.[20] Shareholders only own the capital which they have invested and the share of the company that that investment reflects. David Schrader likens a shareholder to a banker who lends money to the firm, rather than the proprietors of a business who have control over capital.[21] But, this analogy falls down somewhat in that unlike bankers, most shareholders are not entitled to a fixed return whatever happens to the company's fortunes. The benefit obtained by a shareholder very much depends on the profitability of the business.

---

[18] W. Allen, J. Jacobs and L. Strine, 'The Great Takeover Debate: A Mediation on Bridging the Conceptual Divide' (2002) 69 *University of Chicago Law Review* 1067 at 1090.

[19] Roger Gordon, 'Do Publicly Traded Corporations Act in the Public Interest?' (2003) 3 *Advances in Economic Analysis and Policy* 1 at 1. Also, see T. Smith, 'The Efficient Norm for Corporate Law: A Neotraditional Interpretation of Fiduciary Duty' (1999) 98 *Michigan Law Review* 214.

[20] See above at pp. 100–104.

[21] D. Schrader, 'The Corporation and Profits' (1987) 6 *Journal of Business Ethics* 589 at 598. Interestingly Harold Demsetz said that 'shareholders are essentially lenders of equity capital and not owners' ('Toward a Theory of Property Rights' (1967) 57 *American Economic Review* at 358.

As far as protection goes, if the shareholders are unhappy with the company's performance and/or way that it is being managed, shareholders are able to exit the company fairly easily by way of sale on the stock exchange, and this might be seen as a major protection for shareholders.[22] This might mean a loss for the shareholders, but often that is a result of taking evasive action. The loss sustained might be seen as low compared with remaining in the company. Shareholders are also able in many jurisdictions to initiate derivative actions, if they believe that the company has been harmed, and/or oppression/unfair prejudice actions (discussed in Chapter 5).

While shareholders are a critical investor in the company, there are other investors whose future and interests are even more wedded to the company.

3.2 Employees

While in some stakeholder-oriented jurisdictions, like German and Japan, employees' interests are regarded as very important, the same importance is not always attached to them in Anglo-American jurisdictions. Nevertheless, they are able to be seen as critical investors in the company, in that they invest their labour and know-how in their employer company. The point has been made by several commentators that human capital invested by employees in businesses has, in particular, become very important, while there has been a commensurate reduction in the importance of physical assets.[23] In knowledge-based economies, intangible assets, such as human capital, is emerging as the most crucial asset for companies,[24] because, inter alia, there is increased demand for innovation.[25] More and more of business is dependent on human know-how, so that: 'Employees are not merely automata in charge of operating valuable assets but valuable assets themselves, operating with commodity-like physical assets.'[26]

---

[22] Contrast this with shareholders in private companies who are often 'locked in' to their company.

[23] L. Zingales, 'In Search of New Foundations' (2000) 55 *Journal of Finance* 1623 at 1643

[24] Ibid at 1624. Also, see M. O'Connor, 'The Human Capital Era' (1993) 78 *Cornell Law Review* 899; J. Singer, 'The Reliance Interest in Property' (1988) 40 *Stanford Law Review* 611 at 621; D. Millon, 'Redefining Corporate Law' (1991) 24 *Indiana Law Review* 223 at 234–235.

[25] L. Zingales, 'In Search of New Foundations' (2000) 55 *Journal of Finance* 1623 at 1642; M. Blair and L. Stout, 'A Team Production Theory of Corporate Law' (1999) 85 *Virginia Law Review* 247 at 261.

[26] L. Zingales, 'In Search of New Foundations' (2000) 55 *Journal of Finance* 1623 at 1641.

Peter Drucker refers to such persons as 'knowledge workers.'[27] Some have even suggested that employees are the primary stakeholders if knowledge is the pre-eminent productive resource of the company.[28] Bernhard Sharfman makes the argument for the importance of those employees that act as traders and investment bankers, and possessing critical skills for the enhancement of the business of the company. He points out that they are in such strong bargaining positions that they can be guaranteed bonuses each year,[29] and this appears to be the case even after the financial crisis of 2007–09.

Employees make an investment in the company and, like money investors in the company, trust the directors to manage the company well. Employees are, in many companies, viewed as the company's main assets for example, football clubs, companies developing IT programmes (such as Microsoft). It has even been asserted that because of this, the approach of shareholder primacy, with shareholders getting the surplus, is no longer tenable.[30]

Like shareholders, employees might actually increase their investment in their employer/company. They might engage in new training to enable them to do a particular job in the company for whom they work, and this will increase their investment in the company. This training might take place 'in house' during 'company time' or it might be something that the employee does outside of working hours at his or her expense. Whatever the situation, if the training is highly specialised then the employee may be virtually tied to the current employer and reduce his or her chances of working elsewhere. Of course, there could be situations where the training undertaken by the employee is transferable and of value to other employers and this might enable him or her to be able to earn significant salaries elsewhere. But, if an employee is virtually locked into a company then the company can engage in negotiations over salary knowing that the employee's options are severely limited or non-existent. This opens up opportunities for hold-up on the part of the managers of the employer/

[27] *Post-Capitalist Society* (New York, Harper Collins, 1993) and referred to in T. Clarke, 'Introduction' in *Theories of Corporate Governance* (Abingdon, Routledge, 2004) at 23.

[28] R. Grant, 'The Knowledge-Based View of the Firm: Implications for Management Practice' (1997) 30 *Long Range Planning* 450. Also, see L. Zingales, 'In Search of New Foundations' (2000) 55 *Journal of Finance* 1623.

[29] 'When Shareholder Primacy Does Not Apply' and accessible at <http://ssrn.com/abstract=1518597> (last visited, 3 February 2010).

[30] L. Zingales, 'In Search of New Foundations' (2000) 55 *Journal of Finance* 1623 at 1645.

company.[31] Looking at it from the other side, if employees have developed firm-specific skills that the company desperately needs and labour resources in this respect are scarce, then they are able to command better conditions for themselves. In such cases, power and rents are no longer restricted to the top of the management structure, but they are distributed amongst other employees.[32]

Redundancy of employees has often been seen as a way to reduce costs, but it may not enhance entity wealth because the company loses skills,[33] and, perhaps, even more importantly, it creates morale problems in relation to employees that remain,[34] with the possible result that the company will not be able to attract new workers in the future when they are needed,[35] or they may have to pay considerably more to attract employees, perhaps even having to obtain them from further afield.

When a company is short of money to declare dividends it might look at making employees redundant to save money and to obtain the funds that will enable it to pay dividends. As mentioned earlier in this work, Shell appears to have done this in 2009 when it boosted the dollar value of the dividend by five per cent, but axed 5000 jobs.[36] This is not an infrequent move by companies, and it can have other benefits, for it has been said that on average stock prices rise eight per cent when downsizing is announced.[37]

When workers are made redundant it is not only the obvious loss

---

[31] See, M. Gelter, 'The Dark Side of Shareholder Influence: Managerial Autonomy and Stakeholder Orientation in Comparative Corporate Governance' (2009) 50 *Harvard International Law Journal* 129 at 139.

[32] L. Zingales, 'In Search of New Foundations' (2000) 55 *Journal of Finance* 1623 at 1647–1648.

[33] During the present recessionary period BT agreed to grant leave to workers on reduced pay rather than to make them redundant to ensure that when the economic conditions improved they would have a trained workforce ready to go: R. Henry, 'BT in bid to cut staff pay in return for holidays' *The Times*, 4 July 2009.

[34] C. Bull, 'The Existence of Self-Enforcing Implicit Contracts' (1987) 102 *Quantitative Journal of Economics* 147 at 149–154.

[35] J. Macey, 'Externalities, Firm-Specific Capital Investments, and the Legal Treatment of Fundamental Corporate Changes' (1989) *Duke Law Journal* 173 at 192.

[36] C. Mortished, 'Shell to axe 5,000 jobs amid 73% profit fall' *The Times*, 29 October 2009. Also, see N. Daniel, D. Denis and L. Naveen, 'Do Firms Manage Earnings to Meet Dividend Thresholds?' (2008) 45 *Journal of Accounting and Economics* 2 at 2 and referring to A. Brav, J. Graham, C. Harvey, R. Michaely, 'Payout policy in the 21st century' (2005) 77 *Journal of Financial Economics* 483.

[37] L. Mitchell, *Corporate Irresponsibility* (New Haven, Yale University Press, 2001) at 210.

of a salary that occurs.[38] Work is an activity that provides people with meaning, fulfilment, dignity and self-definition.[39] But besides loss of the work and skill that they invested in the company, redundant workers have personal costs related to the loss. For instance, they will experience costs in searching for another job, perhaps moving costs, retraining costs and the emotional cost of leaving a job and colleagues and, possibly, leaving a community.[40]

It is argued by the stakeholder school that employees gain a proprietary entitlement to their jobs after they have worked productively for the company for a certain period of time.[41] Perhaps some workers have passed up the chance of moving to another company out of loyalty to their present employer.

It is contended that employees do not have any motivation to work to their full potential, and so companies need to provide motivation to align their behaviour with company goals,[42] even though this is clearly not the case with all employees. Nevertheless, employee interests have been given relatively little attention,[43] and this places them in a position where they are vulnerable to management caprice.[44]

Protection could differ depending on the particular employee involved. Highly skilled employees and/or senior managers may be able to negotiate personal contracts with clauses granting them some protection, although like all contracts they will suffer from being incomplete. Other employees rarely make individual contracts with companies; they start work subject to very basic terms and many under employment at will. If employees are members of a union they may be able to organise industrial action on a collective basis or benefit from collective bargaining. Withdrawal of labour is the ultimate sanction. It is, perhaps, not the weapon that it

---

[38] A. Carroll, *Business and Society: Managing Corporate Social Performance* (Boston, Little Brown and Co, 1981) at 217.

[39] J. Brummer, *Corporate Responsibility and Legitimacy* (New York, Greenwood Press, 1991) at 223.

[40] See L. Dallas, 'Working Toward a New Paradigm' in L. Mitchell (ed), *Progressive Corporate Law* (Boulder, Colorado, Westview Press, 1995) at 49.

[41] J. Brummer, *Corporate Responsibility and Legitimacy* (New York, Greenwood Press, 1991) at 225. See G. Beisinger, 'Corporate Power and Employee Relations' (1984) 3 *Journal of Business Ethics* 139 at 140.

[42] L. Putterman, 'Ownership and the Nature of the Firm' (1993) 17 *Journal of Comparative Economics* 243 at 253.

[43] K. Wedderburn, 'Companies and Employees: Common Law or Social Dimension' (1993) 109 *Law Quarterly Review* 220.

[44] See M. O'Connor, 'The Human Capital Era' (1993) 78 *Cornell Law Review* 899 at 905–917.

once was, particularly in some jurisdictions such as the UK, Australia and New Zealand due to significant changes in the employment laws over the past 20–25 years. The number of strikes has reduced in the UK over the past decade compared with previous years, perhaps reflecting less employee power. This fall in strike activity might be due to diminished unionisation.[45] Many shareholder primacists argue that employees are well protected by employment, and health and safety legislation, and in some countries, such as the UK, employees will have some protection in the sense that they are entitled to state unemployment benefits if they are made redundant.

3.3 Suppliers

Most companies will depend on some other businesses to supply goods and services to enable them to operate. What is supplied can vary. A typical supplier that is worth mentioning is the supplier that provides a critical component for the product that the company is producing. Such suppliers can vary in their importance. For example, suppliers who supply goods that can be obtained easily elsewhere at roughly the same price are not going to be as prized as the supplier who provides a component for the company's product and is the only one or one of a few who can supply the component. On the other side of the coin, while a supplier who provides goods to the company as well as to a number of companies, will undoubtedly value the company but the company would not be valued more highly than any other customer, unless the value of the contract of supply is significantly more valuable in money terms. But if the supplier acquired special machinery in order to produce goods especially for one company, then the supplier would obviously value the relationship with the company very highly. Also, the supplier could be seen as making a highly specific investment in the company that it would want to protect at all costs. In such a situation the company is in a position where it might be able to force the supplier to reduce its price as the supplier is locked into supplying the company. If the company were to end the relationship voluntarily or due to liquidation, the supplier would, unless it can secure a contract with a similar type of company, lose out. The supplier might be able to salvage

---

[45] D. Bradley, 'Be prepared to act fast when industrial action strikes' *Personnel Today* and accessible at <http://www.personneltoday.com/articles/2007/09/10/42221/be-ready-to-act-fast-when-industrial-action-strikes.html> (last visited, 22 May 2009). See the Department of Business Enterprise and Regulatory Reform statistics <http://stats.berr.gov.uk/UKSA/tu/tum2008.pdf> (last visited, 22 May 2009).

some machinery used specifically for the company's product, but overall it is likely to involve a significant net loss.

As mentioned above, power and rents are no longer restricted to the top of the management structure, but they are distributed among other employees and they are also distributed to those outside of the traditional boundaries of the firm, such as critical suppliers.[46]

Circumstances might be such that some suppliers may expect a company to grant it the chance to match or beat quotes that the company has obtained. The type of case envisaged is where X has been supplying goods to Y Ltd for a period of time and Y Ltd is not unhappy with the standard of X's goods, but receives competitive quotes from other suppliers.

For the most part, except where they have made firm-specific investments in the company, suppliers will be protected, if there is a breakdown in the relationship between a supplier and the company, by the competitive market for their services or goods, for they will be able to offer their goods to the company's competitors, because suppliers are generally indifferent as to who actually purchases their goods.[47] But such a market can protect the company equally.

Some suppliers might be able to protect themselves by including a retention of title clause in their contract with the company, in order to protect themselves in case the company becomes insolvent, but unless there is an arrangement that will be ongoing many suppliers do not have written contracts with those to whom they are supplying, and, in any event, retention of title clauses do not protect suppliers in every eventuality, such as where the company ends the relationship by choice or goods are mixed with other goods to produce something totally different.[48] Suppliers might endeavour to protect the relationship by requiring the company to provide some form of bond, but that might be too costly or commercially unviable.

3.4 Creditors

This class of investor is arguably the most diverse. In this class we can include at the one end creditors such as banks who lend large amounts and institutional investors who hold bonds in the company, all of which finance many of a company's operations, to small trade creditors who

---

[46] L. Zingales, 'In Search of New Foundations' (2000) 55 *Journal of Finance* 1623 at 1647–1648.

[47] W. Carney, 'Does Defining Constituencies Matter?' (1990) 59 *University of Cincinnati Law Review* 385 at 412.

[48] See *Borden (UK) Ltd v Scottish Timber Products Ltd* [1981] Ch 25.

supply some quantities of goods that do not amount to sizeable sums, at the other end. In between there is likely to be an array of creditors including larger general trade creditors, lessors, service suppliers, holders of unexpired intellectual property licences, and tax authorities. The group is so large and diverse that there will be a host of different interests and agendas.

The concern for creditors is often that the conduct of the directors, following the making of the creditor's contract with the company, will increase the risk of a failure to pay what is owed. This might involve poor decisions concerning trading issues, the payment of high dividends to shareholders and also misappropriation or transfers placing property beyond the reach of creditors.

One of the primary concerns of smaller creditors is that they are rarely protected by a detailed contract; the contract simply involves a delivery of goods or services for a certain price. Whereas some creditors, mainly those who are providing finance, not only have contracts with the company but are able to include restrictive covenants in the contracts which they have with companies. These covenants are legion in variety, but prime examples are negative pledge provisions.

Other finance providers, principally banks, will be able to demand security over company assets and that should provide protection even if the company were to become insolvent, provided the value of the security does not become depressed. But other creditors, notably small trade creditors, often lack the necessary bargaining power to be able to obtain concessions in contracts with companies, particularly where the market is highly competitive.[49]

Creditors are able to rely on fraudulent conveyance legislation to recover from persons to whom the directors transfer assets where it is done to defraud creditors.[50] That is, directors of companies might be able to predict liquidation and seek to transfer as many valuable assets to associates before the liquidation actually occurs. Creditors may also seek the liquidation of the company.[51] In the US they can rely on implied covenants of good faith and fair dealing. The viability of taking legal action will depend very much on circumstances, chances of success and resources.

---

[49] M.E. van der Weide, 'Against Fiduciary Duties to Corporate Stakeholders' (1996) 21 *Delaware Journal of Corporate Law* 27 at 49.

[50] For example, see s.423 of the Insolvency Act 1986 (UK).

[51] For example, see s.124 of the Insolvency Act 1986 (UK); ss.459P and 462 of the Corporations Act 2001 (Aust).

3.5 Customers

Obviously large companies are likely to have many customers, perhaps
in the millions. Most of a company's income is likely to be provided by
this class of investor. Customers might depend on the particular product
which a company produces or might not be able to go easily to another
company and purchase a similar product at a similar price. In the former
case customers will be very interested in the affairs of the company, for if
the company fails to produce sufficient products or collapses financially,
customers will be prejudiced. The latter might include those customers who have had to pay a deposit for goods or services that they have
ordered, but not received. Often such deposits will be lost on liquidation,
for unless deposits are able to be said to be held on trust by the company,[52]
customers are merely regarded as unsecured creditors in a liquidation or
administration.

Some customers, purchasing substantially priced goods and services,
will be protected by warranties. Others might find some protection in consumer legislation. Apart from that, and the possibility of seeking goods or
services from the competitors of the company or publicising boycotts of
the company's goods or services, customers often have little protection.

3.6 Managers

We have generally referred to executive directors as managers. Managers
are, as we have seen, critical to the life of a company. They will make recommendations to the board that important decisions be taken, and they
will manage the day-to-day affairs of the company.

Agency theory often leads to managers being given incentives, such as
remuneration packages, that will see their interests aligned with those of
the firm's shareholders.[53] But managers who are able to create value for
their firm might have better outside job opportunities. If managers follow
such a line then this gives them a stake in the financial success of their firms

---

[52] Such as under what is known as a Quistclose trust. This is where a trust
arises when property has been transferred for a specified purpose but that purpose
then fails. See, *Barclays Bank Ltd v Quistclose Investments Ltd* [1970] AC 567
(HL). Also, see, W. Swadling (ed), *Quistclose Trust: Critical Essays* (Oxford, Hart
Publishing, 2004).

[53] C. Loderer, L. Roth, U. Waelchli, and P. Joerg, 'Shareholder Value:
Principles, Declarations, and Actions' April 22, 2009, ECGI – Finance Working
Paper No. 95/2005 at 11 and accessible at <http://papers.ssrn.com/sol3/papers.
cfm?abstract_id=690044> (last visited, 2 September 2010).

and a powerful incentive to create firm value. This very situation, and the fact that they might hold firm-specific human capital in the firm, however, turns managers into residual claimants, and they do not have the same incentive to favour shareholders. Obviously under EMS the idea is that the managers will work for firm value.

The danger for managers is that if a takeover succeeds often they will be replaced. For instance, the key executives of Cadbury left the company very soon after the completion of the takeover by Kraft in January 2010.[54] Arguably, if managers perform well and the company is successful then this is not so likely to occur, although some raiders in a takeover situation will just want to rid themselves of the existing managers for political reasons. Managers will, in event, have probably provided in their contract that they receive a pay-off if they are replaced.

3.7 Local and National Governments

In order to attract or retain companies in a local or national area, governments might offer subsidies and/or tax concessions. As a consequence these governments become investors. The provision of support by the government is usually given pursuant to implicit agreement on the part of the company that it will locate to, and remain for a significant period in, a particular community.

In any event, governments will provide significant infrastructure for companies, such as roads, educational facilities for children and adults, police officers, fire services, health services etc.

Governments might be only able to seek protection by exerting political influence over company officials.

3.8 Community

The notion of the 'community' might be regarded as rather amorphous.[55] It is certainly a concept that is difficult to pin down, and what it entails is not clear. It is generally used to mean the local community in which a company's operations are located,[56] the classic instance being the town in which a company's factory is located. It could well be taken to include the

---

[54] C. Boyle, 'Cadbury executives exit hours after deal closes' *The Times*, 3 February 2010.

[55] W. Carney, 'Does Defining Constituencies Matter?' (1990) 59 *University of Cincinnati Law Review* 385 at 414.

[56] F. Lépineux, 'Stakeholder Theory, Society and Social Cohesion' (2005) 5 *Corporate Governance* 99 at 100.

people, businesses and institutions (including schools, hospitals, national and local governments) located in, and around, the places where the company operates. Of course, for very large companies there will be many communities that are connected to the companies' operations.

The community provides many things for companies, including a place in which their employees can live, and concomitant facilities. A community might even build up its facilities etc to ensure that the company will want to retain its business activities in the community. The benefits for the community can be the employment of its residents by the company, possible donations by the company to community bodies and projects, and the development of better facilities.

The loss of the company may mean that some investment undertaken by the community becomes worthless or certainly not as valuable as it was initially, unless the company is replaced by another company which can provide similar benefits to the community, such as employing a similar number of persons living in the community. The construction of a plant or other buildings by a company, together with investment in any other fixed assets, serves as a bond given by the company that it will not capriciously end operations in the community.[57]

Often the focus in respect of the community is on health issues, ensuring that the company's activities do not affect people adversely. But a community will also be affected if the company decides to close its factory or other operations and relocate elsewhere. Clearly such action would affect employees first and foremost, but the effect can be far wider, especially if the company is large. Closure could mean that small businesses that supplied either the company or its workers (in their private capacities) would have to terminate their activities as well, leading to wide-scale redundancies. Schools and community groups might be affected by the fact that workers might need to relocate with the company or, if made redundant, move elsewhere to obtain new jobs.

The biggest drawback for a community is that unlike individual employees it cannot move location. So, if a large company withdraws or collapses the community will be prejudiced.[58] Communities have few, if

---

[57] W. Carney, 'Does Defining Constituencies Matter?' (1990) 59 *University of Cincinnati Law Review* 385 at 415.

[58] A good example, mentioned earlier, is Longbridge in the West Midlands of England. The car-maker, Rover had a very large plant there and when it collapsed in 2005 the community was harmed. For a detailed discussion of the company and its collapse, see M. Holweg and N. Oliver, 'Who Killed MG Rover?' Centre for Competitiveness and Innovation, University of Cambridge, 25 April 2005 and accessible at <http://www-innovation.jbs.cam.ac.uk/publications/downloads/

any, ways of protecting themselves save for political pressure which might include things like organising demonstrations at the company's plant and lobbying politicians. The extraction of commitments from companies by governments permits communities and groups within communities to free-ride as far as protecting their interests.[59]

4. EMS AND INVESTORS

It is contended that investors, when investing in a company, have the expectation that the managers will operate the company in such a way as to maximise the company's wealth, and thus they would embrace EMS. While with EMS, and unlike stakeholder theory, it must be remembered that the benefiting of investors is not the end, but a means to an end, namely EMS. But for the most part EMS will, indirectly, benefit the investors,[60] and so the investors have an interest in maximising the value of the company.[61] The consequence of this is that the investors would want to see entity maximisation. The approach with EMS is to be contrasted with shareholder primacy where investor interests are also a means to an end, but the end is that mainly the shareholders will benefit.

While investors should benefit from entity maximisation, benefits under EMS cannot be guaranteed. Sometimes one investor, A, will benefit over another, B, and at other times B might benefit over A, and, at other times all will benefit. To create entity value it will be necessary for managers to make decisions that might well affect the position of investors, but all investors must be persuaded that they will, at some point, benefit from entity maximisation or else they will withdraw that investment. If EMS is the focus then the latter course of action should be something that they would not want to embrace. The only proviso to these comments is, as we will see in Chapter 8, that benefiting an investor must contribute in some way to enhancing entity wealth.

---

rover_report.pdf> (last visited, 3 September 2010). Also, see 'Thousands to lose jobs at Rover' accessible at <http://news.bbc.co.uk/cbbcnews/hi/newsid_4440000/newsid.../4449449.stm> (last visited, 11 January 2010).

[59] W. Carney, 'Does Defining Constituencies Matter?' (1990) 59 *University of Cincinnati Law Review* 385 at 414.

[60] Clearly investors are affected by the success or failure of companies: R. Campbell Jr, 'Corporate Fiduciary Principles for the Post-Contractarian Era' (1996) 23 *Florida State University Law Review* 561 at 577.

[61] R. Campbell Jr, 'Corporate Fiduciary Principles for the Post-Contractarian Era' (1996) 23 *Florida State University Law Review* 561 at 578.

As, under EMS, all investors will not be totally satisfied all of the time, it is necessary that directors provide proper explanations for their decisions so as to prevent unnecessary disaffection amongst investors and damage to the company's reputation. This might entail explaining: to a general meeting of shareholders why the dividend paid is not higher; to the employees why there is to be a change in shift patterns or no annual bonuses; to customers why a product has changed.

Investors will all be seeking to better themselves. Employees will seek higher wages and better conditions, suppliers will want timely payment of invoices and be seeking more orders. Lenders and shareholders will want low risk and high returns. Customers will seek low cost delivery of goods or services and a high quality of same, and communities will seek social expenditure, retention of a clean environment, stable employment and increased investment.[62]

The company will hope that the various investors can co-operate to ensure that there is an enlargement of the pie that they will share.[63] But inevitably there will be some conflicts between investors during the life of a company. There is likely to be some squabbling and opportunism on the part of the investors in competition to gain rents. For instance, the employees' interest is in maximising their wages and bonuses and that will conflict with the desire of the shareholders to maximise their investment return through higher dividends and decisions which will lead to an increase in the share price. These, and other investors, may 'confront each other in the political arena, using whatever muscle they have available to persuade the board to favor their claim.'[64] For instance, employees may use the threat to strike. The conflict is resolved in EMS on the basis of the directors having to decide which benefits will maximise entity wealth. This is explained further in the next two Chapters.

---

[62] See M. Jensen, 'Value Maximisation, Stakeholder Theory, and the Corporate Objective Function' (2001) 7 *European Financial Management* 297 at 305.

[63] H. Raiffa, *The Art and Science of Negotiation* (Cambridge, Massachusetts, Harvard University Press, 1982) at 131.

[64] D. Millon, 'New Game Plan or Business as Usual? A Critique of the Team Production Model of the Corporate Board' (2000) 86 *Virginia Law Review* 1001 at 1037.

7. Managerial discretion and accountability

1. INTRODUCTION

In the articulation of EMS in Chapter 4 it was made clear that the managers and directors have the responsibility of fulfilling the objective of the company, and in Chapter 5 there was an examination of the position that should exist if managers or the board as a whole failed to do so; the latter Chapter focused on how investors could enforce EMS against the directors. It would not be a complete study of EMS if we did not consider the position of the managers, for they clearly play an important role in the life of the company under EMS.

There is much that can be said about managers. This Chapter necessarily has to be limited and it merely purports to provide a basic consideration of managers and their role as it is relevant to EMS.

The management of a business by the managers is generally totally in their discretion provided that they do not steal or commit outright fraud.[1] In making decisions and devising strategy the managers are exercising power and authority.[2] Typically, today, the company's articles of association or by-laws will vest the board of directors with general management powers.[3] In some jurisdictions, such as the UK, where directors have been given wide-ranging powers, then they alone can exercise them, and the only thing that the members can do is to pass a special resolution to amend

---

[1] M. Gelter, 'The Dark Side of Shareholder Influence: Managerial Autonomy and Stakeholder Orientation in Comparative Corporate Governance' (2009) 50 *Harvard International Law Journal* 129 at 146.

[2] S. Bottomley, *The Constitutional Corporation* (Aldershot, Ashgate, 2007) at 68; S. Bainbridge, *The New Corporate Governance* (New York, Oxford University Press, 2008) at 34.

[3] For example, see in the UK, The Companies (Tables A–F) Regulations 1985, Art 70 of Table A and The Companies (Model Articles) Regulations 2008, SI 2008/3229, reg 2, Sch 1, art 5 (private companies); reg 4, Sch 3, art 5 (public companies). In the United States, see s.141(a) of the Delaware General Corporation Law (2009) and s.8.01 of the Model Business Corporation Act (2008).

the articles or by-laws.[4] Elsewhere, such as the US, not even a unanimous vote of shareholders can control the directors.[5]

It is a widely-held view that it is appropriate and beneficial for those who occupy positions of power and authority over other people to be accountable to some other person(s) or body for what they do.[6] Where there is flexibility in the role of those holding authority and power, as we have under EMS, there is the possibility of some abuses. The discretion of managers and their accountability for what they do has been the central issue in corporate law for years.[7] Recently Stephen Bainbridge has focused on the issue and had talked of authority and accountability in relation to directors, but noted that the two are irreconcilable for the more one makes a person accountable, the more one restricts his or her discretion.[8] Clearly that is true. Like Bainbridge, I can accept that directors have authority and accountability, and I also accept Bainbridge's assertion that there must be a balance between the two values.[9] Managers must be granted sufficient power so as to get the job done. However, to permit completely unfettered discretion would be placing too much power in the hands of managers and could camouflage self-interest.[10] Just as a public official who has significant power must be accountable and subject to some review, so must managers, to some degree. The difficult issue is prescribing the nature of the accountability and its extent, without making managers' jobs overly onerous. What must be remembered is that the more that there is an adoption of either of the extremes of authority or accountability, there is a greater chance of serious problems materialising.[11]

In the last Chapter we noted that there will be conflict between investors as one investor seeks to gain rents at the expense of other investors.

---

[4]   *John Shaw & Sons (Salford) Ltd v Shaw* [1935] 2 KB 113.

[5]   S. Bainbridge, *The New Corporate Governance* (New York, Oxford University Press, 2008) at 34.

[6]   L. Dallas, 'Working Towards a New Paradigm' in L. Mitchell (ed), *Progressive Corporate Law* (Boulder, Colorado, Westview Press, 1995) at 35.

[7]   D. Millon, 'Theories of the Corporation' [1990] *Duke Law Journal* 201 at 222.

[8]   S. Bainbridge, *The New Corporate Governance* (New York, Oxford University Press, 2008) at 16. See W. Allen, 'Ambiguity in Corporation Law' (1997) 22 *Delaware Journal of Corporate Law* 894 at 895.

[9]   S. Bainbridge, *The New Corporate Governance* (New York, Oxford University Press, 2008) at 108. However, Bainbridge seems to favour authority over accountability.

[10]   Ibid at 67.

[11]   B. McDonnell, 'Professor Bainbridge and the Arrowian Movement: A Review of the New Corporate Governance in Theory and Practice' (2009) 34 *Delaware Journal of Corporate Law* 139 at 186.

The managers are included in the category of investors, as they invest their expertise and labour in the company, and yet they are in the unique position of being able to decide what they actually get as investors, subject to some restrictions, as well as what other investors receive. This obviously raises the issue of opportunism and expropriation of benefits, and that must be addressed. This Chapter focuses first on the wide discretion of the managers, which gives them authority, and then considers their accountability and how it can be provided for.

2. MANAGERIAL DISCRETION

While Chapter 4 explained what directors are to do, in broad terms, namely to maximise entity wealth, managers will retain under EMS an extensive amount of discretion in what they do and how they do it. There is no bright line which informs boards of directors what activity will be acceptable in achieving entity maximisation or what conduct actually constitutes a failure to adhere to that standard.[12] To permit a broad discretion is not a perfect solution, but undoubtedly, and most would agree, the granting of significant discretion to the managers is largely unavoidable. It is clear that the 'core of management decision-making is centered on discretion rather than an application of preset formulas.'[13] It is simply not possible to formulate a single overarching principle or test to guide directors how to act in all situations, as circumstances will be so varied, and the issues that directors encounter are often complex and multifaceted. That is why it is necessary to have flexibility, and to have a model that embraces broad principles rather than specific rules. To perform efficiently managers, and directors in general, have to be granted, to a certain extent, open-ended discretions.[14] The Court of Appeal for the Tenth Circuit in the US, in *Herald Co. v Seawell*,[15] said: 'Within the limits of their legal authority, officers and directors of a corporation, by necessity, possess a large amount of discretionary power.' But while managers must have

---

[12] See, D. Schwartz, 'Objective and Conduct of the Corporation' (1984) 52 *George Washington Law Review* 511 at 530.

[13] R. Nimmer and R. Feinberg, 'Chapter 11 Business Governance: Fiduciary Duties, Business Judgment, Trustees and Exclusivity' (1989) 6 *Bankruptcy Developments Journal* 1 at 36.

[14] M. Whincop, 'A Theoretical and Policy Critique of the Modern Reformulation of Directors' Duties of Care' (1996) 6 *Australian Journal of Corporate Law* 72 at 83.

[15] 472 F.2d 1081 (10th Cir 1972).

discretion, they are guided under EMS by some standard, namely seeking to maximise entity wealth and entity survival. This provides them with a guide but does so without placing them in an inflexible position. It is not unusual to find scholars, coming from different perspectives to this area of debate, accepting that where there are a number of voices proposing the path that a company should follow there is mileage in ensuring the directors maintain their long-standing roles as the primary decision-makers.[16] The point was made in Chapter 4 that directors in most, if not all, models are given wide discretion.

The board of directors will delegate many areas to managers, some who will be members of the board and others who will not. We have to accept that it is a company's management, with its organisational skills, that is the group that is able to decide how to maximise the entity's wealth so as to make a large-scale enterprise productive in the long-run. This comes down partly to trusting them and a dependence on their professionalism.[17] As discussed shortly there are some restrictions on the discretion.

There are several concerns that investors in general might have in relation to managerial discretion. First, the managers are appointed by the board of directors and the directors (including those managers who are members of the board) are appointed by the shareholders. Added to this is the fact that the shareholders have the power in some jurisdictions, such as the UK, to remove the directors. So, the non-shareholding investors might, justifiably, be somewhat concerned that the managers and the directors will do the bidding of the shareholders. Yet, it has been indicated by several commentators that the shareholders do not have much realistic control over, or power to, discipline directors in most jurisdictions, and particularly in the US.[18] Perhaps many investors will

---

[16] For example, see M. Blair and L. Stout, 'A Team Production Theory of Corporate Law' (1999) 85 *Virginia Law Review* 247; S. Bainbridge, 'Director Primacy: The Means and Ends of Corporate Governance' (2003) 97 *Northwestern University Law Review* 547; L. Mitchell, 'The Board as the Path to Corporate Social Responsibility' in D. McBarnet et al (ed), *The New Corporate Accountability* (Cambridge, Cambridge University Press, 2007); V. Ho, '"Enlightened Shareholder Value": Corporate Governance Beyond the Shareholder-Stakeholder Divide' abstract accessible at <http://ssrn.com/abstract=1476116> (last visited, 2 August 2010).

[17] The issue of trust is too immense to discuss here. But see, Blair and Stout, 'A Team Production Theory of Corporate Law' (1999) 85 *Virginia Law Review* 247 at 316. Also, see Blair and Stout, 'Trust, Trustworthiness and the Behavioral Foundations of Corporate Law' (2001) 149 *University of Pennsylvania Law Review* 1735 where the authors consider trust in the wider corporate setting.

[18] For example, see S. Bainbridge, 'Director Primacy: The Means and Ends of Corporate Governance' (2003) 97 *Northwestern University Law Review* 547;

find it attractive that the shareholders are not in control of the directors, and, therefore, are not able to influence them unduly. But, on the other side of the coin, if the shareholders have little or no control and cannot monitor effectively, does anyone else? It is possible that employees could do so by way of negotiation, protest and even withdrawal of labour. We noted in Chapters 5 and 6 other forms of pressure that might be brought to bear by other investors. The primary monitor of the actions of the managers is the board. It is to this body that the managers are directly responsible, and this point is discussed further under the next part of the Chapter.

Second, there is the concern that the directors might use their broad discretion to engage in 'empire building'. By that I mean that while the company may be built up by the managers it might occur in a way that reflects best on the managers rather than providing the optimal maximisation strategy for the entity. Company funds could be used to permit the aggrandisement of the managers, provide them with non-monetary benefits, and to ensure their security of tenure. Motives for this conduct can be varied but is likely to include hunger for: status; power; respect; compensation; and prestige, and to avoid embarrassment and shame.[19] The main thesis often propounded is that managers seek to grow the company and thereby enhance their prestige.[20] In increasing the size and scope of the company the manager becomes indispensable[21] and this provides security of tenure. It must be noted that the results of a study conducted by Marianne Betrand and Sendhil Mullainathan suggest that empire building is not the norm for managers, partially because of the disruption to

---

I. Anabtawi, 'Some Skepticism About Increasing Shareholder Power' (2006) 53 *University of California at Los Angeles Law Review* 561; L. Bebchuk, 'The Myth of the Shareholder Franchise' (2007) 93 *Virginia Law Review* 675; A. Keay, 'Company Directors Behaving Poorly: Disciplinary Options for Shareholders' [2007] *Journal of Business Law* 656; S. Bainbridge, *The New Corporate Governance* (New York, Oxford University Press, 2008); V. Acharya, S. Myers and R. Rajan, 'The Internal Governance of Firms' 1 December 2009 and accessible at <http://ssrn.com/abstract=1350580> (last visited, 19 February 2010).

[19]   For example, see W. Baumol, *Business, Behavior, Value and Growth* (New York, MacMillan, 1959); M. Jensen, 'Agency Cost of Free Cash Flow, Corporate Finance and Takeovers' (1986) 76 *American Economic Review* 323. Also, see M. Kahan, 'The Limited Significance of Norms for Corporate Governance' (2001) 149 *University of Pennsylvania Law Review* 1881.

[20]   R. Stultz, 'Managerial Discretion and Optimal Financing Policies' (1990) 28 *Journal of Accounting and Economics* 3.

[21]   A. Shleifer and R. Vishny, 'Management Entrenchment – The Case of Manager-specific Investments' (1989) 25 *Journal of Financial Economics* 123.

the lives of managers that it might necessitate.[22] Also, provided that the company's wealth and standing is enhanced, investors might not be overly concerned if managers engage in some empire building. Investors might be willing to put up with this if the managers are clearly talented, and any protests might lead to the managers' resignation. All of this is provided, of course, that the empire building is not too costly and does not deflect the managers from the task of developing the company.

Empire building is a kind of agency problem. The concern is that the managers, rather than passing on free cash flow (undistributed liquid funds)[23] to shareholders in the form of dividends, will pump funds into the business of the company, perhaps into what might be regarded as unnecessary areas.[24] Some perceive this as the most critical agency problem encountered by public companies.[25] There are countless stories of managers buying new company jets, building big new ostentatious offices and furnishing offices with extravagant décor, so that they can indulge in 'grandstanding'. Whilst far from foolproof, increasing the number of independent directors on boards can help in preventing empire building and other managerial improprieties, as can the pressure of investors. We will consider more on this point in the next part of the Chapter.

Rather than being concerned about empire building, there might be concern that the directors will decline to take on ventures that might involve some degree of risk because they might be fearful of putting the company in danger and, therefore, their own positions.[26] Another concern is that some managers might avoid any decisions that could involve conflict, hard negotiating or some other difficult tasks, and they will endeavour to seek 'the quiet life'.[27] Empirical research suggests that

---

[22]   M. Bertrand and S. Mullianathan, 'Enjoying the Quiet Life? Corporate Governance and Managerial Preferences' (2003) 111 *Journal of Political Economy* 1043 at 1072.

[23]   L. Bebchuk, 'The Case for Increasing Shareholder Power' (2005) 118 *Harvard Law Review* 833 at 903. Jarrad Harford refers to them as 'excessive cash reserves': 'Corporate Cash Reserves and Acquisitions' (1999) 54 *Journal of Finance* 1969.

[24]   Employees might be equally concerned that they are not receiving pay increases or bonuses.

[25]   For example, M. Jensen, 'Eclipse of the Public Corporation' (1989) *Harvard Business Review* (Sept–Oct) at 61, 66.

[26]   M. Blair and L. Stout, 'A Team Production Theory of Corporate Law' (1999) 85 *Virginia Law Review* 247 at 306.

[27]   Ibid; M. Bertrand and S. Mullianathan, 'Enjoying the Quiet Life? Corporate Governance and Managerial Preferences' (2003) 111 *Journal of Political Economy* 1043.

some managers will avoid closing down factories as part of their attempt to embrace the quiet life.[28]

The limits that one wishes to place on the managers' discretion depend, to an extent, on the view that one takes of managers. As we have seen, the shareholder primacy school generally speaking, as well as those holding to a law and economics approach, take the view that managers are fundamentally untrustworthy souls because human nature is such that it will want to seek self-serving benefits at every possible turn, and managers have that opportunity due to the positions they hold. In contrast, stakeholder theorists and members of the progressive school consider managers to be trustworthy, generally speaking, and as professionals who will take some pride in their work and act as stewards of the company. They take the view that directors will have a moral obligation to stakeholders and will use their powers ethically.[29] Besides placing curtailments on discretion, law and economics advocates propose providing managers with incentives to get them to refrain from engaging in opportunism and/or shirking; this is an effort to align their interests with those of the shareholders. Shortly we will consider the accountability mechanisms that can be employed in relation to directorial power, but whatever is put in place there is a need to place a certain amount of trust in managers and directors.[30] Arguably managers would be trustworthy in an EMS framework as they are not subject to any shareholder pressure to raise the share price and make short-term gains. The trust that is placed on managers and directors is not completely blind, because there are mechanisms that make them accountable. Everyone who exercises authority and power, as managers and directors do, must be accountable.

Undoubtedly, there is room for directors under EMS to act opportunistically, but this is the case also with companies operating under shareholder primacy (and stakeholder theory). Shareholder primacy prides itself on providing the best answers to the agency problem, yet there are

---

[28] M. Bertrand and S. Mullianathan, 'Enjoying the Quiet Life? Corporate Governance and Managerial Preferences' (2003) 111 *Journal of Political Economy* 1043 at 1066–1067.

[29] S. Sharma, 'Managerial Interpretations and Organizational Context as Predictors of Corporate Choice of Environmental Strategy' (2000) 43 *Academy of Management Journal* 581; J. Aragon-Correa, F. Matias-Resch and M. Senise-Barrio, 'Managerial Discretion and Corporate Commitment to the Natural Environment' (2003) 57 *Journal of Business Research* 964; C. Cennamo, P. Berrone and L. Gomez-Mejia, 'Does Stakeholder Management have a Dark Side?' (2009) 89 *Journal of Business Ethics* 491 at 492.

[30] For a discussion of placing trust in directors, see L. Mitchell, *Corporate Irresponsibility* (New Haven, Yale University Press, 2001).

spectacular examples, such as Enron and WorldCom in the United States, Maxwell Communications in the UK and HIH Insurance and One.Tel in Australia, of the failure to monitor and rein in managers. Clearly, managers have, under shareholder primacy, plenty of scope for self-serving activity,[31] and this might go unnoticed for some time.

While managers do enjoy significant discretion, they will be discouraged from shirking, engaging in opportunism, and failing to maximise the entity because they are likely to have to be accountable in one form or another for what they do. Before we move on to a consideration of accountability it is to be noted that while managers have a broad discretion in how they manage the company, this discretion is circumscribed to some extent by matters such as economic pressures. Examples of such pressures are: the cost of capital, the availability of capital, the availability of employees who are sufficiently skilled, the demand for the products of the company,[32] the position of the company in the market place, and whether creditors feel disposed to lend.[33] To a degree managers and directors have an incentive to exercise their discretion fairly for if they do not then certain investors might exit; necessary finance might not be attracted or key employees might become disenchanted and resign. And any or all of the foregoing events could lead to the managers' loss of position due to removal or the winding up of the business.[34]

It must not be forgotten that besides any shareholding that they have, managers have a share in their company. If the company performs poorly or even fails completely and becomes insolvent, then it is probable that they will be out of a job (certainly if the company enters liquidation), and it will, more than likely, adversely affect their reputation, and their chances of securing another post will be reduced significantly.

In managing the business and exercising their discretion, the managers (and the board) would have to ensure that they are not unduly influenced by political power so as to favour a particular investor where that would not contribute to EMS. Examples of political power in this context are the formation of coalitions of shareholders, publicity campaigns, employees'

---

[31] T. Donaldson and L. Preston, 'The Stakeholder Theory for the Corporation: Concepts, Evidence, Implications' (1995) 20 *Academy Management Review* 65 at 87.

[32] M. Blair and L. Stout, 'Director Accountability and the Mediating Role of the Corporate Board' (2001) 79 *Washington University Law Quarterly* 403 at 438.

[33] Ibid; A. Meese, 'The Team Production Theory of Corporate Law: A Critical Assessment' (2002) 43 *William and Mary Law Review* 1629 at 1677–1678.

[34] M. Blair and L. Stout, 'A Team Production Theory of Corporate Law' (1999) 85 *Virginia Law Review* 247 at 283.

industrial action etc. In the framework suggested, it is critical that managers remember that they are not to act either as advocates of any investor group or as part of one. There is always the concern that managers and directors might consider that if they favour the shareholders, their position might be enhanced, especially if they own shares in the company, or if their compensation packages are tied to share prices.[35] On the other hand, managers who are concerned about their reputation and the need to find posts elsewhere in the future, might, under the guise of effecting a balance between conflicting interests, favour creditor and other particular investor interests in an effort to keep a company operating and being able to satisfy creditors so that the managers are not, personally, tainted by a financial collapse of the company. Although not a primary role of managers and directors, it might be necessary for them, at times, to act as referees where there is an apparent conflict between interests,[36] so that the most efficient outcome can be achieved for the entity.[37] Letting conflict become serious is to be avoided as it could lead to either investors losing commitment to the entity or deciding to exit. We have noted earlier in the book that directors would have difficulty in having to engage in balancing exercises involving a great number of stakeholders, especially when those interests are not only to be economic in nature, where there is no specific goal for that balancing. But the essence of EMS is that any balancing that is done occurs with an object in mind and that does at least give the managers and directors a focus. It must always be remembered that managers may see the need to address the existence of conflicting interests as an opportunity to foster their own self-interest.[38]

---

[35] D. Tauke, 'Should Bondholders Have More Fun? A Reexamination of the Debate Over Corporate Bondholder's Rights' (1989) *Columbia Business Law Review* 1 at 65.

[36] W. Leung, 'The Inadequacy of Shareholder Primacy: A Proposed Corporate Regime that Recognizes Non-Shareholder Interests' (1997) 30 *Columbia Journal of Law and Social Problems* 589 at 590.

[37] Ibid at 605; L. Mitchell, 'A Theoretical and Practical Framework for Enforcing Corporate Constituency Statutes' (1992) 70 *Texas Law Review* 579 at 633. This is an approach that has been advocated by the team production theory, as articulated by M. Blair and L. Stout ('A Team Production Theory of Corporate Law' (1999) 85 *Virginia Law Review* 247).

[38] M. Roe, 'The Shareholder Wealth Maximization Norm and Industrial Organization' (2001) 149 *University of Pennsylvania Law Review* 2063 at 2065. In their empirical study Lyn Lo Pucki and William Whitford found that this occurs with respect to companies that are subject to Chapter 11 bankruptcy ('Corporate Governance in the Bankruptcy Reorganization of Large Publicly Held Companies' (1993) 141 *University of Pennsylvania Law Review* 669 at 710).

3. ACCOUNTABILITY

3.1 Introduction

Given the wide discretion of the managers and directors, and the concerns of investors mentioned above, there is clearly a need for accountability. A lack of accountability, as demonstrated by the actions and eventual collapse of the Australian insurance giant, HIH Insurance, can be fatal for the company itself and those who have invested in it and depended on it.[39] The collapse of the company was so much of a concern to the Australian government that a Royal Commission was established to investigate the company's affairs and its slide into insolvency. The Royal Commissioner for the investigation was Justice Owen, and His Honour identified the problem of giving too much discretion for management. He said:

> There were no clearly defined limits on the authority of the chief executive in areas such as investments, corporate donations, gifts, and staff emoluments. In some of these areas the system was out of control but the board did not appreciate it. Nor did the board have a well-understood policy on matters that would be reserved to itself. Apart from obvious things – such as financial statements and approvals for large transactions – matters seem to have come forward at the discretion of the chief executive.[40]

Together with transparency, the UK's Department of Business, Innovation and Skills maintains that accountability is the most important element of good corporate governance.[41]

Accountability has been explained by Anthony Giddens in the following way: 'To be accountable for one's activities is to explicate the reasons for them and to supply the normative grounds whereby they may be justified.'[42] The concept:

> has been viewed as both an end and a means; it has been defined in terms of procedures, results, disclosure of information, recourse, and compliance with

---

[39]   See, *The Failure of HIH Insurance: A corporate collapse and its lessons*, Royal Commission, conducted by Justice Owen, April 2003, vol 1, (Commonwealth of Australia, Canberra) and accessible at <http://www.hihroyalcom.gov.au/finalreport/Front%20Matter,%20critical%20assessment%20and%20summary.HTML#_Toc37086537> (last visited, 31 August 2010).

[40]   Ibid.

[41]   <http://www.berr.gov.uk/whatwedo/businesslaw/corp-governance/page15267.html> (last visited, 19 February 2010).

[42]   *The Constitution of Society: Outline of the Theory of Structuration* (Berkley, University of California Press,1984) at 30.

regulations; and it is often indistinguishable from such concepts as evaluation, efficiency, effectiveness, control and responsibility.[43]

Often accountability is used interchangeably with responsibility.

Accountability is a noble concept but arguably it is lacking in precision. It is of little value in the corporate world unless there are mechanisms that provide for it. Accountability is all about whether the managers and directors' conduct measures up to expectations.[44] Expectations are set by various mechanisms. And every time there is a series of corporate collapses as we had with Enron, Worldcom, Tyco et al in the early part of the first decade of this century, the accountability mechanisms are re-assessed. For instance, after the collapse of these aforementioned companies, the US Congress enacted the Sarbanes-Oxley Act in an attempt to counter a number of problems and, inter alia, to make boards more accountable.

Nearly all will agree that accountability in some form is necessary, but it is probably in relation to how much accountability is imposed on managers and directors where commentators will diverge.

Arguably it is not possible to comprehend the accountability of managers without ascertaining to whom they are accountable and for what. In Anglo-American jurisdictions the directors are generally regarded as being primarily accountable to the shareholders, although this is not the only body to which they are responsible, as we will see below. The managers are responsible ultimately to the shareholders for enhancing shareholder wealth. Under EMS the managers are ultimately accountable to the company, via the board, and they are accountable for maximising the entity and ensuring that it survives.

One other matter that is worthy of mention is when the accountability is to occur. As Stephen Bottomley notes, this can be *ex ante*, before important decisions or actions are taken, or during the process, that is when actions and policies are being put into effect, or, most importantly, *ex post*, that is after the event.[45] Which of the different points of time is

---

[43]   R. Kramer, *Voluntary Agencies in the Welfare State* (1981) at 290 and quoted by S. Bottomley, *The Constitutional Corporation* (Aldershot, Ashgate, 2007) at 68 at 77.

[44]   M. Huse, *Boards, Governance and Value-Creation* (Cambridge, Cambridge University Press, 2007) at 34.

[45]   S. Bottomley, *The Constitutional Corporation* (Aldershot, Ashgate, 2007) at 80 and referring to J. Goldring and I. Thynne, *Accountability and Control – Government Officials and the Exercise of Power* (Law Book Co, Sydney, 1987) at 226.

relevant will depend on the audience to whom accountability is due.[46] The last point, that is, *ex post*, tends to be the most used.

There are different forms that accountability may take. First, the managers may provide accurate information concerning their decisions and actions. This has been referred to as 'accounting for verification'.[47] Second, the managers explain or justify their decisions. Third, the managers are held responsible for what they have done.

We now turn to considering the mechanisms that are provided to make managers and directors accountable.

3.2 Mechanisms

It is not possible to do justice to a consideration of these mechanisms in a general book of this kind. I will deal with the primary ones, and, by necessity, quite briefly.

There is a mixture of accountability mechanisms that exist, and they include board, contractual, regulatory, market and fiduciary constraints on the choices which managers can make, and whilst singly they are arguably not adequate, when seen together they can be seen as sufficient. Certainly it is not possible to arrive at one mechanism that suffices; a variety is needed.[48]

The following mechanisms are designed to prevent, or provide penalties or relief for, unauthorised overreaching of the powers of decision-making. The words of Justice Owen in his Royal Commission report concerning HIH Insurance are most appropriate: 'Despite these [accountability and regulatory] mechanisms, the corporate officers, auditors and regulators of HIH failed to see, remedy or report what should have been obvious.'[49]

---

[46]   J.Uhr, 'Redesigning Accountability: From Muddles to Maps' (1993) 65 *Australian Quarterly* 1 at 4 and referred to by S. Bottomley, *The Constitutional Corporation* (Aldershot, Ashgate, 2007) at 78.

[47]   J.Uhr, 'Redesigning Accountability: From Muddles to Maps' (1993) 65 *Australian Quarterly* 1 at 4 and referred to by S. Bottomley, *The Constitutional Corporation* (Aldershot, Ashgate, 2007) at 80.

[48]   This is the view of Justice Paul Finn (when writing before his elevation to the bench of the Australian Federal Court) concerning accountability in relation to public law: P. Finn, 'Public Trust and Public Accountability' (1993) 65 *Australian Quarterly* 50 at 53.

[49]   *The Failure of HIH Insurance: A corporate collapse and its lessons*, Royal Commission, conducted by Justice Owen, April 2003, vol 1, (Commonwealth of Australia, Canberra) at pxiii, and accessible at <http://www.hihroyalcom.gov. au/finalreport/Front%20Matter,%20critical%20assessment%20and%20summary. HTML#_Toc37086537> (last visited, 31 August 2010).

So, clearly, mechanisms can fail and, therefore, accountability cannot be regarded as foolproof.

3.2.1 Markets

As far as markets go, managers remain subject to the labour market, financial markets, the market for corporate control and the product markets[50] and it is argued by some that these provide highly objective and demanding guidelines.[51] Of particular note here is the first of the markets: the labour market. As we have noted already, managers have to realise that, generally speaking, if they wish to become involved with other public companies in the future they will need to preserve a good reputation.

Some argue that the market mechanisms just mentioned obviate the need for judicial intervention in relation to managerial action as the market mechanisms are able to do a better job.[52] I would take issue with that given the fact that we can have market failure and most, if not all, accept that markets are not perfect.[53] Also, generally speaking, markets cannot require managers to explain or give justifications for their decisions,[54] even though managers might feel compelled to do so for a variety of reasons, not least of which is that if they do not then there might be an implicit presumption that they acted improperly. Even where they do give justifications, managers tend not to provide explanations.

3.2.2 The board

Companies in Anglo-American jurisdictions are controlled by a unitary board of directors. Jonathan Macey refers to them as 'the epicentre' of

---

[50] See, for example, E. Fama, 'Problems and the Theory of the Firm' (1980) 88 *Journal of Political Economy* 228; M. Jensen and W. Meckling, 'Theory of the Firm: Managerial Behaviour, Agency Costs, and Ownership Structure' (1976) 3 *Journal of Financial Economics* 305; E. Fama and M. Jensen, 'Separation of Ownership and Control' (1983) 26 *Journal of Law and Economics* 301.

[51] A. Campbell, 'Stakeholders: The Case in Favour' (1997) 30 *Long Range Planning* 446 at 448. For a succinct discussion of these markets, see A. Meese, 'The Team Production Theory of Corporate Law: A Critical Assessment' (2002) 43 *William and Mary Law Review* 1629 at 1676.

[52] F. Easterbrook and D. Fischel, *The Economic Structure of Corporate Law* (Cambridge, Massachusetts, Harvard University Press, 1991) at 93.

[53] R. Jones, 'Law, Norms and the Breakdown of the Board: Promoting Accountability in Corporate Governance' (2006) 92 *Iowa Law Review* 105 at 121. See H. Hu, 'New Financial Products, the Modern Process of Financial Innovation and the Puzzle of Shareholder Welfare' (1991) 69 *Texas Law Review* 1273 at 1283.

[54] R. Jones, 'Law, Norms and the Breakdown of the Board: Promoting Accountability in Corporate Governance' (2006) 92 *Iowa Law Review* 105 at 118.

corporate governance.[55] Boards of directors will contain both managers
(executive directors) and non-executive directors (independent or outside
directors). In recent years, certainly since the enactment of the Sarbanes-
Oxley Act 2002 in the US and the delivery of the Higgs Report (2003)[56]
in the UK there have been greater numbers of independent directors on
boards. Some will argue that that makes the board a far better accountability mechanism.[57]

Not only do boards of directors play a critical role in EMS, they do so in
all of the models discussed in this book. The directors can be seen as the 'cus-
todians of the enterprise objectives of survival and growth.'[58] Some scholars
maintain that the board is the primary mechanism of accountability. A
leading proponent is Stephen Bainbridge[59] who argues for a director primacy
approach to corporate governance. Certainly, boards of directors may act
as a constraint on managers' actions and a forum for accountability.[60] Of
course, it failed in the case of Enron,[61] and it is only as good as the directors
themselves, their diligence and their tenacity in getting answers to questions
that are raised by the actions of the managers and their plans for the company's affairs. It is notable that the board failed in Enron despite the fact that
it included some apparently very well qualified persons. Simon Deakin and
Suzanne Konzelmann said that: 'Enron's non-executive directors were as
well qualified as almost any group of outsiders could have been to judge the

---

[55] *Corporate Governance* (Princeton, Princeton University Press, 2008) at 51.
Macey says that the directors are the governors of the company.

[56] *Review of the role and effectiveness of non-executive directors*, January 2003,
and accessible at <http://www.ecgi.org/codes/documents/higgsreport.pdf> (last
visited, 5 February 2010).

[57] However, Enron was dominated by independent directors, and yet the company's abuses are legion.

[58] W. Suojanen, 'Accounting Theory and the Large Corporation' (1954) 29
The Accounting Review 391 at 393.

[59] See his book, *The New Corporate Governance* (New York, Oxford University
Press, 2008).

[60] For criticism of the use of boards as accountability mechanisms, see
J. Macey, *Corporate Governance* (Princeton, Princeton University Press, 2008) at
51–68 and 90–104 especially. However, Macey does not suggest that the employment of independent directors is to be abolished: ibid at 102.

[61] This was in relation to the board's oversight duties: *Report of Investigations
by the Special Investigative Committee of the Board of Directors of Enron Corp*, 1
February 2002 at 148ff and accessible at <http://news.findlaw.com/hdocs/docs/
enron/sicreport/> (last visited, 5 February 2010). One of the worrying factors in
Enron was that apart from Kenneth Lay and Jeffrey Skilling, all of the directors
(15) were independent. Additionally, the independent directors were persons of
significant experience and sophistication.

regulatory and business risks . . .'[62] This seems to have been acknowledged in the business world as the publication, *Chief Executive,* voted Enron's board among the best ever in 2000,[63] and that was not long before its demise.

It is clear that the various board committees, such as the audit, remuneration and nomination committees must be independent minded and actually work. It was found by Justice Owen in his report on the collapse of the HIH Insurance Group that the audit committee failed to a degree as it focused almost exclusively on the accounts rather than taking on the critical function of overall risk identification and assessment.[64]

It is hard to know how much we can expect of the non-executive independent directors as they have to act while often subject to several disadvantages. First, they have several roles to play including monitoring the managers[65] and keeping an eye on the development of the company's business, reviewing business decisions, and setting managerial remuneration. Directors have to serve both monitoring and management functions,[66] in that they will oversee what the managers are doing as well as contributing to the setting of company strategy. It is not easy for directors to fulfil both of these contemporaneously. Trying to do so can cause tension and conflict.[67] Second, directors often lack information. Frequently, it is the chief executive officers who control what information is actually given to the board.[68] This is representative of the fact that directors are very much dependent upon management

---

[62] 'Learning From Enron' (2004) 12 *Corporate Governance: An International Review* 134 at 141. The directors had the experience of sitting on 130 boards between them: G. Zandstra, 'Enron, Board Governance and Moral Failings' (2002) 2 *Corporate Governance* 16 at 17.

[63] R. Lear and B.Yavitz, 'The Five Best and Five Worst Boards of 2000' *Chief Executive*, October 2000 and referred to in J. Fuller and M. Jensen, 'What's a Director to do?' Negotiation, Organization and Markets Research Paper, December 2002 at 3, and accessible at <http://ssrn.com/abstract=357722> (last visited, 10 February 2010).

[64] *The Failure of HIH Insurance: A corporate collapse and its lessons*, Royal Commission, conducted by Justice Owen, April 2003, vol 1, (Commonwealth of Australia, Canberra) and accessible at <http://www.hihroyalcom.gov.au/finalreport/Front%20Matter,%20critical%20assessment%20and%20summary.HTML#_Toc37086537> (last visited, 31 August 2010).

[65] A. Cadbury, *Report on the Financial Aspects of Corporate Governance* (known usually as 'the Cadbury Report') (London, Gee, 1992) at para 1.8.

[66] J. Macey, *Corporate Governance* (Princeton, Princeton University Press, 2008) at 53.

[67] Ibid at 54.

[68] J. Fuller and M. Jensen, 'What's a Director to do?' Negotiation, Organization and Markets Research Paper, December 2002 at 3, and accessible at <http://ssrn.com/abstract=357722> (last visited, 10 February 2010).

for information, and managers will often have informational advantages over directors. Managers might be more hesitant about divulging information if they think that directors want it for monitoring purposes rather than to enable them to contribute to consideration of business decisions. However, there is some recent evidence that indicates that directors do have better access to information now,[69] perhaps due to some degree, at least in the US, to the steps made to make boards more structurally independent.[70]

A third inhibiting factor for directors is that they are not usually specialists in the business(es) conducted by the company and so they tend to rely on the managers who have (or should have) significant knowledge and understanding of the business(es) conducted by the company.

Fourth, boards do not necessarily have a direct stake in the enterprise and because of that they may lack motivation to carry out their monitoring duties as carefully and as thoroughly as they might.[71] However, others might argue that as professionals with the need to retain a reputation, directors will not shirk in this regard.

Besides the fact that there are factors which limit the usefulness of directors there are issues related to board dynamics that might attenuate the role of directors. It is said in relation to US boards that they tend to be passive and are subject to capture by managers,[72] and many are often dominated by forthright chief executive officers.[73] It is obviously absolutely critical that to comply with these responsibilities directors should take reasonable steps to place themselves in a situation where they can guide and monitor the management of the company.[74] To enable them to

---

[69] M. Useem and A. Zelleke, 'Oversight and Delegation in Corporate Governance: Deciding What the Board Should Decide' (2006) 14 *Corporate Governance: An International Review* 2.

[70] J. Macey, *Corporate Governance* (Princeton, Princeton University Press, 2008) at 94.

[71] M. Blair and L. Stout, 'A Team Production Theory of Corporate Law' (1999) 85 *Virginia Law Review* 247 at 283–284.

[72] J. Macey, *Corporate Governance* (Princeton, Princeton University Press, 2008) at 57.

[73] D. J. Telman, 'The Business Judgment Rule, Disclosure and Executive Compensation' (2007) 81 *Tulane Law Review* 829 at 859; G. Dent, 'Academics in Wonderland: The Team Production and Director Primacy Models of Corporate Governance' (2008) 44 *Houston Law Review* 1213. This might be due in part to the fact that the CEO often recruits directly or indirectly members of the board: M. Jensen and J. Fuller, 'What's a Director to do?' 19 August 2005, and accessible at <http://ssrn.com/abstract=357722> (last visited, 5 February 2010).

[74] *Dairy Containers Ltd v NZI Bank Ltd* [1995] 2 NZLR 30 at 79; *Sheahan v Verco* [2001] SASC 91 at [101]; *Re HIH Insurance Ltd (in prov liq); ASIC v Adler* [2002] NSWSC 171; (2002) 41 ACSR 72; (2002) 20 ACLC 576 at [372].

be able to do this independently and competently, directors must ensure that they do not allow one or more managers to dominate them, for to allow that situation to occur is for directors to fail in discharging their duties.[75] Often in this regard directors abdicate to domineering colleagues responsibility for certain matters and this means that accountability does not occur, as well as opening up the former to possible liability. Of course, in such circumstances domineering managers often simply refuse to comply with requests for information etc, and so the directors who seek such information are in a difficult position as to what they can or ought to do. Clearly though the 'burying the head in the sand' approach does not work and is fraught with danger; directors cannot, as they once could, be passive in today's commercial world.

There is another aspect to non-executives failing to monitor adequately, or following through on issues that they have discovered from some preliminary monitoring. This is failing to challenge the executives on management issues[76] because of a desire on the part of non-executives not to 'rock the boat.' Directors might not want to be seen as endangering the cohesion of the board,[77] or causing unnecessary work to be done.[78] Further, directors may become overly familiar with managers, and especially the chief executive officer, and this can inhibit their ability to monitor adequately.[79] It is asserted that directors are so influenced by managers that they gradually internalise the managers' perspective on company matters and this of course affects directors' objectivity.[80] These last points are probably true, to a certain extent and from a historical viewpoint, of UK and Australian boards. But in the past 20 years we have seen in the UK and Australia more being required of directors. In relation to the UK, decisions such as *Norman v Theodore Goddard*,[81] *Re*

---

[75] *Re Westmid Packing Services Ltd* [1998] 2 BCLC 646 at 653; [1998] BCC 836 at 842; *Re Landhurst Leasing plc* [1999] 1 BCLC 286 at 346; *Re Queens Moat Houses plc (No 2)* [2004] EWHC 1730 (Ch); [2005] 1 BCLC 136 at [26].

[76] Andrew Hill Lombard ('Deferential directors need to stir up the boardroom' *The Financial Times* 27 September 2007) suggests that there is not enough challenging of executive directors' plans.

[77] See, Felix Robatyn, 'An Agenda for Corporate Reform' *Wall Street Journal*, 24 June 2002.

[78] For instance, see *Gold Ribbon (Accountants) Pty Ltd v Sheers & Ors* [2005] QSC 198 at [105] (Qld S Ct).

[79] See, A. Keay, *Directors' Duties* (Bristol, Jordan Publishing, 2009) at 190–205.

[80] J. Macey, *Corporate Governance* (Princeton, Princeton University Press, 2008) at 58.

[81] [1992] BCC 14.

D'Jan of London,[82] *Lexi Holdings plc (In Administration) v Luqman,*[83] *Re Barings plc,*[84] and *Re Westmid Packing Services Ltd (No 3)*[85] and other important court decisions on directors' disqualification hearings, have raised the bar higher. The same can be said about Australia,[86] and this is the case notwithstanding the advent[87] of a business judgment rule in Australia.[88] In Delaware, where there is, perhaps, the most concern about the role of directors, the courts have emphasised the need for directors to make sure that they are well-informed.[89] Delaware directors are, of course, quite well protected by the business judgment rule. This can mean that directors are not as vigilant as they should be and could weaken the board's role and lessen the amount of managerial accountability. In the report concerning HIH Insurance, Justice Owen made it clear that one of the many failings of the company was that the board failed to set clearly defined limits on the authority of the chief executive in critical areas such as investments, corporate donations, gifts, and staff benefits. In some of these areas the system was out of control but the board did not appreciate it.[90] HIH cannot be seen as a one-off.[91] One only has to look at Enron in the US or Maxwell Communications in the UK for other like examples.

---

82 [1993] BCC 646.

83 [2007] EWHC 2265 (Ch).

84 [1998] BCC 583.

85 [1998] 2 All ER 124; [1998] BCC 836 at 842; [1998] 2 BCLC 646 at 653. A similar view was taken in the disqualification case of *Re Galeforce Pleating Co Ltd* [1999] 2 BCLC 704 which applied *Re Westmid Packing Services Ltd* [1998] 2 BCLC 646; [1998] BCC 836.

86 For example, see *Morley v Statewide Tobacco Services Ltd* [1993] 1 VR 423; *AWA Ltd v Daniels* (1992) 10 ACLC 933; *Re HIH Insurance Ltd; ASC v Adler* [2002] NSWSC 171; (2002) 41 ASCR 72; (2002) 20 ACLC 576; *ASIC v Vines* [2003] NSWSC 1116. . .

87 Introduced by the Corporate Law Economic Reform Program 1999 (Aust).

88 For example, see *Re HIH Insurance Ltd (in prov liq); ASIC v Adler* [2002] NSWSC 171; (2002) 41 ACSR 72; (2002) 20 ACLC 576 (NSW S Ct); *Re One.Tel Ltd (in liq); ASIC v Rich* (2003) 44 ACSR 682 (NSW S Ct); *ASIC v Vines* (2003) 48 ACSR 322 ((NSW S Ct); *Gold Ribbon (Accountants) Pty Ltd v Sheers & Ors* [2005] QSC 198 at [105] (Qld S Ct).

89 See, for example, *Aronson v Lewis* (1984) 473 A. 2d 805 at 811 (Del); *Smith v Van Gorkom* (1985) 488 A. 2d 858 at 872 (Del).

90 *The Failure of HIH Insurance: A corporate collapse and its lessons*, Royal Commission, conducted by Justice Owen, April 2003, vol 1, (Commonwealth of Australia, Canberra) and accessible at <http://www.hihroyalcom.gov.au/finalreport/Front%20Matter,%20critical%20assessment%20and%20summary.HTML#_Toc37086537> (last visited, 31 August 2010).

91 This was something clearly accepted by Justice Owen, ibid, Part 3, 'Corporate Governance'.

Clearly a board cannot be the only measure to ensure that good corporate governance exists.

It might be of some comfort that the decisions of directors, or at least some of them, might be subject to review by the courts. However, as we will see shortly there are significant restrictions on the involvement of courts. This is something that some think is a good outcome.[92]

In sum, boards can and do provide a point of accountability for managers, but given the reasons set out above, it cannot be seen as the only or primary mechanism.

3.2.3   Investors

The managers, via the board, are accountable to the shareholders in general meetings of the company, which may be held only once a year, that is, the annual general meeting. At such a meeting the board will have to account for what it has decided to do as a matter of strategy, the company's performance during the year etc. Although there has been, in more recent times, greater shareholder activism whereby board decisions and strategies have been challenged, and directors either removed or pressured to leave,[93] in diversely owned companies shareholders have little power. The law in most Anglo-American jurisdictions is that the shareholders' meeting may not intervene in the exercise of the powers of management bestowed by the articles or by-laws on the board.[94] The shareholders have the power, in some jurisdictions like the UK, to seek to remove directors, but that is a difficult strategy to bring to fruition for a number of reasons.[95] As discussed in Chapter 5, in some jurisdictions shareholders might file petitions against the board on the basis that it has managed the affairs of the company oppressively or in an unfair and prejudicial manner as far as

---

[92]   For example, see S. Bainbridge, 'The Board of Directors as Nexus of Contracts' (2002) 88 *Iowa Law Review* 3 at 7.

[93]   For example, see A. Jameson, 'Sale hopes up as Scottish Power chief goes' *The Times*, 13 January 2006; S. Butler, 'Patientline hangs up on chief executive amid rebel attack' *The Times*, 14 February 2006; J. Davey, 'Hermes joins rebels calling for Vodafone chief to leave' *The Times*, 24 July 2006; R. O'Connor and C. Seib, 'Emap ousts Moloney as prospect of break-up increases' *The Times*, 18 May 2007; M. Costello, 'Rebel victory as Hirco scraps merger plans,' *The Times*, 2 February 2009; D. Wighton, 'Angry Rio investors stake their claim' *The Times*, 17 February 2009.

[94]   In some jurisdictions, such as Canada (s.137 of the Canada Business Corporations Act 1985), general meetings may pass advisory resolutions concerning management matters that are not within their powers.

[95]   See A. Keay, 'Company Directors Behaving Poorly: Disciplinary Options for Shareholders' [2007] *Journal of Business Law* 656 at 664–675.

the petitioning shareholder(s) is concerned. Such petitions are very rare in relation to public companies.

Under EMS the shareholders are not the only investors who are able to hold directors accountable. In most Anglo-American jurisdictions shareholders are permitted to bring derivative actions if the managers/directors have acted in breach of their duties. As discussed in Chapter 5, under EMS, a range of investors would be able to initiate derivative proceedings against the managers/directors if they were in breach of their duties and the company took no action against them. Of course, before taking such action the investors might call the managers/directors to account for what they have done. Also, investors might be able to bring pressure to bear in the ways discussed in Chapter 5.[96]

3.2.4   The courts

Accountability to the courts is somewhat indirect. Unless an action is brought against the managers then the courts do not oversee the managers and what they do, save for general pronouncements which judges may make in delivering their judgments on the affairs of companies.[97] Some scholars have called for very limited judicial intervention. One is Stephen Bainbridge. He relies on what the former Chancellor of the Delaware Chancery Court, William Allen, said, namely:

> To recognize in courts a residual power to review the substance of business decisions for 'fairness' or 'reasonableness' or 'rationality' where those decisions are made by disinterested directors in good faith and with appropriate care is to make of courts super-directors.[98]

It is questionable whether any reliance can be placed by scholars such as Bainbridge on this judgment. What the judge did not do was surrender all power to directors. The judge's statement left room for him and other judges to decide upon a director's good faith and the care that he or she exhibited.

Bainbridge argues that it is important for efficiency that the decisions of boards of directors are protected from courts (as well as shareholders).[99] He says, in accord with what Chancellor Allen stated above, that court

---

[96]   Above at pp. 240–254.

[97]   Jonathan Parker J did this in the case of *Re Barings plc (No 5)* [1999] 1 BCLC 433 at 489.

[98]   *Re RJR Nabisco Inc* 1989 WL 7036 *13 n.13 (Del Ch 1989) and quoted in S. Bainbridge, *The New Corporate Governance* (New York, Oxford University Press, 2008) at 113.

[99]   S. Bainbridge, 'The Board of Directors as Nexus of Contracts' (2002) 88 *Iowa Law Review* 3 at 7.

review can make judges super-directors. Kenneth Arrow, whose work is relied on by Bainbridge, accepts that directors have to be accountable, but if 'every decision of A is to be reviewed by B, then all we have really is a shift in the locus of authority from A to B and hence no solution to the original problem.'[100] But courts do not regularly get to review the decisions of boards for a number of reasons, such as: no one outside of the board is aware of the decision until it has taken effect and it is often too late to do anything worthwhile; there is no litigant who has standing to take action (it will usually be the company, but the directors will be the ones who will make a decision on behalf of the company); shareholders cannot organise themselves to bring and/or fund a derivative claim; a compromise of any claim is effected; there is not adequate evidence. To say that courts may, on occasions, review directors' decisions is not making them super-directors, as Bainbridge argues.[101]

As mentioned in Chapter 5, some commentators like Bainbridge have had severe misgivings about judges sitting in judgment on what directors have done in making business decisions.[102] David Rosenberg states that: '[w]ealth is maximized when corporations are run by directors who know that their decisions will be reviewed by investors, by analysts, by stockholders, and by business partners – but not by the courts.'[103] Even the Delaware Court of Chancery adopts a similar view. It said in *Re Walt Disney Co Derivative Litigation*[104] that any redress from poor directorial decision-making 'must come from the markets, through the actions of shareholders and the free flow of capital, and not from this Court.'[105]

Courts might not be competent to review the business decisions of directors, but they can hear evidence and based on that make decisions if the evidence is sufficiently probative. In any event, generally courts have been quite generous to directors. In some jurisdictions such as the US, Canada and Australia the business judgment rule exists and this rule is designed to preserve directors' discretion and to protect the directors from courts using hindsight to find them liable. The rule provides, in a nutshell, that

---

[100]　*The Limits of Organization* (1974) at 78 and quoted by S. Bainbridge, *The New Corporate Governance* (New York, Oxford University Press, 2008) at 113.

[101]　S. Bainbridge, *The New Corporate Governance* (New York, Oxford University Press, 2008) at 113.

[102]　Above at pp. 261–265.

[103]　'Galactic Stupidity and the Business Judgment Rule (2007) 32 *Journal of Corporation Law* 301 at 303.

[104]　907 A. 2d 693 (Del, 2005) and this was affirmed on appeal (906 A. 2d 27 (Del, 2006).

[105]　907 A. 2d 693 at 698 (Del, 2005).

courts will not substitute their business judgment for that of the informed, reasonable director who acts bona fide in the best interests of the company.[106] Directors cannot be second-guessed by a court concerning their actions, provided that the directors made informed, reasonable decisions in good faith, and which were based on the details that were available to them when making the decisions. The American courts in particular have tended to be deferential to directors because of the business judgment rule, only making directors liable where there is a clear breach of the requirement of loyalty.[107] But, the Australian courts have not, despite the existence in the past decade of a business judgment rule in statute, been anywhere near as deferential. It is worth noting that notwithstanding the absence of a formal business judgment rule in the UK, UK courts have tended not to second-guess the decisions that directors have made. They have tended to place a generous interpretation on what directors have done at times when they are alleged to have breached their duties. The UK courts, whilst acknowledging that they must not find against directors on the basis of hindsight, have over the last 20 years demonstrated a willingness to assess directors' conduct carefully. This means that review by the UK courts can exist as an accountability measure.

3.2.5   Contract

Investors, although we are generally talking about lenders, suppliers and other creditors, may impose obligations of accountability on the board or the managers in the terms of contracts which they make with the company. For instance, a substantial lender or a bondholder might require the managers to provide some report of what they have done at specified points of time or provide accounts on a regular basis.

---

[106]   For instance, see *Moran v Household International Inc* (1983) 500 A. 2d 1346 at 1356 (Delaware); *Spiegel v Buntrock* 571 A. 2d 767 at 774 (1990) (Delaware); R. Cieri, P. Sullivan, and H. Lennox, 'The Fiduciary Duties of Directors of Financially Troubled Companies' (1994) 3 *Journal of Bankruptcy Law and Practice* 405 at 408. The review of a director's action by a court, applying the business judgment rule, will involve a review of the objective financial interests of the directors, a review of the director's motivation and an objective review of the process by which a decision was reached by the director: *Re RJR Nabisco Inc. Shareholders' Litigation* (unreported, Delaware Chancery Court, 31 January 1989), referred to by A. Tompkins, 'Directors' Duties to Creditors: Delaware and the Insolvency Exception' (1993) 47 *Southern Methodist University Law Review* 165 at 188.

[107]   G. Crespi, 'Maximizing the Wealth of Fictional Shareholders: Which Fiction Should Directors Embrace?' (2007) 31 *Journal of Corporation Law Journal* 381 at 383; M. Blair and L.Stout, 'A Team Production Theory of Corporate Law' (1999) 85 *Virginia Law Review* 247 at 307.

3.2.6 Regulators

An important element of the accountability strategy in some countries is the existence of a corporate regulator which oversees all that is done and which is within its authority. This is the case in the US and Australia, for example, although not in the UK. The American Securities Exchange Commission (SEC) and the Australian Securities and Investment Commission (ASIC) are examples of strong regulators which are given a broad watchdog brief in relation to overseeing company activity. They are well funded and they can be regarded as bodies to which managers are accountable in certain respects. Besides informal contacts with managers and possible administrative action taken by these regulators, these bodies can and do take legal proceedings against managers and directors for breach of duties and other legislative demands. In recent times ASIC has launched substantial proceedings against directors of companies that have collapsed, on the basis that the directors have breached their duties.[108] Of course this does not assist corporate governance on a day-to-day basis, but it might act as a deterrent as far as managers and directors are concerned and cause their conduct to conform to appropriate behaviour. It is arguably a lacuna in the UK's corporate governance system that there is no regulator in the mould of the SEC which oversees corporate life. There are bodies whose remits do touch upon some functions that can be regarded as addressing corporate governance. These include the Financial Services Authority and Companies House (an executive agency of the Department for Business Innovation and Skills). The latter's main functions are to incorporate and dissolve limited companies, to examine and store company information delivered under the Companies Act and related legislation, and provide public registers.[109] The former states that it is:

> the UK's independent regulator responsible for promoting confidence in corporate governance and reporting. We promote high standards of corporate governance through the Combined Code, but *do not monitor or enforce its implementation by individual boards*. We set standards for corporate reporting and actuarial practice and monitor and enforce accounting and auditing standards.[110] (my emphasis)

In some jurisdictions there are other regulators that also oversee directors' roles in a more indirect way. Examples in the US are the Treasury

---

[108] For example, HIH Insurance and One.Tel.

[109] <http://www.companieshouse.gov.uk/about/functionsHistory.shtml> (last visited, 19 February 2010).

[110] <http://www.frc.org.uk/about/> (last visited, 19 February 2010).

and Internal Revenue Service, in the UK there is the Treasury, and in Australia there is the Australian Prudential Regulation Authority.

In most jurisdictions where there is a Stock Exchange this body will provide oversight as to what is being done by company management and require certain information to be disclosed.[111] It is acknowledged that this oversight is not generally strong, and differs widely between countries.

3.2.7 Social norms

Some maintain that social norms can function as a form of accountability mechanism for managers and directors. This is based on the idea that certain social norms prevail in the business world, and they constrain managers and directors as they are concerned about suffering certain social sanctions 'such as shaming, ostracism and embarrassment' being visited on them if they fail to conform.[112] However, there has been criticism of over reliance on social norms as there is some doubt about their impact on directorial behaviour.[113]

3.2.8 Regulation

Regulation can be employed to ensure greater accountability. A prime example of this was the Sarbanes-Oxley Act 2002 in the US which has, inter alia, introduced rules the goal of which was to foster greater independence of directors and auditors so that managerial behaviour will be more aligned with shareholder interests.[114] General companies legislation existing in most countries provides some provisions which require varying degrees of managerial accountability. In most jurisdictions managers and directors have imposed on them several duties by legislation. These usually involve

---

[111] For a discussion of this issue amongst others, see H. Christiansen and A. Loldertsova, 'The Role of Stock Exchanges in Corporate Governance' in *Financial Market Trends*, OECD, No 95 Vol 2009/1 and accessible at <http://www.oecd.org/dataoecd/3/36/43169104.pdf> (last visited, 28 February 2010).

[112] E. Rock and M. Wachter, 'Islands of Conscious Power: Law, Norms and the Self-Governing Corporation' (2001) 149 *University of Pennsylvania Law Review* 1619 at 1641. See the discussion provided in R. Jones, 'Law, Norms and the Breakdown of the Board: Promoting Accountability in Corporate Governance' (2006) 92 *Iowa Law Review* 105 at 124, 129.

[113] R. Jones, 'Law, Norms and the Breakdown of the Board: Promoting Accountability in Corporate Governance' (2006) 92 *Iowa Law Review* 105 at 130–139.

[114] S. Deakin and S. Konzelmann, 'Learning From Enron' (2004) 12 *Corporate Governance: An International Review* 134 at 134. One of the main concerns with the collapse of Enron was the failure of the auditors to identify and publish details of corporate misconduct.

what can be broadly described as fiduciary duties and duties of care and skill.[115] At the heart of fiduciary duties are honesty, good faith and loyalty so they seek to prevent things like conflicts of duty and conflicts of interests. Duties of care and skill naturally seek to require directors to exhibit, in the carrying out of their functions, certain standards of behaviour and action. In the model of enforcement that I developed in Chapter 5 all investors would be able to ensure that if managers breached their duties to the company entity, then, if no action was brought against them by the board acting for the company, investors could do so in the form of a derivative action.

Companies legislation or related legislation in many jurisdictions require directors to provide certain reports. For instance, in the UK the directors must file with the Registrar of Companies the directors' report (including the business review under s.417 of the Companies Act 2006) and annual accounts, as well as the auditor's report on the accounts.[116]

3.2.9 Codes

Some jurisdictions like the UK have a non-mandatory code system (often known as 'soft law'), requiring large public companies to comply with certain requirements or explain if they have not. In the UK it is known as the Combined Code on Corporate Governance[117] which is now overseen by the Financial Reporting Council.[118] The requirement to explain if a board fails to comply is all about ensuring that there is a degree of accountability for decisions not to comply with the Code. The UK approach has been duplicated in many countries around the world.

3.2.10 Auditing

An important element in the corporate governance process is auditing by independent practitioners. This is to ensure there is a balanced picture of the state of the company's affairs. As the Cadbury Report stated:

---

[115]   In the US the latter are subsumed under fiduciary duties.

[116]   Sections 446 (Companies Act 2006) for unquoted companies (not exempt from audit) and s.447 for quoted companies.

[117]   For a recent study of its effectiveness, see S. Arcot, V. Bruno and A. Faure-Grimond, 'Corporate Governance in the UK: Is the Comply or Explain Approach Working?' accessible at <http://ssrn.com/abstract=1532290> (last visited, 9 February 2010).

[118]   The last version of the Code was published in June 2010, and it can be accessed at <http://www.frc.org.uk/documents/pagemanager/Corporate_Governance/UK%20Corp%20Gov%20Code%20June%202010.pdf> (last visited, 31 August 2010)

The annual audit is one of the cornerstones of corporate governance . . . the audit provides an external and objective check on the way in which the financial statements have been prepared and presented, and it is an essential part of the checks and balances required. The question is not whether there should be an audit, but how to ensure its objectivity and effectiveness.[119]

The last point is critical. Clearly on occasions there is not an objective and effective report provided. Of course, Enron is the classic example where this process failed. As a result of this the US legislature passed the Sarbanes-Oxley Act 2002 that provided, inter alia, for a tightening up of the auditing requirements.[120]

The existence of the auditing requirement should, one would think, ensure, more often than not, that managers are not going to indulge in improper activity.

3.2.11 Summary

Clearly there are flaws with all of the mechanisms listed. But arguably having a single one is not possible, and to ensure that there is better corporate governance having more mechanisms within reason is sensible provided that that does not lead to imposing too many restrictions on managers. On this point it is necessary for there to be a reasonable trade-off between authority and accountability, because to do their jobs properly managers must retain a substantial amount of authority and discretion.

While it should not deter us from trying to improve the process of accountability, we have to acknowledge that no legal, organisational or regulatory sanctions are able to prevent all forms of improper or undesirable practices as we lack perfect information and it is not possible to define every activity that might be detrimental to good corporate governance.[121]

4. CONCLUSION

In this chapter it has been acknowledged that the managers of companies are granted wide discretion under EMS, but to deal with the concerns that emanate from that discretion there is accountability built into the

---

[119] *Committee on the Financial Aspects of Corporate Governance* (Cadbury Report) (London, Professional Publishing Ltd, 1992) at para 5.1.

[120] S. Deakin and S. Konzelmann, 'Learning From Enron' (2004) 12 *Corporate Governance: An International Review* 134.

[121] E. Elhauge, 'Sacrificing Corporate Profits in the Public Interest' (2005) 80 *New York University Law Review* 733 at 748.

model. The primary mechanisms are provisions in contracts, the board of directors, the courts, the markets, and the regulators. It is to be readily acknowledged that these devices are not foolproof and none of the aforementioned is adequate on its own, but a combination of them does provide reasonable accountability. Managers who are willing to act opportunistically or to shirk are not able to be concerned with only one or two mechanisms that might find them out. It is far more difficult to act improperly where there are several mechanisms that can ascertain wrongdoing.

8. Allocation of profits

1. INTRODUCTION

Clearly it is hoped that companies will make profits. Indeed, many see profits as the feature which distinguishes companies from other human organisations.[1] If companies do not make profits then they are going to be in serious trouble. One of the main issues in dealing with the corporate objective is resolving what directors are to do with the profits that their company makes. The issue does not go to the determination of the objective of the company, but it is so critical that it cannot be ignored in any serious consideration of the objective of the company.

Enlightened shareholder value, the concept introduced by s.172 of the Companies Act 2006, captures the importance of dealing with what companies earn, in saying that the directors are to manage so as to promote the success of the company, but it then qualifies this by stating 'for the benefit of the members as a whole.'[2] Under s.172, the success of the company and the benefit of the members cannot be separated, and this suggests that the fruits of the company's business will go to the members/shareholders. In contrast EMS purports to separate the benefits to shareholders and benefits to the company. Maximising entity wealth should benefit the members (and all investors in some way), but indirectly.

When companies make profits there is the possibility of squabbling amongst the investors and an attempt to engage in rent-seeking.[3] Effectively shareholder primacy provides that the money that remains after discharging all obligations, such as paying creditors, general over-

---

[1] For example, R. Eells and C. Walton, *Conceptual Foundations of Business* (Homewood, Illinois, Richard D. Irwin, 1969) at 535.

[2] The UK's Company Law Review Steering Group, in its review of UK company law, accepted shareholder primacy as the objective of the company, so one assumes that this involves direct benefits for members. See, Company Law Review, *Modern Company Law for a Competitive Economy: The Strategic Framework* (London, DTI, 1999), at para 5.1.5.

[3] M. Blair and L. Stout, 'Director Accountability and the Mediating Role of the Corporate Board' (2001) 79 *Washington University Law Quarterly* 403 at 420.

heads, and any money that is needed for capital improvements or to be kept in reserve, should go to the shareholders. It is uncertain what would happen under stakeholder theory. Presumably the directors would have to distribute funds after balancing the interests of the stakeholders. The book has already rehearsed the problems that exist in balancing when there is no goal established which is to be achieved by the balancing. In Chapter 4 it was explained that under EMS the goal of a company is to maximise the total value created by the entity, that is to produce as much wealth as possible for the entity, and at the same time ensure the survival of the operation of the company; so directors must deal with the profits in such a way that will achieve those goals.

This Chapter, after dealing briefly with the rather thorny issue of profits, explains how profits are allocated in accordance with EMS.

2. PROFITS

Profit is not a precise term. Daniel Greenwood distinguishes between two kinds of profit: economic and accounting. Successful companies produce profits, that is, they are able to get in more from the sale of their products/ services etc than they pay out for inputs (employee wages, payments on debt capital, purchase of raw materials etc) to keep the companies going. This profit, the economic profit, is known as the residual, and we noted in Chapter 2 that the shareholder primacy theory holds that the shareholders are entitled to that, or at least a major part of it. Accounting profit is the amount over and above a company's overheads that is paid out by way of dividends and that which is retained by the company (retained earnings).[4] Interestingly, while the payments to employees as wages, payments to creditors and all other payments made to investors to compensate them for their inputs, reduce the amount of the accounting profits, payments by way of dividends to shareholders do not. Dividends are not regarded as costs per se, even though the cost of capital is a cost to the company, in that just like employees' labour the company needs money to be con-tributed by shareholders in order for it to operate and make profits. It might be argued that the amount of dividend that is needed to ensure the shareholders remain with the company is a cost and not to be seen as being paid out of the accounting profits. Payments that exceed that which is paid as dividends and that are set aside as retained earnings are part of the

---

[4] D. Greenwood, 'The Dividend Puzzle: Are Shares Entitled to the Residual?' (2007) 32 *Journal of Corporation Law* 103 at 111.

economic profits of the company. For the purposes of this Chapter when there is a reference to profit, economic profit is in view.

Of course, profits can be increased by reducing elements of the company's outgoings. Prime in this respect is the reduction of the labour cost, usually by retrenching workers.[5] A reduction in the interest payable to lenders is, of course, another possible way of reducing outgoings, as is streamlining the production process (for manufacturing companies).

Profit-making is critically important, of course, but it is not an end. Making profits simply enables a company to continue to exist and develop. What it does with the profits is a crucially important question.

3.   ALLOCATION

What we focus on in this Chapter, assuming that companies have made economic profits, is what do they do with those profits? It has been said that there is 'no greater policy issue in corporate law than to whose benefit corporate production is intended to redound.'[6]

The starting point is to acknowledge the fact that the economic profit belongs to the company itself. This is critical as far as corporate existence is concerned.[7] No one has a right to participate in its distribution. This statement even includes the shareholders. They have no right to dividends until dividends have been declared by the general meeting,[8] and this is usually after the directors have recommended a dividend to the meeting. This power is usually set out in either the articles of association or a statute.[9] The company's economic profit constitutes rents to which no one has a moral or legal right.[10] It is the company's board, as part of its role of managing the company, which will have to decide what to do with the profit. The only thing that can be done to challenge the board's decision is for the shareholders, if they are able, to bring a derivative action against

---

[5]   Shell appears to have done this in 2009 when it boosted the dollar value of the dividend by five per cent, but axed 5,000 jobs: C. Mortished, 'Shell to axe 5,000 jobs amid 73% profit fall' *The Times*, 29 October 2009.

[6]   C. Brunner, 'The Enduring Ambivalence of Corporate Law' (2008) 59 *Alabama Law Review* 1385 at 1426.

[7]   D. Greenwood, 'The Dividend Puzzle: Are Shares Entitled to the Residual?' (2007) 32 *Journal of Corporation Law* 103 at 113.

[8]   For example, see *Re Accrington Corporation Steam Tramways Co* [1909] 2 Ch 40. Also, see the US's Revised Model Business Corporations Act, s.8.01.

[9]   For example, see s.170 of Delaware's Corporations Code.

[10]   D. Greenwood, 'The Dividend Puzzle: Are Shares Entitled to the Residual?' (2007) 32 *Journal of Corporation Law* 103 at 115.

the directors for breach of their duties, such as not using funds for proper purposes and/or (in some jurisdictions like Australia) not acting bona fide in the best interests of the company. The directors have a broad discretion in determining how the company's profits will be used and who will get what.[11] There has to be significant latitude granted to directors in deciding what should be done with the profits of a company. Kent Greenfield has voiced concern about the distribution of profits being solely in the hands of the board, as it is elected by the shareholders.[12] Obviously the concern is predicated on the fact that directors might favour shareholders unreasonably as the latter have the power to oust the former. It must be noted that Greenfield's concern is expressed in the context of a corporate culture dominated by shareholder primacy.

When profits are made, it is possible that there will be rent-seeking by the investors. It is likely that the directors will come under pressure from investors to benefit them. All, or at least most, investors usually have some lever which they can try to use to influence managers into awarding them benefits. Some of these were discussed in Chapters 5 and 6. Directors would have to be sufficiently independent so that investors are not able to influence them, certainly in a way that could not be consistent with entity maximisation and sustainability. It has been said that this can easily turn into 'a war against all as each seeks the largest portion.'[13] Concern has been voiced that this could produce an impasse, and this state of affairs could affect the company's future.[14] Certainly it could be divisive, but it is the task of the directors to distribute fairly and in a way that will enhance the company's wealth and at the same time ensure the survival of the operation of the company. The directors must devise a scheme of distribution that will ultimately enhance the company in the long run and permit it to continue as a going concern. Importantly, the directors' decision in considering what benefits, if any, to bestow on investors, must be based not on consideration of the personal interests of the investors (or, of course, the personal interests of the directors), but based on what will enhance

---

[11] Sally Wheeler refers to the situation where there is a distribution to investors other than just shareholders as 'corporate social intervention': *Corporations and the Third Way* (Oxford, Hart Publishing, 2002) at 134. However, she believes that how the profit is distributed depends on a company's desire to aspire to be virtuous.

[12] 'Reclaiming Corporate Law in a New Gilded Age' (2008) 2 *Harvard Law and Policy Review* 1 at 23.

[13] A. Kaufman and E. Englander, 'A Team Production Model of Corporate Governance' (2005) 19 *Academy of Management Executive* 9 at 13.

[14] Ibid.

company interests. The difficulty for directors in some cases is that there may be some uncertainty as to whether providing a benefit to a particular investor will in fact translate into corporate wealth. Determining whether it will do so is going to be problematical on occasions. In this whole process investors have to realise that if directors succumb to pressure then that could have a deleterious effect on the company in the near or medium term and eventually be counter-productive for them as directors.[15] It could also ultimately be detrimental for most, if not all, investors.

The wealth generated is usually seen as profits, but profits do have a short-term bias as they relate to the current accounting period.[16] Profits do not take into account the fact that there is a need for investment by the company to ensure long-term development, for example there is a need to provide for research and development, employee training, new equipment etc.

There are many options available to the directors, such as: the retention of all or part of the profit in its bank account as an investment or set aside for contractual obligations in the following accounting period (the latter known as 'provisions'); extend more credit to its trading partners; the payment of dividends to shareholders; investment in new plant and equipment; repay creditors earlier than required under the relevant credit contracts (which may provide benefits in terms of a reduction in payments or the securing of goodwill with creditors); increase wages and pay bonuses to employees; reducing the cost of its products or services so its customers pay less; buy-back its shares, where permissible; make donations to local community projects, and so on.[17]

Whilst no one has a particular right to the profits, investors might feel that they are entitled to something from their contribution to the company's success. The investors most likely to feel this way are the shareholders and employees. If shareholders do not see any of the funds by way of dividends there is likely to be unrest and this might lead to a variety of actions being taken by individual, or groups of, shareholders. But generally speaking it is likely that shareholders would look to sell their shares. If a number of shareholders did this it is probable that that would affect

---

[15]   For example, see the comments of Elaine Sternberg in relation to shareholders: E. Sternberg, *Just Business*, 2nd ed (Oxford, Oxford University Press, 2000) at 218.

[16]   Ibid at 46.

[17]   For example, the large UK company, JCB, made a large donation to the reconstruction programme in Pakistan due to the 2010 floods that devastated the country. (see, <http://www.jcb.com/PressCentre/NewsItem.aspx?ID=821> (last visited, 1 September 2010).

the share price and it could well compromise the company's ability to raise further capital as potential investors might be apprehensive of the managers' intentions and the company's viability.[18] The options available to shareholders and other investors are discussed, albeit in a different context in Chapters 5 and 6.[19]

A distribution of profits could be made on the basis of people getting what they deserve – using the concept of distributional justice. The problem is that it is generally impossible to determine what are in fact an investor's just deserts in a corporate situation,[20] especially when we are talking about large public companies with complex affairs. To be sure it is likely that an investor's contribution has been an element in the success of the company, but to what extent? How would one assess the impact of a particular investor's input? Getting into an examination of what each investor deserves is fraught with problems. It is exceptionally difficult *ex post* to assess to what extent each investor has contributed to the success of the company, and who is responsible for what. Rather than engaging in this process, EMS provides that directors should apportion profits in such a manner that will permit the company to survive and to go on and maximise its wealth in the future. For example, the company might decide not to pay as high a dividend as it could because it wishes, perhaps, to pay a bonus to employees, feeling that this strategy might win the company important goodwill with the employees. All of this can be justified on the basis of ensuring the company is economically and financially sound. This will involve some balancing, but that must be founded on what will eventually maximise the entity and sustain it. What is done as far as distribution is concerned is likely to affect, in a not insubstantial way, the future of the company.

There are obviously market-driven baselines that may well dictate how the board distributes funds. For instance, dividends will usually have to be paid out to ensure both retention of shareholders and a keenness amongst shareholders to take up any new share issue. There might be a need to pay a bonus to certain skilled workers who might be head-hunted by other companies. At this time, as Margaret Blair and Lynn Stout indicate, it is

---

[18] S. Bainbridge, 'In Defense of the Shareholder Wealth Maximization Norm: A Reply to Professor Green' 50 *Washington and Lee Law Review* 1423 at 1441 (1993).

[19] See above at pp. 240–256 and pp. 280–291.

[20] See D. Millon, 'New Game Plan or Business as Usual? A Critique of the Team Production Model of Corporate Law' (2000) 86 *Virginia Law Review* 1001 at 1025. In this respect the situation under team production might be no different than under shareholder primacy theory (ibid at 1026–1027).

the task of the directors to balance competing interests in such a way as to keep everyone happy,[21] but unlike Blair and Stout who see the divvying up of the profits as dependent somewhat on the result of the use of political power,[22] rather than any principle, EMS lays down the principle for any distribution. As mentioned above, the principle is that the distribution must be done in such a way as to produce entity enhancement. As alluded to above, Blair and Stout believe that if there is no fixed sharing rule, then at the time of the divvying up of profits there will be rent-seeking which will be costly.[23] However, with EMS while there might be such attempts by investors, directors can always point to the fact that they have to do that which will foster the company's wealth. Also, pragmatically directors would need to understand that if rent-seeking was not controlled and directors gave into pressure, then this is likely both to dissuade others from investing in the company and to cause existing investors to consider withdrawing, especially if they felt that they had little clout or opportunities to wield some political power. But EMS is in accord with the team production approach of Blair and Stout when it is asserted that there is a need to reward contributors (investors) in order to keep them involved in the company. While team production suggests the company gives contributors what they want, EMS provides that the company benefits investors to the extent that that action will enhance the company's wealth in due course. Blair and Stout seem to see retention of contributors, as they call them, as critical, but while the retention of many investors is a critical issue, it might be beneficial to the entity if a particular investor were not retained. Also, if an investor's importance is marginal then directors might not be concerned if the investor decided to withdraw from involvement with, or in, the company.

Obviously, those who adhere to shareholder primacy would not agree with the above approach. Some would take issue with it because they regard the shareholders as the owners of the company. If the shareholders are seen as the owners of a company, then it is an easy step to regard what remains after discharging outgoings, such as buying goods and employing people etc, as the profits, and they are to go to the shareholders. But the concept of profits is more than the sums that are paid to shareholders as dividends each year or are reinvested in the company. Profit can be seen as the portion of the income of the company less that which has to be used

---

[21]   M. Blair and L. Stout, 'A Team Production Theory of Corporate Law' (1999) 85 *Virginia Law Review* 247 at 281.

[22]   Ibid at 323–326.

[23]   Ibid at 266.

to pay what are often referred to as 'overheads,' namely the costs associated with borrowing money, payment of employees, purchasing materials needed to pursue the development of the business etc. On the basis that the shareholder is merely one investor, albeit an important one, it is appropriate to see dividends as business expenses (needed to be paid to satisfy shareholders and retain them) rather than to be perceived as something that is paid after the meeting of business expenses,[24] or as returns on their ownership of the company.

Intuitively the above system would be fairer as investors are benefited to the extent that they can enrich the company entity; that is, if they are critical to the entity surviving and developing then they should be rewarded.

To say that employees are entitled to share in the profits is based on the idea that any wages and fringe benefits which they have been paid are not sufficient to discharge the value of the employees' contribution to what the company produces.[25] Implicit in this might be the fact that in many situations employees have firm-specific expertise that is not going to be beneficial elsewhere. It might also be argued that employees invest their efforts and whole career (in some cases) in their employment with the company and the market does not take this into account ordinarily.[26] The contractarian theorist is probably going to argue that employees should ensure that all of these factors should be taken into account when the employment contract is accepted. The riposte is that there is usually inequality of bargaining power and, in any event, employees do not always foresee what might happen during the period of the employment, and this is partially due to information asymmetry.

If a company has struggled and is in danger of collapsing, investors like employees and creditors might be willing to make sacrifices. Employees might take a reduced salary or, as workers decided to do in 2009 at the JCB company in Uttoxeter, England, agree to a reduced working week with less pay. Creditors might be willing to grant the company a repayment holiday or to compromise their claim. But where a company has been profitable investors might rightly expect some benefits. The employees might seek a wage increase. In such a case the company has to determine what will foster entity wealth. If the workers took some form of industrial action, and even withdrew their labour, the company's immediate future would probably be affected, at least to some degree.

---

[24]   D. Schrader, 'The Corporation and Profits' (1987) 6 *Journal of Business Ethics* 589 at 599.
[25]   B. Shenfield, *Company Boards* (London, George Allen and Unwin, 1971) at 155.
[26]   Ibid.

A company may choose to retain a portion of their profits for various reasons. The prime reason is probably that it will make the company more economically stable and enable it to deal with fluctuations in market conditions by using it as a hedge against unprofitable, or at least less profitable, periods. Other reasons could be to build up capital to enable it to purchase new assets, such as equipment, plant and buildings, or to be able to satisfy commitments or liabilities which are contingent or prospective. There is evidence that large public companies do retain a substantial amount of earnings,[27] and some would say that it is rational to do so in order to ensure the maintenance and growth of the company.[28] Such companies tend to utilise these earnings rather than obtaining funding from bond or equity issues or from banks.[29] These provide the financial assets that form the basis of investing in fruitful capabilities that can lead to innovation and economic development.[30] Franklin Allen and Douglas Gale have said that provided that retained earnings are reflected in the value of the equity of the company, paying out dividends to shareholders is not necessary for the shareholders to benefit.[31] However, Michael Jensen maintains that efficiency determines that funds should be distributed to the shareholders rather than being retained.[32] The concern that investors might have in relation to the retention of profits is that they may be used to enable managers to engage in 'empire building' as discussed in Chapter 7.[33] It is likely that there are sufficient accountability mechanisms that this danger might be averted in many cases.

It has been suggested that while large companies have traditionally retained earnings and reinvested, in more recent years managers have employed the approach of 'downsize and distribute'.[34] An example of this

---

[27]   E. Fama and H. Babiak, 'Dividend Policy: An Empirical Analysis' (1968) 63 *Journal of American Statistics Association* 1133 at 1156 and referred to by Blair and Stout, 'A Team Production Theory of Corporate Law' (1999) 85 *Virginia Law Review* 247 at 292.

[28]   K. Iwai, 'Persons, Things and Corporations: The Corporate Personality Controversy and Comparative Corporate Governance' (1999) 47 *American Journal of Comparative Law* 583 at 618.

[29]   F. Allen and D. Gale, *Comparing Financial Systems* (Cambridge, Massachusetts, MIT Press, 2001) at 342.

[30]   M. O'Sullivan, 'The Innovative Enterprise and Corporate Governance' (2000) 24 *Cambridge Journal of Economics* 393 at 394.

[31]   F. Allen and D. Gale, *Comparing Financial Systems* (Cambridge, Massachusetts, MIT Press, 2001) at 360.

[32]   'Eclipse of the Public Corporation' (1989) *Harvard Business Review*, September–October 61 at 66.

[33]   Above at pp. 297–298.

[34]   W. Lazonick and M. O'Sullivan, 'Maximizing Shareholder Value: a New Ideology for Corporate Governance' (2000) 29 *Economy and Society* 13 at 14 and 18.

is the decision, referred to elsewhere in this book, of Shell in late 2009 to boost the dollar value of the dividend by five per cent, notwithstanding a large decrease in profits. This occurred only after the company had axed 5,000 jobs.[35]

Stephen Bainbridge might criticise EMS, based on what he has said elsewhere,[36] because non-shareholder investors might appear 'to get a second bite of the cherry,' in that they can negotiate contractual rights when investing and then they get benefits after profits have been earned. He resolutely denies any benefits to investors that are not contracted for. A main plank of his reasoning is that the law, like God, helps those who help themselves. First, that is erroneous theology (the scriptures in Christianity, Judaism and Islam indicate that God clearly helps anyone and especially those who cannot help themselves (the scriptural bases for that are too many to cite)) and second, the law, in places, does specifically help those who cannot help themselves. For example various jurisdictions vitiate contracts where there is undue influence of certain persons. Leaving that aside, in EMS, people only benefit from the profits when it is likely to enhance company wealth.

Why would managers think that benefiting investors would produce corporate wealth? One answer is that human beings are 'reciprocators' in that they tend to treat others the way that they are treated by others,[37] and so if a company is reasonable and respects their input then investors will respond positively. So, if, for example, workers are benefited they are more likely to remain loyal and work harder.[38]

4. CONCLUSION

The central issue in the whole debate about the objective of the company is: who gets the benefits generated by the company? This Chapter has sought to address that issue from the point of view of EMS. Unlike shareholder primacy which is committed to ensuring that shareholders are those who ultimately benefit from what the directors do, or stakeholder theory

---

[35] C. Mortished, 'Shell to axe 5,000 jobs amid 73% profit fall' *The Times*, 29 October 2009.

[36] 'In Defense of the Shareholder Wealth Maximization Norm: A Reply to Professor Green' (1993) 50 *Washington and Lee Law Review* 1423 at 1433.

[37] For example, see D. Dickinson, 'Ultimatum Decision-Making: A Test of Reciprocal Kindness' (2000) 48 *Theory and Decision* 151 at 153.

[38] K. Greenfield, 'Saving the World with Corporate Law' (2008) 57 *Emory Law Journal* 947 at 977.

which asserts that directors are to consider the interests of all stakeholders in giving out benefits, EMS provides that directors are to allocate benefits of trading in such a way as to enhance the company. The questions that directors have to address are: how can we best distribute the profits to enhance the company? Will providing these benefits to this investor foster the strength of the company in some way? Obviously, directors have to be able to justify the answers that they provide to these questions.

9. Epilogue

It is not intended to compose a long conclusion, but after a journey through many concepts, theories and ideas a few words are appropriate and necessary. There have been years of debate concerning the objective of the public company and still we have no resolution. The law offers ambiguities.[1] Argument over the years has revolved around two dominant positions, the shareholder primacy approach and the stakeholder approach. Commentators have tended to be polarised, robustly holding to one of the two extremes, shareholder primacy or stakeholder. There has been little inclination, relatively speaking, to look at other approaches or even to be more bold and devise new approaches. Some have sought to modify aspects of the two dominant theories.

After providing a long, but important, opening Chapter that sought to set the scene for the ensuing discussion and to raise many of the issues broached later in the book, Chapters 2 and 3 sought to examine the shareholder primacy theory and the stakeholder theory respectively, and to do so in some depth. The conclusion from the two Chapters was that they both had significant shortcomings. In Chapter 4 a new model was proposed, the entity maximisation and sustainability model (EMS), which differed in important ways from the two aforementioned theories. As well as providing some justification for the model, the Chapter introduced the model and set out in general terms how it would work.

The book then sought to explain EMS and some of the practical issues that are raised in relation to its implementation. In Chapter 5 the book considered the issue of enforcement. What if the directors neglected to adhere to EMS? We saw that stakeholders under a stakeholder theory approach, in particular, had significant problems in enforcement. The Chapter sought to explain how EMS could be enforced. What was proposed was the amendment of the statutory derivative provisions in jurisdictions where only shareholders are entitled to seek leave of the court to take derivative action on behalf of the company. The amendment

---

[1] B. Coudary, 'Serving Two Masters: Incorporating Social Responsibility into the Corporate Paradigm' (2009) 11 *University of Pennsylvania Journal of Business Law* 631 at 673.

proposed was to permit anyone interested in the company being able to apply to bring or continue derivative proceedings. It was noted that this state of affairs exists already in Canada and Singapore. In Chapter 6 it was acknowledged that a company cannot achieve its objective unless those whose activities are essential to the company's operations, namely the people I have referred to here as the investors, play their various parts. The Chapter identified investors and discussed their role, and where they fit in the EMS model.

Chapter 7 discussed the position of the managers in the EMS model. Emphasis was placed on the fact that they needed to be granted discretion, but this had to be balanced by making them accountable for what they were doing or not doing. The Chapter identified various accountability mechanisms that can be employed and these were discussed. The conclusion that was drawn was that there are many accountability mechanisms and while each one of them has shortcomings, the mechanisms as a whole mean that directors are able to ensure a reasonable level of accountability.

Finally, Chapter 8 explored the issue of profits and how they are distributed. The discussion centred around the fact that under EMS, profits are allocated to investors on the basis of what will benefit the company entity the most. The questions that directors have to address are: how can we best distribute the profits to enhance the company? Will providing these benefits to this investor foster the strength of the company in some way? The answers to these questions must be consistent with enabling the company to maximise its position and, at the same time, ensure the company's survival.

What the book has not sought to do is to address the responsibility of companies. There is significant debate about whether companies have responsibilities or not (outside of legal ones) and to whom, and if it is agreed that they do, there is further debate about what those responsibilities actually are. The book has endeavoured solely to address the objective of the company. This is not to say that the issue of responsibility is unimportant. On the contrary, it is very important. Simply though, as maintained throughout, objective and responsibility are separate issues, and arguably the latter depends on the former.

It is maintained in this work that ascertaining the objective of the large public company is critical for many reasons. These include the fact that identifying the objective is important as it underpins the kind of corporate governance that needs to be implemented and determines what responsibilities are imposed on directors. It also gives guidance to directors to know what they should be doing. Furthermore, it informs shareholders and other investors in companies what these entities should be doing and what direction they should be taking.

Notwithstanding the volume of material that has been written concerning the corporate objective there is probably still going to be much written in forthcoming years. It would be pretentious to think that this work is the last word. It clearly will not be. To begin with there is still more to be said about aspects of EMS that need to be developed further, and EMS may have to be considered in the light of new developments in the commercial world, especially as a consequence of the financial crisis of 2007–2009.

The value of the work is not necessarily in that it will change practical management in the short term. It is submitted that it might, however, form the foundation for further work and consideration by academics, law-makers, lawyers and managers. Work like this invariably contributes to a wide-ranging debate in which it takes time for the academic world and those immersed in the commercial world to appreciate what is being said. I think that the likely strength of the results of my proposal is to be seen in theoretical terms, providing an underpinning for the development of corporate governance guidelines or regulation in the future.

Index